WISCONSIN POLITICS AND GOVERNMENT

D0886019

*Politics and Governments
of the American States*

General Editor

John Kincaid
Robert B. and Helen S. Meyner
Professor of Government and
Public Service, Lafayette College

Founding Editor

Daniel J. Elazar

Published by the University of
Nebraska Press in association
with the Center for the Study
of Federalism at the Robert B.
and Helen S. Meyner Center
for the Study of State and Local
Government, Lafayette College

JAMES K. CONANT

Wisconsin Politics and Government

AMERICA'S LABORATORY OF DEMOCRACY

UNIVERSITY OF NEBRASKA PRESS
LINCOLN AND LONDON

Library of Congress
Cataloging-in-Publication Data
Conant, James K.
Wisconsin politics and government :
America's laboratory of democracy /
James K. Conant.
p. cm.—(Politics and governments
of the American states)
Includes bibliographical references and index.
ISBN-13: 978-0-8032-1548-1 (hardcover : alk. paper)
ISBN-10: 0-8032-1548-7 (hardcover : alk. paper)
ISBN-13: 978-0-8032-6456-4 (pbk. : alk. paper)
ISBN-10: 0-8032-6456-9 (pbk. : alk. paper)
1. Wisconsin—Politics and government.
I. Title. II. Series.
JK6016.C66 2006
320.9775–dc22
2005017844

For Susan, whose loving support made possible
the completion of this work and whose intellectual contributions
made this a better book than it otherwise would have been

CONTENTS

MAP, TABLES, AND FIGURES

Acknowledgments

During the course of researching and writing this book, many individuals and institutions provided help and support, for which I am very grateful. The Wisconsin Academy of Sciences, Arts, and Letters granted me writer-in-residence status at the beginning of this project, and the Evjue Foundation, Inc., awarded a grant to the Academy to support my work. Carol Toussaint, an early advocate for this project, was instrumental in securing this award. During the later stages the Department of Public and International Affairs and the College of Arts and Sciences at George Mason University (GMU) provided support in the form of graduate research assistance.

My wife, Susan, and my friend and professional colleague, Hal Bergan, read and offered many useful substantive and editorial suggestions on all of the chapters prepared for the first draft. Susan also read and edited several revised versions of the chapters. Sharon Van Sluijs provided editorial advice on the third draft of the manuscript.

John Kincaid provided a wide range of valuable substantive recommendations and many useful editorial suggestions on several drafts of this manuscript. I particularly want to thank John for encouraging me to give the thematic focus of the book special emphasis and to use it to link chapters together. Reviewers selected by the University of Nebraska Press also made helpful suggestions.

Dennis Dresang wrote the first draft of chapter 5, and about half of the current chapter 5 is taken from that draft. Tim Conlan, Tom Corbett, Bob Evanson, W. Lee Hansen, Gerhard B. Lee, Tim Nixon, Jim Pfiffner, John Sacco, and Tom Walz each read a draft of one or more various chapters and made many recommendations for improvement.

My daughter, Jennifer Lee Conant, provided research support for chapters

3, 5, and 9, and she did all of the formatting work required to submit the entire manuscript to the University of Nebraska Press. Jennifer Teal served as a graduate research assistant for chapters 3, 5, 7, and 12.

For assistance with data collection and for calling my attention to useful source materials, I want to thank Legislative Reference Bureau staff members Pete Cannon, Mike Keane, Clark Radditz, Dan Ritchie, and Gary Watchke. Others who provided valuable assistance include Cindy Ashley, Dan Caucutt, William De Soto, Tom Kaplan, Bob Lang, Larry Meade, R. David Myers, Tim Nixon, Bradd Pfaff, Tom Solberg, David Scheler, Bob Thomasgard, John Torphy, William Volkert, Tom Walz, and David Wegge. Interviews or conversations with Dale Cattanach, Governor Anthony Earl, Bob Lang, Governor Patrick J. Lucey, Senator Gaylord Nelson, Senator Fred Risser, Don Schneider, and Representative Dave Travis are gratefully acknowledged.

The resources of the Wisconsin State Historical Society, the Legislative Reference Bureau, and Memorial Library and Geography Library at the University of Wisconsin–Madison were of great value to me throughout this project. Additionally, employees in a variety of Wisconsin state agencies and institutions responded expeditiously to my questions and requests for information; these agencies include the Departments of Administration, Agriculture, Public Instruction, Natural Resources, Tourism, the Ethics Board, Elections Board, Wisconsin Supreme Court, Wisconsin State Assembly, Wisconsin State Senate, Legislative Audit Bureau, Legislative Fiscal Bureau, and Legislative Reference Bureau. Staff at the Wisconsin Taxpayers Alliance and the *Wisconsin State Journal* also provided assistance.

For supporting my research and writing projects on Wisconsin government and politics that predate the invitation to write the present volume, I want to thank Charles Anderson, Dennis Dresang, Sheila Earl, R. Booth Fowler, W. Lee Hansen, Bob Haveman, Jack Huddleston, Alice Honeywell, and the late Bob Lampman. Undergraduate and graduate students in my classes on state government also contributed to this book on Wisconsin. My goal was to introduce the students to individual states and to engage them in the comparative study of state politics and government. By working with them, and by using books in the University of Nebraska Press series on the states, I developed a good sense of what seemed to be essential material for their "education" in state politics and government.

I owe a debt of gratitude to the many fine journalists who have reported on Wisconsin politics and government over the years. I also want to express my appreciation to the many authors and scholars whose works of literature, history, geography, environmental studies, economics, and political science preceded mine. It is Wisconsin's particular good fortune that wonderful stories of its people, its environment, and the interaction between the two exist in the pages of Laura Ingalls Wilder's *Little House in the Big Woods*, Carol Ryrie Brink's *Caddie Woodlawn*, Sterling North's *Rascal*, and Aldo Leopold's *A Sand County Almanac*.

For their ongoing interest in and their support for this project over the many years required to complete it, I want to especially thank my wife, Susan, my daughters, Jennifer and Stephanie, my mother, Audrey Conant, my brother, Dave, my in-laws, Gerhard and Mildred Lee, the late Carlos Stitgen, other family members, and my good friends Nick Berg and Bob Evanson.

My only regret in finishing this study of Wisconsin politics and government is that I did not complete it in time for my father, Roger Conant, to see the final results. I know he would have enjoyed reading this book and discussing its contents with me.

Introduction

The most important feature of Wisconsin's society, government, and politics during the twentieth century was its progressive nature. Wisconsin had a highly developed civil society, its elected and administrative officials continuously attempted to improve the state's political institutions, and they attempted to enhance the economic and social circumstances of the state's citizens. Throughout the century Wisconsin's politics were issue-oriented, state government institutions operated free of scandal, and the administration of state policies and programs was conducted efficiently and effectively. Wisconsin's citizens usually turned out to vote in large numbers, and many participated in political activity in ways that extended beyond elections.

In short, Wisconsin's civil, political, and governmental experience during the twentieth century seems to correspond with the democratic ideal posited by Alexis de Tocqueville in his classic work, *Democracy in America*.[1] When Tocqueville used the term "democracy," he "used it much as we use it today to embrace social and economic as well as political practices and institutions."[2] More modern students of democracy than Tocqueville have associated a model form of democracy with such factors as high rates of electoral participation, clean politics, the responsiveness of elected leaders, and the administrative capacity to implement public laws. In all of these measures Wisconsin fared well, too.

Wisconsin first became visible as a model polity within the American governmental system in the early 1900s, when many of its institutional and policy innovations were adopted by the national government and by other states. For these innovations, Wisconsin won praise as a "laboratory of democracy." The state continued to produce important initiatives throughout the remainder of the twentieth century, which solidified and extended its reputation. Thus Wisconsin's contributions to American democracy during the twentieth century were distinctive—and perhaps even unique—among the fifty states.

Wisconsin's political experience during the past century is all the more remarkable because it might have turned out very differently. Although the Progressive influence was very strong from the state's earliest days, other factors and circumstances almost permanently altered the state's Progressive political trajectory. Thus it is conceivable that Wisconsin's twentieth-century experience might have paralleled that of other Midwestern states to its south and east, like Illinois, Indiana, and Ohio, rather than that of its Progressive neighbor to the west, Minnesota.

When Wisconsin entered the Union in 1848, it was a pioneer society on the northwestern edge of the young American Republic. The majority of Wisconsin's early settlers were from New England and New York, and they held what scholar Daniel J. Elazar called a "moralistic" conception of government.[3] These settlers believed that government ought to serve the interests of the community as a whole, rather than the interests of a few.

The state's 1848 constitution clearly reflects the framers' commitment to this moralistic conception of government. For example, the document not only prohibited all forms of gambling but also included provisions intended to prevent large economic entities from gaining control of the state or from using its financial credit. Also noteworthy were the economic protections extended to the state's citizens. Considered in the context of their times, these constitutional provisions and protections seem remarkable.

Despite the constitutional framers' intentions, however, the state's developmental path was interrupted and nearly altered permanently in the post–Civil War period. During the 1870s and 1880s the railroads and lumber industry gained dominant positions in the state's economy. When these economic interests aligned with Republican Party bosses, the result was "machine"-type politics.

Machine politics was found in many states during this era, but historian Richard Current maintains that it was nearly perfected in Wisconsin. According to Current, Wisconsin's party bosses maintained a smooth-running machine in the state.[4] Patronage was a key part of keeping it oiled. Jobs in the party and in government were given as rewards to those who did faithful service for the party, and big businessmen benefited handsomely for their support of the party and its leaders.[5]

Opposition to the machine was galvanized and led in Wisconsin during the 1890s by Robert M. La Follette Sr. and those who supported his Progressive ideals. "Fighting Bob," as he would come to be known, characterized the struggle with the machine as a fight to save democracy in the state. After a bitter, decade-long contest La Follette finally won the governorship in 1900, and Progressive Republicans won control of the assembly. It was not until 1904, however, that La Follette and the Progressive Republicans finally gained control of the Republican Party.

Immediately after La Follette and his supporters gained control of state government, they began the task of restoring democratic institutions and processes. La Follette and the Progressive Republicans in the legislature also engaged in a series of policy experiments designed to improve the social and economic conditions of the state's citizens. These were the institutional and policy "experiments" that won for Wisconsin national visibility and praise.

It is worth noting, however, that in addition to the many benefits associated with the rise of La Follette and the Progressive spirit, there was at least one important cost. During the machine era the party bosses held key positions on congressional committees, and they were able to earmark a substantial share of the national government's pork-barrel appropriations for the development of Wisconsin's railroads, harbors, and rivers.[6] To the Progressive reformers, who focused intensely on open, clean government, this was anathema. Thus one of the great ironies of Wisconsin politics is that the only time the state enjoyed a favored position in the distribution of national government appropriations was during the machine era.

In addition to returning the state to the political path set by Wisconsin's constitutional framers, La Follette and the Progressives of the early 1900s also set the premises and boundaries for politics and policymaking in the future. True to this course, Wisconsin's elected officials continued the effort to improve democratic institutions and processes throughout the twentieth century. State officials also experimented with policies designed to improve the economic and social life of the community as a whole. Only toward the end of the twentieth century were some of the Progressive premises or boundaries severely tested or broken, with the overturning of the constitutional prohibition against gambling serving as perhaps the most important example.

CYCLES OF INSTITUTIONAL AND POLICY EXPERIMENTATION

Although Wisconsin's institutional and policy innovation was almost continuous during the twentieth century, four major periods of experimentation can be identified. Each of the four can be associated with and understood in relationship to important developments at the national level:

- the early 1900s to 1915, during the Progressive era
- the 1930s, during the Great Depression-New Deal era
- the late 1960s through the 1970s, during the era when liberal Democrats seemed to dominate institutional and policy development in the national government
- the mid-1980s through the 1990s, when the rise of Ronald Reagan and conservative Republicans in Congress seemed to reflect and, in turn, generate a counterreaction to the policies of the liberal Democrats.

The first period of institutional and policy experimentation in Wisconsin is the best known to historians, political scientists, journalists, and elected officials. As already noted, the state's visibility during this era was the result of the political, economic, and social reforms that Robert M. La Follette and his Progressive-era colleagues developed and implemented in the state. This package of reforms won for Wisconsin the title of the Progressive State, and it won praise from a wide range of observers, including former president Theodore Roosevelt.

After visiting Madison in 1910, Roosevelt said: "I felt like congratulating the country as a whole because it has in the state of Wisconsin a pioneer blazing the trail along which we Americans must make our civic and industrial advance during the next few decades."[7] Two years later Roosevelt offered additional praise: "Thanks to the movement for genuinely democratic government, which Senator La Follette led to overwhelming victory in Wisconsin, the state has become literally a laboratory for wise experimental legislation, aiming to secure the social and political betterment of the people as a whole."[8]

The second era of great experimentation in Wisconsin, the early and mid-1930s, was in many ways a logical extension of the first. State governments, like the national government, were looking for ways to cope with the tremendous economic, social, and political dislocation caused by the Great Depression. Led by newly elected governor, Philip La Follette, the son of Robert La Follette Sr., Wisconsin's legislators and administrators responded with a series of innovations in institutional design and public policy. The most important of these innovations were in two areas: social welfare policy and administration, and employment policy and administration.

Consequently when members of Franklin D. Roosevelt's administration were launching the New Deal in the mid-1930s, Wisconsin was an obvious place to look for institutional and policy responses to social and economic problems. Daniel Elazar summed up the state's national visibility and role in this way: "Wisconsin's pioneering efforts in social welfare before the New Deal are well known. They became models for many of the new federal aid programs that were often drawn so as to minimize the dislocation to that state's established programs."[9]

The third major period of institutional and policy experimentation in Wisconsin was the late 1960s and 1970s. The policy innovations of this period can be viewed as a logical extension of the Progressive and New Deal eras, when Wisconsin's elected and administrative officials attempted to improve democracy in its economic, social, and political forms. The institutional and policy "experiments" undertaken during the late 1960s and 1970s included efforts to expand economic opportunity, enhance social justice, and increase citizen participation in the democratic process.

The leading figure in these institutional and policy innovations of the 1970s was Democratic governor Patrick Lucey. National government policy, federal and state court decisions, and strong economic growth not only provided a conducive climate for Lucey's initiatives but also helped to propel them forward. Lucey also had strong support from Democratic legislators, who gained control of the state assembly during the late 1960s and the state senate during the early 1970s.

The fourth period of significant institutional and policy experimentation in the state occurred during the late 1980s and early 1990s. Significantly, many of the innovations that took place during this period can be viewed as a reaction to what happened within the state and the nation during the 1970s. Ronald Reagan's election in 1980 and the rise of the conservative Republicans in Congress during the decade set the stage for this period of innovation in Wisconsin, but the deep national and regional economic recession of the early 1980s propelled it forward.

The leader of the most recent set of institutional and policy innovations in the state was Republican governor Tommy Thompson. Ironically Thompson was sometimes quoted as saying that he learned much of what he needed to know about being governor from Patrick Lucey. Yet in his approach to policy, politics, and administration, Thompson was very different from Lucey. Indeed Thompson made Wisconsin visible among the states and within the nation by taking significantly different approaches to some key institutional and policy matters than those taken by Lucey.

states.[3] People travel to Wisconsin to hunt and fish, boat on the Mississippi River, hike or camp in the state's beautiful state parks and forests, traverse its marvelous system of bike trails, canoe or go "tubing" down its rivers, take vacations on one of its thousands of inland lakes, lie on the beautiful sand beaches of Lake Michigan, sail the cold, clear waters of Lake Superior, or drive Wisconsin's rustic country roads.[4]

What factors have contributed to the exceptional quality of life in Wisconsin? The state's varied geography, its settlement patterns, regional setting, historical development, and diversified economy have all played a role. The most important factor, however, may be the progressive, or positive, role that state government has played in the society. Throughout much of Wisconsin's history, its politics and public policy have been shaped by those who believe that government's proper role is to protect its citizens and to advance the interests of the community as a whole rather than the interests of a few.

This "commonwealth," or "moralistic," conception of the proper role for government has not gone unchallenged in the state, however. Opposition to it has come from those who view politics and government as an extension of the marketplace, rather than as something separate from it. In the "marketplace," or "individualistic," view of politics and government, the primary role for government is to serve the interests of those who control it; that is to say, members of the party in power, as well as the individuals (party members) and business organizations that support them. They all expect to gain tangible rewards from government.

The competition for control of state government between leaders, citizens, and groups who have held these differing conceptions of government has sometimes flared up during election campaigns and legislative sessions; at other times, the struggle has been less visible. Whether visible or not, the results of the electoral competition between those who hold the commonwealth and marketplace views has had profound consequences for the state and its people. In fact, while social, economic, and political conditions in Wisconsin seemed almost ideal in the latter half of the twentieth century, conditions in the late 1800s were dramatically different.

At that time the state and its policies were controlled by those who favored the marketplace model, and this contributed to an economic and environmental crisis that emerged during the 1870s and continued through the 1880s and 1890s. National economic recessions set the stage for this crisis, but internal economic and environmental conditions helped to ignite it. Less than thirty years after Wisconsin entered the Union as a frontier society in 1848, exploitative lumber, mining, and farming practices had significantly altered and severely damaged a natural landscape that had once been covered with large prairies, beautiful freshwater lakes and streams, fertile marshlands, vast forests, a remarkable range of plant species, and large populations of wildlife. In many parts of the state, intensive wheat farming led to a dramatic decline in the ability of the soil to support any crop, and mining practices led to pollution of lakes, streams, rivers, and marshes.

Clear-cutting the vast tracts of old-growth forests that covered the northern three-fifths of the state, however, had the deadliest consequences. The cutting not only destroyed the habitats for plants, fish, and wildlife but also set the stage for infernos that overwhelmed human settlements. The remains of the clear-cutting, as well as the tangled masses of brush that grew quickly after the trees were removed, provided fuel for the fires.[5] Almost all of the state's northern counties experienced at least one major conflagration. The greatest loss of life occurred during the Peshtigo fire of 1871, which swept through six counties and killed more than one thousand people.

Because state government was controlled at the time by interlocking railroad and timber interests, state policy tended to provide explicit or tacit support for these exploitative practices. With more than 80 percent of the state's population dependent for their livelihoods on the land and the state's other natural resources, however, these environmental, economic, and political conditions had an adverse effect on most of the people. For some of the state's residents these exploitative practices and the state policies that supported them had devastating consequences.

Resistance to the economic monopoly and political control of the railroad and timber interests first emerged in the early 1870s. Farmers, who joined together under the banner of the Patrons of Husbandry, or Grange movement, voiced their grievances against the railroad monopoly and the high rates charged for shipping grain to markets.[6] They also challenged both the Democratic and Republican parties to denounce corruption in government and they demanded state regulation of railroads.[7] Farmers alone, however, did not have the political strength required to bring about a significant change in state policy.

Nearly twenty years passed before a broad-based effort to wrest control of the state from the railroad and timber interests was initiated. The key figure in that effort was Robert M. La Follette Sr. In 1891, La Follette broke with the Republican Party bosses, known as the "Stalwarts." The Stalwarts were supported by and catered to the big economic interests.[8]

After a bitter, decade-long fight with the Stalwarts for control of the Republican Party, La Follette finally won the party's nomination for the governorship in 1900.[9] In that same year, he won the general election for governor. He was reelected governor in 1902 and 1904. In 1906 La Follette was elected to the U.S. Senate.

La Follette, his successors in the governorship, James O. Davidson and Francis McGovern, and other Progressive Republican legislators broke the stranglehold of the railroad and timber interests on state government. With the political support of the Social Democrats from Milwaukee and the expertise of faculty from the University of Wisconsin–Madison, the Progressives opened up state government through election reforms, redesigned and invigorated government institutions, and effectively changed policy.[10] Among the new policies the Progressive reformers ushered in were a workmen's compensation act, a state income tax, a law establishing maximum hours of labor for women, an apprenticeship act and related vocational education programs, a minimum-wage act for women and children, a pension act, a retirement fund for teachers, and a corrupt-practices act that limited and publicized campaign expenses.[11]

More than a century after La Follette and his allies gained control of Wisconsin government, the Progressive legacy remains an important factor in the state's politics, government institutions, and public policy. Wisconsin citizens expect openness in government and honesty from their elected officials; that government will protect them from some of the excesses of the private sector; and that government will be an effective steward of the state's natural resources. Wisconsin's citizens also expect state (and local) government(s) to provide a high level of service in education, transportation, public safety, social welfare, and health care.

At the same time it is important to note that throughout the twentieth century those who held the marketplace (individualistic) view of politics and government remained a competitive force within the state. They not only provided an opposition to Progressive policies but also served as a counterweight to the moralistic (commonwealth) view of politics and government. In functional terms this counterweight may have served a useful purpose.

For example, during the early 1900s the initiative and referendum were advocated by Progressives throughout the country as a means of returning control over the election process to the people. These measures were approved in California, Oregon, and a number of other states where the Progressive movement was strong, but they were rejected in Wisconsin. Rejection of initiative and referendum may be the single most important factor in the relatively stable and moderate nature of politics in Wisconsin during the 1970s, 1980s, and most of the 1990s. Conversely during the same period, politics in California and Oregon were relatively turbulent and radical.

Also worth noting is that the strength and influence of those holding the marketplace conception of government and politics were renewed in Wisconsin during the 1980s and 1990s. National politics and economic circumstances set the stage for this renewal. Ronald Reagan's election as president in 1980 was an important contributing factor, as were international, national, and regional economic trends. During the early 1980s the nation suffered its worst economic downturn since the Great Depression, and that recession was particularly severe in the Midwest and most of the older industrialized states of the Northeast and Mid-Atlantic regions.

Within Wisconsin the improved electoral fortunes of those holding the marketplace view of government were both led and personified by Republican governor Tommy Thompson. After serving as a member of the minority party in the state assembly for almost twenty years, Thompson ran for the governorship in 1986 and won election by a narrow margin. He was reelected in 1990, 1994, and 1998 by large margins. Thompson resigned the governorship in January 2001 to take the job of secretary of the Department of Health and Human Services in the George W. Bush administration.

Thompson's fourteen-year tenure in the governorship, his staunch allies in the legislature, the strong support he had from business, his aggressive use of the partial-veto power, and the Wisconsin Supreme Court's apparent reluctance to constrain the governor's actions all contributed to a remarkable accumulation of power by the Republican governor in both the legislative and administrative arenas.[12] In turn, these powers gave Thompson the opportunity to reshape state policy and its implementation in a variety of ways.

In support of some of his most controversial policy changes, particularly in social welfare, Thompson claimed that he was employing the same principles that the Progressives employed to shape government policy during the beginning of the twentieth century. Although Thompson may genuinely have believed this was the case, it also seems clear that he was attempting to employ a powerful symbol to diffuse opposition to his policy proposals. In doing so he followed a tactic that President Reagan employed as he pursued his conservative agenda by frequently invoking the name of Franklin Roosevelt.

Democrats in the legislature, however, were more likely to associate some of Thompson's policy initiatives with the marketplace philosophy and his tactics with the old Stalwart Republicans. Some bristled at Thompson's attempt to claim the Progressive mantle. Yet particularly in the area of social welfare reform, a case can be made that Thompson was employing some of the key Progressive beliefs, including the strong value placed on work and education.

The remainder of this chapter will provide an overview of Wisconsin—its geography; climate; exploration, settlement, and early development; economy; and politics and political culture—so as to better situate the more particular political discussions that follow in later chapters.

GEOGRAPHY

Wisconsin sits in the north-central part of the United States, and it covers 56,066 square miles.[13] Wisconsin's land area is larger than that of Michigan to the east, but slightly smaller than those of its southern and western neighbors, Illinois and Minnesota, respectively. Overall Wisconsin ranks in the middle among the states in physical size.[14]

Wisconsin has an irregular border. Its shape, however, resembles the top side of a person's left hand—with the thumb separated somewhat from the fingers. The irregularity of its shape is due in large part to the fact that on three sides the borders are defined by water. Lake Michigan and Green Bay define the state's eastern border; the St. Louis, St. Croix, and Mississippi rivers together define the western border. Lake Superior and the Menominee, Brule, and Montreal rivers define most of the northern border.[15] Only Wisconsin's southern border, which separates the state from Illinois, is drawn across soil.

One of the most interesting features of Wisconsin's geography is that pre-historic forces left a huge dome or mound somewhat south of the midsection of the state. Because this high point of the state is close to its center, the state's major river systems run in several different directions. For example, the Fox River, in the east-central part of the state, runs north into Green Bay. By simply looking at a map of the state, one might assume the opposite—that Green Bay runs south into the Fox River and Lake Winnebago. Some river systems, like the Brule, run north into Lake Superior, while others, like the Apple, run southwest into the Mississippi River. Still other rivers, like the Rock, run south into Illinois.

Geographic Regions of the State

Wisconsin is divided into seventy-two counties, with numerous cities, towns, and villages. Geographers, however, divide the state into five major regions: Eastern Ridges and Lowlands, Central Plain, Western Upland, Northern Highland, and Lake Superior Lowland.[16]

The Eastern Ridges and Lowlands consist of 13,500 square miles running from Door County in the north to Walworth County in the south. This area is bordered on its eastern side by the Niagara escarpment (made of Niagara limestone), which extends all of the way across the country to Niagara Falls. Lowlands make up most of the region, and they consist of smooth plains and glaciated lakes. Green Lake, one of the most interesting of these lakes, is nestled in a glacial bowl. The lake is more than seven miles long, two and one-half miles across, and nearly three hundred feet deep. Viewed from atop the hills that surround it, the lake has the appearance of a Scottish loch.

The largest glaciated lake in the Eastern Ridges and Lowlands is Lake Winnebago. Its north-south axis extends for more than sixty miles, and at its widest point the Winnebago is twenty miles across. The Fox River connects Lake Winnebago with Green Bay to its north, and the state's heaviest concentration of industrial cities can be found along this river and the lake.[17] Other prominent glacial lakes in the Eastern Ridges and Lowlands include the Oconomowoc group and the Madison chain of lakes. The latter consist of Kegonsa, Mendota, Monona, Waubesa, and Wingra.

The crescent-shaped Central Plain consists of 13,000 square miles lying between the Western Uplands and the Eastern Ridges and Lowlands. The Central Plain consists of both glaciated and unglaciated areas. Although there are some glaciated lakes in this region, swampland is a more common legacy of the glaciers. In fact, there are nearly 750,000 acres of swampland in the Central Plain. Not all of this land is left unused, however. Cranberries and other products are grown in many acres of these marshes. Finally, other prominent physical features of the area include hills, some large with others low and rounded, and numerous moraines.

The Western Upland consists of approximately 13,250 square miles extending from the southern part of Polk County in the north to the Wisconsin-Illinois border in the south. The Western Upland widens out as one moves south, and, at the state's southern border, it extends from the Mississippi River to the middle of the state. Most of this area was not covered by glaciers; thus it retains its early rugged landscape. Glaciers did extend into the eastern part of the Baraboo range, however, leaving behind what is now one of the

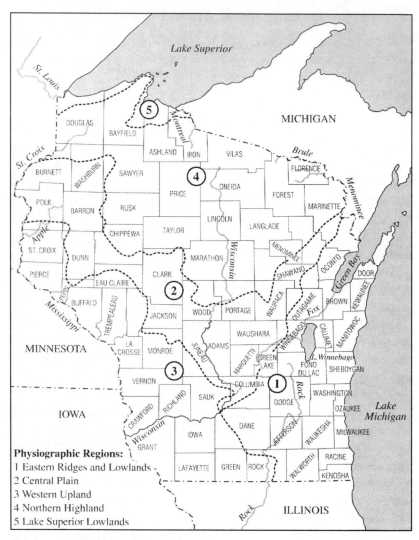

Physiographic Regions:
1 Eastern Ridges and Lowlands
2 Central Plain
3 Western Upland
4 Northern Highland
5 Lake Superior Lowlands

Physiographic Regions of Wisconsin

state's top tourist attractions, Devil's Lake. Set between ancient mountains that are now breaking apart, Devil's Lake and the state park that surrounds it attract more than four million visitors per year.[18]

The Northern Highland consists of 15,000 square miles and is shaped something like a shield. It is part of a great upland region that reaches beyond Wisconsin into Canada, Labrador, and Hudson Bay. Its Precambrian rock provides evidence that the area was once covered by lofty mountains, but for the most part there are only remnants of that early landscape left. One of those remnants is the Penokee-Gogebic Range in Northern Ashland and Iron counties. Most of the area was once glaciated, and most of its lakes sit in kettles or moraines that were formed by melting ice.

The fifth and smallest region of the state is the Lake Superior Lowland. It consists of only 1,250 square miles, all within three counties: Douglas, Bayfield, and Ashland. The area is essentially a plain, and most of it was once covered by Lake Superior.

CLIMATE

Wisconsin's climate is influenced by its physical geography, its location deep within the interior of the United States, and its prevailing atmospheric conditions. Labeled a "temperate continental" climate by geographers, Wisconsin and surrounding states have a climate found in only a few regions of Eurasia and nowhere in the Southern Hemisphere.[19] The key to the state's climate—and its variability—is "the relatively unique combination of climate controls."[20] As a land mass situated far from the ocean, it tends to heat and cool more rapidly than states found in coastal locations that receive similar solar radiation. Additionally, while Wisconsin is most frequently affected by the mild Pacific air mass coming from the west, the state is also "open to invasion by extremely cold arctic air masses from the north and warm and humid tropical air masses from the Gulf of Mexico and the tropical Atlantic."[21]

The tropical air masses, a mean annual precipitation ranging from thirty-one to thirty-nine inches, and the large numbers of rivers and lakes that lie within the state can make summers relatively humid. When July and August temperatures reach into the upper eighties and lower nineties, high levels of humidity can make the days seem oppressive. Lakes Superior and Michigan do moderate summer temperatures somewhat for adjacent land areas, but they seem to have less effect on cold temperatures during the winter.

Arctic air masses can make Wisconsin's winters very long and very cold. In fact, winters in Wisconsin are comparable to winters in northern Sweden and central Russia.[22] While average daily winter temperatures may vary by as much as twenty degrees between the northern and southern parts of the state, it is not unusual for any part of the state to have days, or sometimes even weeks, with temperatures running from ten to thirty degrees below zero. During the winter of 1995, temperatures in the northern part of the state reached fifty degrees below zero—as they have on many other occasions.

The state's winter temperatures are often among the coldest in the nation, and national television and radio coverage of them seems to have made a deep impression on a good share of the country's population. One of the very first questions someone from out of state is likely to ask a Wisconsinite is, "How do you survive those winters?" If the truth be known, even Wisconsinites do, from time to time, complain about the cold. Yet many of the state's inhabitants think of winter as a special season—a time to play in the snow, skate, play hockey, ski, go sledding or tobogganing, ice fish, ice boat, or snowmobile.

EXPLORATION, SETTLEMENT, AND EARLY DEVELOPMENT

Archaeological evidence shows that parts of Wisconsin were occupied by peoples sometimes referred to as Paleo-Indians as early as 10,000 BC. As the last of the glaciers was receding, these Indians were moving in to hunt and gather. Over the course of the next ten centuries, a variety of peoples immigrated to and emigrated from Wisconsin. At the time the state was discovered by Europeans in 1634, three major tribes of Native Americans and a number of smaller tribes inhabited the territory. The dominant tribe was the ferocious Winnebago, who largely eliminated other tribes that once lived in the northeastern part of the state.[23]

Wisconsin's discovery by Europeans was the result of the search for a northwest passage to China—and the search for furs. Samuel Champlain, the governor of New France (Canada), sent an expedition to the West to find a "People of the Sea."[24] Champlain's envoy, Jean Nicolet, traveled via canoe from Canada through the Great Lakes to Wisconsin in 1634. He first set foot on Wisconsin land when he ascended the area now known as Red Banks, located approximately twelve miles northeast of the city of Green Bay. This historic Door County site has been preserved, and visitors to it still enjoy a stunningly beautiful view of the large body of water known as Green Bay. Nicolet's encounter with the Winnebago was both dramatic and successful, but further exploration was probably facilitated more by the near-term demise of the Winnebago than by Nicolet's skillful diplomacy.[25]

The next European visitors to Wisconsin were the fur traders Grollier and Radisson, in 1660, followed by Father Menard and Father Allouez in 1671–72, and Father Marquette and the explorer Louis Jolliet in 1673. Marquette and Jolliet canoed down the Fox River, portaged to the Wisconsin River, and reached the Mississippi River on June 13, 1673. Their trip marked the opening of the area to an influx of explorers, missionaries, fur trappers, and traders. The most famous of the explorers was Robert La Salle, who overcame tremendous obstacles and ultimately followed the Mississippi all the way to its mouth in Louisiana.[26]

The territory that became Wisconsin was highly valued by the French as both a fur-trading area and a passageway to the Far East. To ensure their command, the French built forts on the Great Lakes and other key locations. Although relations with the Indians were sometimes stormy, the French controlled the area until the end of the French and Indian War in 1763. English control meant an expansion of fur trading, which remained the area's principal economic activity until the War of 1812.

Passage of the Northwest Ordinance of 1787 by the Continental Congress marked the beginning of a new step in settlement and economic development. The ordinance provided for the establishment of three to five states in the Northwest Territory beyond Ohio. Prior to 1800, however, there were no more than two hundred Europeans living in the area that eventually became Wisconsin.[27] In 1818, Wisconsin became part of the Michigan territory, and in the 1820s, lead mining developed rather rapidly, particularly in what is now the southwestern part of the state.

The 1832 defeat of Black Hawk, last of the great Indian chiefs in the territory, both advertised the territory and opened it up for more rapid European settlement. Settlers poured in from New England and New York in particular, and the "Territory of Wiskonsan" was organized in 1836. The new territory included not only what is now Wisconsin, but also what are now the states of Minnesota and Iowa. Henry Dodge, a leading citizen of the mining area, was appointed governor of the territory by President Andrew Jackson.

Not long after the Territory of Wisconsin was established, the movement for statehood began. This movement was driven by a number of factors, but the need for boundary protection and internal improvements were probably the most important. In 1834 Congress moved the Illinois border north to include Chicago, so that Illinois had an outlet on the Great Lakes. Then Congress turned over the northern peninsula of Wisconsin, an area rich in copper and iron, to Michigan as a repayment for land lost to Ohio. The

Wisconsin Territorial Legislature petitioned Congress to return the borders to their earlier status, but this appeal was rejected. The loss of territory accelerated the drive for statehood.

On August 6, 1846, an enabling act for joining the Union was passed by Congress, and the first constitutional convention was held in Wisconsin. Entry into the Union was delayed by a year, however, when on April 6, 1847, voters rejected the proposed constitution, which contained a set of provisions that generated strong opposition from business interests and other groups.[28] These "radical" provisions allowed married women to retain property after marriage, prohibited state borrowing to finance internal (infrastructure) improvements, prohibited the confiscation of homesteads in cases of bankruptcy, prohibited the establishment of banking corporations, and made elections the basis for selecting judges.

A second constitution was drafted later in 1847, which included all of these provisions except banking formation and regulation and the married women's property clause.[29] These controversial issues were to be decided by referendum after the voters approved the constitution. The 1847 document was approved by voters on March 13, 1848, and, by an act of Congress, Wisconsin became the thirtieth state to join the Union on May 29, 1848.

During the years that immediately preceded and followed statehood, Wisconsin's population grew rapidly. A large influx of German and Scandinavian immigrants, coupled with the movement of people from New York, Vermont, Pennsylvania, and Ohio, caused the state's population to grow from 44,478 in 1842 to 210,546 in 1847. Between 1847 and 1850 the population grew 150 percent to 305,390. During the 1850s the population more than doubled, reaching 775,881 in 1860.[30] So rapid was Wisconsin's growth that its 1860 population was larger than Michigan's and that of all of the New England states except Massachusetts, ranking fifteenth overall out of thirty-four states.[31]

Economic activity also grew rapidly. The extension of rail lines opened the state's interior to farmers; the Fox River Valley became the site of many flourmills; and Milwaukee became an important port for shipping wheat to the East. Wheat replaced lead as the state's principal economic product.

The 1850s was also a time of important political developments. On February 28, 1854, dissident members of the Whig, Free Soil, and Democratic parties joined together in Ripon, Wisconsin, to form a new political party.[32] Alvan E. Bovay, "a lawyer born in New York and college-educated in Vermont, proposed the name 'Republican' for the new party."[33] The resolution adopted at the meeting called for the formation of a "great Northern party," that would, among other things, protest the extension of slavery into the Union's territories and agitate for its prohibition.[34]

On July 13, 1854, more than one thousand delegates from around the state attended a party convention in Madison, Wisconsin. They approved a party platform and the proposed name for the new party.[35] The new Republican Party achieved immediate success with the election of two congressmen in 1854, and a U.S. senator and a governor in 1855. In 1856 the majority of the state's electorate voted for John C. Fremont, the Republicans' first presidential candidate, and in 1860, a majority voted for Abraham Lincoln.

In 1861, several months in advance of the events at Fort Sumter, the Wisconsin legislature prepared for the coming conflict by giving the governor special powers to cooperate with the national government.[36] As a result of this action, Governor Alexander Randall was able to muster sixteen Wisconsin regiments within a week of Lincoln's call for volunteers. During the Civil War, Wisconsin sent more than 91,000 men to fight for the Union cause. Among the troops that distinguished themselves during battle were those of the Iron Brigade. Their remarkable performance at Second Manassas is documented by historian Shelby Foote in his book, *The Civil War: Fort Sumter to Perryville*, and the critical role they played in slowing the Confederate advance during the first day of Gettysburg has been commemorated by a monument on the battlefield and documented by historians.[37] Almost 11,000 Wisconsinites died during the Civil War, and the state's war expenses exceeded $11.5 million.

During the post–Civil War period, the state's population continued to grow rapidly with new waves of immigration from Europe, New York, New England, Pennsylvania, and the Ohio Valley. The pace of industrialization increased, and expansion of the railroads made lumbering profitable. By 1880 lumber was second only to wheat among the state's economic products. Also during this period, economic and political power became increasingly concentrated in the hands of the railroads, timber companies, mining companies, and banks. The rise of a strong Progressive reform movement in the 1890s finally provided a basis for checking, and eventually reducing, the powerful grip these interests had on both state government and the state's people.

ECONOMY

Through its early developmental stages in the seventeenth and eighteenth centuries, Wisconsin's economy was based first on fur and then on mining.

Before the middle of the nineteenth century, mining gave way to agriculture as the state's principal economic activity. By the late 1880s, wheat farming had seriously depleted much of the state's agricultural soil, and farming nearly lost its number-one position to lumber production. Agriculture's place ahead of lumbering was retained, however, largely as a result of the movement from wheat to dairy farming.[38] Early in the twentieth century manufacturing became the state's primary economic activity, and it remains so today.

Two important factors behind the rapid development of Wisconsin's manufacturing sector were its geographic location and settlement patterns. A substantial portion of Wisconsin's workforce was European in origin, and many, particularly among those who were German-born, had the knowledge and skills needed to establish manufacturing enterprises or to work in them. Additionally, the raw materials for manufacturing, both coal and iron ore, were abundant in or near the Great Lakes region. In fact during the first half of the twentieth century, only one other region of the world was known to have similar concentrations of coal and iron ore comparable to the Great Lakes: the Ruhr-Lorraine-Luxembourg district in Western Europe.[39]

By 1910, Wisconsin was one of the top ten states in manufacturing production. The state remained in this category for all but one year up to 1960. During that fifty-year period, heavy machinery produced in Wisconsin played key roles in major development projects both at home and abroad, including the Panama Canal and the Boulder Dam. For example, 70 of the 102 steam shovels used to dig the Panama Canal were made in Wisconsin by Bucyrus Erie. In the case of Boulder Dam, the enormous turbines used to generate hydroelectricity were produced in Wisconsin by Allis Chalmers.[40]

For all of the years since 1960, Wisconsin has remained among the top fifteen states in manufacturing. This seems rather remarkable, given the fact that the effects of the national recession of 1979–82 were exacerbated for Wisconsin by a severe regional recession. Thus, like most of the Great Lakes states, Wisconsin lost a disproportionately large number of manufacturing jobs between 1979 and 1982. Statewide, approximately 80,000 manufacturing jobs were lost during this period, with more than half of those jobs lost in the Milwaukee area alone.[41] A national television news broadcast highlighted the bleak conditions in Milwaukee during 1982. The broadcast showed more than 30,000 unemployed workers standing in line for two days in temperatures that reached twenty degrees below zero—just to apply for one of the two hundred jobs advertised by an area firm.

The loss of manufacturing jobs during the late 1970s and 1980s had a powerful ripple effect throughout Wisconsin's economy. A standard rule of thumb for calculating the effect is that, for each manufacturing job lost, an additional three jobs are likely to be lost in other sectors of the economy, such as wholesale and retail trade, construction, and services.[42] Probably the single most important reason for the loss of manufacturing jobs in Wisconsin was the same as for the Midwest–Great Lakes region as a whole: the decline of the U.S. automobile industry. Other reasons included:

- changes in technology, which in turn changed the types of products needed as manufactured goods
- competition from other states, some of which offered "tax incentives" or new factories as a carrot to persuade Wisconsin's industries to relocate
- overseas competition, and
- the decision by American companies to move jobs based in Wisconsin overseas

In contrast to most of the 1980s, the 1990s were good years for Wisconsin's economy. Wisconsin's unemployment rate was consistently one of the lowest in the nation, and more new jobs were created in Wisconsin than in all but a few states. The most dramatic employment growth came in the service sector, which surpassed manufacturing in 1992 as the state's number-one employment sector.[43] This occurred despite the fact that the manufacturing sector regained most of the jobs lost during the recession of the early 1980s. To be sure, the state's manufacturing base had changed significantly, and heavy manufacturing production, in particular, no longer constituted the share of jobs it once did.[44] Wisconsin nevertheless continued to produce and export large amounts of manufactured goods.[45]

In addition to service and manufacturing, a number of other sectors, including lumber and paper products, construction, and agriculture, contributed to Wisconsin's economic performance during the 1990s. During that decade, Wisconsin retained its position among the top five states in the production of lumber and paper products. The construction sector, which had not enjoyed the boom conditions experienced in other states during the 1970s and 1980s, was very strong. Additionally, the agricultural sector continued its traditionally strong performance.

In each year of the 1990s Wisconsin ranked first or second among the states in the production of cranberries, milk, and cheese, and it ranked between first and third in the production of sweet corn, soybeans, carrots, oats, peas, and snap beans for processing.[46] The top national rankings for milk and cheese have traditionally provided the basis for the state's claim to be "America's Dairyland."[47]

Wisconsin's good economic performance during the 1990s was reflected in the national rankings of income per capita. In 1999 average per capita income in Wisconsin was $27,421, ranking 22nd out of the fifty states. The 1999 rank compares favorably to the 1990 ranking of 24th, and even more favorably to the 1985 rank of 26th. Yet the 1999 ranking for average per capita income was still slightly below Wisconsin's 1970 rank of 21st.[48]

For most Wisconsinites, the economic recovery of the 1990s meant improved incomes and purchasing power. Yet it is worth noting that a majority of the jobs created nationally during the first half of the 1990s were service jobs that paid wages below or only slightly above the poverty line.[49] Wisconsin did have solid employment in both the manufacturing and construction sectors, and these jobs paid substantially higher wages than did service jobs.[50] Nevertheless, in Wisconsin, as in other states, some of the workers who lost manufacturing jobs during the late 1980s and 1990s were unable to find new jobs in manufacturing and thus lost their middle-class status.

POLITICAL CULTURE

Political culture can be described as the "particular pattern of orientation to political action in which each political system is embedded."[51] According to Daniel J. Elazar, American national political culture consists of two contrasting conceptions of the political order: marketplace and commonwealth. Each of these conceptions places primary emphasis on one of the two poles: power or justice. These poles, Elazar elaborates, define the "basic political concerns of all civil societies." In the marketplace conception the primary emphasis is on who gets what, when, and how (power). In the commonwealth conception the primary emphasis is on the development of the good society (justice).

Within the states Elazar finds both the marketplace(individualistic)and commonwealth (moralistic) political cultures. In addition, he finds a third culture, which he calls "traditionalistic." These cultures, Elazar argues, shape the operation of a state's political system in three key areas:

- perceptions of what politics is and what can be expected from government
- the kind of people who will participate in politics and government, and
- the way in which the art of government is practiced

In the marketplace or individualistic culture, politics is viewed as a bargaining process among self-interested individuals and groups. Politics is seen as a sometimes dirty business, and it is to be left to professionals. Those who participate expect to gain rewards for their efforts, and they can be expected to distribute benefits to the people who help them.

In the traditionalistic culture there is ambivalence toward the marketplace and a presumption that only an elite few can govern. Family or social ties usually determine who will be a part of the self-perpetuating elite. The elite use government to advance their own economic interests and to protect their political interests.

In the moralistic culture politics is viewed as an important, even noble, enterprise. Participation in politics by all citizens is viewed as highly desirable. Politics is focused on issues, and the purpose of political activity is to create and maintain a government that advances the interests of the whole society.

As noted earlier in this chapter, Wisconsin's dominant political culture is the commonwealth (moralistic) culture. The moralistic political culture was brought to the state during the early and middle 1800s by Yankees from New England and New York, and it was reinforced by immigrants from Scandinavia and Germany during the middle and late 1800s.

The influence of the state's moralistic political culture can be seen in its constitution and governmental institutions and in the day-to-day operation of its political system. Wisconsin's constitution was built in part upon the presumption that government has an important, positive role to play in society. Governmental institutions were, for the most part, given enough energy to carry out that work, but strong popular control over elected officials was to be maintained.

Electoral and legislative politics in Wisconsin tends to be issue-oriented. Wisconsinites turn out in large numbers to vote, and government officials have been careful to minimize barriers to electoral participation. Many Wisconsinites participate in political activity beyond the ballot box, and they expect their elected officials to be responsive—and to conduct themselves in a responsible manner. Minor indiscretions by elected officials that would not be noticed in most other states have cost Wisconsin legislators their jobs.

As mentioned previously, Wisconsin's citizens have very strong expectations about both the quantity and quality of services government should provide. They expect state (and local) government to manage the state's natural resources carefully and to protect the environment vigilantly. They expect to have good schools at all levels of education.

Wisconsinites expect government to ensure that they work in a safe workplace, can travel quickly and safely throughout the state, and have a wide range of high-quality outdoor recreational opportunities. Last but not least, Wisconsin's citizens have traditionally assumed that state (and local) governments would protect them from the excesses of the marketplace and provide assistance for those who are not able to compete fully in the marketplace.

It is important to note that Wisconsin's citizens have traditionally been willing to pay for these services. In fact Wisconsin's state and local tax rates have typically placed the state among the top ten in the country. Although some may consider this a dubious distinction, it does highlight something important. Because Wisconsin is only an average state with respect to income per capita, the state's taxpayers have to pay more than taxpayers in wealthier states do just to provide the same level of services. As described here, however, Wisconsin's citizens have insisted on a higher level of services than is provided in most wealthy states—which translates into high taxes.[52]

Although the moralistic political culture is the dominant culture in Wisconsin, the individualistic culture also has strong roots in the state. This is not surprising, given the fact that fur trading and then mining were the state's principal economic activities for the first two hundred years of European settlement, and lumbering was a major activity during the next one hundred years. During the 1800s the individualistic culture came with settlers from Pennsylvania and Ohio, and Ireland, Poland, and other Central and Southern European countries.

From time to time over the past century and a half, the state's institutions have come under the control of elected officials and interest groups whose approach to politics and government has resonated more closely with segments of the state's population that favor an individualistic or marketplace approach to politics and government. In historical terms the high-water mark of the marketplace, or individualistic, orientation was the 1870s, 1880s, and 1890s. During that era political and governmental power was consolidated in the hands of a few, and directed by an interlocking set of businesses for their own interests.

In short, for much of this thirty-year period, what might be described as an extreme version of the marketplace model was in place. During this era the "machine" politics often associated with places like New York City and Chicago was largely perfected on the state level in Wisconsin. The Republican Party was closely tied to the lumber and railroad interests, and the party itself was a very smooth-running machine.

Historian Richard Current argues that the strong and capable leadership of the Republican Party bosses, Philetus Sawyer, Henry C. Payne, and John C. Spooner, was the key to the party's finely tuned operation. According to Current these men "were a triumvirate such as no other state could boast."[53] Of course, Wisconsin was not the only state that fell under the control of those who owned the railroads or lumber companies during that era, nor, as mentioned, was it the only state that experienced "machine" politics.

In modern times the most successful and robust period of dominance by those whose orientation toward politics and government fit the marketplace model was probably the last decade of the twentieth century. During that decade the state's executive branch was headed by Tommy Thompson, a Republican governor whose orientation seemed much more compatible with the marketplace culture than the commonwealth culture. In addition, the Republican Party controlled at least one house of the legislature during the decade.

Although Thompson proudly declared himself a pro-business governor, established a highly disciplined party organization, and aggressively used the chief executive's powers, he did not attempt to reinstate the "machine"-style control of state government that existed in the latter part of the 1800s. Like the Stalwarts of old, however, Thompson enjoyed the active and generous support of the business community, he benefited from the disarray of the Democratic Party in the state, and he used the levers of state policy and state administration to reward friends and punish enemies. All of these factors helped to make Thompson Wisconsin's most powerful governor, and his power enhanced his ability to bring to office elected representatives and administrators who favored the marketplace orientation.[54]

CONSTITUTION AND GOVERNMENTAL INSTITUTIONS

Wisconsin continues to operate under its original 1848 constitution. Like the U.S. Constitution, the document establishes the principal government institutions and distributes powers among them; it also establishes protections for citizens in the form of a bill of rights. Unlike the constitutions of many other states, Wisconsin's 1848 document was neither excessively long nor filled with detailed instructions about the operations of government. As a result Wisconsin lawmakers have been able to respond to changing economic, social, and political circumstances with less difficulty than lawmakers elsewhere in the country.

Having said this, however, it is important to note that Wisconsin's constitution was amended 132 times between 1848 and 2002. As a result, only two of its fifteen articles remain unchanged. These changes have occurred even though the state's constitution is relatively difficult to amend. All constitutional amendments must originate in the state legislature, and a majority of both houses of two successive legislatures must approve the proposed constitutional amendment. Then the amendment is put to a vote of the people during a regularly scheduled election. Seventy-five percent of the 174 amendments approved by the state legislature have also been approved by voters.[55]

Some of the 132 amendments approved by voters involved minor, uncontroversial housekeeping items; others emerged from bitter political struggles that have had important institutional and policy consequences. Some of the latter are discussed below; others are discussed in the chapters on the state constitution, the legislature, the governor, and the Wisconsin Supreme Court. Also discussed in these chapters are the ways in which Wisconsin's constitution has been changed through practices that have stretched constitutional language in ways that the framers of the document would probably find objectionable. This form of constitutional change underlies some of the most interesting and important political and institutional conflict that occurred during the last three decades of the twentieth century.

Wisconsin's legislature is an active and professional institution. Among the factors contributing to the institution's reputation and performance are its membership, organization, and staffing patterns. The legislature has traditionally attracted capable representatives, and it has served as a pioneer and model for other states and the Congress in the area of legislative organization.

Wisconsin's legislature consists of two houses: the assembly and the senate. There are ninety-nine assembly representatives and thirty-three senators. Each senate district consists of three assembly districts. A majority of districts are competitive two-party districts.[56] In fact during the 1990s there was fierce competition for majority control of both houses of the legislature. One result was that campaign spending escalated rapidly during the decade, particularly in what are sometimes called "marginal" districts. In these districts the number of Democrats and Republicans who are registered to vote is relatively equal. It is often in these districts where partisan control of the assembly or senate has hung in the balance.

In addition to changes caused by increased party competition, the makeup of the membership has also changed over the past thirty-five years. The influence of rural Wisconsin has declined, and the influence of cities and suburbs has increased as a result of redistricting conducted every ten years to comply with the "one man, one vote" principle contained in the state constitution. During the 1970s, 1980s, and 1990s, the number of women and minority members serving in the legislature grew substantially. The number of full-time, "professional" legislators grew also.

Wisconsin's legislative pay currently ranks in the top 25 percent among the states. All legislators have their own office and at least one full-time staff person. Committee chairs have two or more full-time staff members. Legislative leaders have between three and six staff members.

From the 1960s through the 1990s, both parties in the legislature also had their own "caucus" staffs. The caucus staffs were disbanded in 2002, however, after Wisconsin's Ethics and Election Board began an investigation into staff activities.[57] It turns out that some staff members, who were paid from the state treasury rather than by either party, were participating in election campaigns. This practice was a violation of Wisconsin election law, and it was an unfortunate aberration from a long tradition of clean government and politics.

Both houses of the legislature—and their committees—are served by a number of agencies. Among the foremost of these agencies are the Legislative Reference Bureau and the Legislative Fiscal Bureau. The Reference Bureau provides bill-drafting and other services. The Fiscal Bureau provides analytic services with respect to budget and policy matters.

Wisconsin was the first state to establish a Legislative Reference Bureau (1900). This agency served as a model for both the national government and other states. When the analytic functions related to budget- and policymaking were placed in a separate agency (the Fiscal Bureau), Wisconsin again pioneered an institutional change that was followed by other states. In addition to the Legislative Reference and Fiscal Bureaus, the Wisconsin legislature has another important agency that has served as a model for other states—the Legislative Council. Many of the major policy issues taken up by the legislature are examined by the Legislative Council before they are introduced in a standing committee for formal consideration.

Wisconsin's legislature has traditionally been very active in the budgetary process. The key budget committee is the Joint Committee on Finance. The committee introduces and then examines the biennial budget proposed by the governor. Membership on the committee consists of eight members of the assembly and seven members of the senate. The committee has more prestige and influence than any other committee, and positions on it are highly coveted by legislators. The committee (and its staff) gives the legislative body exceptional institutional expertise and potential leverage in its budget negotiations with the governor. In practice, however, committee votes are often along partisan lines, with the party controlling the governorship voting for the governor's budget proposals.

Wisconsin's governor is generally described in political science texts and articles as having moderate or moderately strong formal powers. The six powers on which these ratings are based include: length of term in office; opportunity for reelection; budgetary powers; veto powers; appointment powers; and powers of organization. In the first four areas, the Wisconsin governor's powers are actually quite strong.

For example, the governor has a four-year term of office, and there are no constitutional or statutorily prescribed limits on the number of terms that can be served consecutively. The governor's budgetary powers are also substantial, in part because all expenditures of more than $100,000 must be included in the budget bill. Thus the executive budget, which the governor prepares with the help of the State Budget Office, includes most appropriation and most major policy initiatives. Finally, in addition to the standard veto authority over legislation, Wisconsin's governors have a form of the item-veto power that is unique among governors. The latter allows the governor to line-out or eliminate appropriations numbers or language in the budget bill. In Wisconsin's state government documents and publications, this power is called the "partial veto."[58]

The four-year term, the budgetary powers, and the partial-veto power give Wisconsin's governor the opportunity to be a very powerful player in the state's political life and policy decision making. In fact, recent governors, such as Patrick J. Lucey, Lee Sherman Dreyfus, and Anthony Earl, not only exploited the latter two powers but also found clever ways to extend their reach beyond the points exercised by their predecessors. When unlimited tenure is combined with these powers and a governor aggressively stretches them, Wisconsin's chief executive can be a dominating player. Governor Tommy Thompson forcefully demonstrated this fact.

In contrast to the four powers discussed above, the governor's appointment and organizational powers are limited. Some of the state's key departments and many independent agencies are headed by independently elected officials, boards, or commissions, and the members of the boards and commissions select the secretary or head of the agency. In almost all cases, however, the governor appoints the members of the boards or commissions. Even so, it often takes a full term or more for a governor to appoint a majority of a board or commission. Likewise, the governor's ability to reorganize an executive branch agency is limited by state statutes and the state constitution. Thus reorganization initiatives are taken only very selectively.

Wisconsin's executive branch structure can be classified as a "traditional" form of organization.[59] In the traditional model the governor's control over the executive branch agencies is limited and shared with independently elected officials and boards and commissions. Only in the case of cabinet departments does the governor have the authority to appoint the secretary of the department and remove the appointee at any time.

Since the 1960s governors have made an effort to move toward a "cabinet" form of organization by reducing the number of agencies, the number of independently elected officials heading agencies, the number of advisory boards and commissions, and expanding the number of departments headed by gubernatorial appointees. In the Public Administration literature, the "cabinet" model of executive branch organization is often described as the ideal model because the governor has direct control over the executive branch departments.

In 1967 Governor Warren Knowles initiated a comprehensive reorganization of Wisconsin's executive branch, which reduced the number of agencies from 85 to 32.[60] The new structure included four constitutional offices, fourteen operating departments, and fourteen independent agencies. Over the next thirty years, some additional agencies were added, some were consolidated into departments, and some boards and commissions were eliminated.

In 2002 the state had eighteen executive branch departments and thirteen independent agencies. The governor appoints the heads of fourteen of the eighteen departments. Two departments, Justice and Public Instruction, were headed by independently elected officials, and two departments, Employee Trust Funds and Veterans Affairs, were headed by part-time boards that appoint a secretary. All of the independent agencies were headed by a full-time commission or a part-time board. The governor appoints most commission and board members.

Another way to describe the executive branch and its administrative agencies is through employment data. Approximately 50 percent of the state's 60,000 employees work in the thirty-one executive branch departments and agencies. Only 5 percent of the employees work in the three principal governmental institutions: office of the governor, the state legislature, and the state's supreme court. More than 45 percent of the state's employees work in the University of Wisconsin system.

Wisconsin's court system, like the state's other institutions, has been known nationally for its clean and effective operation. Yet the courts have not had the national visibility during the twentieth century that the state's legislatures and governors have enjoyed. Among the reasons for this circumstance is that courts in Wisconsin have not often been important innovators or pioneers. An important exception, however, may be the Progressive era of 1900–1915, when the Wisconsin Supreme Court showed a greater willingness to accept Progressive reforms (statutory changes) than either the U.S. Supreme Court or many other state high courts.

The state's courts were reorganized in 1977 to conform to the model advocated by the American Bar Association and the Council of State Governments. A major purpose of the reorganization was to simplify and streamline court organization and thereby provide a more expeditious process for coping with ever increasing litigation. The workload increases in civil disputes and in criminal cases—due in large part to increases in alcohol and drug abuse—have prompted the need for more courts and additional organizational changes.

A review of decisions and citations demonstrates that Wisconsin justices rely heavily not only on the strictures of state law and federal preemptions but also on the leadership of courts in California, New Jersey, and Ohio. Wisconsin's current chief justice, Shirley Abrahamson, has been a visible leader in the "new judicial federalism."[61] Her efforts to revitalize the importance of state constitutions in the federal system have not, however, been endorsed enthusiastically by a majority of her colleagues.

Over the past 150 years there have been several occasions on which the Wisconsin Supreme Court has been required to serve as a referee in the struggle for power between the legislative and executive branches. Particularly in the period from 1985 through 1999, a host of such cases were brought before the court. Like most supreme courts, Wisconsin's has usually been reluctant to be drawn into matters sometimes described as "political." Among the consequences of this predisposition was that executive power was substantially expanded, while legislative power was reduced. Another was that the chief executive and some executive branch agencies, usually with the support of the legislature, were allowed to take actions that seemed to be in direct conflict with the language of the state's constitution.

In the chapter treating the constitution, we will discuss a number of cases that underscore the ways in which some of the key provisions of this document have been stretched—or perhaps even subverted—by elected and administrative officials. In some cases this occurred because the officials wanted to avoid the time-consuming and sometimes hazardous path of pursuing a constitutional amendment. In other cases elected officials seem to have ignored the boundaries of the constitution or provided novel inter-pretations of the constitution's provisions because their attempts to secure a constitutional amendment did not succeed.

POLITICAL INSTITUTIONS

Political parties and interest groups are the two main political institutions operating in Wisconsin politics. The brief overview of parties presented here will be followed by a brief discussion of interest groups. Wisconsin's politics have often been described as "issue-oriented," especially in drawing a contrast between the machine, or patronage-type, politics of some other states. The description remains as fitting today as it was during the early years of statehood. This does not mean, however, that political parties are or have been unimportant. Rather, it defines the boundaries or political culture within which party competition has taken place throughout most of the state's history.

As noted previously, during the early years of statehood a large part of Wisconsin's population came from New England, Germany, and Scandi-navia. A substantial portion of these immigrants were educated and politi-cally sophisticated. While these groups, and others that followed, tended to settle in identifiable enclaves or communities, a party's stand on issues was likely to be as important as ethnic or religious heritage. Similar conditions can be identified today, although they are less pronounced. Population enclaves can still be identified throughout the state; the state's population is still highly educated and politically sophisticated; and many voters continue to put a party's or a candidate's position on an issue above party loyalty or ethnic considerations.

In addition to immigration patterns, state politics and the fortunes of the state's political parties have been affected by national economic problems and issues, national elections, state issues, and the personalities of state party and elected officials. For example, the advent of the Great Depression in 1929 had a significant adverse affect on the fortunes of a state Republican Party that had been recaptured and revitalized by anti-Progressive interests during the middle and late 1920s.

Yet it was the Wisconsin Progressives, rather than Democrats, who bene-fited from the Republicans' problems. Indeed, despite the improved fortunes of Democrats nationally during the 1930s and early 1940s, no significant reconstruction or revitalization of the Democratic Party occurred in Wisconsin during this period. One of the principal reasons for this circumstance was the close connection between President Franklin Roosevelt, the Democratic president, and the Progressive Party, which was formed in 1934.

Attempts to revitalize Wisconsin's Democratic Party began in earnest after World War II, but progress was slow. The Republican Party's national problems in the aftermath of Watergate, however, helped Democrats make major statewide election gains during the 1970s. Then, in the 1980s, the election of Ronald Reagan to the presidency provided an impetus for state party members to reenergize the Republican Party.

Wisconsin's electoral and party history has been divided into four key eras by Leon Epstein, one of its foremost students.[62] Five periods are designated here in order to highlight the rise and decline of the Progressives and the Progressive Party. During the first period, 1848–54, the state had two-party competition. Democrats were dominant; the Whigs were the principal opposition. During the second period, 1855–1900, the Republican Party was in control. Founded in Ripon, Wisconsin, in 1854, the antislavery Republican Party quickly replaced the Whig Party and eclipsed the Democratic Party. From 1860 to 1900, Republican candidates won the governorship in all but three elections.

The third period, 1900–1934, was an era when Stalwart Republicans and Progressive Republicans fought for control both of the Republican Party and statewide offices. The fourth period, 1934–1946, marked the formation of the Progressive Party and, ultimately, its demise. In this period, competition for statewide offices consisted of a battle between a revitalized Republican Party and the Progressive Party. The Progressives' opposition to United States involvement in World War II, however, was among the keys to its collapse in 1946.

The fifth period, from 1947 to the present, can be described as a realignment of the parties along national lines. After the Republican Party rejected Progressive efforts to rejoin it, large numbers of Progressives moved into and rejuvenated the Democratic Party. In 1957 William Proxmire was elected to the U.S. Senate, and the Democratic Party's statewide fortunes began to improve. Today, Wisconsin can properly be considered a two-party state.

Like political parties, interest groups play an important role in Wisconsin politics. As is the case nationally, interest groups in Wisconsin are primarily aligned with one party or another. Business groups tend to support Republicans; labor groups, including public employees and teachers, typically support Democrats. In addition to these traditional groups, a number of grassroots organizations exist and play important roles in Wisconsin politics. Most of these organizations are distant from either political party. Some focus on issues like Indian treaty rights, while others articulate general philosophies, such as opposition to any form of government whatever.

THE STATE BUDGET

Budgets not only provide a record of who gets how much of the state's financial resources but also a record of who pays how much for state spending. Thus a budget provides an important record of a government's priorities and the relative influence various interests have on governmental decision making. Since the early 1900s Wisconsin's commitment to education and social welfare has been reflected in the state budget, and from the 1920s onward, the state's commitment to transportation and natural resource management has also been reflected in the budget.

While economic and social circumstances changed over time, these commitments remained very firm. In fact throughout most of the 1980s and 1990s, eleven policy and program areas accounted for 88–90 percent of state general-purpose revenue spending.[63]

Some program names and structures were changed in the late 1990s, but the top ten programs in the FY 2003 budget still accounted for 85 percent of general-purpose spending. These programs included:

- school aids
- the University of Wisconsin system
- medical assistance (Medicaid)
- corrections
- property tax credits
- shared revenues (state revenues shared with local governments)
- community aids (for various human service programs)
- tax relief for individuals
- Wisconsin Works (income-maintenance and job-training support), and
- Supplemental Security Income.[64]

Substantial state expenditures are also made for highway construction and maintenance and for transportation aid to local governments. These expenditures are not general-fund expenditures, however, because they are supported by intergovernmental aid from the national government and from state gasoline taxes, rather than state general-fund taxes like the sales and income tax. Consequently they do not appear in the top-ten list provided above.

The extraordinary commitment the state has made in education, social welfare, and other policy areas, however, does have a cost. Specifically, it requires a high level of state and local spending. Because Wisconsin is a state of only moderate per capita wealth, high levels of spending can only be sustained through relatively high levels of state and local taxation. During the thirty years from 1970 through 1999 Wisconsin consistently ranked among the top ten states in state and local spending and state and local taxes.

The income tax, the corporate income tax, and inheritance taxes were important sources of revenue for most of the twentieth century. These tax sources were established during the Progressive era of the early 1900s, and they gave the state the capacity to finance its services. Since the 1960s, the sales tax has been an increasingly important revenue source.

The rationale for establishing the general sales tax was to give the state the capacity to provide additional financial aid to local governments. By the 1970s more than 40 percent of all the money the state raised was going back to local governments in direct aid, grants, property tax relief, and other support. Despite the unusually high level of state aid for local governments, however, the demand to reduce local property taxes continued to be a major driving force in state political and financial decision making throughout the 1980s and 1990s. As governors and legislators continued to respond to these demands the percentage of state expenditures going to local governments continued to rise over the years, reaching almost 60 percent in the late 1990s.

Maintenance of the state's commitment to high-quality services and high levels of aid to local governments was seriously tested when the state's economic fortunes declined during the 1980s. These conditions played into the hands of citizens, interest groups, and elected officials with a marketplace orientation. Their preference for less governmental activity and for lower levels of spending and taxation seemed to resonate with many voters during this period.

Indeed the electoral success of those holding the marketplace orientation had significant policy consequences during the 1980s. It led to a modest reduction in the progressivity of the state's income tax, the start of state-sponsored gambling as a means of generating state revenue, and a phasing out of the inheritance tax, which was converted to an estate tax. In the 1990s the revival of the marketplace orientation led, among other things, to a drive to cut individual income taxes and lower corporate income tax rates.

Wisconsin's commitment to local governments was tested again at the beginning of the twenty-first century, as the effects of the national and international economic downturns took their toll on the state's economy. Attempts to balance the budget during these difficult economic times not only included reductions in spending for state operations but also included a phase-out of state aid to local governments via the Shared Revenue Fund. At the same time this extraordinary change was taking place, state support for K–12 schools continued to grow. Indeed it appears that the dramatic increases the state made in K–12 aid during the middle and late 1990s was a key factor that tipped the state budget out of balance in the first place. Tax cuts made during the late 1990s and the recession that officially began in March 2001 were also key causes of the state's fiscal problems.

CONTINUING TRADITIONS AND EMERGING ISSUES

The foundation upon which Wisconsin's contemporary political culture, government institutions, and public policy have been built is the Progressive tradition. Perhaps the single most important dimension of this tradition is that it established a set of citizen expectations for and a set of boundaries within which state politics are conducted and policy choices are made. At the same time, within those boundaries there has been great tension between citizens and elected officials whose view of politics and government fits within the moralistic and individualistic camps—particularly in areas like state and local finance and social welfare. Competing values lie at the heart of these differences, and so do the fiscal consequences of state policy.

Wisconsin's high service levels and its generous support to school districts and local governments require high levels of state spending. Given that Wisconsin is a state of only moderate wealth, high levels of taxation are required to sustain state policy choices. This presents some difficult problems. First it can put Wisconsin at a disadvantage in the interstate competition for wealthy individuals and for businesses. Second it contains the seeds for citizen discontent, which could boil over into sharp policy changes. Conservative legislators and business interests have repeatedly objected to high levels of state taxation and spending during the past thirty years. The fact that governors and the state legislature placed levy limits or cost controls on local governments and school districts during the 1970s, 1980s, and 1990s suggests that concern over the issue has important political implications.[65]

In addition to the emerging pressure to address state spending and taxation levels, there are several other issues that will remain important in the future. At least two of these issues, gambling and lobbying, will continue to test the boundaries established by the Progressive tradition in even more significant ways than the state-local finance issue. For example, in the middle 1990s the state's attorney general, James Doyle, expressed concerns about the hundreds of thousands of dollars that gambling interests were pouring into election campaigns.[66] Even Governor Thompson, a strong supporter of the constitutional amendment that allowed the establishment of dog tracks and a state lottery, acknowledged during his second term that an effort had to be made to control gambling in the state.[67]

Although state-sponsored gambling has been limited for the time being to a state lottery and dog tracks, many proposals to expand state activity in this area have active sponsors. Additionally, the constitutional amendment that allowed gambling in the state opened up a Pandora's box. Removing the 1848 prohibition against any state-sponsored gambling also removed the prohibition that had limited Indian tribes to running bingo parlors. Since the 1987 amendment overturning the gambling prohibition, a host of Indian tribes have set up casino operations, and gambling has become a major industry in the state.

Another issue with considerable implications for the state is lobbying. While Wisconsin has relatively strict rules about lobbying, data collected by the state's Ethics Board showed that $44.4 million was spent on lobbying during the 1999–2000 legislative session.[68] Even with rules perceived to be "tight," citizens might suspect that their government—or at least pieces of it—is for sale to the highest bidder.

A related problem for Wisconsin is the critical role that money now plays in election campaigns. Money not only provides the vehicle for lobbying but also for securing the "access" to elected officials that many lobbyists enjoy. Specifically, private interests and interest groups provide campaign donations that elected officials need in order to run television advertisements. In response to such "favors," legislators may be sympathetic to or even active advocates for these interests and interest groups.

Wisconsin is not the only state in which gambling, lobbying, and campaign financing present significant problems for or challenges to the independence and integrity of state politics and government. Indeed, because Wisconsin has traditionally had a vigilant press and a political culture that has provided a fairly clear boundary between private interests and policymaking activities, it is conceivable that these challenges will be confronted in a more straightforward manner in Wisconsin than in many other states. Nevertheless, even Wisconsin's history shows that when large amounts of money flow into politics, the outcome can be very corrosive to the Progressive values and premises that Wisconsinites have traditionally embraced.

Finally, in addition to the emerging issues noted above, Wisconsin faces ongoing competition from other states for business enterprises and wealthy individuals. Press reports regularly contain stories about the way in which a particular state landed a new manufacturer or new business enterprise, at least in part, through giveaways of tens or even hundreds of millions of dollars of "incentives." Likewise, states regularly promote themselves on the basis of "favorable" tax climates. While low taxes are not the only, or perhaps even the single most important, factor in the relocation of businesses or wealthy individuals from one state to another, they do play a role.

Wisconsin cannot sustain its high service levels without high taxes. Yet it may be difficult to sustain a strong state economy in the long run if businesses view taxes in the state as excessively burdensome while, at the same time, other states promise generous incentives to companies if they relocate from Wisconsin. This challenge, combined with the issues identified above, begs an important question: Has the Progressive legacy reached—or perhaps even passed—its peak in Wisconsin? It can be argued, of course, that the external environment has forced, and will continue to force, Wisconsin policymakers to move away from the commonwealth model and toward the marketplace model.

Collectively the challenges Wisconsin faces seem substantial enough that an observer who knows the state's history can scarcely avoid thinking about the 1870s and 1880s. During that era Wisconsin was dominated by a few economic interests and party bosses, and the state's circumstances were relatively typical of those in a majority of the states. After one hundred years of the Progressive legacy in Wisconsin, however, it seems difficult to imagine that the state's citizens would allow their political institutions to be captured once again by narrow economic interests that manipulate the levers of government for their own gain. History shows, however, that while tradition may shape the choices of each generation, it does not provide absolute guarantees.

CHAPTER TWO

The Constitution

> Wisconsin's Constitution has stood the test of time longer and better than any other in the western three-fourths of the country.
>
> Milo Quaife, *The Movement for Statehood, 1845–1846*, 1918

> Power is divided and limited because those elected to high office will exercise every bit of power they are granted and no less. And the limits on power, if they are tested and seem elastic, will be stretched and stretched some more.
>
> Tom Loftus, *The Art of Legislative Politics*, 1994

Like the U.S. Constitution, state constitutions are compacts between the governed and their governors. State constitutions delineate the rights of citizens, establish the basic governmental institutions, distribute powers among those institutions, and define how the process of electing the people's representatives will work. State constitutions are also legal and political documents. They are legal documents because they establish the basic rules within which all other state activity—including lawmaking—is supposed to take place. They are political documents because they tend to reflect a particular orientation toward government and governmental activity that grows out of a state's historical experience, political culture, and regional setting.[1]

Wisconsin's constitution of 1848 emerged from a two-year struggle that reflected some deep-seated differences among political parties about the proper role of government in a civil society. The central point of contention was whether Jacksonian reforms designed to limit the power that large financial interests had over government, politics, and individual citizens would be incorporated into the constitution.[2] The proponents of the Jacksonian reforms won the initial battle in 1846, but the opponents won the second round, as their campaign against the constitutional document formulated in 1846 led to its defeat at the polls in the early months of 1847. Yet the Jacksonian reformers seem to have prevailed in the contest because the constitutional document written in 1847 and approved in 1848 incorporated most of the provisions of the 1846 document.

Wisconsin still operates under its 1848 constitution. Only five states, all in New England, operate with older constitutions.[3] Wisconsin's constitution, like the U.S. Constitution on which it was partially modeled, was written mostly in broad terms to prevent the need for constant amendment. Furthermore, the processes established for amending the document were made relatively difficult. Nevertheless, the constitution was amended 131 times in the 150 years between the state's founding in 1848 and its Sesquicentennial in 1998.[4] One additional amendment occurred in 1999. As a result of these amendments, only two of the fifteen articles contained in the original document remain unchanged.

This chapter begins with background on the types of state constitutions that exist in the United States. Additional historical background on Wisconsin's constitution comes next, followed by an outline of the document's contents. A description of constitutional amendments passed between 1848 and 1930 comes next, followed by a similar section for the period from 1931 to 2002. The fifth section contains an overview of other ways in which the state's constitution was changed or stretched between 1960 and 2002. The chapter concludes with some reflections on constitutional change and the vulnerability of constitutional protections.

TYPES OF STATE CONSTITUTIONS

Under the U.S. Constitution states are free to establish whatever kind of constitution they wish, as long as the government is of a republican form.[5] In a republic, sovereign power resides in the hands of the citizens who are entitled to vote for representatives. The representatives exercise power on the citizens' behalf and govern according to law.[6] In the American constitutional context, republican government also implies three separate branches of government (legislative, executive, and judicial). Despite these common institutional requirements, however, state constitutions differ in a variety of important ways. In fact, Daniel Elazar has identified at least six different types of state constitutions: commonwealth, commercial republic, southern contractual, French civil code, frame of government, and managerial.[7]

The frame of government (or Far West) constitutional type was used by several of the states that, like Wisconsin, were originally part of the Northwest Territory established in 1787.[8] This type of constitution places emphasis on the "structure of government and the distribution of powers within that structure."[9] Given that Wisconsin was the last of the states formed from this territory, its constitutional framers undoubtedly were aware of the forms adopted by other states.

Yet despite the state's regional setting, Wisconsin's constitution of 1848 is, perhaps, more appropriately described as a commonwealth form. The document contains a philosophic assumption about the proper role of government in a civil society, and it sets a direction for that society.[10] As already noted, the constitution was designed to limit the influence that large economic interests had over state government and to protect citizens from those economic interests. The document also contained a vision of what was and was not appropriate in the social sphere. For example, one of the articles contained in the 1848 constitution positioned the state firmly in opposition to divorce and prohibited the state from sponsoring lotteries.

During the remainder of the 1800s, several attempts were made to expand the state's role in regulating the economy and in delimiting social activities. Constitutional amendments were proposed to regulate railroads and to limit the consumption of alcoholic beverages. Taming the power of the railroads proved to be an uphill struggle, however, and the effort to limit drinking created a strong negative response from the state's large German population. In fact, the drinking issue played an important role in several legislative and gubernatorial elections. During the twentieth century, efforts to use the constitution to extend economic regulation continued, but efforts in the social area moved primarily into the arena of statutory law.

TERRITORIAL STATUS, STATEHOOD, AND THE STRUGGLE OVER THE FIRST CONSTITUTION

The "Territory of Wiskonsan," a name some historians associate with an old Native American word meaning "a gathering of the waters," was organized in 1836. The territory included what is now Wisconsin, Iowa, Minnesota, and part of the Dakotas.[11] Prior to this time, the area that became Wisconsin was first operated under the laws of the Indiana Territory. After Indiana became a state, the area of Wisconsin was operated under the laws of the Michigan Territory. Attempts to establish a constitutional convention, and thus begin the process of applying for statehood, were rejected by the voters in referendums held in 1840 and 1842, by votes of 499 to 92 and 1,821 to 619, respectively.[12] In 1843 and 1844 the territorial legislatures defeated statehood initiatives.[13] Rejection of the referendums is thought to have been due, in large part, to fears that taxes would have to be raised to pay for the new government.

In January 1846, however, the referendum for a constitutional convention was finally approved by a vote of 12,332 to 2,487.[14] The need for internal improvements and concerns about boundary-protection seem to have turned public opinion in favor of statehood. As a territory, large sections of Wisconsin land were lost through two actions taken by the U.S. Congress: the Illinois boundary was moved north to include Chicago, in order to give that new state access to the Great Lakes; and the northern peninsula of Wisconsin, which had rich copper and iron deposits, was given to Michigan, as repayment for land Ohio had taken from Michigan.[15]

These events and others led to the affirmative vote for statehood in 1846. The build-up to that vote and the remarkable debate over the state's first proposed constitution are described by historian Milo Quaife in his 1918 study:

> With the suddenness, seemingly of a western hurricane, there developed in the latter part of 1845, a demand on the part of the voters for admission of Wisconsin to the Union. For about a year and a half the storm of political discussion raged without a single lull. During this time the ideas of the voters as to the kind of government desired were formulated, the election of delegates to the first convention (that of 1846) and the convention itself were held, and the great debate over the question of ratifying the convention's work was fought out. . . . Probably never since then have the people of Wisconsin been absorbed in a political issue to the degree which prevailed from January 1846 to the election of April 1847.[16]

The 1846 constitutional document was written in Madison, the territorial capital, by 126 delegates. These delegates were elected from the counties of the Wisconsin Territory, after Governor Henry Dodge called for a constitutional convention. The convention's delegates were described as "thoroughly representative."[17] Forty-six delegates were New York natives, 42 were natives of New England, 29 were from Mid-Atlantic states, 9 from southern states, and 16 were foreign-born. Sixty-nine delegates were farmers, 26 were lawyers. The oldest delegate was 65, and the youngest 23.[18]

On the basis of the delegates' origins, some historians have described the 1846 convention as "predominantly an assemblage of young Yankee farmers."[19] Historians have also emphasized the "distinguished nature of the delegates," as they point out the large number of delegates who had served in the territorial legislature and local government and the number who were to be future officials in Wisconsin, including judges, legislators, congressmen, and governors.[20] Still other historians have emphasized the party or partisan make-up of the convention, by pointing out that a large majority was drawn from the Democratic Party, while the Whig Party was in the minority.

Each factor emphasized by historians provides a basis for understanding the dynamics and the outcome of the 1846 convention. First, many of the delegates had carefully fashioned views about the type of state government they wanted.[21] Second, partisan differences, aligned in part with national political parties, came into play during both the convention and its aftermath. Third, many of the delegates had similar ideas about how the convention should work and what the constitutional document itself should look like. The delegates' model was New York, specifically "the New York convention that sat during the summer of 1846" and the "constitution and political practice" of that state.[22] Even with these models as guideposts, however, the delegates to the Wisconsin convention are generally given high marks for their "independence of thought and readiness to experiment."[23]

The 1846 document has been described as largely the product of the Progressive Democrats. The members of this group were inspired by the Jacksonian reform initiatives designed to limit the power that economic interests had over the national government. Economic events and their effects also shaped the vision the Progressive Democrats had of politics and government. These events included the 1835–47 depression and its catastrophic effects on farmers and citizens, the financial collapse of states bordering Wisconsin that had invested heavily in canal (infrastructure) development, and bank scandals in Wisconsin itself.[24]

The Progressive Democrats wanted to avoid the corruption of state affairs by monied interests, particularly banks. They also wanted to avoid what they viewed as excessive control by financial interests over the lives of citizens.[25] Among the provisions they installed in the 1846 document were a prohibition against the incorporation of banks, a prohibition against the contracting of state debt for internal improvements, a prohibition against the seizure of homesteads in cases of bankruptcy, and the popular election of judges. The latter was seen as an essential part of blocking control of the courts by monied interests.

All of these provisions were controversial, and most members of the Whig Party objected to them. The Whigs in Wisconsin were closely aligned with the national party, and were viewed as the party of property and finance.[26] The Whigs' foremost interest seemed to be economic growth and land development. They viewed banks and internal improvements as critical to the economic development of the state and to the potential profits they could make on their landholdings. Additionally, the Whigs believed that judges should be appointed, not elected, and they opposed homestead protection in cases of bankruptcy.[27]

Two other matters addressed by the convention stirred controversy, and the Progressive Democrats' positions on these issues contributed to the defeat of the 1846 document at the polls. Progressive Democrats put a provision in the 1846 document that allowed women to maintain property—even after they were married. This was a radical idea for its time, and Retrograde Democrats and Whigs found it highly objectionable. One opponent of the measure, Edward V. Whiton, "predicted that the married women's rights provisions would lead to the 'utter destruction of the home and the annihilation of the marriage contract itself.' "[28]

The other issue that created controversy was suffrage for blacks. The abolitionist Liberty Party objected to the 1846 document because it did not contain provisions for "Negro suffrage." Both the Progressive Democrats and Whigs were largely antislave, but the Liberty Party pressed for a more dramatic response to slavery than the Progressive Democrats, or, for that matter, the Whigs, were prepared to provide.[29]

Each of the five controversial provisions and the failure to establish Negro suffrage provided a basis for mobilizing opposition to the 1846 document created by the Progressive Democrats, and the combined opposition of the Whigs, Retrograde Democrats, and of the Liberty Party proved too much. The 1846 document was rejected by the voters on April 6, 1847; 14,199 voters supported the document, but 20,321 voted against it.[30]

Not long after the defeat of the document, Governor Dodge called for another constitutional convention. This time, however, he called for a smaller number (sixty-nine) of delegates. Most members of the first convention refused to serve again, and only six of the sixty-nine delegates elected from the counties were returnees. As in the first convention, however, most of the delegates were natives of New York and New England, most were farmers and lawyers, and their ages ranged from twenty-five to sixty-nine. The similarity in demographic profile of the two groups is quite striking, but at least one historian reports that the second convention "was thought to represent a more conservative element than the first."[31]

The constitution approved in the 1848 convention was a new document,

chapter, are those pertaining to lotteries, divorce, and the use of public debt to fund internal (infrastructure) improvements.

The executive article provides for both a governor and a lieutenant governor, who are to be elected at the same time every two years. Unlike the constitutions of some other states, Wisconsin's constitution provides the governor with sufficient power to serve as more than a mere ceremonial figurehead. Among those "[p]owers and duties" is the responsibility for seeing that "the laws be faithfully executed." The governor is further granted the power to veto bills passed by the legislature, subject to a two-thirds override by both of its houses.

The administrative article provides for the offices of secretary of state, state treasurer, and attorney general. These officers are to be elected every two years. The duties of these three administrative officers, however, are, by and large, left to the determination of the legislature. The administrative article also contains provisions for the election of sheriffs, coroners, registers of deeds, and district attorneys in each county, and it grants the governor the power to remove any of these officers for cause.

The judiciary is to include a supreme court and five circuit courts. The supreme court is to have appellate jurisdiction only, and its five justices are to be drawn from the circuit courts. The term for these supreme court judges is to be five years. All circuit judges are to be elected and to serve terms of six years. The legislature is given the power to establish more circuit courts and judgeships as it sees fit. The legislature is also empowered to establish a permanent supreme court, "whenever the legislature may consider it necessary." Removal of judges for misconduct is also established in the 1848 document.

Article VIII is titled "Finance" and contains provisions affecting that topic on both the state and local governmental levels. Among the key requirements for state government is that all taxation "be uniform." Key prohibitions, as already noted, include that against the use of state debt for internal (infrastructure) improvements. Among the important provisions regarding local government finance is the authority given to state government to regulate local finance and to limit local government borrowing to 5 percent of annual revenue.

Article IX is titled "Eminent Domain and Property of the State" and Article X "Education." Article IX treats state jurisdiction on waterways and territorial property, and gives the state the power of eminent domain (that is, the power to take private property for public use). Article X provides for a state university, and it requires local governments to assess taxes to support education for those from ages four to twenty in order to secure state aid for primary and secondary education.

Article XI is titled "Corporations"; Article XII "Amendments"; Article XIII "Miscellaneous Provisions"; and Article XIV "Schedule." The Corporations article forbids the legislature from chartering or incorporating banks unless the public approves of such action through a referendum. Amendments are to be made through only two means: a convention, or a process in which two consecutive legislatures and then the voters of the state approve a change. The Miscellaneous Provisions article proscribes, among other things, both dueling and the simultaneous occupancy of both U.S. government and state government offices. Most notable in the article detailing matters of schedule is identification of the process through which the constitutional document is to be approved.

CONSTITUTIONAL AMENDMENTS AND INSTITUTIONAL DEVELOPMENT, 1848–1930

As noted earlier, Wisconsin's 1848 constitution was free of much of the detail included in many other state constitutions. As a result Wisconsin's governors and legislators could usually respond to changing circumstances and citizen demands by modifying statutes or creating new ones, rather than going through the difficult process required to amend the constitution.

In one important area, however, Wisconsin's constitutional framers did provide detailed instructions on some operational matters. For example, salaries for legislators, governors, and judges were fixed in the constitution. As a result the type of amendment voters were asked to consider most often during the first eighty-two years of statehood was raises for state officials in each of the three branches.

Pay Changes for State Officials

The first constitutional amendment designed to change the pay of an elected official appeared on the ballot fourteen years after statehood, in 1862.[37] At issue was whether the governor's pay would be raised from $1,250 per year to $2,500 per year. The proposed amendment was soundly defeated. In 1869, however, voters approved an amendment that increased gubernatorial pay from $1,250 to $5,000 per year. Forty-seven years later, in 1926, voters approved an amendment to repeal the constitutionally established salary and set gubernatorial pay by statute. Problems with the language of the amendment, however, meant that the process had to be repeated. Six years later, in 1932, the amendment was approved. From that point forward gubernatorial pay was set by statute.

The first-time voters were asked to approve a pay raise for legislators was in 1867. In that year, voters approved an amendment that raised legislators' pay from $3.50 per day to $350 per year. Fourteen years later, in 1881, voters approved another pay increase for legislators. This time the amendment called for an increase of $150, moving legislative pay up from $350 to $500. At that point, however, voter generosity seemed to come to an end. Pay increases for legislators were rejected in amendments voted on in 1909, 1914, 1923, and 1925. Additionally, an amendment that would have moved changes in legislative pay from a constitutional to a statutory process was rejected in 1919. The stalemate was finally broken, in 1929, when voters approved an amendment repealing the constitutionally fixed salary and authorized the setting of salaries by statute.

Salary for Wisconsin judges was set in the 1848 constitution at $1,500 annually. Thus, the starting salary for judges was higher than the governor's salary and considerably higher than the salary for legislators. The governor's salary moved higher than that of judges in 1869, as a result of a voter-approved amendment, but legislative pay continued to lag far behind. Interestingly, no amendment attempting to change the salary of judges was put to the voters until 1912. In that year voters approved an amendment that repealed the constitutionally fixed salary and gave the legislature the authority to set judicial salaries by statute.

In addition to changes in the pay of state officials, other important matters, such as the design, operation, and powers of the legislature, the courts, and the chief executive, were also the focus of proposed amendments between 1848 and 1930. Some of the most important are described below.

Changes in Legislative Operation

In 1854, only six years after the constitution was ratified, three proposed amendments dealing with the legislative branch were put to a vote of the people. The first amendment would have increased the term for assembly representatives from one to two years. The second amendment would have increased the term for senators from two to four years, and the third would have changed legislative sessions from an annual to biennial status. All three amendments were soundly defeated.

Twenty-five years later, however, in 1879, the same three provisions were packaged into a single amendment. That amendment was approved by two consecutive legislatures in 1880 and 1881. It was then put to a vote of the people, who approved the changes in the referendum of 1881.

Changes in the Supreme Court

The first attempt to make changes in the constitutional provisions (Article VII) for the judicial branch began in 1871. In that year, a proposed amendment to create a separate supreme court with four associate justices and a chief justice passed both houses of the legislature. As noted earlier in this chapter, the 1848 constitution provides for a supreme court whose justices would be drawn from the five circuit courts. It also stipulates that the legislature can modify the original arrangement at the end of five years. Thus, in 1853, the legislature used statutory means to establish a supreme court with a chief justice and two associate justices, all of whom were to be elected.[38]

Some citizens and legislators, however, believed that the foundation for the supreme court should be a constitutional provision rather than a statute. A proposed amendment passed in 1871 was passed for a second time by both houses of the legislature in 1872. The voters, however, rejected the amendment in 1872 by a vote of 29,755 to 16,272.[39]

Only four years after the 1872 amendment was defeated at the polls, however, the advocates of a separate supreme court with five justices again put forward their proposal. The proposed amendment was approved by the state legislatures of 1876 and 1877. Then, in 1877, voters approved the amendment by a vote of 79,140 to 16,763.[40] The amendment created a constitutionally chartered supreme court with a chief justice and four associate justices, with each justice elected to a ten-year term.

Two years later, in 1889, another constitutional amendment was passed that affected the state's highest court. This amendment stated that the justice with the longest continuous tenure would be the chief justice of the supreme court. Then, in 1903, voters approved an amendment that expanded the supreme court to six associate justices and a chief justice.

Changes in the Chief Executive

In contrast to the legislature and the supreme court, important constitutional changes in the powers and duties of the chief executive did not occur until after the turn of the century. In 1908 voters approved an amendment that required the governor to sign legislative bills within six days, lest the bill become law. The original language in the constitution did not have a time limit, so governors could sit on a bill passed by the legislature without taking any action. In short, the 1908 amendment seems to have been designed to curtail gubernatorial power by making the governor more responsive to the legislature.

In contrast to the 1908 amendment, a constitutional change approved by voters in 1930 substantially expanded the chief executive's power. The 1930 amendment gives the governor what, in political science texts, is commonly referred to as "item-veto" power, but is referred to as "partial-veto" power in Wisconsin Supreme Court decisions and other official sources, such as the *Wisconsin Blue Book*. The term "partial veto" seems to have its origins in the language employed in the 1930 amendment, which empowers the governor to approve bills of appropriation "in whole or in part."[41] The part of the appropriation bill not vetoed becomes law.

Proponents of the 1930 partial-veto amendment wanted to give Wisconsin's governor the means to cut out specific appropriations that contained pork-barrel spending. In an attempt to ensure that they did not give too much power away in the 1930 amendment, however, legislators reserved some recourse for their institution. Specifically, the amendment gives the legislature the opportunity to overturn the governor's partial veto with a two-thirds vote of both legislative houses. As a practical political matter, however, this is a very high hurdle for a legislature to meet.

Philip La Follette campaigned against the amendment when he ran for governor in 1930. He believed that the partial veto would give the chief executive too much power. Ironically, Philip La Follette ended up winning the election; thus he became the first governor to have the partial-veto power. True to his initial concerns, however, La Follette used this new power very sparingly.

CONSTITUTIONAL AMENDMENTS AND INSTITUTIONAL DEVELOPMENT, 1931–2002

With the exception of the amendment giving the governor partial-veto authority over appropriations in 1930, no amendments that significantly altered the powers, duties, or operations of any of the branches were approved during that decade; the same can be said of the 1940s and 1950s. Several amendments that affected the courts and the legislature were approved, but none had a significant effect.

It was not until the 1960s and 1970s that voters approved amendments that contained important institutional provisions. In 1967, two amendments were approved that affected the chief executive: one establishes joint election of the governor and lieutenant governor; the other increases the term for both the governor and the lieutenant governor from two to four years.

The change to the four-year term for the governor (and lieutenant governor) is made all the more important because no limit is set on the number of terms a governor (or lieutenant governor) can serve. This amounts to a crucial contrast with the actions of most states in the latter half of the twentieth century. Typically, when a four-year term for governors has been adopted, this change has been accompanied by a two-term limit.

A third amendment approved during this period (1977) had an effect on both the executive and legislative branches. The amendment removes the lieutenant governor from the position of presiding officer for the state senate and gives the senate the authority to choose its own presiding officer. This step diminishes both the visibility and relative importance of the lieutenant governor's role in the state.

During the 1970s four amendments were adopted that affected the courts. All four were approved by voters in the same year: 1975. The four amendments establish a unified (statewide) court system; create a new appeals court; designate by statute a retirement age for supreme court justices and other judges; and detail court-system disciplinary procedures. Patrick J. Lucey, the first Wisconsin governor to serve a four-year term (1970–77), pressed very hard to bring about a unified court system supported by state tax revenues.

During the 1980s and 1990s several constitutional amendments had an effect on the powers, duties, or operations of the legislature, chief executive, or judiciary. Of these, the most important is the 1990 amendment that limits governors' use of the partial-veto power. The amendment was initiated during the 1980s by legislators from both parties who believed that Governor Tommy Thompson had abused the powers granted by the constitution.

Thompson was using the partial veto to strike letters, words, or even sentences from the budget bill. By this means, he was able to create new words and thus new programs or appropriations without legislative involvement. Thompson was not the first governor to use the partial-veto power in this manner. During the 1970s, Governor Lucey began to employ some of these tactics, and his successors in the executive office, Sherman Dreyfus and Anthony Earl, expanded the use of the tool.

Governor Thompson's use of the partial veto, however, was a dramatic escalation over past practices. The expansion is illustrated by increases in the frequency with which the partial veto was used and the extent of the substantive changes made in legislation. It is noteworthy that Thompson himself expressed satisfaction with the aggressive way in which he used the partial veto. For example, Thompson, in his *Power to the People: An American State at Work* (1996), reports on the changes he made in the legislatively approved budget bill by using the partial veto. Thompson said, "I held a press conference to announce my vetoes. There were 290 in all—far more than any governor had done before."[42]

Given the way in which the partial veto was being used to strike letters, words, and sentences from budget bills, it was probably fitting that the amendment to constrain the chief executive's partial-veto power was labeled the "Vanna White Amendment," so named after the *Wheel of Fortune* television game show hostess, Vanna White, who revealed letters chosen by participants on a large game board (the game board letters were, of course, used to "create" words). In any case the amendment approved in 1990 included the following language: "In approving an appropriation bill in part, the governor may not create a new word by rejecting individual letters in the words of the enrolled bill."[43]

OTHER CONSTITUTIONAL DEVELOPMENTS, 1848–1930

The issue that generated the most heated debate during the constitutional conventions of 1846 and 1847 was whether banks would be allowed to form and incorporate under Wisconsin law. The convention of 1846 decided to prohibit banks from forming or incorporating. This prohibition was the single most important factor in the defeat of that document. The 1847 convention put language in the constitution that gave the legislature the power to charter banks if the people of the state approved of such action in a referendum. In other words, a favorable vote in an advisory referendum, rather than the more difficult constitutional amendment process, would be sufficient for bank operation to begin. On this basis, those who opposed the 1846 document supported the 1847 document, and their support led to the document's ratification in 1848.

An advisory referendum on the matter was held in 1851, and, by a margin of three to one, the voters said yes to banks. Then, in 1852, a referendum was approved that provided language under which banks could be incorporated and operated. That was far from the end of statewide votes on banking provisions, however. Additional referendums on banking were put to a vote of the people seven more times over the next forty years. In all cases except the last, the proposed banking provisions were approved. The only defeat came in 1898, when a referendum calling for the oversight of banks by a commission went down by a small margin.

In 1902, the constitutional provision (Article XI, section 5) that required a referendum on banking-law changes was repealed. From that point on, the matter could be handled through statutory changes alone. There is a small irony worth noting here. The constitutional amendment of 1902 came to fruition while Robert La Follette was governor and his Progressive supporters had a prominent voice in the legislature.

As champions of democracy in both its political and economic forms, La Follette and his legislative supporters were the direct descendants of the Progressive Democrats of 1846. It was those early "Progressives" who were determined to prevent the incorporation of banks, in order to protect state citizens from abuse by large economic interests. Yet a mere half-century later, La Follette and the other Progressives of the early 1900s seemed to be more concerned about making banking services available to citizens than they were about the risks that banks posed to those citizens.[44]

A second issue of great importance addressed by both the 1846 and 1847 constitutional conventions was whether the state could participate in internal (infrastructure) improvements. The constitutional documents produced by both conventions contain provisions that prohibit the use of state debt for internal improvements. Indeed, Article VIII, section 10, of the 1848 constitution says: "The state shall never contract any debt for works of internal improvement, or be a party in carrying on such works: but whenever grants of land or other property, shall have been made to the state, especially dedicated by the grant to particular works of internal improvement, the state may carry on such particular works, and shall devote thereto the avails of such grants, and may pledge or appropriate the revenues derived from such works in aid of their completion."[45]

This prohibition against internal improvements was not formally changed until 1908. The amendment was supported by the Progressives, who were determined to expand state services for citizens. The amendment adds a new sentence to the end of Article VIII, section 10, reading: "Provided, that the state may appropriate money in the treasury or thereafter to be raised through taxation for use in the construction or improvement of public highways."[46]

This new provision opened the door to the contracting of state debt for highway construction. Two years later, in 1910, an amendment was approved by voters that gave the state authority to borrow for the development of state water power and for the regeneration of state forests. The 1910 amendment, however, was declared invalid by the Wisconsin Supreme Court on procedural grounds.[47] Fourteen years later, in 1924, voters again approved the forestry provisions.

Other important issues addressed by the 1846 and 1847 constitutional conventions included whether judges would be elected or appointed, whether property rights would be established for married women, and whether suffrage would be extended to blacks. The first issue was decided in favor of election of judges, and no amendments were put forth in the state's first eighty years—or thereafter for that matter—to challenge this decision. Property rights for married women are established in the 1846 document, which was rejected by voters in 1847, and those rights are not included in the constitutional articles of 1848.

In 1849 an attempt was made to "extend suffrage for colored persons" through a referendum. The vote was 5,265 for the measure and 4,075 against, but the operating practices of the state apparently were not changed. Another referendum for the same purpose was defeated in 1857. In 1866, however, one year after the end of the Civil War, the Wisconsin Supreme Court ruled that the referendum of 1849 was valid. This time, state practice was brought in line with the referendum.

In 1876 women's political rights were extended when, through constitutional amendment, they were given the opportunity to vote on school-related matters. Then, in 1919, women were given suffrage rights for presidential elections, but this was done through statute rather than constitutional amendment. The other suffrage issue addressed by constitutional amendment during this period was the right of certain (white) alien males to vote. In 1908, an amendment was approved by voters that limited the right to vote to full citizens.

OTHER CONSTITUTIONAL DEVELOPMENTS, 1931–2002

Suffrage matters and the issue of whether the state ought to contract debt for infrastructure improvement also received attention through constitutional amendment processes during the period 1931–98. A constitutional amendment granting full suffrage for women was approved by legislative bodies in 1931 and 1933. Then, in 1934, it was approved at the polls by a vote of

411,088 to 166,744.[48] This affirmative vote came fourteen years after full suffrage rights were given to women through an amendment to the U.S. Constitution, and this rather tardy approval of full women's suffrage seems a bit at odds with Wisconsin's Progressive heritage.

With respect to state financing for infrastructure, amendments to the constitution during this period expand the categories of improvements for which state debt can be contracted. In 1945 aeronautical programs were added to the list of exceptions to the original constitutional prohibition in Article VII. In 1948 an amendment for veterans' housing was approved, and in 1960 an amendment that authorized state appropriations for port development won majority support at the polls. Then, in 1975, an amendment was approved to include transportation facilities among the internal improvements in which the state could invest.

A third area of constitutional change that occurred between 1931 and 1998 involved gambling. Specifically, the constitutional prohibition against lotteries was overturned in 1987. Article IV, section 24 (1), of the 1848 constitution says: "The legislature shall never authorize any lottery or grant any divorce." The 1987 amendment approved by state voters, however, opened the door for a state lottery.

After the passage of the amendment, Article IV, section 24 (1), of the constitution was modified to read: "*Except as provided in this section*, the legislature shall never authorize any lottery or grant any divorce."[49] The 1987 amendment also creates the following language in section 24 (6): the "legislature may authorize the creation of a lottery to be operated by the state as provided by law."[50] Soon after this 1987 provision was in place, the legislature passed the statutory authority for a state lottery.

Accompanying the 1987 lottery amendment was an amendment that prohibits the legislature from barring pari-mutuel betting. Although state sponsorship of pari-mutuel betting is forbidden in Article IV, section 24 (5), of the 1848 constitution, the legislature used the new constitutional language to give a green light to this form of gambling. Shortly after the amendment was passed, the legislature set out, by statutory means, the terms under which pari-mutuel betting could take place.

One other consequence of the lottery and pari-mutuel gambling amendments of 1987 is worth noting. By eliminating the gambling prohibition, the legislature and the voters provided an opening for Indian tribes to run casino gambling enterprises. It was an opening that many Indian tribes quickly used to their advantage, and casino gambling is now a big business in the state.

OTHER CONSTITUTION-RELATED ACTIVITIES, 1960–2002

In addition to amending state constitutions through the formal constitutionally prescribed procedures, there are several other ways in which state constitutions can be changed. For example, U.S. Supreme Court decisions and state supreme court decisions may overturn state constitutional provisions. Another way constitutional change comes about is through "custom and usage."[51] The latter type of change occurs informally, through changes in the practice of government office holders, administrators, and employees.

Some of these informal changes may be of little importance, while others may be significant. In functional terms these informal changes can be viewed as a lubricant for state governments that have old, outdated, detail-laden constitutions.[52] These constitutions may make it difficult or impossible for elected and administrative officials to respond to changing economic, social, and political circumstances in a timely manner. From a more formal, legal perspective, however, such informal changes might be viewed less charitably.

A third way in which constitutions can be changed is through new statutes. In some cases, the language of the statute may seem to fall outside of the boundaries established by constitutional language, but the new statutory language either goes unchallenged or it provides a basis for the courts to reinterpret the constitution. Like informal changes these statutory changes may be of little importance or, conversely, very important. Judgments vary about whether such changes involve "stretching" the constitution or finding ways to adapt constitutions to changing circumstances.

A number of highly publicized cases of constitutional adaptation or stretching took place between 1960 and 1999. Both "informal" means, or changes in practice, and statutory change were employed. The cases involved efforts to get around constitutional prohibitions on the use of state debt, to expand use of the partial veto, and to enhance gubernatorial authority to reorganize and manage one of the executive branch agencies.

The first case, involving both informal and statutory means to get around prohibitions on state debt, was considered a departure from the approach lawmakers took during the first half of the twentieth century. Beginning in the early 1900s and continuing for more than fifty years, a series of amendments were adopted that established state authority to borrow money for specific types of internal improvements, such as the construction and maintenance of highways, the management of forests, and improvements to ports. The history of these amendments shows, however, that they were approved only after many years of effort were invested by governors and legislators.

In 1960 state officials took a new approach toward using the state's credit for internal improvements. Rather than pursuing a constitutional amendment, they created a quasi-governmental corporation called the Wisconsin Housing Finance Authority. The initial purpose of the authority was to construct housing for the economically disadvantaged. Although there may have been a good moral argument for this state activity, the formation of this entity opened the door for those who wanted to expand the use of state debt for other forms of internal improvements. In 1983, for example, the authority's mission was expanded by statute to include economic development projects, and its name was changed to the Wisconsin Housing and Economic Development Authority (WHEDA).[53]

After 1983 WHEDA's mission was expanded to include loan guarantees as part of its economic development activities. Perhaps the most remarkable use of WHEDA's new powers occurred in 1996, when its borrowing authority was used to help finance a new $280 million domed stadium with a retractable roof for the Milwaukee Brewers baseball club. Through WHEDA up to $50 million of bonds or notes were committed for this purpose.[54] State officials also found another way to supply an additional $160 million of bonds to finance the stadium.

Although Wisconsin was neither the first nor the last state to invest in a stadium for a professional sports team, the way in which this financing was put together is a rather remarkable story. Indeed the public officials who backed this move, including Governor Thompson and a group of state legislators, had to overcome a series of setbacks to arrange the deal. The most important and visible of those setbacks was the defeat of a 1995 constitutional amendment that would have established a sports lottery as the financing mechanism for the stadium.[55]

Public rejection of the sports lottery probably would have stopped state officials who were less determined or creative than the stadium supporters. This group, however, found alternatives to the sports lottery. They used WHEDA as one of the alternatives. Specifically, a WHEDA loan was the source for $50 million of the $90 million the Brewers were to pay as their part of the stadium costs.[56] The second part of the financing package was a new mechanism created in Wisconsin Act 56. Commonly known as the Stadium Act of 1995, this act declares that the stadium has an important public purpose: economic development. The act also authorizes the creation of a "stadium district," which, in turn, is authorized to sell up to $160 million worth of bonds.[57] Wisconsin Act 56 also gives the stadium district authority to establish a 1-percent sales tax as the means to repay the bonds.[58]

What makes this case interesting is that language contained in Article VII (sections 10 and 3) of the state constitution seems to prohibit such actions. For example, section 3 states that "the credit of the state shall never be given or loaned in aid of any individual, association, or corporation."[59] In this case, however, it appears that the state's credit was used in aid of a corporation—the Milwaukee Brewers.

Whether the constitution allowed such action was one matter. A related issue was the credit-worthiness of the private corporation the state was going to support. According to the legislature's own study, the Milwaukee Brewers Corporation may have had no net worth, or may even have had a negative net worth, at the time the state's resources were committed.[60] Net worth is, of course, one of the key factors used by banks to determine whether a loan should be made. Thus, in simple financial terms the state-supported "loan" for the Brewers was rather unusual.

In 1996 the constitutionality of the Stadium Act was challenged by the Libertarian party of Wisconsin.[61] The supreme court, however, rejected the challenge. Among the reasons the court gave for rejecting the plaintiffs' objections to WHEDA's involvement in the stadium's financing was that the legislature had specified that a public purpose was to be served in building the stadium—that is, economic development.[62] The court also maintained that the "stadium district," the agency set up to collect sales taxes to pay off the bonds used to finance the stadium, was not a state agency. Given the supreme court's decision, the constitutional stretching that seems to have occurred here was validated, in part because the legislature provided statutory authorization for the actions.

The elastic qualities of constitutional language were also underscored in a case involving the partial veto. As previously noted in this chapter, Governor Thompson was using the partial veto to create new laws without legislative participation. He did so by excising digits, letters, and words included in the state budget bill to create new words and new meanings.

In 1987 the legislature asked the supreme court to stop Thompson from using the partial veto to change legislative intent. In a four-to-three decision in 1988, however, the court upheld Thompson's actions.[63] The court's decision motivated the legislature to take action on its own. After passage by two consecutive legislatures, in 1989 and 1990, an amendment was approved by the voters in 1991 that prohibited use of the partial veto to create new law.

In two other cases where constitutional stretching seemed to have taken place during the 1980s and 1990s, the Wisconsin Supreme Court made judgments showing that there are indeed limits to the constitution's elasticity. In the first case, the court curtailed the governor's power regarding other constitutionally elected officials. The case grew out of a dispute between Governor Thompson and another constitutionally elected executive-branch official, State Superintendent of Public Instruction John Benson. The two men not only disagreed about public policy in the field of education but also its implementation. At the request of Thompson, the legislature passed a statute in 1996 that created a Department of Education, with a secretary that served at the pleasure of the governor.[64]

This action essentially disenfranchised Benson, who, as part of his official duties, was the chief administrator of the Department of Education. The action was challenged in state court. In a 1996 decision the supreme court ruled that the governor and the legislature could not strip a constitutionally established administrative official of his duties or his department.[65]

In the second case, the supreme court set limits on the use of the partial veto. The antagonists in the case were the legislature and Governor Thompson. The state senate objected to the governor's use of the partial veto for revenue matters in the state budget bill (1995 Assembly Bill 557). In its 1997 decision, the court said that the governor could not use the partial veto in matters related to revenue. Here is language from the court's decision: "At the core our tripartite system of government is the principle that the power of each branch must know limits. Wisconsin governors have perhaps more extensive power to alter legislation than do any other state governors. But a governor's power to craft legislation necessarily must have constitutional limits. A write-in veto power which extends beyond the reduction of appropriation amounts intrudes too far into the constitutional grant of legislative power vested in the Senate and the Assembly."[66]

Elasticity and Its Limits

The cases outlined in this section illustrate important factors about state constitutions. These cases show the "elasticity" of state constitutions; they also demonstrate that there may be limits to the amount of stretching that can be done. Additionally the cases highlight the fact that the state supreme court may be asked to delineate those boundaries. Finally, the cases seem to show that the court may be reluctant to intervenc in disputes between the legislature and the governor.

For some readers, the most interesting case material presented here may be the court's apparent reluctance to stop a governor from using the partial veto to create laws that were neither considered nor passed by the legislature. One can only speculate about the long-term effects this circumstance might have had on Wisconsin politics and government if it had not been constrained in 1997. It is also important to note that efforts to constrain this power were initiated by the opposition party in the senate. If the governor's party had controlled both houses of the legislature, the outcome of this power struggle between two branches of government might have been different.

Is court reluctance to intervene in disputes between the legislature and the governor unique to Wisconsin? It may be the rule rather than the exception. Supreme court justices may view these disputes as political struggles rather than as legal or constitutional matters. At the same time, there are risks associated with this type of interpretation. If a state supreme court does not intervene to stop the stretching of the state constitution by one of the branches, the whole notion of the court as a protector of the constitution could be open to question.

CONSTITUTIONAL PROTECTIONS AND THEIR LIMITATIONS

Because constitutions both limit and permit government activity, distribute powers among the government institutions and actors, and shape and constrain the ways in which public laws are made, they ultimately shape the distribution of benefits and burdens in a state. Consequently it is not surprising that attempts to amend state constitutions are an important and ongoing part of state politics. Here we have looked at attempts to modify Wisconsin's constitution through processes prescribed in the document itself. We have also discussed other means by which state constitutions are modified or ignored.

The examples of extraconstitutional activity described in this chapter illustrate some of the rather dramatic ways in which constitutional provisions can be stretched by actors inside and outside of the governmental system. This concept may be surprising to those who assume that matters of constitutional law are straightforward legal, rather than political, matters. At the same time, these examples highlight both the vital importance and the limitations of constitutional documents.

Nor are these illustrations of the sometimes elastic nature of certain constitutional protections limited to recent times. An example from the state's early history underscores in a most remarkable fashion the ways in which the intent of the constitutional framers was breached. At the beginning of this chapter, we noted the efforts made by Wisconsin's constitutional framers to prevent large economic interests from taking over the state's governmental machinery and using it to oppress state citizens. Yet not even ten years after the Wisconsin Constitution was approved, the railroads and timber industry began their assault on that constitutional assumption.

As the United States government gave land it owned to the state for development purposes, the state in turn gave the land to the railroads for infrastructure improvement.[67] The railroads then used the land and the tracks they put on it to control the flow of goods from farm to market. The railroads charged exorbitant rates for the transport of goods, and those rates often prevented the farmers from making a profit on their crops.

As the railroads' economic power grew, so too did their political power. By the late 1850s they were found to be bribing legislators.[68] Yet this discovery did little to slow the growth in their economic and political power. Furthermore, as the railroads joined forces with the lumber barons, they essentially gained control over the state government. As a number of Wisconsin historians have noted, no matter of consequence was decided without the approval of the bosses.

The net effect was that the railroads and timber bosses controlled much of state policymaking for almost thirty years. Had it not been for Robert La Follette and the legislators and voters who supported him, the control these economic interests had over state government and state citizens would not have been broken in the early 1900s. Nor, without La Follette and his supporters, would the state have emerged, during the early 1900s, to serve as a Progressive (moralistic) model for the nation.

The constitutional framers had put the state on the right course, but it was up to a future generation to move the ship of state back onto the course the framers had charted originally. Indeed the challenge of keeping the ship of state on course is ongoing. Perhaps it is not surprising that La Follette himself made such an observation when in 1887 he noted that "to every generation, some important work is committed."

CHAPTER THREE

The Legislature

The Progressive Republicans dominated both houses of the (1911) Legislature . . . (and they) had a coherent ideology. . . . They focused on the most important problems confronting the state and resolutely attempted to solve them.

Jack Stark, "Useful Lessons from the 1911
Legislature," *State Legislatures*, July–August 2000

A person newly elected to the legislature enters an institution that has a well-established organizational structure: complex rules of procedure, a division of labor that is largely preordained, patterns of leadership, unwritten rules of the game, and time-honored traditions. New members . . . have to "learn the ropes," make new friends, and adapt themselves to conflicting demands and pressures.

Samuel C. Patterson, "Legislative Politics in the States," 1996

Wisconsin's capital city, Madison, is a congenial setting for lawmaking.[1] The city's downtown is located on an isthmus between Lakes Mendota and Monona, and the Capitol occupies a hill near the center of this isthmus. The Capitol is graced by a large and beautiful dome, and its four wings extend out from the building's center toward the four points of the compass. The Senate Chamber is located on the second floor of the south wing; the Assembly Chamber is located on the second floor of the west wing.[2] The other two major governmental institutions, the Office of the Governor and the Wisconsin Supreme Court, are located in the east wing.

In part because it has, after the U.S. Capitol, the tallest dome in the country, and in part because of its natural setting, Wisconsin's Capitol is visible from many miles away. Whether one is driving up East Washington or West Washington Avenue toward the Capitol during the daytime, or looking toward the lighted dome at night across Lake Mendota or Lake Monona, the view is breathtaking. The prominence of the Capitol seems well suited to a state in which strong governmental institutions are highly valued and public service is held in high esteem.

This chapter begins with a brief overview of the legislature's Progressive foundations and its modern reputation. Then the two houses of the institution, the senate and assembly, are described and compared. Next, membership in the legislature is discussed, with emphasis given to members' resources and compensation, party affiliation, demographic characteristics, and careers. Legislative organization and operation is the fourth topic examined, with emphasis placed on the process by which a bill becomes a law and on the roles played by legislative committees, leadership, and support agencies. Legislative activity, which consists of policymaking, oversight, and constituent casework, is examined next. The chapter concludes with a discussion of some of the important challenges facing the legislature.

PROGRESSIVE FOUNDATION, REPUTATION, AND PROFESSIONALISM

An integral element of Wisconsin's Progressive heritage has been the drive of its leaders to improve the social, economic, and political circumstances of the state's citizens. There has also been the drive to improve the effectiveness of governmental institutions through experimentation and innovation. Since the early 1900s the Wisconsin legislature has been a pioneer in developing important institutional and procedural innovations that have been widely adopted by other states. For example, Wisconsin was the first state to provide professional staff assistance to its legislature (1901; Legislative Reference Library), to adopt a plan for continuous revision of its statutes (1909; Revisor of Statutes), and to establish a permanent legislative body to study "subjects affecting the welfare of the state" (1947; Legislative Council).[3]

Wisconsin was also among the first states to require fiscal notes for all legislative bills (1953; Legislative Fiscal Bureau), and to have a joint legislative committee for the review of administrative rules (1955; Joint Committee for Review of Administrative Rules).[4] Today the legislature continues to be innovative in such areas as bill drafting and automation of its internal processes. The legislature is also pioneering ways of enhancing communication between the state's citizens and their legislators.[5]

Another important element of Wisconsin's Progressive heritage is that the state's citizens expect openness in the legislative process, and they expect their elected representatives to be honest and hard-working. To ensure that all representatives do act responsibly, legislators have enacted open-meetings laws and strict ethics rules. The latter prohibit the state's elected representatives from taking anything of value from a lobbyist or citizen— including so much (or little) as a lunch or a drink. These formalized institutional norms, coupled with high citizen expectations, mean that violations of those standards do not happen very often. A less attractive aspect of this circumstance, however, is that missteps by legislators that might be considered minor indiscretions in most states may be presented as scandalous by Wisconsin's press.

Historically, Wisconsin's legislature has a good reputation. For instance, the 1911 legislature, which was dominated by Progressives, won national visibility and acclaim for its remarkable record of accomplishment.[6] A study of state legislatures published in 1970 ranked Wisconsin's among the top five in the country.[7] Since that study was conducted, staff and agency support for the legislature has been steadily strengthened.

More recent rankings that are of interest to students of state legislatures identify Wisconsin as one of nine states that have highly professional legislatures; the others are California, Illinois, Massachusetts, Michigan, New Jersey, New York, Ohio, and Pennsylvania.[8] All of these states, as reported in a 1994 National Conference of State Legislatures study, had relatively long legislative sessions, high salaries for legislators, high levels of staff support, and high numbers of legislators who were employed full-time. In contrast, sixteen mostly rural states had short sessions, low pay, low staff support, and few full-time members. The remaining twenty-five states ranked between the high and low groups.

Among the institutional attributes legislative scholars, such as Samuel C. Patterson, have associated with professional legislatures are legislative expertise, legislative capability to respond to citizens' wishes and demands, and legislative capability to engage in oversight of the administrative agencies.[9] For comparative purposes, readers of this chapter will find a wonderful portrait of the rural legislature in Diane D. Blair and Jay Barth's *Arkansas Politics and Government* and an excellent example of a legislature that falls in between the professional and rural legislatures in Cole Blease Graham Jr. and William V. Moore's *South Carolina Politics and Government*.[10]

THE SENATE AND THE ASSEMBLY

The senate has thirty-three members; the assembly has ninety-nine members. The formal requirements for election to both houses are the same: a person must have been a resident of the state for at least one year, and must be a qualified voter from the district he or she wishes to represent. To be a qualified voter, a person must also be at least eighteen years of age. Each senator and each member of the assembly represents a single district. The districts are drawn in such a way that each senate district contains three assembly districts.

Members of the assembly serve two-year terms, while members of the senate serve four-year terms, with half of the senate elected every two years. The sixteen senators representing even-numbered districts are elected in the same year the U.S. president is elected; the seventeen senators from odd-numbered districts are elected in the same year that Wisconsin's governor is chosen. Districts range in size from those that cover only a part of a city (Milwaukee or Madison) to those that cover several counties. The ideal population size for senate districts was established as 162,536 during the 2002 redistricting undertaken by the U.S. District Court for the Western District of Wisconsin; the ideal size for an assembly district was set at 54,179 people.[11]

Wisconsin's 1848 constitution requires the legislature to redraw districts for both legislative houses after each U.S. decennial census. The objective of this provision is to have each legislator represent an approximately equal number of citizens. Consequently, Wisconsin did not experience the dramatic urban-rural realignment in legislative seats that occurred in many states after the U.S. Supreme Court's decisions in 1962 (*Baker v. Carr*) and 1964 (*Reynolds v. Sims*).[12]

Nevertheless, the redistricting efforts that followed those Court decisions and the 1970 census were particularly contentious.[13] Difficulties arose in the efforts to redraw legislative and congressional districts because of the need to comply with all of the U.S. Supreme Court's principles; the requirement to reduce the number of assembly seats from one hundred to ninety-nine; and the task of making three assembly districts fit within each senate district. An additional complicating factor was that Democrats controlled the governorship and the assembly, but Republicans controlled the senate. After extended negotiations, the 1971–73 legislature finally passed a redistricting plan, and the governor signed it. Because the lines for the legislative districts were drawn primarily to protect incumbents of both parties, the plan appeared to be a "hodgepodge" with "no logic."[14] For this reason and others, the redistricting plan was challenged in the state supreme court, but the court refused to invalidate it.[15]

The map presented to the court in 1972 included some important changes in district geography and party-registration figures, which led to some changes in membership in the senate, the assembly, and the U.S. House of Representatives. In fact, turnover rates for the election that followed the 1970s redistricting were a good deal higher than rates in years that preceded it. Turnover rates were also higher after redistricting in the early 1980s and 1990s than in years that preceded or followed those changes.[16] It is worth noting that this pattern matches the national pattern, in which turnover peaks occurred after redistricting in the 1970s, 1980s, and 1990s.[17]

Senate and Assembly Differences

The senate and assembly differ in a number of ways, including, as noted previously, the number of people represented, length of terms of office, and even the size of the legislative houses themselves. The senate is more formal and orderly than is the assembly. It has fewer committees and fewer members on each committee than does the assembly; there are also fewer people to participate in floor debates than there are in the assembly. Consequently, a senator is likely to have more influence over any given piece of legislation than would a representative in the lower house.

Another difference between the two houses is the perception of time that guides the two institutions. Members of the senate can take a long-term view in responding to constituent needs or demands. In contrast, members of the assembly are generally more likely to feel the pressure to make rapid changes, and to do things that will enhance their reputations prior to their upcoming reelection campaign. These factors may make the assembly seem both more dynamic and more boisterous than the senate.

Thus, the tempo, focus, and priorities of the senate and the assembly tend to differ. These differences can also lead to competition for control of the legislative agenda, and they sometimes lead to open conflict between the two houses. Of course conflict between the two bodies is most likely to occur when the houses are not under the control of the same party. Competition for power between the leaders of the two houses can also accentuate interinstitutional differences and spur conflict. Both of these factors have come into play during recent decades. One former leader, however, Assembly Speaker Tom Loftus, maintains that the party leaders in both houses made concerted efforts during the late 1980s and 1990s to find common ground.[18] Fred Risser, senate president during the years that Democrats held a majority in the senate during the 1990s, contends that these efforts enabled relatively smooth transitions to occur during the 1995–96 legislative session, when there were three changes in majority control of the senate.[19]

MEMBERS

Whether an elected state representative is serving in the upper or lower house, the resources available to that legislator play a key role in how effectively he or she can function. Among such resources, two are particularly important: office space and staff assistance. In some states, legislators have had to work out of the trunks of their cars because they have not had office space. They have also had to work without staff assistance for important tasks like responding to constituent mail, scheduling appointments in the Capitol, arranging meetings in the home district, preparing speeches, and evaluating legislation.

Resources

In comparison to their peers in other states, Wisconsin's legislators fare very well when it comes to office space and staff support. During the 2003–4 legislative session, all members of the senate had private offices—something senators have enjoyed since the mid-1980s. In addition, all senators had at least three staff members. Committee chairs were given one additional staff person, for a total of four. The principal officers of the senate, including the president, president pro tempore, majority leader, assistant majority leader, minority leader, and the assistant minority leader, each had five staff members. As a practical matter, this distribution of staff means that all members of the majority party end up with four or five staff assistants because they all hold either committee chair or leadership positions.

All members of the 2003–4 assembly also had private offices. This was not always the case; in fact, it was not until renovation of the Capitol was completed in 1998 that all members enjoyed this luxury. Like their senate counterparts, members of the assembly are provided staff support.[20] All representatives have an average of one and one-half staff assistants; committee chairs have two. The majority leader has five staff members, and the assistant majority leader has three; the minority leader has five staff members, and the assistant minority leader has three. The Speaker has six staff assistants, and the speaker pro tempore has five.

In the area of compensation, like offices and staff, Wisconsin legislators are better off than most of their counterparts in other states. Members of both the 2001–2 assembly and senate received the same pay, $45,569 per year.[21] Although this is far from the highest pay among the states, the compensation level puts Wisconsin in the top 25 percent. More importantly, it is sufficient compensation to allow Wisconsin legislators to be full-time legislators if they choose to be.

Members of both houses are also reimbursed for travel and living expenses. This is very important for most legislators because the state capital is not their home. Specifically, legislators qualify for $88 for living expenses for each day of the legislative session if they certify that Madison is their temporary residence. Additionally, legislators receive reimbursement for one round trip per week from the state capital to their homes.

Party Affiliation

Studies of state legislatures conducted by political scientists often focus on members' party affiliation, a variable presumed to have an important connection to the types of public laws or public policies made by a legislature. For example, since the 1949 publication of V. O. Key's pioneering study, *Southern Politics in State and Nation*, there has been reason to believe that single-party control of a legislature is likely to yield policies that are adverse to the needs and circumstances of both lower economic classes and particular groups, such as African Americans.[22] Thus data on party affiliation is generally examined to determine whether membership in the legislature reflects two-party competition.

Historically, most members of the Wisconsin legislature have been drawn from the Republican Party, and indeed Ripon, Wisconsin, claims the title of "Birthplace of the Republican Party." A meeting to organize a new party was held in Ripon on February 28, 1854, and a statewide party convention followed in Madison on July 13, 1854. While Wisconsinites are justifiably proud of Ripon's claim, it is only fair to acknowledge that Jackson, Michigan, offers a competing one.[23] That city's claim seems to be based on the date of the statewide party convention held on July 6, 1854, one week before the statewide party convention held in Madison, Wisconsin.

In any case, only a year and a half after the February 28, 1854, meeting in Ripon, Wisconsin's Republican Party enjoyed electoral successes, and it quickly became the dominant party in the state. Yet even during the nearly one hundred years of Republican dominance, from 1860 through the late 1950s, it is at least arguable that two-party competition existed because the Democratic Party served "as the political agency for an occasionally effective mobilization of opposition to the ins."[24] Nevertheless, for most of this period, control of both legislative houses was firmly in the hands of the Republicans.

"Wisconsin's dominant [r]epublicanism," says Leon Epstein, "resembled that of most north central states." Largely as a result of the Civil War, republicanism was equated with "patriotism and respectability," especially in "Wisconsin counties settled by Yankees from New England and upstate New York." The liquor issue, Epstein says, "also served to solidify support with the temperance minded, native American Protestant."

Conversely, traditional Democratic support came primarily from those citizens who found themselves outside of the value system represented by the Yankee conscience, such as German and Irish immigrants. Nevertheless, because it was "at least as conservative as the Republican [P]arty," Epstein says, the Democratic Party did not serve as a vehicle for generating economic protest or political reform.

The weakness of the Democratic Party in the 1890s and early 1900s was further exacerbated by the rise of Robert La Follette and the Progressive movement within the Republican Party. La Follette's hard-fought victory within the Republican Party in 1900 and his subsequent election as governor "rendered nearly impossible," says Epstein, the "vitalization of the Democratic [P]arty as a liberal opposition." Thus from the early 1900s through 1932 Wisconsin politics was conducted largely within the Republican Party, and the Progressive faction was in control of the party for most of these years.

In 1934 the Progressives split from the Republican Party and formed their own party. Subsequently, the Progressive Party enjoyed some success in gubernatorial and legislative elections. For several reasons, however, including the opposition of its leader, Robert M. La Follette Jr., to America's entry into World War II, the party's fortunes declined, and its members disbanded in 1946.[25] Many Progressives returned to the Republican Party; others moved to the Democratic Party. This change finally gave the Democrats the opportunity to become the liberal opposition party. Although the reconstituted Democratic Party did not win a statewide race until 1957, when William Proxmire was elected to the U.S. Senate, the party gained majority control in the assembly in 1958. This victory marked the revival of two-party competition in the state.

Since the late 1950s there has been two-party competition for control of the legislature. In the state assembly, for example, majority control changed hands four times during the eighteen elections held between 1958 and 1996.[26] No change occurred in the 1998, 2000, or 2002 elections. In the senate, majority control changed hands four times between 1958 and 1996.[27] No change occurred in the 1998 or 2000 elections, but majority control did change again as a result of the 2002 election. The shifts in majority control have largely paralleled the national electoral fortunes of Democrats and Republicans, but circumstances specific to Wisconsin have also played an important role.

A snapshot of party affiliation in Wisconsin's legislature is presented in table 1. The table contains data for the years 1965, 1975, 1985, 1995, and 2003.

The data in table 1 show that Republicans had majorities in both the senate and the assembly in 1965. In 1975 and 1985, Democrats held majorities in both houses. In 1995, Republicans had a majority in both houses. During the 1995–96 legislative session, however, Republicans lost control of the Senate.

Winning and Losing Majority Status in the Senate

The method by which the Republicans captured and then lost majority control of the senate during the 1995–96 legislative session is a fascinating story of lucky breaks and high-stakes political intrigue. The roots of the contest extend back to 1992. The year began with Democrats holding an eighteen-to-fifteen majority in the senate. During the November elections, however, two incumbent Democratic senators won congressional election victories. Russ Feingold won a U.S. Senate seat, and Peter Barca won a U.S. House seat.[28]

These victories created two vacancies in the Wisconsin Senate, and Republican Governor Tommy Thompson managed to create a third vacancy by luring Democratic senator Marvin Rochelle out of his senate seat by offering him a higher paying job in an executive branch agency.[29] As a result, the party lineup in the senate was evenly divided (fifteen seats each), and the Republicans only needed to win two of the three special elections held to fill the empty seats and gain control of the senate.

In the spring of 1993 the Republicans did win two of the three special

Table 1. The Wisconsin Legislature, 1965–2003: Party Affiliation and Demographic Characteristics

	1965		1975		1985		1995		2003	
	Senate	Assembly	Senate	Assembly	Senate	Assembly	Senate	Assembly	Senate	Assembly
Party										
Democrat	12	52	18	63	19	52	16	48	15	41
Republican	20	48	13	36	14	47	17	51	18	58
Age										
Average	55	48	45	41	43	42	48	45	51	49
Youngest	26	25	27	20	29	24	31	26	33	27
Oldest	75	75	78	72	61	72	67	69	75	75
Education										
Beyond H.S.	17				4	14	2	15	29	87
Bachelors Degree		43	22	57	14	43	18	38	24	61
Advanced Degree			16	28	12	30	8	26	8	32
Occupation										
Full-time Legis.					8	37	12	40	13	39
Attorney	10	23	12	14	9	14	6	10	3	8
Farmer	4	17	0	14	4	14	1	14	3	9
Other			19	71	9	22	14	35	15	45
Gender										
Male	32	97	30	90	29	77	25	75	25	72
Female	0	2	1	9	3	22	8	24	8	27
Race										
White	32	95	31	97	32	96	31	93	31	92
African American	0	2	1	2	1	3	2	6	2	6

Sources: "Personal Data on Wisconsin Legislators," *Wisconsin Blue Book* for 1965, 1975, 1985–1986, 1995–1996, 2003–2004; "Members of State Legislature," *Wisconsin Blue Book* for 1965, 1975, 1985–1986, 1995–1996, 2003–2004

election contests. By doing so, they ended nineteen years of Democratic control in the senate, dating back to 1974. During the 1994 elections Republicans retained a one-seat majority in the senate. Thus the 1995–96 legislative session began with the Republicans holding a seventeen-to-sixteen majority in the senate and a three seat (fifty-one to forty-eight) majority in the assembly. Midway through the session, however, the Democrats gained a one-seat majority in the senate.

The mid-session change in the senate was the result of a highly unusual recall election in which the incumbent Republican senator, George Petak, was defeated by Democratic challenger Kimberly Plache. The recall resulted from constituent dissatisfaction over Senator Petak's tie-breaking vote in support of what his opponents described as a $160 million state subsidy for the Milwaukee Brewers' new baseball stadium, and an additional $50 million of construction loans. One "cost" of the deal was a sales-tax surcharge levied on five southeastern Wisconsin counties.[30] Part of all of these counties were in the district represented by Senator Petak. Petak had promised his constituents that he would not support this deal, and he did work against it in the legislature. At the eleventh hour, however, he changed his position and voted for the bill. Consequently, Petak was recalled by his constituents, and he lost his bid to retain his seat.

Demographic Characteristics

Demographic data on legislative members, such as age, education, occupation, gender, and race, are examined for several reasons. The data are used to compare legislatures across states and to track changes in the demographic makeup of legislatures. Demographic data are also used to see how closely the elected representatives reflect the composition of the state's population. Some political scientists, as well as others outside of academe, believe that the more closely a representative body fits the demographic characteristics of its constituents, the more representative its actions will be.

Specifically there is a presumption that legislators whose demographic characteristics most closely resemble their constituents will be better able to understand and pursue the wishes of those citizens in the state legislature. Like the data on party affiliation contained in table 1, the data on age, education, occupation, gender, and race contained therein yield an interesting portrait of the Wisconsin legislature.

For example, the data for the 2003–4 legislature show that the majority of legislators are white males who are college-educated and in their mid-to late forties. This demographic profile is similar to that of legislators in most other states.[31] In one important respect, however, the current profile of Wisconsin legislators appears to differ significantly from most states. The most commonly held occupation of legislators in other states is that of lawyer or businessman. The occupation listed with greatest frequency in Wisconsin is "full-time legislator."[32]

In the 2001–2 legislature, for example, fifteen of the thirty-three senators (45 percent) and forty of the ninety-nine representatives (40 percent) identified themselves as "full-time legislators."[33] Several observers of the legislature estimate that the number of full-time legislators may actually be as much as 50 percent higher than those totals. At least one study put the percentage of full-time legislators in Wisconsin at 60 percent.[34] Since the percentage of full-time state legislators on a national basis is less than 16 percent in the lower house and 14 percent in the senate, Wisconsin's numbers for the 2001–2 legislature were somewhere between two and three times higher than the national figures.[35]

It is worth noting, however, that data on the 2003–4 legislature show that fewer members (thirteen senators and thirty-nine representatives) identified their occupation as "full-time legislator" than did so in the 2001–2 legislature. This change could be the result of changes in the membership, or it could be the result of a growing reluctance on the part of legislators to identify themselves as "full-time legislators." In either case "full-time legislator" remained the number one occupation of Wisconsin legislators.

Just as the data in table 1 can be used to make comparisons with other states, they also provide a basis for looking at whether the makeup of the Wisconsin legislature has changed over time. Here, too, there is an interesting pattern. Perhaps the most dramatic change over the forty-year period is the sharp increase in the number of women members in both the senate and the assembly. In 1965 there were no women serving in the senate, and there were only two women serving in the assembly. The numbers of women serving in both chambers rose steadily during the 1970s, 1980s, and 1990s, reaching peak levels in the 2001–2 legislature.

During the 1990s the number of women serving in the legislature put Wisconsin among the top tier of states in that category.[36] In the 2001–2 legislature there were eleven women in the senate (33 percent) and twenty-two women in the assembly (27 percent). Although the numbers of women were lower in the 2003–4 legislature than in the 2001–2 session, Wisconsin was one of twenty states in 2003 in which women made up at least one-quarter of the state legislature.[37] In 2003 there were eight women in the senate (24 percent), twenty-seven (27 percent) in the assembly, and women held leadership positions in both the senate and the assembly.

Another change that has occurred in legislative membership is the number of African Americans who are members of the senate and assembly. In 1965 there were no African American members of the senate, and there were only two African American members of the assembly. In 2003 there were two African Americans in the senate and six in the assembly. These numbers make the percentage of African Americans in the legislature a little over 6 percent, a percentage that matches the African American share of the statewide population. Perhaps even more important is that these African Americans represent districts in Milwaukee, and, in one case, Racine, that have a substantial African American population base. Wisconsin's black representation in the state legislature is the same as the national average of 6 percent.[38]

Also worth noting is the fact that the first Latino representative was elected to the Wisconsin legislature in 1998 as the representative of the assembly's Eighth District. Pedro Colón was reelected in 2000 and 2002, and he faced no opposition in the 2004 election. The largest ethnic group in the Eighth Assembly District is Hispanic (39 percent).[39] On a statewide basis, however, only 3.6 percent of the Wisconsin population identified themselves as Hispanic or Latino in the 2000 census.

Finally, some interesting changes took place in average age, education, and principal occupation of legislators over the nearly forty-year period covered by table 1. The average age of legislators in both houses declined during the 1970s and 1980s, but it rose again during the 1990s. In 2003 the average age of senators was somewhat lower (fifty-one) than it was in 1965 (fifty-five), but the average age of representatives in 2003 (forty-nine) was slightly higher than it was in 1965 (forty-eight).

The number of legislators with bachelor's degrees rose steadily during the 1960s, 1970s, 1980s, and 1990s, reaching a high point in the 2001–2 legislature. In the 1965–66 legislature 52 percent of the senators and 43 percent of the assembly representatives had college degrees. In the 2001–2 legislature, by contrast, 85 percent of senators and 68 percent of assembly representatives had college degrees.[40] Interestingly the percentage of senators holding college degrees dropped to 76 percent in the 2002–3 legislature, and the percentage among representatives fell slightly to 66 percent.

In terms of occupation the number of legislators who identified themselves as practicing attorneys and farmers declined between 1965 and 2003.

In 1965 nearly a third of the senate and a quarter of the assembly said they were practicing attorneys. In 2003 only 9 percent of senators and 8 percent of assembly representatives said they were practicing attorneys. During this same period, the number of senators who said their principal occupation was farming declined from four to three; the number in the assembly fell from seventeen to nine. Even at the reduced levels of 2003, however, the percentage of farmers and attorneys in the legislature substantially exceeded the share these occupations represent in the state's economy.

Recruitment, Careers, and Turnover

Legislative careers in Wisconsin, like those in other states, can be divided into three stages: recruitment, advancement, and departure or exit. The first stage involves the decision a potential candidate makes about whether to run for the legislature. This decision is always a highly personal decision. Time and energy that might have been spent with family, friends, or in the development of careers or hobbies is often sacrificed. Additionally, particularly for some of the candidates who are running for an assembly seat or a senate seat for the first time, the risks of losing the election can be high. With such a loss can come feelings of public humiliation or rejection.

The variables that may influence the potential candidate's decision to run for office include previous electoral experience, party recruitment efforts, the recruitment efforts of legislative leaders, and/or interest group support. For example, more than one-half of the members serving in the 2003 assembly previously served in local government. Some of these legislators were actively recruited by their party organizations.[41] Some were recruited and supported by the Speaker or minority leader in the assembly or the majority and minority leaders in the senate. Last but not least, some were supported by specific interest groups.

For newly elected legislators the primary objective is to keep the seat they have just won; thereafter members can think about advancing within the legislature itself. For most members, advancement involves getting the committee assignments they want and developing expertise in the committees' business. The next step may involve becoming a committee chair or winning a position of institutional leadership, such as majority or minority leader. The fact that the majority party controls all committee-chair positions means that members have a stake in sustaining or improving their party's electoral fortunes.

For some who are elected to the legislature, career advancement will mean election to a higher office and an exit from the institution. For most assembly representatives, the next step is the senate. Indeed, data show that two-thirds of the 2003 senate's members served in the assembly.[42] For members of the senate, the next step on the career ladder might be a run for a congressional seat or a statewide office. Still others might decide to exit the assembly or senate and put what they know and whom they know to use as a lobbyist or as a member of a corporation's public affairs staff. These positions typically pay far more than the modest salary earned by a state legislator.

Incumbents who seek to remain in the assembly or senate usually have a very good chance of staying in office and advancing their careers within these institutions. Like their counterparts in Congress, incumbent legislators usually have a substantial advantage over their challengers. Incumbents in Wisconsin typically win more than 90 percent of the time—a figure comparable to national statistics.[43]

For example, data assembled by Wisconsin's Legislative Reference Bureau show that only a small number of those who served in the 2001 legislature were defeated in the primary or general election; additionally, only one incumbent senator was defeated in the primary election and only three were defeated in the general election of 2002. In the assembly, the incumbent success rate was even higher; only one was defeated in the primary and two were defeated in the general election.[44]

The high rate of success enjoyed by incumbents in the states and in the U.S. Congress generated substantial discussion during the 1980s and early 1990s. Some political scientists, journalists, interest groups, and citizens expressed concerns about whether the advantages of incumbency distorted the democratic process because citizens are not given a "true" choice among contestants, and whether it created a class of professional politicians that is out of touch with the real needs of constituents. These concerns, coupled with other motives such as the Republican Party's efforts to "uproot Democratic majorities in many legislatures," fueled efforts to set term limits for legislators.[45]

Described by some scholars as an "assault" on state legislatures, the term-limit movement gained momentum and received a great deal of public and press attention between the early 1980s and mid-1990s.[46] Ultimately, by 2001 some form of term limits had been adopted in twenty-one states for members of the state legislature. Similar term-limit efforts were mounted for congressional seats, but they were unsuccessful because the U.S. Supreme Court struck down state-enacted term limits for members of Congress in a 1995 decision.[47]

Despite its visibility and potential appeal, however, term limits were not an important issue in the public debate about government and politics in Wisconsin. Some Republican candidates for federal and state offices took the pledge to support term limits or to limit their own time in office, but these pledges seemed to have little effect. No serious movement emerged within the state legislature to limit the terms of office holders.

There are a number of reasons for this circumstance. Among them is the fact that public expectations about government and politics are rooted in Wisconsin's moralistic political culture. In this culture there is an underlying presumption of respect for governmental institutions and their members. A second reason is that Wisconsin does not have initiative or referendum, the key device through which term limits were put on the ballot in most states that adopted them.[48] Of the twenty-one states that had some form of term limits in 2001, only one did not have initiative and referendum.[49]

Turnover and the Need for Legislative Stability

While incumbent legislators enjoy a substantial advantage in electoral competition if they run for reelection, electoral defeat is just one of many reasons incumbent legislators leave office. Indeed journalists and political scientists have often pointed to the problems associated with high turnover rates in legislatures. Specifically, experience and expertise are often considered key assets that enable legislators to make good decisions on legislation. A high rate of turnover can result in an inexperienced legislature with inadequate levels of expertise.

In historical terms the turnover rate of legislators in Wisconsin has been neither exceptionally high nor low compared to that of other states. For example, in the six elections from 1978 through 1988, on average about 23.3 percent of the membership in the Wisconsin legislature turned over each legislative session.[50] This figure is close to the national average for that time period.

In the 1990s, however, turnover in Wisconsin declined to an average of 16.2 percent. Turnover rates also declined during the 1990s in other states where, like Wisconsin, the institution of the legislature was professionalizing.[51] In states where term limits were established and began to take effect during the latter half of the 1990s, however, turnover rates were much higher than were Wisconsin's.[52]

While the lower rates of turnover in Wisconsin in the 1990s deserve attention, some important insights into legislative careers and legislative turnover in Wisconsin can be gained by considering the full range of data included in table 2. The data show that between 1963 and 2001, 116 senate incumbents did not return and 428 assembly incumbents did not return. Thus, between 1963 and 2001 there were 544 new members of the legislature.

Of the senators who did not return, 7 took appointments in the executive branch of state government; 27 ran for other offices; 19 lost in a primary election; 22 lost in a general election; and 41 quit for other reasons. Among assembly members who did not return, 22 took other appointments in state government; 110 sought other elective office; 46 lost in a primary; 101 lost in a general election; and 133 quit for other reasons.

It is worth noting that in both houses approximately one-third of those who did not return left the legislature for "other reasons," including the frustration experienced by legislators as a result of the tension between governing and legislating, the financial costs of serving as a legislator, the burden of being confronted by too many demands, the high costs a legislative career can have on family life and jobs, and the sense that their public service contribution had been fulfilled.[53]

Whatever the reasons legislators have for leaving office, the turnover in Wisconsin's legislature has traditionally been sufficiently high to ensure that there will be fresh faces and new ideas every session. At the same time, the turnover rate has been low enough to ensure that a majority of legislators will have both experience and expertise.

LEGISLATIVE OPERATION AND ORGANIZATION

In 1970 Wisconsin voters adopted a constitutional amendment allowing the state legislature to meet annually. Prior to 1970 the legislature could only meet in the second year of the legislative term if it was called into special session. Today the plan for the biennial session is established by the Joint Committee on Legislative Organization.[54]

The committee's two-year plan is structured around floor periods. In 2003 there were nine floor periods; they began in January and ended in November. In 2004 there were four floor periods. The first was in January, the last was in May. During floor periods, the legislature usually meets Tuesday through Thursday, with floor sessions starting at 10:00 a.m. for the senate and 9:00 a.m. for the assembly. The early afternoon hours are usually reserved for committee meetings; the late afternoon hours are used for floor sessions. Toward the end of each legislative session, both houses are likely to meet

Table 2. The Wisconsin Legislature: Legislators' Reasons for Not Returning 1963–2001 Sessions

Session	Sought Other Office		Defeated in Primary Election		Defeated in General Election		Accepted Other Govt. Position		Other Reasons		TOTAL	
	Senate	Assembly	Senate	Assembly	Senate	Assembly	Senate	Assembly	Senate	Assembly	Senate	Assembly
1963	2	1	1	10	1	8	–	–	2	13	6	32
1965	–	6	2	4	–	7	–	2	4	2	6	24
1967	3	4	1	5	1	6	–	–	–	11	5	26
1969	–	6	3	4	1	15	–	1	4	4	8	30
1971	2	10	3	4	–	5	–	3	2	7	7	29
1973	–	7	–	2	2	9	–	–	4	5	6	23
1975	1	4	1	1	3	1	–	3	1	8	6	17
1977	3	6	4	2	–	7	–	3	1	3	8	21
1979	2	4	1	3	1	2	–	2	1	1	5	18
1981	3	6	–	4	2	11	–	1	4	12	9	34
1983	1	9	–	–	1	5	–	–	4	12	6	26
1985	3	4	1	3	–	3	1	–	–	3	5	13
1987	1	3	–	–	–	5	–	1	1	7	2	16
1989	2	8	–	1	2	2	1	2	3	5	8	18
1991	–	6	–	1	2	3	2	–	2	12	6	22
1993	2	9	1	–	–	3	–	1	1	4	4	17
1995	–	6	–	–	1	3	1	–	3	–	5	12
1997	1	6	–	1	–	3	2	3	1	10	4	23
1999	–	1	–	–	2	1	–	1	1	8	3	11
2001	1	6	1	1	3	2	–	–	2	6	7	16

Note: "Other Reasons" includes members who died during their term of office

Source: Wisconsin Legislative Reference Bureau

in continuous floor sessions. The calendar for the 2003–4 legislature is presented in table 3.

During the legislative session, each house keeps a daily journal of its actions. All business before the house, including procedural actions on bills, roll-call votes, communications from the governor or the other house, and special committee reports are recorded. During floor sessions the business before the legislature and the actions taken by it are published weekly in a five-part report called *The Bulletin of the Proceedings of the Wisconsin Legislature*. Additionally, during each legislative session, the chief clerks of each house publish a *Weekly Schedule of Committee Activities*, which lists the time and place of committee hearings for the upcoming week.

Each house also issues a daily calendar listing the business to be taken up on the floor of the house that day.[55] All written records are on file at the Legislative Reference Bureau and other libraries throughout the state. These records may also be purchased by individuals and organizations.

How a Bill Becomes a Law

A bill is a proposal to add to or change the general statutory laws contained in the *Wisconsin Statutes*. Before such a proposal can be introduced, it must be drafted by the Legislative Reference Bureau. A bill can be introduced by a single member of either house, a group of members, or by a legislative committee; it can also have co-sponsors from the other house. Each bill must go through the "normal procedures and be passed by the house of origin before it can go to the other house, where the process is repeated."[56]

After it is introduced, each bill is given a number by the chief clerk and "read the first time." This reading consists of the bill's "relating clause," which briefly describes the subject matter of the bill. The bill is then referred to a standing committee, whereupon the committee chair makes the decision on whether a hearing should be held. All hearings are open to the public, and testimony may be submitted in person or in writing. After the hearing has been held, the committee chair decides whether to take action on the bill. Bills that receive a favorable vote by a majority of the committee are reported to the house.[57]

In the 2003 legislature, all bills reported by senate standing committees were sent to the Committee on Senate Organization; all bills reported by assembly standing committees were sent to the Committee on Rules. These two committees scheduled all floor debate. Floor debate is preceded by a

Table 3.   2003–2004 Session Schedule

Jan. 6, 2003	2003 Inauguration
Jan. 7, 2003	*Floorperiod*
Jan. 28–30, 2003	*Floorperiod*
Feb. 18–20, 2003	*Floorperiod*
March 11–20, 2003	*Floorperiod*
April 24, 2003	Deadline for sending bills to governor
April 29–May 8, 2003	*Floorperiod*
May 28–June 27, 2003 (or until passage of budget)	*Floorperiod*
Aug. 14, 2003	Deadline for sending nonbudget bills to governor*
Sept. 23–Oct. 2, 2003	*Floorperiod*
Oct. 21–23, 2003	*Floorperiod*
Nov. 4–13, 2003	*Floorperiod*
Dec. 11, 2003	Deadline for sending bills to governor
Jan. 20–Feb. 5, 2004	*Floorperiod*
Feb. 24–March 11, 2004	*Last general-business floorperiod*
April 15, 2004	Deadline for sending bills to governor
April 27–29, 2004	*Limited-business floorperiod*
May 4, 2004	Deadline for sending bills to governor
May 11–12, 2004	*Veto review floorperiod*
May 26, 2004	Deadline for sending bills to governor
May 13, 2004–Jan. 3, 2005	Interim committee work
Jan. 3, 2005	2005 Inauguration

Note: Any floorperiod may be convened earlier or extended beyond its scheduled dates by majority action of the membership or the organization committees of the two houses. The Committee on Senate Organization may schedule sessions outside of floorperiods for senate action on gubernatorial nominations, but the assembly does not have to hold skeleton sessions during these appointment reviews. The legislature may call itself into extraordinary session or the governor may call a special session during a floorperiod or on any intervening days.

*Deadline for budget bill depends on bill's passage

Source: *Wisconsin Blue Book* 2003–2004, p. 247

"second reading" of the bill; then amendments can be offered, debated, and voted upon. A vote to "engross" the bill ends this debate. Engrossment consists of rewriting the bill to incorporate all amendments that were adopted and all technical corrections that were approved in the house.

After engrossment the bill is ready for a "third reading." After the third reading, the bill is put to a vote. In the senate the vote is preceded with: "This bill having been read three separate times, the question is, 'Shall the bill pass?' " In the assembly, the vote is preceded with: "This bill having been read three separate times, the question is, 'Shall the proposal be passed?' " At this point, no amendment is possible and the vote is taken.[58]

Bills passed in one house are sent to the other house, where they go through the same procedure. Some bills, however, are referred directly to the calendar of the second house, rather than going to a standing committee. If the bill is approved by the second house, with or without amendments, it is sent back to the house of origin. If the bill has amendments, the first house must vote on the amended bill. If, conversely, there are no amendments, the bill is directed to the Legislative Reference Bureau for enrollment. In cases where the house of origin does not concur in amendments of the second house, a conference committee is set up to work out the differences. Then each house votes on the compromise version; no amendments are allowed at this point.

The enrolled bill is then signed by the clerk of each house, and by the Speaker if the house of origin was the assembly. The bill is then forwarded to the governor. The governor has six days (excluding Sunday) to take one of three actions on the bill: sign it; veto it in whole, or, if it is an appropriation bill, in part; or not sign, in which case it becomes law in six days without the governor's signature. Over the years, however, a tradition has developed by which an enrolled bill will not be sent to the governor until the chief executive is ready for it. Thus, in practice, the governor typically has more than six days in which to act. If a governor does veto a bill in whole or in part, the bill can become law if two-thirds of the members of both houses vote to override the veto. This type of supermajority requirement, however, means that few vetoes are overridden.

In the ten Wisconsin legislative sessions that preceded the 2001–2 legislature, an average of 1,800 bills were introduced. Of these bills, approximately 22 percent (396) passed both houses. Over these same ten legislative sessions an average of fifteen bills were vetoed in whole by the governor, and an average of fifteen were vetoed in part.[59] For purposes of comparison, we can also look at the 1995–96 legislative session. During that session, 1,799 bills were introduced, and 475, or 26.4 percent, passed both houses. Governor Thompson exercised his full veto power on four of these bills; he used his partial veto on twenty-one of them. None of the vetoes was overridden by the legislature.[60]

Wisconsin's legislative activity can also be compared to that of other states. In the legislative sessions between 1997 and 1999, for example, Alaska was the state in which the fewest bills were introduced (356) and enacted (142). New York was the state in which the most bills were introduced (17,667) and enacted (3,846). In a state of more comparable size to

Wisconsin, Minnesota, 3,051 bills were introduced and 1,157 were enacted. In Oregon 3,103 bills were introduced and 1,170 enacted, and in Virginia, 2,150 bills were introduced and 902 enacted. In short, the number of bills introduced in Wisconsin is somewhat lower than states of similar size, but the percentage of bills passed is close to the national average of 25 percent.[61]

Committees

A large part of the work of the legislature is done in committees. Most of the legislation considered on the floor of the senate and the assembly is prepared in committees. Consequently the structure and operation of the committee system, as well as the power and status of various committees, is very important. In the Wisconsin legislature, the number, names, and tasks of the committees are determined by the majority party. As a result the committee structure can vary from legislature to legislature. In the 2003–4 legislature the senate had fifteen standing committees and the assembly had forty-two standing committees. In addition there were eleven joint (senate/assembly) committees and one joint research committee.

Ron Hedlund, a scholar who has studied Wisconsin's legislature, observed that "the committee system and the involvement of members are quite different between the [s]enate and [a]ssembly."[62] These differences, Hedlund maintains, result in higher levels of specialization, expertise, continuity, commitment, and participation in the senate. In addition the way the majority party treats the minority party seems to vary significantly between the two chambers.

In the senate, committees have broad and clearly defined jurisdiction over the development of legislation. Furthermore, the committee structure is adjusted to fit the knowledge, expertise, and preferences of the senators.[63] In contrast, Hedlund argues, there "has never been clear-cut jurisdiction for [a]ssembly committees."[64] Additionally, assembly personnel are fit to the committee structure established by the Speaker. The size of committees in the senate tends to range from five to eight members, with each member serving on two or three committees. In the assembly, the size of committees ranges from three to seventeen members, with members serving on as few as two committees or as many as nine.[65]

In the senate, committee assignments are made by the five-member Committee on Senate Organization. This committee tends to honor the preferences of incumbent legislators who wish to hold on to existing committee assignments. Additionally, the committee is bound by senate rules to honor the committee assignments submitted by the minority caucus.

In contrast, the Speaker of the assembly makes all committee appointments. The Speaker may honor the requests of incumbent party members, but he or she is not bound by any seniority presumption or rule. In fact, committee assignments, and particularly committee chair assignments, may be part of the "resources" exchanged for votes as the Speaker runs for election or reelection. Furthermore, the Speaker is not bound by any rules regarding the appointment of minority party members. The minority party is not guaranteed committee assignments proportional to its numbers in the chamber, and the Speaker does not have to honor the requests of the minority caucus.

The importance and status of a committee may vary from legislative session to legislative session, depending on the agendas of the governor and the legislative leaders. One committee whose status does not change, however, is the Joint Committee on Finance. This committee, made up of nine members drawn from the assembly and nine from the senate, is the most powerful and important committee. Consequently, for most legislators, it is the most desirable committee assignment.

The special status of the Joint Committee on Finance stems from the statutory provision 16.47 (2) governing legislative and budgetary matters. Any proposed legislation that is expected to increase state costs or reduce state revenues by more than $100,000 biennially cannot be passed until the budget bill is passed. Thus, rather than simply dealing with appropriations for existing legislation, the budget bill in Wisconsin also contains funding for all new legislation that has an estimated biennial cost (or revenue reduction) in excess of $100,000.

Leadership

Each chamber of the legislature elects its own presiding officers and party leaders. In the senate the presiding officer is the president.[66] The senate president is elected for a two-year term at the beginning of each legislative session. While all members of the senate vote for this officer, the election that really counts is conducted in the previous month (December) in the majority party caucus.

The presiding officer in the assembly is the Speaker. Here, too, the vote in the majority party caucus is the key to selection. The members of the majority party caucus in both houses also elect two floor leaders, identified as the majority and assistant majority leaders. The minority caucus in both houses selects the minority and assistant minority leaders.

The assembly Speaker and the senate president usually preside over floor debate. On a temporary basis, however, they may designate another member to handle this job. In both chambers the presiding officers are bound by a set of rules established by the members, but substantial discretion remains. Thus it is not surprising to see the debate managed in a way that is favorable to the interests of the majority party. The majority party leader and assistant leader help the presiding officers coordinate legislative activity.

The assembly Speaker is often referred to as the second most powerful official in Wisconsin state government, after the governor. The size of the Speaker's power base, as well as the ability to make all committee appointments, select committee chairs, and assign legislation to committees gives the Speaker tremendous influence in the legislative process. In recent years these powers have been substantially enhanced by the Speaker's involvement in efforts to maintain an electoral majority. Speakers now actively engage in recruitment of candidates, the assignment of technical (campaign) experts, and fundraising for candidates.

The senate president's powers are more circumscribed by chamber rules and organization than are those of the assembly Speaker. Generally, the senate president's campaign activity is not likely to be as extensive as the Speaker's. The senate president nevertheless can be influential in a variety of ways, not least in the kind of tone he or she sets for the chamber. In the senate, the norm is for the president to preside in an evenhanded way, to keep things running smoothly, and ensure that a proper degree of decorum is maintained during floor sessions.

During the 2003–4 legislative session, the senate president was Republican Alan Lasee. In the 2001–2 session, when the Democrats had the majority in the senate, Democrat Fred Risser was president. Risser held the president's job for almost all of the 1970s, 1980s, and 1990s. In 2001 Senator Risser had the distinction of being the longest-serving member of that legislature, and he continued his public service in the 2003–4 legislature. It is worth noting here that Risser was following in the footsteps of his father, grandfather, and great grandfather, all of whom had served in the Wisconsin legislature.[67]

The assembly Speaker for the 2003–4 legislative session was Republican John G. Gard. The assembly Speaker for the 2001–2 legislative session was Republican Scott Jensen, who served as chief of staff to Governor Tommy Thompson before he won a special election for an assembly seat in 1992.

Legislative Agencies

In addition to legislative committees and leaders, five legislative agencies play a key role in the legislative process. The exceptional quality of these nonpartisan agencies is an important factor in the overall institutional capacity of the Wisconsin legislature. Both the quality and stability of the leadership in these agencies contributes to their strong performance.

Of these five agencies the Legislative Audit Bureau is the largest, with a 2003–4 staff of eighty-seven.[68] For many years the bureau was run by Dale Cattanach, a highly respected veteran of state service.[69] The director in 2004 was Janice Mueller. The Legislative Audit Bureau conducts both financial and program audits. These audits are used in legislative oversight activities.

The second largest of the five legislative agencies is the Legislative Reference Bureau, with fifty-eight staff members. This agency provides bill drafting as well as research and library services for the legislature. The bureau was founded in the early 1900s by Charles McCarthy. During the 1970s and 1980s, Rupert Theobold was the head of the agency, and in the mid-1990s, it was Peter Dykman. During the 2003–4 legislature, Stephen Miller was its head.

The Legislative Fiscal Bureau is responsible for revenue and expenditure estimates, as well as all other fiscal matters. The agency, comprising thirty-five employees, supports the Joint Committee on Finance as it assembles the budget bill. The head of the agency during the 2003–4 legislative session was Robert Lang, a highly regarded veteran of legislative service; his work in the bureau extends back to the 1970s.

The Revisor of Statutes Bureau had a staff of ten in 2003–4. The agency's most important duties include the editing and publishing of the *Wisconsin Statutes and Annotations* and the *Wisconsin Administrative Code and Register*. The head of the agency during the 2003–4 session was Bruce Munson.

The Legislative Technology Service Bureau was formed in 1997. Its mission is to provide information-technology support to legislators and legislative agencies and to coordinate the planning and execution of electronic-information programs and services. The agency had twenty-five employees during the 2003–4 legislative session; Mark Wahl was the head of the agency.

LEGISLATIVE ACTIVITY

Legislators' work can be divided into three main areas: lawmaking, oversight of the executive branch agencies, and casework.[70] Lawmaking is often assumed to be the most important, most difficult, and most time-consuming part of a legislator's job. As previously noted, during any given two-year legislative session in Wisconsin an average of 1,800 bills are introduced. On the basis of volume alone, one might conclude that a legislature functions something like "an assembly line in a factory where many products are manufactured in a short period of time."[71] One negative consequence of this volume is that even full-time legislators can devote only a small amount of time to study each bill.

Volume is only one aspect to be considered in the lawmaking process. Other factors include the complexity of the proposed legislation, the scope of its likely effects, and the saliency of the proposed legislation for citizens and interest groups. Some bills, such as minor housekeeping matters and those with limited scope, may move through the legislature smoothly. Other bills, however, may be controversial, and the process of legislative review may become slow, tedious, and conflicted.

A question that has been of particular interest to political scientists is, How do legislators decide to vote on a bill that has reached the floor of their house? Among the factors Samuel C. Patterson has identified that might influence a legislator's decision making are:

- party and party leaders
- committees
- staff
- lobbyists representing private interest groups and executive branch agencies
- the governor, and
- citizens in their legislative districts.

Still other factors might include press coverage of an issue, conscience, and public opinion polls.

Some research conducted by political scientists seems to show that the primary influence on decision making is other legislators, including party leaders, party members, committee members, and friends. Other research indicates that influence might vary on the basis of the type of legislation being considered, the strength of parties in the state, the level of legislative professionalism, or whether a legislator's self-conceived role is what political scientists call "delegate," "trustee," or "politico."

In the case of a legislator who thinks of himself or herself as a delegate, for example, the views of the district's constituency may be the most important factor in a voting decision because this type of legislator sees his or her job as representing the views of constituents. On the other hand, a trustee may vote his or her conscience, while a politico may be heavily influenced by political factors such as party leaders or opinion polls. In highly professional legislatures, committees and staff may be primary influences. In legislatures where parties are strong, the primary factor is likely to be party leadership; where parties are weak, interest groups might be key.

Legislative Oversight

In addition to making law, legislative bodies usually oversee the implementation of the laws they pass to ensure that taxpayers' money is spent properly. Sometimes referred to as a financial audit function, this part of the legislature's oversight role is supported in Wisconsin by the Legislative Audit Bureau.

Other types of oversight responsibilities undertaken by the legislature are program audits or performance audits, which are conducted to ensure that the executive branch agencies are implementing the law in the way the legislature intended.[72] Statutes are often written broadly to ensure their passage by the legislature. When a statute is written in this way, those in the executive branch agency charged with implementing the new law face a difficult challenge. In order to implement the law, they must first establish operational rules and procedures, and must often face problems the legislature avoided, such as balancing conflicting goals and balancing the demands of interest groups that expect very different things.

In Wisconsin the Legislative Audit Bureau is the legislative agency that actually performs the financial and program-performance audits. The bureau then feeds the results of its work to the Joint Legislative Audit Committee. This committee consists of the co-chairs of the Joint Finance Committee, plus two majority and two minority party members from each house. The Joint Legislative Audit Committee operates under the supervision of the Joint Committee on Legislative Organization.[73]

Case Work/Constituency Relations

Casework, or constituency relations, is the third major function performed by legislators. Casework is generated by citizen requests for assistance. Sometimes the request is simply for information; sometimes it is a request for help in getting a response or action from an executive branch agency. In still other cases a citizen writes asking that a legislator overturn a decision by an agency.

Legislators typically view casework as an important function. It is an opportunity to perform an important public service, as well as a way to build support for reelection. Nevertheless, legislators may spend only a small part of their time on casework. For example, in his study of the Minnesota and Kentucky legislatures, Richard Elling found that only 18 percent of a Minnesota legislator's time was devoted to casework; in Kentucky the figure was 13 percent.[74] The principal explanation Elling gives for his finding is that staff members do most of the work.

No one has conducted a formal study like Elling's in Wisconsin so it is impossible to say with confidence whether the time Wisconsin legislators spend on casework is similar to that of Minnesota and Kentucky. Because members of Wisconsin's assembly and senate do have office staff to handle much of the casework, however, it seems reasonable to think that Elling's average findings might be close to the mark.

Until recently the U.S. Postal Service was the principal vehicle of communication for citizens' requests for legislative assistance, but telephone calls were an important source, too. While the mail and telephone calls continue to be important channels of communication for citizens, the number of requests for assistance made through e-mail has been growing rapidly in recent years. This new technology has made citizen access to legislators easier in some respects. From a legislator's point of view, however, this can be a mixed blessing. While legislators may be able to give more help to more citizens as a result of this technology, the volume of contacts from a small number of individuals may increase dramatically, and consume much more staff time.

CURRENT CHALLENGES

Wisconsin's Progressive legacy is easy to see in the development and ongoing operation of the legislature. The state's legislative institution has a long history of important institutional and policy innovations that have served as models for other states and for the national government. In recent decades Wisconsin's legislature has become one of only a handful of state legislatures defined as having a high degree of professionalism. Despite this legacy and its wonderful institutional capacity, however, Wisconsin's legislature has not escaped from some of the difficult institutional problems that afflicted other state legislatures during the latter part of the 1980s and 1990s.

For example, a decline in the legislature's institutional power vis-à-vis the governor is a visible part of its legacy during the latter part of the 20th century.

Like some of its counterparts in other states, Wisconsin's legislature was not an equal partner with the governor in the process of lawmaking during the late 1980s and the 1990s.[75] The departure of four-term governor Tommy Thompson for Washington DC and President George W. Bush's cabinet in 2001 opened the door for the legislature to reclaim some of its lost power, but whether the institution's leaders are capable of doing so in a constructive manner remains an open question.

In addition to its balance-of-power problems with the chief executive, Wisconsin's legislature experienced growing levels of internal partisan conflict, increasingly aggressive efforts by legislative party leaders to maintain or secure majority control of each legislative chamber, rising levels of political action committee (PAC) election activities, campaign contributions by lobbyists, and a blurring of distinctions between legislators and lobbyists during the 1990s. Each one of these problems reflects powerful forces operating in contemporary society, and these forces seem to be deeply rooted.

While these forces and problems are not unique to Wisconsin, events that occurred in the state during 2001 and 2002 seemed to show that they manifested themselves in a surprising and disturbing way during the 1990s and the first part of the twenty-first century. The *Wisconsin State Journal* in May of 2001 published an investigative report disclosing that full-time state employees of the Democratic and Republican Party caucus staffs were secretly campaigning "for legislative candidates on state time and from their offices, in apparent violation of the law." Among the key findings of the report was that "state caucus offices serve as campaign central for many legislative races," with caucus staff "performing a variety of functions in their government offices including coordinating advertising, selecting campaign consultants, providing lists of registered voters, and designing brochures and giving out advice and information." Some caucus staff acknowledged that, particularly during the election season, they were out of the office working on campaigns all of the time.[76]

Ironically, the caucus staffs, one for each party in both legislative houses, were created during the late 1960s as part of a Ford Foundation–sponsored reform initiative designed to strengthen state legislatures.[77] Each caucus staff was to be supervised by party leaders, and the purpose of the caucus staff was to conduct research on policy issues, bills pending before the legislature, and so forth. The cost of the employees working on the caucus staff in 2001 was estimated to be $3.9 million, and the use of these taxpayer supported personnel in election campaigns seemed to be a clear violation of the 1960s reform objectives, the state's ethics rules and laws, and the state's campaign finance and elections laws.[78]

The *Wisconsin State Journal* report stimulated two additional investigations: one a joint investigation by the Wisconsin Ethics Board and the Wisconsin Elections Board, and the other by Dane County District Attorney Brian Blanchard. The Ethics and Election Board investigation was brought to a conclusion in October of 2001 when legislative leaders agreed to disband the caucuses in return for an end to the investigations. The "deal" with legislative leaders "failed to name names or provide details of specific incidents of misconduct, as the state Ethics and Elections boards left that to an investigation being conducted by Dane County District Attorney Brian Blanchard and Milwaukee District Attorney E. Michael McCann."[79]

In May of 2002 the first indictment stemming from Blanchard's investigation was announced. Senator Brian Burke, a highly regarded Democrat from Milwaukee, co-chair of the Joint Finance Committee, and a candidate for attorney general, was charged with eighteen felonies. The charges against Burke for his attorney general's campaign included the use of his State Capitol office for raising campaign funds, charging campaign related expenses to taxpayers, and an attempt to withhold or conceal subpoenaed records.

During the press conference in which the indictments against Burke were announced, Blanchard also acknowledged that a "secret John Doe investigation was continuing into allegations that others engaged in illegal campaign activity at the Capitol and traded votes for campaign contributions."[80] The investigation was focused on evidence that lobbyists had been "asked to make campaign contributions to get favorable consideration of their issues—pay to play, in the jargon of the Capitol."[81]

In October of 2002, just six weeks before the November elections, additional indictments were announced. Blanchard charged assembly Republican Majority Leader Scott Jensen with three felony counts of misconduct in office and one misdemeanor for allegedly "converting the taxpayer funded [a]ssembly Republican Caucus and his own Capitol staff into powerful campaign machines aimed at assuring his grasp on power." Assistant Republican Majority Leader Steve Foti was charged with one felony misconduct count related to supervising a full-time state employee hired by Jensen whose only task was fundraising for the Republican Party Caucus. Assistant Republican Majority Leader Bonnie Ladwig was charged with one misdemeanor for use of caucus staff for partisan election campaign purposes.[82]

Milwaukee County Assistant District Attorney David Feiss charged senate Democratic Majority Leader Charles Chvala with twenty felony counts.

The charges against Chvala were part of a sixty-seven-page criminal indictment, and they included alleged "extortion, money laundering and illegal schemes to exceed donation limits to candidates." Three of the felony charges against Chvala were for use of Senate Democratic Caucus staff for partisan election campaign purposes; the extortion charges were for allegedly "demanding cash for favors, punishing or rewarding certain interests based on payments," and creating "elaborate schemes to hide money trails."[83]

Senator Brian Burke was the only legislative leader to resign his office in the immediate aftermath of these indictments; he also abandoned his campaign for attorney general. Jensen, Foti, and Ladwig continued their reelection efforts; Chvala did not have to run for reelection in 2002. All three Republican legislators were returned to office in the November 2002 election. Neither Jensen nor Ladwig faced a competitor from the other party.

After completing their terms in the 2003–4 legislature, however, Foti, Ladwig, and Chvala decided not to run for reelection in 2004. Jensen, on the other hand, filed the papers necessary to be a candidate. He faced no opposition in the 2004 Republican primary election, and it appears that state Republican Party leaders did not make an effort to find a candidate to oppose him. Even more surprising is the fact that Democratic Party officials did not find a candidate to oppose Jensen in the general election.

As of the date of this writing (May 2005) none of the cases against these legislators had gone to trial. A principal reason for the delay was that all were appealing their cases before they went to trial. For example, Burke insisted that he had done nothing wrong, and he sought dismissal of the eighteen felony counts against him.[84]

Dane County District Judge Bill Foust responded to part of Burke's petition by dismissing five counts related to efforts to raise money for the aborted attorney general's campaign at the State Capitol. Judge Foust "declared that the law barring the solicitation of campaign money in state buildings was so broad that it 'applies to everyone in the world.' " Thus, Foust asserted, "it would be unfair to single out Burke for felony prosecution."[85] The logic of this decision , however, was beyond the grasp of some observers in the capital.

Jensen, Foti, and Chvala attempted to overturn by appeal the charges that they had illegally used state resources for campaign work. Jensen and Foti's attorneys challenged the felony indictments against their clients arguing "that state statutes offer no clear distinction between legislative work and campaign work, making it impossible for them to know that what they were doing was against the law."[86] Chvala's attorney offered a similar argument. Attorneys for the three legislative leaders also contended that "local prosecutors cannot judge the conduct of an elected lawmaker."[87]

In early 2004 Wisconsin's Fourth District Court of Appeals refused to overturn the charges against Jensen, Foti, and Chvala. The court ruled that state "statutes clearly prohibit using state resources for political work," and that the defendants "had ample warning their alleged conduct violates Wisconsin law."[88] In June of 2004, however, the Wisconsin Supreme Court agreed to hear the three lawmakers' appeal of the appellate court ruling.[89] Foti's lawyer described this result as a very good sign for his client; Chvala's attorney had a similar response, even though the court's order only applied to four of the felony counts against Chvala.[90]

What is an observer of Wisconsin's legislature or Wisconsin politics and government to make of all this? Journalist David E. Rosenbaum, who covered the scandal for the *New York Times*, offered a comparative perspective. First, he noted that the use of party caucus staff for campaign purposes might be common practice in many states, but it was far outside the accepted norms, rules, and laws in Wisconsin. Second, he stated that shaking down lobbyists was considered inappropriate or illegal, even in the most freewheeling states. Third, he said that the indictments represent the most serious scandal in Wisconsin since "Robert La Follette formed the Progressive movement in the early 1900s and rooted out political bosses and corporate influence."[91]

Another way to put the recent scandals into perspective is to compare events in the 1970s and the 1990s. Consider, for example, what happened in the 1970s to legislators who committed seemingly minor infractions of state ethics and election laws. One state senator was prosecuted after he accepted $100 to cover expenses for a speech he gave at an upstate resort; another was charged with accepting food and drinks at a Green Bay Packers football game. Two other legislators were defeated for reelection after they used their state credit card for personal phone calls that cost much less than $100 dollars.[92]

In contrast to these perhaps overzealous responses to minor infractions, grievous and widespread violations of state rules and laws were apparently taking place during the 1990s that may have cost state taxpayers millions of dollars. Yet even though these activities were considered "an open secret" in the Capitol, no one blew the whistle and no one investigated. Indeed, the executive director of the Ethics Board, Roth Judd, acknowledged during the *Wisconsin State Journal*'s 2001 investigation of improper legislative caucus activity that "such activity has been rumored for years," yet no complaints were filed with the Ethics Board, and the Board launched no investigations.[93]

How is all this to be explained? How could the long established moral presumptions about and legal barriers to these activities apparently have been dissolved? How could it be that no "complaints were filed" with the Ethics Board and the Board itself did not launch an investigation into activities so widely and persistently rumored? How was it, as *Wisconsin State Journal* reporter Dee J. Hall noted when she broke the caucus story in 2001, that regulators, lawmakers, and the press turned a blind eye to these activities for so many years?[94]

One explanation is that the normal institutional checks designed to stop these activities simply broke down; another is that the pursuit of funding for election campaigns became such an overriding priority for some legislative leaders that they lost track of all of the other implications of what they were doing. These explanations are useful, but they miss some of the important texture of what apparently happened, including shared assumptions of key participants, secretive behavior on the part of some legislative leaders, the growth of a culture of denial, and a surprising ignorance among legislative staff and candidates of the state's ethics rules and election laws.

The "culture of denial" was on full display when a spokesman for Speaker of the Assembly Scott Jensen denied that caucus staff were campaigning on state time.[95] Additionally, as noted earlier, the indicted legislative leaders claimed that they did not have ample warning that what they were doing was illegal. Yet press commentary and press reports indicate that these same leaders were very secretive about some of their dealings related to caucus meetings and activities and that they made efforts to conceal caucus election activities.[96]

Some caucus staff members who were interviewed during the *Wisconsin State Journal*'s investigation seemed aware of state rules and laws that prohibited campaigning on state time, in state buildings, and with state supplies, but they apparently did so because it was required and because they wanted to help their parties. Nearly all acknowledged that almost all of the work performed by caucus staff was on election campaigns. Only one of the staff members interviewed reported complaining to her boss about doing the campaign work on state time and requesting a transfer out of the caucus.[97]

Similarly, some legislative candidates who benefited from the help of the party caucus employees claimed that they did not know where their help was coming from. A majority of the candidates said that they did not know caucus staff were prohibited from working on campaigns during state time or in state offices. One Republican candidate expressed surprise and disbelief that the assembly Republican Caucus, the source of his campaign help, was part of state government.[98]

Some of these responses sound eerily similar to reactions expressed by workers and managers in corporations like WorldCom and Enron, where major scandals were exposed in 2001 and 2002. For example, the response of legislative leaders to the charges brought against them seems to parallel the defense offered by top executives in these corporations: innocent of any wrongdoing and ignorant of any illegal activities in the organizations over which they presided. It also seems ironic that, because both major political parties in Wisconsin were apparently using the same tactics to pursue legislative campaign victories, neither party blew the whistle on the other.

Another unpleasant dimension of the apparent scandal in Wisconsin is that the legislative leaders who were ultimately indicted in 2002 had already decided in 2001 to bill the state for the costs of the lawyers they used to defend themselves and their staff during the caucus investigations. By May of 2002, when this story first broke, those costs had already totaled $664,000.[99] To make matters worse, Governor McCallum refused to let the attorney general go to court to attempt to block the use of state funds to pay for these legal bills.[100] In examining the record one is struck by the apparent lack of contrition on the part of the indicted legislative leaders. Only one resigned office immediately, four served an additional two years in the legislature before resigning, and one, former Speaker of the Assembly Scott Jensen decided to run for reelection in 2004.

IN SUMMARY

The legislative scandal that came to light in 2001 and 2002 is shocking to Wisconsin residents and to longtime observers of Wisconsin politics and government who assumed that the state's history, culture, and laws were sufficient protection against these types of scandals. Yet the scandal illustrates once again how even long-standing norms, ethics rules, and election laws can fall victim to forces operating within society and on governmental institutions. Perhaps Gaylord Nelson, a former Wisconsin governor and U.S. Senator, offered the most penetrating assessment of the effects of these scandals when he said: "When I was in the [U.S.] Senate, it was very common for someone who knew politics to say to me 'You come from the clean state.' . . . We had a tradition in Wisconsin. Now we've become like every other state. It's disgusting. It's a damn disgrace."[101]

A key question the recent scandal seems to beg is whether Wisconsin's citizens and elected and appointed officials in the three branches of government have made a firm commitment to stop all of the allegedly illegal behavior identified in indictments and investigative press reports. To do so will require tightening state ethics rules and election laws, strengthening their enforcement and adjudication, and pushing all who played a leading role in the scandal out of public life. If effective antidotes for these scandals are developed and implemented, and if the antidotes are used as part of a thorough cleansing of the corrosive influences that contributed to this scandal, some of the state's lost political luster as a laboratory of democracy might be recovered.

On the other hand, if the state's citizens and officials are unwilling or unable to take all of the steps necessary to restore the integrity of election processes and the way citizen tax dollars are spent, Wisconsin may serve as a key barometer of the way in which the powerful economic and political forces currently operating in society will play out in other states. In this way Wisconsin might indeed serve as a "laboratory," though not a "laboratory of democracy."

CHAPTER FOUR

The Governor

With the legislature at last on the administration's side, La Follette's program was secure. But it could not have succeeded without a civil service law, because the whole Progressive program depended on confidence in the administrators.

Wisconsin: A Guide to the Badger State, 1949

Nothing in state government, and the institution that is the Office of the Governor, is the same as it was in January 1987, when Republican Tommy G. Thompson came into office. . . . Power is so consolidated in the hands of the governor and key aides that no cabinet secretary makes a major decision without first checking with the governor's office.

Steven Walters, *Milwaukee Journal Sentinel*, December 24, 2000

The twentieth century opened with Robert M. La Follette Sr. taking office as governor of Wisconsin; it ended with Tommy G. Thompson concluding his thirteenth year in the executive office. La Follette is the most important and Thompson is the most powerful of the governors in Wisconsin's history. The juxtaposition of these two men puts into sharp relief the competing currents of Progressive and Stalwart that have flowed through Wisconsin politics for the past 155 years, and it reveals the important role a single powerful individual can play in a state's political history when that person holds the office of governor.

This chapter begins with a brief comparison of these two men. The chapter also contains many references to the other seven governors who, along with Tommy Thompson, served as Wisconsin's chief executive during the last forty years of the twentieth century, and it contains information about the two men who served as Wisconsin's governor at the beginning of the twenty-first century. The chapter also includes a discussion of the factors that political scientists tend to emphasize in studies of governors, such as the formal legal requirements that must be met to become a candidate for governor; the party affiliation and demographic characteristics of those who have been elected governor; the governor's pay, benefits, and staff support; the governor's formal responsibilities and powers; and the roles that governors play in the state and the intergovernmental system. Special attention is given to the ways in which Wisconsin's recent governors exerted influence on state politics, policy, and administration. The chapter concludes with an examination of what the state's chief executives have done after leaving the governorship.

A COMPARISON OF THE FIRST AND LAST
GOVERNORS OF THE TWENTIETH CENTURY

Robert M. La Follette Sr. was the twentieth governor of Wisconsin; Tommy G. Thompson was Wisconsin's forty-third governor. La Follette was a Progressive Republican and Wisconsin's most important governor. Thompson was Wisconsin's longest-serving and most powerful governor. Thompson claimed to be the heir of the Progressive heritage, but some observers think he was the heir of the Stalwart Republicans.[1] Although La Follette and Thompson were members of the same political party, their political philosophies and policy preferences differed sharply. Other differences between the two include the route they traveled to the governorship, the kind of political opposition they faced, the formal powers they held, the power they actually wielded, and the approach they took to the administration of state government.

La Follette came to power after a decade-long struggle within the Republican Party for control of the gubernatorial nomination. The Stalwart Republicans had managed the party for more than thirty years, and they were not about to yield quietly to a young rebel. Furthermore, La Follette's six years as governor were marked by an ongoing, fiercely contested struggle with the "machine" for control of the state's governmental institutions and public policy. La Follette's political philosophy was articulated in many of his speeches, but it can be summed up in a single sentence: the cure for the ills of democracy is more democracy.[2] His principal objective was to ensure that the state's resources were used for the benefit of all of the people, rather than for the enrichment of a few.

La Follette attempted to decentralize political and administrative power in order to ensure popular control over governmental institutions. He sponsored the Civil Service Reform Act of 1905, and he worked hard to strengthen the capacity of the state's administrative agencies to enforce regulatory policy and to deliver services. La Follette only achieved part of his policy agenda during his six years as governor; when he left the governorship for the U.S. Senate, the task of pursuing that agenda was given over to his Progressive successors, James O. Davidson and Francis E. McGovern.

Conversely, Tommy Thompson's rise within the Republican Party and the state occurred with the support of the party's powerbrokers, and yet his electoral success may be viewed as something of a surprise. Although Thompson had served in the assembly for almost twenty years before he pursued his party's gubernatorial nomination, there was little in his record to suggest that he could win a statewide election or become an effective governor. Indeed, because he so frequently and stridently objected to new initiatives proposed for state government, Thompson was commonly known within the State Capitol as "Dr. No."[3] He nonetheless emerged from the 1986 primary election as the Republican Party's gubernatorial candidate.

Thompson's November 1986 upset of incumbent Democrat Anthony Earl in the general election can be attributed to many factors, including Earl's feud with Milwaukee's mayor, Henry Maier; the powerful negative effects the recession of the early 1980s had on the state's economy and budget; the strong financial support Thompson had from the business community; and the strong backing he had from the Republican Party faithful. Equally important was the fact that Thompson reinvented himself during his run for the governorship, while his opponent, Anthony Earl, was unable to shed the negative image he had developed with many voters, particularly blue-collar Democrats, during his first year in office.[4] For example, the shrill, negative tone that seemed to characterize Thompson during his years in the assembly was replaced by a new, more positive outlook, and his "bombastic" style was replaced by a more moderate persona.[5] Earl, however, was unable to regain the confidence of many voters who found some of his early actions as governor disturbing or even threatening.[6]

In contrast to La Follette, Thompson's political philosophy seemed to be built on the presumption that what is good for business is good for the state.[7] Indeed Thompson seemed fond of proclaiming, "I am a pro-business governor."[8] Thompson also seemed driven to concentrate power in his own hands, rather than to share it with the legislature or to delegate it to administrators. Thompson was very open about his distrust of "bureaucrats," and his approach to running the executive branch seemed to be more compatible with the patronage-style politics of the Stalwarts than with the Progressives' approach to government.[9]

Thompson had more formal power than did La Follette, in large part as a result both of having the partial veto added through constitutional amendment in 1934 and the gubernatorial term changed from two to four years in 1968. Thompson used this power very aggressively, and he achieved a position of dominance in both the legislative and administrative arenas never before attained by any other Wisconsin governor. This dominance was viewed very positively by most of Thompson's supporters and very negatively by most of his opponents.

Thompson, no longer "Dr. No," would soon become known to both his opponents and supporters as "King Tommy."[10] The title was used derisively by Thompson's Democratic opponents but affectionately by many of his Republican supporters. Thompson was not generally viewed as a friend of civil service, and he was taken to court by the League of Women Voters for violations of the civil service laws. Unlike La Follette, Thompson remained in office long enough to complete his own policy agenda. By the end of 1999 his tenure in office exceeded the number of years served by La Follette and his two Progressive successors, Davidson and McGovern. Through the aggressive use of both legislative and administrative means, Thompson had realized most of his most important policy objectives.

FORMAL REQUIREMENTS, TERM LENGTH, AND SUCCESSION

The formal legal qualifications for the governorship are spelled out in Article V (2) of Wisconsin's 1848 constitution: "No person, except a citizen of the United States, and a qualified elector of the state, shall be eligible to the office of the governor." In Article V (1) the governor is given a two-year term of office, with no limit on the number of terms that can be served. Section 1 also says that the governor and lieutenant governor will be elected at the same time, but it does not require that they be from the same party. Rather it specifies that the candidate getting the highest number of votes for each office be declared the winner. Additionally in section 3 of the Executive Article, the time of election is left to the legislature to determine. Finally in section 7 there is language specifying that the office of the governor "shall devolve upon the lieutenant governor for the residue of the term" if the governor is impeached, removed from office, dies, resigns, or is unable to perform the duties of the office due to mental or physical disease.

The eligibility requirements spelled out in 1848 remain the same today as they were 155 years ago, though several other provisions concerning the office of the governor have changed since then. In 1968 a constitutional amendment increased the governor's term to four years and required that the governor and lieutenant governor be elected together. A 1979 constitutional amendment clarified the lines of succession to the offices of both governor and lieutenant governor. In the event that the governor leaves office, the lieutenant governor becomes governor, rather than acting governor. If a vacancy occurs in the lieutenant governor's office, the secretary of state becomes lieutenant governor.

These constitutional changes were designed to address several problems that arose over the years, among them that governors had little time to govern during a two-year term. Shortly after election they had to again focus their attention and energies on an election campaign. Although concern about this situation emerged relatively soon after the constitution was adopted in 1848, the urgency of the problem continued to grow over the years as the state government grew larger and more complex.

A second problem was that the separate election of a governor and a lieutenant governor could result in candidates from competing parties holding the state's two top offices. This happened in 1960 when Gaylord Nelson (Democrat) was elected governor for a second time, and Warren Knowles (Republican) was elected lieutenant governor. In 1962 John Reynolds (Democrat) was elected governor and Jack Olson (Republican) was elected lieutenant governor. Then, in 1964, Warren Knowles (Republican) was elected governor and Patrick Lucey (Democrat) was elected lieutenant governor.

There were several ways in which this cross-party arrangement created, or had the potential to create, tension. First, the lieutenant governor became acting governor whenever the governor was out of the state. Second, in the event the governor died, resigned, or was disabled, party control of the chief executive's office could shift. Third, the position of lieutenant governor could be used as a platform to attack the governor and then launch an election campaign to unseat the incumbent.

These strains were certainly visible when Warren Knowles and Patrick Lucey held the governorship and lieutenant governorship, respectively. From Inauguration Day forward, the relationship was not particularly cordial. The tension worsened when Knowles grew worried about traveling outside of the state, lest he give Lucey opportunities to make mischief with the levers of power. The relationship ultimately became hostile when, part of the way through Knowles's first term, Lucey's intention to run against Knowles in the 1966 election became known.[11]

The 1968 constitutional change putting the governor and lieutenant governor together on the ballot eliminated these real and potential cross-party troubles. Likewise the constitutional change to a four-year term gave the governor more opportunity to govern. The four-year term also provided a greater degree of insulation from national politics than before.[12] Because the four-year term began in 1970, an off-year for the presidential election, the gubernatorial race never coincides with the presidential race.

While all of these effects might be considered salutary, the recent constitutional changes did not address an important governance issue that probably should have been addressed: gubernatorial term limits. Wisconsin's 1848 constitution did not establish a term limit, and no term limit was included in the 1968 constitutional amendment that extended the term from two to four years. Perhaps this potential problem was overlooked because, as of 1968, no governor had ever served more than three terms, or a total of six years.[13] Whatever the reasons for the failure to establish a term limit in 1968, however, it has had a very powerful effect on Wisconsin politics, government, and public policy. Specifically the absence of a term limit made it possible for Tommy Thompson to win reelection for a third, and then a fourth, four-year term. As a result, he was able to consolidate and use power in a way that none of his predecessors in the governor's office had been able to do.

PATHWAYS TO POWER

Among the important questions that are regularly addressed in studies of the states' elected chief executives is whether there is a highly defined pathway to the executive office. In Wisconsin, as in many other states, party affiliation has been a key factor in determining who becomes governor. Additionally a set of demographic characteristics and a particular form of professional experience also seem to correlate with the rise to power. As part of the discussion of these factors, the long-term historical record is presented here, with special emphasis on the past forty years.

Party Affiliation

For most of Wisconsin's history party affiliation has been a key to the door of the executive office. During the first fifty years of statehood, Republicans dominated the governorship in Wisconsin. After the founding of the Republican Party in 1854, Democrats won the office only three times during the remainder of the century. Thus competition for the office was largely within the Republican Party, and, during the 1870s and 1880s, only candidates who had the blessing of the Stalwart machine (railroad and timber bosses) would be nominated by the party or elected governor.

As noted earlier, Robert La Follette and the Progressive Republicans battled the railroad and lumber barons (Stalwart Republicans) for control of the Republican Party during the late 1890s and early 1900s. After La Follette's election in 1900, Progressive candidates won the Republican Party nomination for much of the next twenty years. It is important to note that this type of success for Progressive Republicans—or those who believed in the Progressive agenda—was not unique to the state. Teddy Roosevelt, a Progressive Republican, was elected to the presidency during this era; so too was Woodrow Wilson, a Democrat with strong Progressive views. Additionally, candidates with Progressive views were elected to the executive office in a number of states, including Oregon and California.

During the 1920s, however, the pendulum swung the other way within the Republican Party at both the national and state levels. In the 1930s Wisconsin's Progressives split from the Republicans and formed their own party. Thus competition for the governorship within the state became three-sided: Republican, Progressive, and Democrat. Robert La Follette's son, Philip, was elected governor in 1934, but third-party status was difficult for the Progressives to maintain. The powerful effects of national elections and national issues during the Great Depression exerted a strong pull in the direction of the two national parties. The Progressive Party disbanded after World War II.

As noted previously, some of the Progressives moved back into the Republican Party; others became Democrats. The latter movement was a key factor in the rejuvenation of the Democratic Party. Election victories in statewide contests did not come quickly or easily for the changing Democratic Party. More than a decade of rebuilding was needed before Gaylord Nelson was elected governor in 1958. It is worth noting, however, that two others who played leadership roles in the post–World War II rebuilding of Wisconsin's Democratic Party, John Reynolds and Patrick Lucey, were also elected to the governorship.[14]

A profile of governors who have been elected during the modern, two-party competitive era is provided in table 4. During the last forty years of the twentieth century, there were eight governors; three were Republican, and

Table 4. Profile of Wisconsin Governors: 1959–2000 and 2001–2003

Governor Name, Party, Years	Birthplace	BA or BS Degree	Advanced Degree	Local Govt.	State Legislature	Statewide Office	Other Prof. Experience	Age When Elected Gov.	Years Governor	Post-Govshp.
Nelson (D, 1959–1963)	Clear Lake	X	Law		Senate[1]			42	4	U.S. Senate
Reynolds (D, 1963–1965)	Green Bay	X	Law			Atty. Gen.	Nat. Govt./ Fed. Court	41	2[3]	Fed. Judge
Knowles (R, 1965–1971)	River Falls	X	Law	County Board	Senate[1]	Lt. Governor		56	6	Law Firm
Lucey (D, 1971–1977)	La Crosse	X	Law		Assembly[1]	Lt. Governor	Business/ Party Chair	53	7	Ambassador[7]
Schreiber (D, 1977–1978)	Milwaukee	X			Senate[1]	Governor		39[2]	1[4]	Business
Dreyfus (R, 1978–1982)	Milwaukee	X	Ph.D.				Chancellor UW–SP	52	4	Business
Earl (D, 1982–1986)	Lansing MI	X	Law		Assembly[1]		DNR Secretary	45	4[3]	Law Firm
Thompson (R, 1986–2001)	Elroy	X	Law		Assembly[1]			45	14	Sec. of HHS
TOTALS	7 / 8	8 / 8	7 / 8	1 / 8	6 / 8	4 / 8	4 / 8	Avg.= 46.6	Avg.=3.8[5] Avg.=5.2[6]	8 / 8
McCallum (R, 2001–2002)	Fond du Lac	X	M.A.		Senate	Lt. Governor		52[2]	1.9[4]	
Doyle (D, 2003)	Washington DC	X	Law			Attorney General	Law, Nat. Govt.	58		

Source for Columns 1–10: Wisconsin Blue Book for the years 1960, 1964, 1970, 1981–1982, 1985–1986, 1995–1996, 2001–2002, 2003–2004

[1] Designates leadership role in senate or assembly   [2] Age when moved from lieutenant governor to governor due to elected governor's resignation   [3] Defeated in bid for election   [4] Defeated in bid for second term   [5] Average without Thompson   [6] Average with Thompson   [7] U.S. Ambassador to Mexico

five were Democrats. On February 1, 2001, Republican Scott McCallum succeeded Thompson for the remaining year of his term. On January 1, 2003, Democrat Jim Doyle took office after he defeated McCallum in the November 2002 election.

Birthplace, Gender, Age, and Education

The data in table 4 show that being a Wisconsin native is a key factor associated with those who become governor. Seven of the eight people who served as governor between 1959 and 2000 were born in Wisconsin. The only governor who was not a native, Anthony Earl, was born in neighboring Michigan. McCallum was born in Wisconsin; Doyle was born in Washington DC, but grew up in Oshkosh and Madison, Wisconsin.

The longer-term historical record of the twentieth century also shows the importance of being a Wisconsin native. Between 1901 and 1958, fifteen of eighteen governors were born in the state. Prior to 1900, however, none of Wisconsin's nineteen governors were born in the state; sixteen were born in other states, and three were born in other countries. This pattern is not surprising, given the fact that between statehood in 1848 and 1900, large parts of the state's population consisted of immigrants from other states or other countries.

A related geographical fact is that most of Wisconsin's governors have come from counties in the southern half of the state.[15] One explanation for this circumstance is that the southern half of the state is, and always has been, much more heavily populated than the northern half. Nevertheless the first three governors who came to office after 1958—Nelson, Reynolds, and Knowles—were from the northern half of the state. The next four governors who were Wisconsin natives—Lucey, Schreiber, Dreyfus, and Thompson— were born in the state's southern half. McCallum was born in the southern half of the state, while Doyle was raised in it.

All eight of the governors who served during the last forty years of the twentieth century were white men, as are McCallum and Doyle. The same was true of the twenty-five governors who served between 1848 and 1958. Indeed the record indicates that as of 2003, no black male and no female of any race had ever run for the governorship.

With respect to age, the data in table 4 show that recent governors have been relatively young when they were first elected to or assumed the office. Four of the eight men who served as governor during the period from 1959 to 2000 were forty-five or younger when they were elected; three were in their early or mid-fifties. The youngest of the eight governors was Martin Schreiber, who was thirty-nine. Schreiber was not elected to the office; he became acting governor when Patrick Lucey resigned to serve as President Carter's ambassador to Mexico. Scott McCallum was fifty-two when he moved into the executive office after Tommy Thompson resigned to become Secretary of Health and Human Services; Jim Doyle was fifty-eight when elected in 2003.

The last eight governors of the twentieth century were an average of five years younger than the men who were elected from 1866 to 1946. The average age during that period was fifty-two.[16] The average age of the eight governors is, however, a good deal higher than that of the nine men elected in the state's first twenty years. The average age of those men elected between 1848 and 1868 was only thirty-eight. Interestingly, the range of ages at which governors have been elected to or assumed office over the past 150 years is rather wide: from thirty-eight to eighty.[17] The oldest of these men, Walter Goodland, assumed office in 1943 at the age of eighty when the governor elect, Orland Steen Loomis, died before he was inaugurated.

The eight men who held the governorship from 1959 to 2000 were all well educated. All eight had bachelor's degrees, and seven also held an advanced degree. Of the seven advanced degrees, six were in law, and one was a Ph.D. It is worth noting that four of the eight bachelor's degrees were from the University of Wisconsin–Madison, and four of the six law degrees were from the University of Wisconsin–Madison's Law School.[18] McCallum and Doyle both had advanced degrees; Doyle's was in law.

The historical data on governors show that nineteenth-century governors did not commonly hold college degrees. The data also show that after World War II all Wisconsin governors had a college degree.[19] During the 1970s, 1980s, and 1990s, scholars and journalists regularly noted the fact that modern governors have been much better educated than were their predecessors. Nevertheless, even by this standard the credentials of Wisconsin's recent governors seem quite remarkable.

Professional Experience

Among the eight governors who served from 1959 to 2000, seven had substantial professional experience in government and politics. Lee Dreyfus was the only recent governor who could be labeled an "amateur." Six of the eight served in the state legislature before they ran for the governorship.

Furthermore, all six held a leadership position in that institution. John Reynolds did not serve in the state legislature, but he had solid governmental-political credentials. Before he ran for governor, he had played a leadership role in the state's Democratic Party, held two important administrative posts in the federal court system, and served as state attorney general. McCallum served in the state senate and as lieutenant governor; Doyle had served as attorney general.

In terms of professional experience the historical record shows that most governors were in public service before they ran for governor. Most held positions in local government, and then in the state legislature, before they ran for chief executive. As noted, many also held or ran for a statewide office, such as attorney general or lieutenant governor, before they ran for governor. Edward J. Miller notes that only eight "amateurs" won election to the governorship between 1848 and 1958.[20] In the academic literature, "amateurs" are defined as people who had not made elective office or other public service their primary career. Most of the eight amateurs were well-known industrialists, such as Julius Hiel and Walter Kohler Jr., who capped off their private-sector careers with a run for the governorship. Interestingly all eight amateurs were Republicans, and the average age at which these businessmen were elected governor was fifty-six.[21]

Why has the legislature been such an important stepping-stone to the governorship? By winning and then defending a seat in the legislature, these men became seasoned veterans of election campaigns. As legislative leaders, they developed statewide visibility, built friendships and a support network in the legislature, gained knowledge of state policy, and developed key connections within their political party. Last but not least, they developed an understanding of the state's principal media sources and the resources and influence that various interest groups can bring to bear on public policy issues. All of these assets are generally considered to be important for gubernatorial campaigns.

Of the eight governors who were elected between 1958 and 2000, Lee Dreyfus was the only one who had not previously run for and won elective office. Ironically, among the reasons Dreyfus was able to win the Republican nomination for the governorship in 1978 was that other Republicans, including the Republican leadership in the legislature, apparently thought the odds of beating Acting Governor Martin Schreiber were too long. It is also important to note, however, that even Dreyfus had an important connection to public service. He spent most of his professional career in Wisconsin's state university system, where he worked as an administrator and faculty member. When he ran for governor, he was serving as chancellor at the University of Wisconsin–Stevens Point.

On the basis of the historical data from 1848 to 2000, then, there seems to be a more or less clearly defined pathway to the governorship. It begins with one's birth in the state and moves on to elective office in local government. It then traverses a run for the state legislature, and then perhaps an attempt to win statewide office to better position oneself for a run at the governorship; for some, the path passes directly from the legislature to the governorship.

The path for modern governors resembles the longer historical pattern, but it varies in several interesting ways. The modern path begins with birth in the state, but is followed by an undergraduate degree. After graduation it is on to law school, most likely at the University of Wisconsin–Madison. When the law degree is received and the bar exam passed, the push begins to win a seat in the state legislature. Soon after election to the legislature, it is time to push further for a leadership position. Running for governor may come next, or there may be a step or two in between, including a run for lieutenant governor.

A key presumption held by those who observe and those who serve in state legislatures is that the pathway is either up or out—especially for those who are ambitious. This presumption gains credence when one examines the careers of the men who held the Wisconsin governorship during the last forty years of the twentieth century.

There is, however, one caveat against concluding that there is a relatively direct line from legislative leadership to the governorship. At any given time, there are at least six people holding leadership positions in the legislature: three in each chamber. Only a fraction of these people have taken the risk of competing for a statewide office.

The nature of risks faced by these legislative leaders when they step into the statewide political arena can be put into sharp relief by what happened to two of them during the 1990s. In 1990 Tom Loftus, a Democrat and powerful and effective assembly speaker, challenged incumbent Governor Thompson. The results for Loftus, his supporters, and the members of the Democratic Party were not pretty. Thompson won the contest by a wide margin. Then, in 1994, the Democratic majority leader in the senate, Charles Chvala, challenged Thompson. Chvala suffered a defeat that was even more one-sided than that experienced by Loftus.

Yet in some respects Chvala was the luckier of the two. He did not have to seek reelection for his senate seat when he challenged Thompson in 1994.

Consequently he returned to the senate, where he continued to serve in a leadership position. Loftus, however, could not run for an assembly seat while he was running for governor. His election defeat in 1990 left him without a job. In 1993 Loftus returned to public service when President Clinton appointed him Ambassador to Norway.

PAY, OFFICE QUARTERS, STAFF SUPPORT, AND BENEFITS

Those who pursue the governorship rarely do so with the goal of maximizing their income. That objective is more likely to be fulfilled by achieving a high-level management position in the private sector. In 2002, for example, the salary for Wisconsin's governor was $122,406. This is very modest pay for a chief executive who oversees an entity with more employees than all but a relatively small number of American corporations. Yet the pay gap between the public and private sectors is underscored by the fact that the Wisconsin governor's salary is usually listed in the top half of gubernatorial salaries nationwide.

The governor's office is located in the east wing of the State Capitol; the personal suite is located on the second floor. The suite is commodious, with deep mahogany walls, and a large, ornate chandelier hanging from the ceiling. From this suite the governor can look out through large and gracefully arched windows across the lovely Capitol grounds.

The entire executive office consists of two floors, and is tightly packed with staff. In the 1999–2001 budget, forty-eight staff members were officially authorized for the office of the governor, and the amount appropriated for the executive office was $6.7 million. The growth of staff over the last thirty years of the twentieth century was substantial, as were the resources given to the governor. In 1970, for example, the official staff was twenty-two, and the corresponding funding was $1.4 million.

The inner core of the governor's staff is usually made up of five or six members. Most modern governors have had a chief of staff, policy advisor, scheduler, press secretary, legislative director, legal counsel, and director of national relations. The structure of this inner core reflects both the scope of the responsibilities and the pressures that fall upon the governor. Most of the remainder of the staff report to one of these top-level gubernatorial assistants.

Among the tasks that consume a good deal of staff time are responses to correspondence, casework, and appointments to boards and commissions. On any given day, the governor may receive four hundred to five hundred pieces of mail. Sometimes as much as half of this correspondence requires casework investigation before a response can be generated. The task is also large in the matter of appointments because the governor may have to fill three hundred to five hundred positions during any given year. The vast majority of these vacancies occur when a sitting board member or commission member completes his or her term. When a state board or commission is in the throes of dealing with a difficult public problem, these appointments require a special sensitivity to political factors. At other times the appointments are relatively routine.

In addition to having an impressive office in the Capitol and a large staff, there are some other important perquisites that come with the job of governor. Perhaps the most important of these is the opportunity to live in the Governor's Mansion. The large, white mansion is located in Maple Bluff, a community situated on the northeast side of Madison. The front of the mansion faces a quiet road that is graced with other large and handsome houses; the back of the mansion faces Lake Mendota. During the summer, the view from the back terrace of the mansion is likely to include sailboats skipping across the waters of the state's fifth-largest lake. During the winter, the view from the glass dining area in the mansion is likely to include ice boats skimming across the lake and dozens of people ice fishing. Beyond its function as a formal meeting place, governors also use the mansion for social events.

RESPONSIBILITIES AND FORMAL POWERS

In Wisconsin's 1848 constitution, Article V is the Executive Article. In this article the principal responsibility assigned to the governor is to "take care that the laws are faithfully executed." In other words the governor is the state's chief administrator. Yet the formal powers given the governor in that article are focused on the governor's relationship with the legislature, not on the executive branch agencies. Specifically, the governor is given the power to veto legislation, call the legislature into special session, and recommend to the legislature whatever he or she believes is appropriate.

Perhaps this focus on executive-legislative relations, rather than on the management of the executive branch, should not be a surprise. In 1848 state government was small and simple. State expenditures for all government operations, including the legislature and the court system, were only $13,472.[22] In addition, the constitution provided for the independent election of a state treasurer, secretary of state, and attorney general—officials who could oversee most of whatever state activity was undertaken.[23]

Along with the powers granted in Article V for dealing with the legislature, the governor is given command of the state's militia and the power to grant reprieves, commutations, and pardons for all crimes except treason. In Article VI the governor is given the power to remove from office any elected county official, provided that he give that official a written statement of the charges. The governor is also empowered to fill vacancies for most local elected offices whenever they occur. Thus, the formal powers for the oversight of local government seem greater than for the oversight of the state executive branch.

Some of the key powers needed to ensure that the laws are faithfully executed are granted by statute rather than by the constitution. Such powers include the ability to appoint the secretaries of key departments and the immediate subordinates of those secretaries, the power to assemble a state executive budget recommendation, and the power to appoint almost two thousand officials to boards and commissions that oversee the implementation of state law or contribute to state policy development.

Despite the modest grant of constitutional powers given to the chief executive, Wisconsin's governor is generally described in the political science and public administration literature as having moderately strong formal powers.[24] The powers on which these ratings are based include length of term in office, opportunity for reelection, budgetary powers, veto power, appointment powers, and powers of organization. In the first four categories, the governor's powers are actually quite strong; in the latter two, they are more constrained.

Wisconsin's governor has a four-year term of office, with no limits on the number of terms that can be served consecutively. The governor also prepares an executive budget, with the help of the State Budget Office. Additionally, Wisconsin's governor has partial-veto authority. It is important to understand the difference between Wisconsin's partial veto and the item veto available to governors in many other states. The item veto only gives a governor the power to eliminate particular lines in a bill, while the partial veto allows Wisconsin's governor to eliminate part of a line or even particular letters or numbers in a line or bill. The partial veto is a very important tool for Wisconsin governors when it comes to the state budget.

Conversely, the Wisconsin governor's appointment and organizational powers are more limited. Some of the state's key departments and agencies are headed by independently elected officials, and boards or commissions head a number of the independent agencies. In almost all cases where boards or commissions operate, the governor appoints the members of the boards or commissions. It often takes a full term or more, however, for a governor to appoint a majority of the board or commission. The governor's ability to reorganize an executive branch agency is likewise limited by state statutes and the state constitution. Thus reorganization initiatives are undertaken somewhat selectively.

ROLES AND INFLUENCE

Defining a governor's formal responsibilities, powers, and spheres of influence is one way to describe what governors do and what tools they have at their disposal. Another approach is to outline the various roles they are called upon to play during their term in office. Wisconsin's governor, like governors in other states, serves as head of state, party leader, chief legislator, intergovernmental representative, and chief administrator.

Given the fact that governors have limited time, energy, and resources, some of these roles will be given more emphasis than others. Which of the roles a particular governor emphasizes most will depend on two key factors: personal characteristics and external factors. The personal characteristics include the governor's personality, interests, professional experience, knowledge, and skills. The external factors include economic conditions, the climate of the times, and issues that are at the top of public and governmental agendas.

The role of head of state is often associated with ceremonies, ribbon cutting, speech making, and photo opportunities. The ribbon-cutting ceremonies may involve the opening of a new school, factory, bridge, road, or park. The ceremonial role may also involve giving graduation addresses, delivering speeches at conventions, making presentations at lunch-time events, or hosting recognition ceremonies for sports teams that have won championships. Most governors enjoy these ceremonial duties. These occasions not only give the governor visibility but also provide an opportunity for the governor to celebrate the state's achievements and to make social connections.

Opportunities to engage in these activities are plentiful. On any given day a governor may be invited to dozens of events. This is where an astute scheduler in the office of the governor can help immensely. The scheduler has to find ways to link events together in order to minimize travel time and maximize exposure. Even with a state patrol officer driving the governor from place to place, a trip from the southern end of the state to the northern end can take more than five or six hours, and a trip across the state from east to west can consume three or four. The governor can, of course, use the state airplane to reduce trip time, but the logistics of airports and airtime can also be very time-consuming.

The role of party leader can also be time-consuming.[25] As party leader the governor may want to ensure that the person selected as state party chair has compatible views. The governor may also want to be involved in the recruitment process for the state party executive council and the various county party apparatuses. Governors usually participate in large events sponsored by the state party, and they may also participate in county events. Although these events may include fundraising dinners, the governor may also engage in party fundraising as a separate stream of activity. All of these activities may need to be coordinated with party leaders in the legislature, as well as other key party constituencies.

Finally, as party leader, the governor may be involved in recruiting candidates and in campaigning on behalf of those who are running for office. Particularly when a governor is popular, candidates for the senate and assembly seek his or her endorsement. They may also ask the governor to appear with them during campaign stops. This support can be very important to candidates in closely contested general election races. The candidates hope that the governor's reputation and status will give their campaigns a boost. While governors may enjoy such activity, there is also some risk involved when they put their prestige on the line for a particular candidate. If that candidate loses, the opposition party may claim that the governor's influence with voters is overrated.

As chief legislator, the governor's task is to focus on statutory law and the politics of the legislative process. Specifically, a governor may be engaged in matters involving the reauthorization of programs, amendments to statutes, or the creation of new statutory law. As previously noted, the state biennial budget bill is the largest and most important of the bills that move through the legislature. It is also the bill that will receive the most focused and sustained attention of the governor and the governor's staff.

The governor must further be prepared to accept petitioners from the legislature, who come to ask for help with matters of key importance to their districts and/or to them personally. These matters may involve the need to straighten a deadly curve on a state highway or the desire to have a new state park. The governor and his legislative director must also work closely with legislative leaders. This relationship may be key to getting what the governor wants and to blocking or stopping legislation the governor does not want to have to veto.

The governor's role as intergovernmental representative has become increasingly important over the past couple of decades, as state-local, state-to-state, state-national, and state-international relationships have developed in scope and complexity. Local government officials regularly request time on the governor's calendar to discuss matters related to their city, county, or school system. Wisconsin's governor serves on a number of formally chartered interstate commissions, such as the Great Lakes Compact Commission. The governor must also represent the state in such important associations as the National Governors' Association. Because a substantial part of the state's revenue comes from the national government, and because U.S. statutes and administrative rules can either constrain or enable state activity, governors may also need to invest large blocks of time in working with the state's congressional delegation, the president, or cabinet secretaries. Particularly when the president is from the opposition party, the establishment of these important links can be difficult.

As chief administrator, Wisconsin's governor oversees a large governmental apparatus established to implement state law. In 2000 more than sixty-seven thousand full-time employees and almost seven thousand part-time employees worked in the state's executive branch departments and agencies. The largest of these institutions was the University of Wisconsin system, with approximately 45 percent of all state employees and about half of all part-time employees.

The executive branch is organized into eighteen departments and thirteen independent agencies. The governor appoints the heads of thirteen of the eighteen departments. Two departments are headed by independently elected officials, and three are headed by part-time boards that appoint a secretary. All of the independent agencies are headed by a full-time commission or a part-time board. Most commission and board members are appointed by the governor.

Given the tremendous scope and complexity of state activity, as well as the number of executive branch departments, agencies, boards, and commissions, the role of chief administrator can be demanding, time-consuming, and frustrating. Some governors seem content to limit their focus to the appointment of departmental secretaries. Others may be more directly involved in oversight of the executive branch agencies, while still others may become heavily involved in attempts to enhance the performance of individual agencies or the executive branch as a whole.[26]

Of these roles, the two that many recent governors were most comfortable playing were those of ceremonial head of state and chief legislator. These are the two roles that correspond most closely with the governors' professional experience. As former members of the legislature and former legislative leaders, most became skilled at working the crowd at social gatherings and at taking advantage of photo opportunities. The role of ceremonial head of state is thus just a larger version of what they had already done. The same is the case with that of chief legislator. As legislative leaders, they were used to moving—or attempting to block—the governor's policy agenda. In the role of governor, they are simply a bit farther forward on the policy chain.

Most governors are least likely to feel comfortable in their capacity as chief administrator. Most people who run for political office are likely to be more interested in the political than administrative dimensions of public issues. Furthermore, most governors have little, if any, professional experience as administrators. Even those who ascend to the governorship from business soon learn that public administration is very different than private administration.[27] Additionally, even governors who have an interest in administration quickly learn that attempting to manage a huge and highly varied administrative apparatus is both tremendously time-consuming and frustrating.[28] Thus, they too are likely to focus their attention elsewhere.

Some examples of recent Wisconsin governors who have played one or another of these five roles particularly well might help to illustrate how personal factors and external factors come into play. Warren Knowles played the role of ceremonial head of state exceptionally well. He had a pleasant manner, he was very photogenic, and he had a dignified countenance that the press and the cameras seemed to love. Indeed, the press came to make a habit of printing front-page pictures of Governor Knowles cutting ribbons, convening meetings, and signing important state documents.

For different reasons, Lee Dreyfus also was exceptionally good in the role of ceremonial head of state. He had a special stage presence, and he seemed to relish opportunities to give speeches to both small and large crowds. Audiences in turn seemed to enjoy listening to him. By means of his speechmaking, and his trademark red vest, Dreyfus boosted his visibility and popularity throughout the state.

Patrick Lucey, on the other hand, did not play the role of ceremonial head of state very well. He often seemed uncomfortable giving speeches to large audiences, and more than once his delivery was described as "wooden." Even in small-group settings, he often seemed ill at ease making a formal presentation. On numerous occasions, he told some of his staff members that he much preferred grappling with difficult policy or administrative problems to spending time at ceremonies.

Gaylord Nelson, Warren Knowles, Patrick Lucey, Anthony Earl, and Tommy Thompson all seemed to play enthusiastically the role of legislative leader and each showed substantial skill in pursuing his policy objectives. Yet the fact that all of these governors had experience as legislative leaders did not mean that they all handled the role of chief legislator in the same way. Earl, for example, came out of the legislature with a deep respect for the institution and the people elected to serve in it. As a result he was reluctant to be too heavy-handed in his dealings with legislators. In contrast, Thompson was extraordinarily aggressive in demanding support and loyalty from members of his own party, and he effectively used tools at his disposal to reward or punish.

At least two of the eight Wisconsin governors who served between 1959 and 2000 made a substantial investment of time and energy in the role of party leader: Warren Knowles and Tommy Thompson. Knowles's presence at party events seemed to reassure both leaders and the rank and file. He was willing to give his time to party activities; as a result state and county officials sought him out. Additionally Knowles seemed to have a good working relationship with the legislative leaders of his party.

The drive and energy Thompson committed to building the party apparatus may have been motivated by the many frustrating years he spent in the assembly while Republicans were in the minority. Thompson certainly had a clear understanding of the benefits that would accrue to him if he had a majority in both houses, and he worked hard to build that majority. Thompson's approach to party leadership in the legislature was somewhat different than that of Knowles. Thompson was more demanding of that leadership, but he was also more successful in influencing who would hold the position. He even took a variety of steps to ensure that a loyalist led the Republicans in the assembly, and he made a concerted effort to gain a similar degree of responsiveness from Republican leaders in the senate.[29]

Each of the eight governors who held office between 1959 and 2000 engaged in the role of intergovernmental representative, but some invested more time and energy than did others. The degree of involvement seems to be, at least in part, a function of the policy or budgetary issues in which governors took a particular interest. For example, John Reynolds was interested in the intersection of national and state law and court decision making.[30] He also had a good network of connections in the national justice system. Thus he actively represented the state's interest in this area. Patrick Lucey and

Anthony Earl were both actively engaged in efforts to reduce pollution going into Wisconsin's lakes and rivers. One of the ways they could focus on this objective was to be active participants in the Great Lakes Compact Commission.

Transportation was a particular interest of Tommy Thompson. Road building was an area where he could reward those who supported him, and he aggressively pushed his road-building agenda. A key to road building is the amount of national government revenue that flows to a state. Thompson worked hard, as several of his predecessors had, to improve the ratio of gas-tax money returned to the state for every dollar that went to the federal highway trust fund. He strove to influence U.S. transportation legislation and to get the formula changed through which these monies were distributed. He had more success in this than did his predecessors, in part because, and fortuitously for his purposes, a consensus had emerged nationally that more "fairness" was needed in the distribution of gas-tax funds. Thompson also became a highly visible representative for the state in regional and national discussions of high-speed rail transportation.

Governors do not have the time, inclination, experience, or skill to play all of the five roles equally well. Nor are they always free to choose how much time they will invest in each role, because external events may force them to spend more time on one than another. While overinvestment in one role may bring particular benefits, underinvestment in others may have negative consequences. Lucey, for example, loved playing the role of chief legislator and chief administrator. In his years as legislator, legislative leader, lieutenant governor, and state party chair, he acquired a tremendous command of the technical dimensions of a wide range of state programs.[31] He also had a wide knowledge of the state's administrative machinery and well-formed views about which parts of it performed well and which did not. He also seemed to have a clear grasp of the important connection between policy and administration.

Lucey was criticized by some for spending too much time managing his policy agenda and overseeing the executive branch departments and agencies. Some party loyalists seemed hurt by the lack of attention he paid to them, and they were surprised by how little he invested in the Democratic Party. Yet many of the legislators, administrators, and staff members who saw Lucey at work understood the benefits of having a governor with his breadth and depth of knowledge.

Lucey's keen intellect and his willingness to make hard decisions also made a positive impression.[32] No matter who participated or how many people participated in policy-issue or budget-briefing sessions with Governor Lucey, there was rarely any doubt about who would make the final decision. Nor, for that matter, was there much doubt about who *ought* to be making the decision. In contrast, other governors, both in Wisconsin and elsewhere, have arrived in office with a very limited knowledge of state policy and administration and a great reluctance to be pulled into issues that require hard choices be made in those areas.

GOVERNORS AS FREE AGENTS OR CAPTIVES OF FATE

Being governor of a state can be a high-profile and even glamorous job, and governors can have a big impact on a state's politics, public policy, and administration. Yet this is only one side of a multifaceted picture; others may be less appealing. Governors often feel a sense of acute frustration over the constraints they face. They may also be hemmed in by forces beyond their control. Such forces could include decisions made by preceding governors and legislators and/or by economic recession. The former conditions may leave a governor little or no wiggle room in policy decision-making; the latter condition may put a governor in a position where any choice made will offend some or all of the state's voters.

Anthony Earl was the governor who, among the eight who held office between 1959 and 2000, seems to have been most adversely affected by these forces. When Earl took office in 1983, he inherited a sizable structural budget deficit. That is, spending commitments substantially exceeded what could be supported with the existing revenue stream in the current fiscal year and in the foreseeable future.

The budget problem had been carefully masked by the Dreyfus administration, and it came as a big surprise to the newly inaugurated Earl administration in January of 1982. Indeed shortly after he took office Governor Earl learned that the state was likely to have a deficit in the current (1982) fiscal year. With the fiscal year more than half over, Earl had to make some quick decisions. His options were to cut spending, increase taxes, or do some of both. Because spending cuts were more easily made at that point in time than tax increases, he put the primary emphasis on expenditure reductions.

The adjustments Earl made in spending were a short-term response to the immediate problem, but the larger structural issue still needed to be addressed in the biennial budget. To make matters worse, a downturn in the national economy had set in, and this downturn was exacerbating the new governor's fiscal problems. In order to respond to the situation, Earl decided to hold the line on salaries for state employees in his FY 1982–84 budget. This created a storm of protest from what might be considered a natural constituency for a Democratic governor who was favorably disposed to civil service.

As the fiscal situation deteriorated, Earl also opted for an income tax surcharge of 5 percent. The surcharge was to be temporary—designed to be in place only until the economy improved and the deficit cloud lifted. It was a courageous decision by Earl, who could have used the sales tax for the same purpose. After all, a sales-tax increase has a less direct or visible effect on individual taxpayers. Yet Earl did not take this path, largely because the sales tax was more regressive in its effects. While this may have been a good public policy decision, it did not win Earl many friends.

These decisions, as well as others Governor Earl had to make, put his reelection prospects at risk. In the campaign of 1986 Tommy Thompson made good use of these risk factors. A key Thompson campaign theme was that the only thing wrong with the state of Wisconsin was its governor. New leadership, he argued, could dispose of all other problems. Thompson went on to defeat Earl in 1986. Thus Earl paid a high price for his good stewardship of state finances. He received little public credit for solving the state's fiscal crisis, and the challenger who defeated him at the polls reaped the benefits. The new governor, Tommy Thompson, inherited a sound fiscal foundation from which to pursue his agenda.

AFTER THE GOVERNORSHIP

What happens to governors after they leave office? Do they, as Douglas MacArthur said of old soldiers, simply fade away? This was decidedly not the case for the eight Wisconsin governors who held office between 1959 and 2000. As the data in table 4 show, all eight men had active careers after they left the governorship. Gaylord Nelson went on to represent Wisconsin in the U.S. Senate. John Reynolds was appointed by President John F. Kennedy to a federal judgeship in the state. Warren Knowles returned to the practice of law, as did Anthony Earl. Patrick Lucey served as ambassador to Mexico under Jimmy Carter. He later established a consulting practice with clients in a number of states. Martin Schreiber and, later, Lee Dreyfus accepted high-level positions in one of the state's largest insurance companies, but neither remained in these positions very long.[33]

Perhaps an equally important question is whether these governors continued to play an important role in their parties or in state politics and public policy. As a U.S. senator, Gaylord Nelson continued to be a major figure in the Democratic Party, but his focus shifted from state to national politics and policy. As a federal judge, Reynolds's ability to engage in politics was limited, but through decisions he made from the bench he certainly had an effect on public policy. Knowles maintained a connection to the Republican Party as senior statesman, but he was not actively engaged in politics or policy development.

Within a year of the time he left the governorship, Lucey was actively engaged in a presidential campaign as part of a third-party ticket. John Anderson was the presidential nominee, and Lucey was the vice-presidential nominee of the Independent Party. This move cost Lucey dearly with Democrats inside Wisconsin and across the nation. Yet during his ambassadorship in Mexico, Lucey developed a strong antipathy toward President Carter. Because he could not support a Republican presidential candidate, he took what he viewed as the only viable option.[34] After a respectable showing on the third-party ticket, he put his energy into consulting activities and managing the substantial financial portfolio he had developed in the private sector before he was governor.

Schreiber and Earl maintained their connection to the Democratic Party, but neither played a significant leadership role. Additionally, both continued to be involved in the shaping of public policy, but again in a very limited way (representing the interests of specific clients in the legislative process). Lee Dreyfus apparently had little active engagement in state politics or public policy after he left the governorship.

Finally, we turn to the case of Tommy Thompson. In the summer of 1999, while he was serving his fourth term as governor, Thompson announced that he would not seek a fifth term. It was widely believed at the time that Thompson's ambition was to serve in a Republican presidential administration in 2000. In December of 2000 that hope became a reality when President-elect George W. Bush offered Thompson the opportunity to serve in his cabinet as secretary of the Department of Health and Human Services. Thompson apparently preferred Transportation to Health and Human Services, but he accepted the president-elect's offer.[35]

Thompson's own doubts about whether the move was a good one for him were echoed by others inside and outside of Wisconsin. Among those who knew Thompson well or had watched him operate as governor, there were doubts about whether he could successfully make the transition from chief executive of Wisconsin to departmental secretary in Washington DC.

Yet given the remarkable way in which he moved from conservative ideologue to a more moderate and sophisticated politician during his years in elective office, it did not seem farfetched to think that Thompson would find the formula required for effective leadership in Washington DC. The fact that he relatively quickly became a favorite of many reporters in the capital lends credence to this view. At the same time one of the most interesting press accounts about Thompson was one published in the *Washington Post* after a meeting the paper's editors and reporters had with him. The article was titled "Government in Molasses." The central theme, perhaps not surprisingly, was the frustration Thompson felt over the difficulties of getting anything done in the capital city.[36] It was a frustration Thompson apparently shared with his famous predecessor, Robert M. La Follette, who went to Washington DC to serve in the U.S. Senate.

CHAPTER FIVE

The Courts

Most of the law under which an American lives is the law of his state. His marriage, his property, his will are all governed by state law. If he gets into a lawsuit about a business contract or a real estate deal or an automobile accident, the result will ordinarily be determined by state law—law laid down in state and local statutes and by decisions of state courts.

Anthony Lewis, Gideon's Trumpet, 1964

Courts are an enigma to most people. Unlike the governor's office, they are not the focus of intense political party activity. Unlike legislatures, they are not surrounded by lobbyists nor are they the constant object of interest group activity. Yet they are the third branch of government, an integral part of the same political system in which governors and legislatures play such a prominent role.

Herbert Jacob, "Courts," 1983

There are two competing views of courts in American political thought and in the practice of American politics.[1] One is the belief that the courts' role is to settle legal disputes in an impartial and evenhanded manner, with the underlying presumption that courts can perform this role only if they are insulated from politics. The other is the belief that courts, like other democratic institutions, should be responsive to the electorate. The underlying presumption here is that because courts make policy decisions, they must be accountable to the people.

The conflict between these two perspectives can be seen in historical and contemporary disputes over whether judges should be elected or appointed. For example, during the state constitutional conventions of 1846 and

1847 Wisconsin's Progressive Democrats insisted on the election of judges, while Whig party members wanted judges to be appointed. The Progressive Democrats won the battle, and, had they lived long enough, would have been pleased to see the results. During the Progressive era from 1900 to 1915, the elected members of the Wisconsin Supreme Court generally rejected pleas that they overturn most of the new political, economic, and social reform legislation. Given the scope and scale of these statutory changes, the court's response was remarkable.

This chapter begins with a brief review of the way the courts responded to the Progressive reforms of the early 1900s; it also includes a description of the way in which the Progressive legacy influenced Wisconsin's courts. The second section contains a brief overview of the way state citizens may view the courts and an example of the way in which Wisconsin courts engage in policymaking. A description of the structure of the state's judiciary comes next, followed by an examination of the judicial selection process. The fifth section describes the "other actors" apart from judges who play important roles in court proceedings. The chapter is concluded with a short review of some of the important policy issues decided by the Wisconsin Supreme Court.

THE COURTS IN THE PROGRESSIVE ERA

Most histories of the 1900–1915 period in Wisconsin, known as the Progressive era, say little about the courts. These histories usually focus on the other two branches of state government: the executive branch and the legislature. Political parties, party leaders, individual entrepreneurs, and corporations may also get significant attention.

There is one exception to this general rule, however. Most historians report a story about the courts told by Robert M. La Follette. La Follette contends that his decision to make a break with the bosses of the Republican Party in 1891 came after he was asked to carry a bribe to a judge.[2] La Follette had recently lost his seat in Congress in the Democratic landslide of 1890; it was a seat he had held since 1885.[3]

Neither La Follette nor others at the time claimed that corruption was a widespread problem in the courts, and reform of the courts was not a focus of Wisconsin Progressives. Yet there were some good reasons for Progressives nationally and in Wisconsin to be concerned about the courts. As much of the national historical record for the 1890s and early 1900s shows, judges at the time tended to ignore calls for economic reform, tax reform, and social reform. Historian John D. Buenker provides the context for the courts' response by arguing that judge-made law from previous decades "sanctioned government promotion of private enterprise and hamstrung measures aimed at regulation, taxation, redistribution, or protection of the disadvantaged."[4]

The doctrine the U.S. Supreme Court and other state courts used to overturn reform legislation was "substantive due process." According to legal scholar Joseph A. Ranney, the "term was a catch-all term for a variety of provisions the courts used to scrutinize state and federal use of 'police power'—that is, use of regulatory powers to promote public welfare."[5] The basic presumption was that "any state statute, ordinance, or administrative act which imposed any kind of limitation upon private property raised the question of due process of law."[6]

Yet this context makes the reaction of Wisconsin's supreme court to Progressive legislation seem all the more remarkable. The court did overturn some reform legislation, such as conservation bills of the 1911 legislature relating to reforestation and waterpower regulation.[7] The majority of the cases decided by the court, however, indicate that, by and large, the majority of the justices were not overtly hostile to the Progressive reforms. For example, the court rejected challenges to the Progressives' political reforms, including the direct primary; civil service reforms; tax reforms, including the income and inheritance tax; and reforms aimed at worker protection, including the workmen's compensation law.[8]

How can the Wisconsin Supreme Court's generally positive response to the Progressives' legislation be explained? Several key factors have been identified by Ranney and other scholars. First, in Wisconsin, precedent for state regulation of economic activity had been established via the Potter Law of 1874 and upheld by the Wisconsin Supreme Court. Indeed, the court's chief justice, Edward G. Ryan, gave energetic support to this law.

Second, most of the Progressive legislation was drafted by Charles A. McCarthy, the head of the new Legislative Reference Library, and John R. Commons, a faculty member at the University of Wisconsin.[9] As they designed reform legislation, these two men carefully studied what was going on in congress and in state legislatures and courts across the country. McCarthy in particular was determined to draft legislation in a manner that would meet any constitutional challenge.

Third, John Winslow, who was appointed to the court in 1891 and reelected in 1895 and 1905, became chief justice in 1907. It was Winslow, Ranney contends, who "ensured that the court struck down only a few

Progressive measures."[10] Winslow believed that the court's response to reform legislation should be one of "constructive conservatism." He thought that the court should "curb the most serious excesses created by reform, and, for the rest, stay out of reform's way."[11]

Lastly, the justices of the supreme court had to stand for election; thus they could only ignore the growing public demand for reform legislation at some risk. One justice who did ignore this chorus, Roujet D. Marshall, was defeated in 1917. Marshall was the main opponent of Progressive reforms, and he took the lead role in persuading the other justices to declare unconstitutional the Progressives' 1911 legislation aimed at conservation and reforestation. In the *Forestry* case, *State ex rel. Owen v. Donald* (1915), Marshall wrote the court's opinion. In it he insisted that it was individuals, rather than government, that would provide for the common good.[12] The case was "probably the most controversial supreme court decision of the Progressive era," and Marshall became publicly associated with it.[13]

Progressive Legacy

In addition to the Wisconsin Supreme Court's relatively supportive responses to Progressive reforms, it is also worth noting that the legacy of the Progressives' approach to government and politics remains visible in all of the state's courts. For the past one hundred years Wisconsin's courts have been among the cleanest in the nation, and, like other institutions of Wisconsin state government, the courts have a well-deserved reputation for high ethical and professional standards. Concerns about jury tampering or judges for sale have been virtually nonexistent. In short, the Progressive tradition has put Wisconsin courts in a position to be respected by the state's citizenry and to earn respect from around the country.

OVERVIEW OF CITIZEN PERSPECTIVES, TRIALS, AND POLICYMAKING ACTIVITIES

While Wisconsinites can be justifiably proud of the "cleanliness" of the court system, this should not be interpreted to mean that encounters with courts are something to be desired. It is more likely that citizens of Wisconsin, like those of other states, simply want to avoid being in court as a litigant. Some Wisconsinites may feel the same way about jury duty, but many others accept their responsibility to perform this important civic duty. Yet whether one is a litigant or a juror, participation in a trial can be an annoyance and a disruption to the routines of life. For litigants the personal and financial consequences of an unfavorable judgment can be disastrous.

Citizens may also associate courts with social drama and tragedy. News coverage of trials exposes the details of ghastly crimes and reveals the intrigue of clever attempts to bilk people out of money or property. The uncertainty of how a jury might rule is itself captivating. Of course courts not only determine guilt and resolve conflicts but also engage in relatively routine activities such as the registration of name changes and adoptions.

While trial courts are largely engaged in what Herbert Jacob calls "norm enforcement" or the application of law in a wide range of areas, appellate courts may be involved in policymaking.[14] One reason appellate courts make significant policy decisions is that they are called upon to interpret language in statutes or constitutions. Sometimes this language is vague or ambiguous. A second reason is that appellate judges may see their role as one of interpreting law rather than of merely implementing statutory or administrative law.[15] According to Jacob, it is "a fundamental tenet of American law that appellate courts possess the right to interpret statutes, to alter past judicial rulings, and even to declare legislative enactments as contrary to the Constitution."[16]

One of the most visible recent examples of policymaking occurred in the 1990s, when the Wisconsin Supreme Court was asked to decide whether allowing parents to use publicly funded vouchers to pay to send their children to religious schools violated the constitutional prohibition against state support for religious institutions. Initially the justices tied, 3–3, with one member not participating in the decision because of a conflict of interest.[17]

In 1996, however, shortly after the tie vote, Chief Justice Nathan Heffernan, who voted against the use of the vouchers, retired. The election to fill his seat was waged in part on how candidates would vote on the voucher case. N. Patrick Crooks, who favored allowing religious institutions to get the vouchers, won. In reconsideration of the voucher case after this election, the justices voted 4–2 (again, with one justice not participating) in favor of the voucher program.

While appellate courts can play an important role in establishing public policy, however, their opportunity to do so is limited by the way in which their agenda is set. Unlike legislators or governors, judges cannot initiate policy changes on their own. Judges only rule on the cases brought before them; thus they are dependent on lawyers litigating for their clients and on district attorneys prosecuting someone charged with a crime.

In fact, courts sometimes serve as the agenda-setter for other institutions, rather than as the final decision maker. A good example is the 1981 case of *State v. Quality Egg Farm*. The issue was what constitutes a "public nuisance." In 1967 a farmer in tiny Bristol, Wisconsin, started an enterprise with 60,000 chickens. In seven years, the chickens multiplied to 140,000, and by 1980 he had 300,000 chickens producing eggs.

In addition to eggs, the 300,000 chickens produced fifteen tons of chicken manure every day. The few neighbors considered the manure a nuisance, especially on warm summer days with the breeze blowing in a certain direction. Did Quality Egg Farm violate the state law against being a public nuisance? Does the adjective "public" refer to a community, such as Bristol, or did legislators use that term to refer to a large number of people, which then would not apply to Bristol?

The county circuit court ruled against Quality Egg Farm in favor of the concept of community, even when that community consists of a small number of people. The appellate court disagreed and reasoned that the legislature must have meant "public" to refer to a relatively large number of people. The supreme court reversed the appellate court decision and upheld the community-based definition.

The supreme court's decision took explicit note of the lack of clear legislative intent and invited the legislature to pass legislation providing more precise guidance. The issue was hotly debated in the legislature for over a decade. Finally, in 1995, the Right to Farm Act was introduced and adopted, establishing a priority for agricultural activities over small-town comfort. The court, in short, put an issue on the calendar of the legislature.

STRUCTURE OF THE JUDICIARY

The state constitution gives the governor and legislature the power to establish the structure of the judiciary. The governor and the legislature have the constitutional authority to determine the number of courts in the state and what, if any, limits there are on the cases they may hear. Until 1959, however, the elected officials in these two branches did not attempt to establish a statewide structure, and each county had its own arrangement. Some had specialized courts for traffic or small claims or family issues; others only one court. Jurisdictional boundaries sometimes overlapped and were confusing.

In 1959 the legislature passed a law creating a uniform system throughout the state. In 1977 legislation was passed that more fully articulated the state structure and also addressed the critical issue of financing for the courts; in this act Wisconsin followed the general model of court reorganization that was advocated by the American Bar Association and the Council of State Governments. As a result, Wisconsin's court system now includes municipal courts, circuit courts, courts of appeal, and a supreme court.

Municipal Courts

Cities, villages, and towns have the authority to create municipal courts individually and jointly. Two hundred and twenty-five municipal courts existed in Wisconsin as of September 2003.[18] These courts rule only on cases involving local ordinances. There are no jury trials in municipal court; judges decide all cases. Both the defendant and the municipality, however, have the right to a jury trial, which is available in the circuit court.[19] The majority of municipal court cases involve traffic violations, including first-time drunk-driving offenses. In recent years, juvenile matters, including underage drinking and drug offenses, have also become a large part of municipal court caseloads.[20]

Municipal judges are elected in nonpartisan elections in the spring, and take office May 1. Municipalities may set the terms for their judges at two to four years. State law does not require that municipal judges be attorneys, but nearly 50 percent are.[21] Most municipal judgeships are part-time positions, but Milwaukee and Madison have full-time judges. Milwaukee has the largest municipal court, with three full-time judges and three part-time court commissioners. The Milwaukee court handles more than 190,000 cases annually.[22]

Circuit Court

Each county has a circuit court, but six rural counties have been paired and share three circuit courts. The number of judges per circuit court ranges from one to forty-six, depending on the population in the county. The state's 241 circuit court judges are elected for six-year terms in nonpartisan elections. Vacancies are filled by gubernatorial appointment, but the appointee must stand for election in the spring following appointment.[23]

Circuit courts have original jurisdiction, meaning lawsuits can be initiated at this level. A single judge presides, and litigants typically have a choice between a jury and a bench trial. In urban areas, circuit courts have established specialized commissions to deal with some of the high-volume cases, such as traffic, probate, small claims, and divorce and custody. Circuit courts also take appeals from state administrative tribunals, typically when there is a dispute about whether an administrative law judge acted within his or her authority and/or followed proper procedure.

Throughout the circuit court system, more than a million cases were filed in 2002. Of these, 428,049 were contested cases filed in the trial courts, while 637,266 were uncontested and disposed without trial. The largest part of the total caseload (53 percent) comes from forfeiture cases (which include traffic cases), followed by civil (25 percent), criminal (14 percent), juvenile (5 percent), and probate cases (4 percent).[24]

Court of Appeals

Any ruling by a circuit court may be heard by one of four courts of appeals in the state. Each court of appeals consists of several judges, each of whom is elected for a six-year term. Two of the courts of appeals have four judges each. One (a rural part of the state) has three judges, and the other (which includes the state capital and a number of medium-sized towns) has five. The expectation is that a three-judge panel will consider each case that is appealed. When the caseload is particularly heavy, the process may involve one judge considering the appeal in depth and then seeking review and approval by two other judges. Attorneys present their arguments in oral and written form, but without the witnesses and evidence used at the original trial.

A total of 3,342 cases were filed in courts of appeals in 2002. Civil cases made up 55 percent of this workload, while criminal cases made up 45 percent. Also worth noting is the fact that only 37 percent of the cases filed ended in an actual opinion, while a majority (56 percent) of the case decisions came in the form of either a summary disposition or a memorandum opinion.[25]

Supreme Court

The Wisconsin Supreme Court serves as the "court of last resort" in the state. The court is also responsible for the administration of the entire state court system and for regulating the legal profession in Wisconsin. Since 1907 the supreme court has had seven members; the longest serving member assumes the position of chief justice.

In 2003 the chief justice was Shirley S. Abrahamson; the other six justices (listed in order of length of term on the court) were William A. Bablitch, Jon P. Wilcox, Ann Walsh Bradley, N. Patrick Crooks, David T. Prosser

Table 5. Wisconsin Supreme Court Caseload, 1980–2003

	1980	1985	1990	1995	2000	2003
Total Matters Docketed	459	1047	1068	1426	1471	1591
Civil	345	747	754	599	864	982
Criminal	114	300	314	527	607	609
Total Carried Over from Previous Year	232	94	105	118	101	137
Civil	166	71	83	93	70	108
Criminal	66	23	22	25	31	29
Total Matters Considered	123	287	299	319	331	424
Civil	n/a	226	243	265	252	363
Criminal	n/a	61	56	54	79	61
Total Matters Denied	429	601	621	920	943	914
Civil	n/a	415	403	513	497	466
Criminal	n/a	186	218	407	446	448

Source: Wisconsin Supreme Court, "Supreme Court Monthly Statistical Report," December, 1981–2004

Jr., and Patience D. Roggensack. Supreme court justices are elected on a statewide basis to ten-year terms. Elections for the supreme court, like all other Wisconsin judgeships, are nonpartisan and held in the spring.

A major feature of the court-reform legislation passed in 1977 is that the supreme court does not have to take all of the appeals submitted to it. While the courts of appeal cannot refuse cases, the supreme court can select which ones it wants to hear and let the appellate court rulings be the final decision for all the others.

This discretion gives the supreme court the ability to set its agenda by making selections from the pool of appealed cases. The cases that are prime candidates for consideration by the supreme court tend to be those with high political and policy significance, such as the case involving public vouchers for religious schools, and those where rulings by different courts of appeal conflict with one another.

The opportunity to accept appeals or let lower court decisions stand also gives the supreme court a means through which to maintain a reasonable and manageable workload. The court seems to be using this tool effectively. The number of cases docketed with the supreme court has risen steadily since 1980, and the number of cases considered by the Court has grown. The proportion of cases considered in 1980 and 2003, however, was the same.

An example of the cases docketed with the court between 1980 and 2003, the types of cases docketed, and the number and type of cases the court has considered is provided in table 5.

Among the points of interest one can glean from the data is that the court denies, or refuses to consider, approximately two-thirds of the cases docketed, that more criminal cases are docketed than civil cases, and that the court carries over a substantial number of cases from one year to the next.

Director of State Courts

Since 1961 the courts have been able to rely on an administrative unit, headed by a director of state courts, for various managerial services. The director is responsible for making sure judges have courtrooms and office space, clerical support, equipment, and the like. These support services would seem to be uncontroversial, and they are generally handled in a professional manner.

In a matter related to this apparently nonpolitical and nonpartisan function, however, the 1999 elections for a seat on the supreme court took on something of the character of a comedy. One justice opposed the reelection of his colleague in part because she asked the director of state courts to remove the game programs on computers in supreme court offices. This was offered as an example of how the judge was micromanaging the court administrative staff.

Judicial Commission

In 1972 the supreme court adopted a Code of Judicial Ethics to guide all judges in the state; the court also created a nine-member judicial commission to implement the code. The Judicial Commission was established by statute in 1977, and it has the authority to conduct confidential investigations of allegations of misconduct and to consider petitions related to the permanent disability of a judge or court commissioner. The commission reports its findings to the supreme court and prosecutes those cases where it finds cause for disciplinary action. On the basis of commission recommendations, the supreme court has taken a variety of disciplinary actions, ranging from reprimands to suspensions, but it has not exercised its authority to remove a judge from office.

Recall

Occasionally judges have been removed from office before their term expired. In recent years one judge suffered that fate through the recall process. The recall provision in the state constitution applies to all elected officials, including judges. This provision gives voters the opportunity to remove elected officials from office through petition and balloting. Recall was added to the constitution through amendment in 1926. It was one of the Progressive reforms of that decade.

The first successful recall of a judge in Wisconsin was the ouster of Archie Simonson as a circuit court judge in Madison in September 1977. The community was outraged when Simonson imposed a light sentence on three men found guilty of gang-raping a high school student. The judge then lectured the young woman from the bench, blaming her for inciting the assault because of the clothes she was wearing. In short order petitions for recall were circulated and signed, and under a national spotlight the recall election resulted in the replacement of Simonson with Moria Krueger, one of the first female judges in the state.

In May 1982 voters came close to recalling a circuit judge in Grant County. He, too, blamed a victim for an assault on her. In this case the victim was a very young girl, whom the judge found to be very sexually provocative. Although the effort to recall him fell short of its goal, the controversy did lead to his failure to get reelected for another term. This is noteworthy because virtually all incumbent judges running for reelection in Wisconsin are successful. In fact, throughout the 1990s, 87 percent of those who ran for another term did not face an opponent.

JUDICIAL SELECTION

Wisconsin is one of sixteen states that elects its judges on nonpartisan ballots.[26] As mentioned previously, the elections are always held in April when other nonpartisan races occur in an effort to place distance between judicial races and party politics. There are, of course, instances when there are apparent links between a candidate and a party. William A. Bablitch, who has been on the Wisconsin Supreme Court since 1983, was a Democratic state senator and majority leader prior to running for the bench. The person who ran N. Patrick Crooks's campaigns, first unsuccessfully and then successfully, for a seat on the state's highest court is Scott Jensen, a Republican member of the state assembly and Speaker of the assembly from 1998 to 2002. Representative Jensen, moreover, has never concealed his own goal of becoming governor.

The usual pattern, however, is for a judicial candidate to assemble a campaign organization that includes visible members of both parties and to seek endorsements from professionals associated with the law, such as lawyers, police officers, and prosecutors. In her 1999 bid for another ten-year term on the supreme court, Chief Justice Abrahamson lined up public support from former governors, Democrats and Republicans, the wife of the incumbent Republican governor, prominent attorneys throughout the state, police unions, and district attorneys in each county. Her opponent, Sharren Rose, was not able to do that. Rose's most visible supporters were some Republicans and, interestingly, several other justices on the Wisconsin Supreme Court.

Typically judicial campaigns in Wisconsin are uneventful. Candidates tend to accept an informal agreement that it is inappropriate to discuss specific cases, especially those that are pending. Rarely does someone indicate how he or she will rule even in hypothetical cases. Instead the contests are over credentials: education, experience, civic involvement, and the like. Endorsements and name recognition are also important.

Campaign spending is significantly lower than in partisan elections, and interest group contributions are minimal. In the 1994 judicial contests, for example, only 8.1 percent of the campaign spending was by interest groups. The remainder was by the campaign organizations of the candidates, funded by personal contributions and the candidate's own funds. By contrast, interest groups were responsible for 91.9 percent of campaign spending in the partisan elections in the fall of 1994. Not surprisingly, almost all the interest group spending in judicial contests is by the legal community.[27]

There are exceptions to the general pattern of dull, credential-based electioneering. The 1996 campaign that won N. Patrick Crooks a seat on the supreme court gave a clear impression, although not an explicit promise, that he would vote with those who favored allowing public vouchers to go to religious schools. Likewise, although Wisconsin has a low crime rate, a contest that involves more than credentials is likely to involve the question of who is going to be "tougher" on criminals.

Voter turnout in April elections is usually about one-third that of the partisan elections in the fall. This puts a premium on efforts by candidates to get their supporters to vote on election day. It also means that judicial candidates can be affected by extraneous issues, such as a referendum or a controversy between other candidates on the ballot. Despite the uncertainties, incumbents in Wisconsin, like those in other states, are likely to be reelected, and, as noted earlier, may not even have opponents.[28]

The advantages of incumbency place special significance on the process of selecting a judge to fill an unexpired term. In Wisconsin the governor has authority to appoint someone to a vacancy that occurs on the bench—whether in the circuit courts, courts of appeal, or on the supreme court—in the middle of a term. Consent of the Wisconsin Senate is required. By tradition governors appoint an advisory committee to review applications and make recommendations.

Not surprisingly, governors use the opportunity to appoint someone they find politically and personally acceptable. It is not uncommon for judges to resign or retire, rather than complete a term, in order to allow the governor to make an appointment. The governor initially appointed three of the seven members of the 1999 supreme court. This was true as well for 25 percent of the justices in the courts of appeal and 26 percent of those in circuit courts.

OTHER ACTORS IN JUDICIAL PROCEEDINGS

While judges are an obvious focus of attention and concern in the judicial process, the work of the courts also depends heavily on attorneys and prosecutors.

Attorneys

Wisconsin's ratio of people per lawyer is relatively low, as there are many lawyers in the state. According to the American Bar Association, there are 624 citizens for each attorney, placing Wisconsin thirty-sixth among the states on this index.[29] In order to practice law in the state, one must either earn a law degree at the University of Wisconsin–Madison or at Marquette University in Milwaukee, or simply pass the state bar exam. One function of the state courts is to admit and, when necessary, to discipline lawyers.

When attorneys file a case they set the agenda for the courts. Attorneys are also key in removing cases from the agenda when they settle a dispute on their own. Settlements are possible at any point before there is a ruling. Estimates of most lawyers and judges are that only about 10 percent of the cases filed are not settled before a verdict is reached.

Office of Lawyer Regulation

In 2001 the Wisconsin Supreme Court created the Office of Lawyer Regulation to receive and evaluate all complaints, inquiries, or grievances related to attorney misconduct or medical incapacity. The office replaced the Board of Attorneys' Professional Responsibility, which was established by the legislature in 1978. The director of the Office of Lawyer Regulation is appointed by the Wisconsin Supreme Court. The Board of Administrative Oversight and the Preliminary Review Committee are part of the office and work under the supervision of the supreme court. The board monitors the system for regulating lawyers but does not handle individual complaints or grievances. The Preliminary Review Committee handles complaints forwarded to it by the director of the Office of Lawyer Regulation. If the committee decides that there is cause to proceed, the director may seek a range of disciplinary actions by the supreme court, including license revocation.[30]

The political sensitivity of regulating lawyers can be illustrated by events that took place under the Office of Lawyer Regulations' predecessor, the Board of Attorneys' Professional Responsibility. In 1996 the board initiated a number of policy and procedural changes that raised concerns from staff members and supreme court justices. These concerns led to the resignation of the staff administrator and became an issue in the 1999 supreme court race between Chief Justice Abrahamson and Sharren Rose, who served as chair of the board. The charges were that the board was moving to protect lawyers rather than to pursue serious client complaints. Among the specific charges were:

- scheduling open meeting times of the board in ways that made it difficult for the public to attend
- refusing to let people who file a complaint see the lawyer's response and changing minutes of meetings
- letting board members participate in disciplinary decisions in which they had a conflict of interest, and
- allowing board members to secretly strike people from the list of attorneys who might be hired to prosecute disciplinary cases.

If these charges were true, the basic purpose for which the board was established would have been compromised, and the actions would run counter to Wisconsin's Progressive, clean governmental traditions. According to a newspaper investigation, Rose's candidacy against Chief Justice Abrahamson directly stemmed from steps the chief justice was taking to respond to objectionable board actions.[31] The chief justice and Wisconsin's traditions prevailed.

Prosecuting Attorneys

In criminal cases district attorneys prosecute on behalf of the state. Each county has an elected district attorney. The races for this office are partisan and scheduled in the fall. The term is two years. As with judges, the governor may appoint someone to a partial term if a vacancy occurs between elections. That happens, but it is unusual, in part because the term is so short. District attorneys may, if authorized by their county board, appoint assistants to help with the workload.

The attorney general represents the state in civil cases and also handles criminal cases that are appealed, either to the state courts of appeal or to the federal courts. Wisconsin law, however, does give the governor the opportunity, under some circumstances, to select other counsel. Some interesting examples are provided below.

The attorney general is elected in a partisan contest at the same time voters elect the governor. The offices are separate, and it is not unusual to have a governor of one party and an attorney general of another. In fact, as a highly visible, statewide official, the attorney general may come to be a candidate for governor. These institutional and partisan circumstances can take on a special character when an attorney general decides that a law is unconstitutional or for some other reason not worth defending.

For example, a highly publicized conflict occurred between Attorney General Jim Doyle and Governor Tommy Thompson during the mid-1990s involving the state superintendent of public instruction. As reported in chapter 2, at Governor Thompson's request the legislature passed a statute that created a Department of Education, with a secretary that served at the pleasure of the governor. The attorney general took the position that the governor and legislature could not make such a change through statutory means. Thompson responded by hiring an attorney to oppose the attorney general and defend the statute. As a result, the attorney general and the governor dueled in court. The attorney general won this dispute with a unanimous decision from the supreme court overturning the new law.

Governor Thompson also hired an attorney in 1998 to defend a different state law. The governor's decision was based on doubts about how enthusiastic and effective the attorney general would be in this particular case, and not because the attorney general refused to defend the law. The case was the one already cited involving public vouchers for religious schools. Attorney General Doyle made it clear that he thought the law was unwise, but he also expressed the belief that the law did not violate the state constitution. He thus felt obliged to defend the statute. Thompson, however, used discretionary funds to hire someone in whom he had more confidence to argue the case in court alongside the attorney general.

Governors can also use discretionary funds to hire attorneys to work on cases that the attorney general is pursuing. Governor Thompson exercised this option when the state was suing tobacco companies—the workload was so heavy that the attorney general's staff needed assistance.

The attorney general is also the executive head of the state's Department of Justice, which provides criminal-investigation services to district attorneys, maintains fingerprint and criminal-record information, provides training to law enforcement officials, and works with local and federal officials on drug issues. Until 1995 another function of the department was consumer protection. In that year, Governor Thompson and the Republican-controlled legislature removed this function from the attorney general's office and placed it within the purview of the Department of Agriculture, Trade, and Consumer Protection. The latter department, in contrast to the Department of Justice, is a cabinet agency headed by a secretary who serves at the governor's pleasure.

State Public Defender

Wisconsin has an independent agency that provides legal services to individuals who cannot afford an attorney; it reports to a citizen board. The nine-person board is appointed by the governor, with the consent of the Wisconsin Senate, and must include six members who are licensed attorneys in Wisconsin. The Public Defender Board establishes the criteria for determining who may receive services. They have included children, for example, who in some circumstances are involved in litigation against their parents.

The board also hires and supervises the state's public defender, who heads the agency and serves at the pleasure of the board. The University of Wisconsin Law School operates a separate but related program known as Legal Assistance for Institutionalized Persons. This organization provides supervised assistance from law school students to inmates in state prisons and to patients in state mental health institutions.

POLITICS, POLICY ISSUES, AND THE COURTS

The structure of the courts and the content of public policy issues that arise in a state can influence the role of the judiciary. For the most part, Wisconsin's judiciary is competent, nonpartisan, well run, and respected. To gain a more complete understanding of the role of Wisconsin courts and their place in the policymaking process, however, one might look at recent key legislative and court actions.

The first two policy issues, "truth in sentencing" and "three strikes," show the ways in which the governor and the legislature can limit the discretion of the court. The next policy issue, school choice and religion, illustrates the way in which the supreme court can use either the state constitution or the U.S. Constitution as the basis for decisions about individual rights. The final three policy issues, all related to due process, show the ways in which the supreme court attempts to balance police powers with individual liberties.

Limiting Court Discretion
"Truth in Sentencing"

In 1998 the Wisconsin legislature and governor acted to end parole, sponsoring a measure known as "truth in sentencing." The major motivation behind this measure was to "get tough" on criminals. The law was adopted in response to a highly publicized case in which someone who was on parole after serving about 40 percent of his sentence committed a murder. Other states, often in a similar situation, had already passed a truth-in-sentencing law. North Carolina was cited most frequently as an example.

An important result of truth in sentencing is that it takes discretion away from the courts. Prior to the passage of this law, a judge considered the circumstances of a crime or the record and personal background of someone who had been convicted, and then imposed a sentence that fell between a minimum and maximum established by the legislature. The correctional system also had discretion to reward someone for good behavior or to recognize rehabilitation and release the person before the term expired. Under the new measure these options have been foreclosed: crime X receives sentence Y, and sentence Y means sentence Y and nothing less. Formulas, rather than judges or parole boards, are used to determine how much time a convicted person serves. Discretion exists only prior to conviction, and it is exercised by prosecuting attorneys in plea bargains rather than by judges at trial.

"Three Strikes"

The "three-strikes" law, initiated in California, similarly removes discretion from judges and expands the role of prosecuting attorneys. Wisconsin's three-strikes law requires a more serious level of felony than does California's in order to make a life sentence mandatory. The limitations placed on the authority of the courts are nonetheless considerable.

Individual Rights and the Court
School Choice and Religion

In *Jackson v. Benson* (1998) the Wisconsin Supreme Court allowed publicly funded vouchers to be used for tuition at religious schools.[32] A major implication of the supreme court's ruling was the reliance of the majority opinion on the U.S. Constitution rather than on Wisconsin's constitution.[33] Article I, section 18, of the Wisconsin Constitution is much more restrictive with respect to the separation of church and state than is the First Amendment to the U.S. Constitution, and a key tenet of "judicial federalism" is that states may be more protective of individual liberties than the federal government if they so desire.[34] Thus, Wisconsin's supreme court could have used the state constitution as the basis for its ruling but chose not to do so.

Contrast the U.S. Constitution:

Congress shall make no law respecting an establishment of religion, or prohibiting the free exercise thereof.

with the Wisconsin Constitution:

The right of every person to worship Almighty God according to the dictates of conscience shall never be infringed; nor shall any person be compelled to attend, erect or support any place of worship, or to maintain any ministry, without consent; nor shall any control of, or interference with, the rights of conscience be permitted, or any preference be given by law to any religious establishments or modes of worship; nor shall any money be drawn from the treasury for the benefit of religious societies, or religious or theological seminaries.

As Chief Justice Abrahamson and Justice William A. Bablitch, the minority on the Wisconsin Supreme Court pointed out, if one applies the restrictions of the state constitution it is impossible to permit the use of publicly funded vouchers for fees at religious schools. The majority, as has been noted, chose, however, to base its decision on the U.S. Constitution. They interpreted the broader language in the U.S. Constitution as allowing government to give tax-supported vouchers to parents and then allow parents to choose to send their children to a religious school. (A procedural problem in the Wisconsin case is that the voucher is not redeemable with just the signature of the parents. The receiving school must also sign; the money is then sent directly to the school.)

Regardless of the merits of the case, the decision of the majority on the state supreme court to rely on the U.S. Constitution instead of the state constitution is significant. Depending on one's point of view, the decision to adopt national standards for this decision, rather than state, could be praised or criticized. Parents who want to send their children to parochial school might see the decision as a vindication of their individual rights. Those opposed might complain that Wisconsin's supreme court abandoned the protection of their rights, which were guaranteed in the more restrictive language of the state constitution.

Due Process

In a series of cases in the mid-l990s, the Wisconsin Supreme Court favored giving discretion to police officers over protecting individual privacy. In each case, the issue was how to balance the need to fight crime with the need to maintain personal liberty.

In *State v. Morgan* (1995) Michael T. Morgan objected when police officers stopped his car at 4:00 a.m., frisked him, and searched his car, even though there was no probable cause that he was committing or had committed a crime.[35] Police justified their action on the basis that he was in a high-crime area. Indeed, in *Terry v. Ohio* (1968) the U.S. Supreme Court ruled that police may stop individuals and conduct a limited search in high-crime areas.[36] The majority on the Wisconsin Supreme Court sided with the police, despite the contention by the minority that the factual standards required by the *Terry v. Ohio* ruling were not met.

The issue in *State v. Andrews* (1996) was whether police could search the belongings of a visitor when they executed a search warrant in someone's home.[37] Michael Andrews was a guest in a friend's apartment when police came in with a drug-sniffing dog as part of an authorized search. The dog reacted to a duffel bag belonging to Andrews, in which there was marijuana and drug paraphernalia. The entire court agreed that the evidence found in this circumstance could be used to prosecute Andrews. Everyone on the court further agreed that even if the objects named in the search warrant are found on persons not named in the warrant or in their possessions, the evidence can be used by the prosecution.

In another case where the majority ruled in favor of the police, the U.S. Supreme Court unanimously sided with the lone dissenter on the Wisconsin Supreme Court. In *State v. Richards* (1996) the dispute was whether it was necessary for police to knock and announce their presence before entering a premise to execute a search warrant.[38] Specifically, police entered a motel room without knocking and announcing their arrival because they feared any warning would allow those suspected of engaging in a drug deal to dispose of the evidence.

Chief Justice Abrahamson argued that allowing this practice threatened the privacy and sanctity of individuals' homes. She recognized the concern about the destruction of evidence, but feared the implications of a blanket "no-knock" rule. While the majority on the Wisconsin Supreme Court disagreed with her, the entire U.S. Supreme Court upheld her argument and overturned the state action.

PERSPECTIVES ON THE WISCONSIN SUPREME COURT

In general, the rulings in the due process cases cited in the previous section seem to show a conservative tendency in the Wisconsin Supreme Court during the 1990s. The majority did not seem inclined to extend rights to individuals at the expense of the prerogatives of police or the traditions of society. Critics of the court could argue that federal courts have been more protective of individual liberties in such cases than have the state courts. Yet, caution, or even conservatism, on the part of a state supreme court, particularly one to which the justices are elected, seems neither surprising nor unreasonable. For scholars who would like Wisconsin's judicial branch to be more innovative in cases dealing with individual rights, however, the court's reluctance to experiment boldly has been a source of disappointment. The Wisconsin Supreme Court's reluctance to innovate contrasts with the experimentation evinced in recent decades by the supreme courts of California, New Jersey, and Ohio.

To put such discussions in a broader context, however, it is worth noting that over the past twenty years, scholars and members of the legal community have had an animated discussion about the "new judicial federalism." As previously noted, the new judicial federalism "allows state courts and legislatures to set rights standards that are higher, but not lower, than those established under the U.S. Constitution."[39] Wisconsin's chief justice, Shirley Abrahamson, has been very active in national discussions and scholarly examination of this topic.[40] This fact, taken together with her opinions in some of the cases previously discussed, seems to indicate that she has been an advocate for court decisions that take advantage of the possibilities offered by the new judicial federalism.

Whether Wisconsin's supreme court has been a leader in the new judicial federalism is, however, only one basis for developing a perspective on the role of Wisconsin's court system, and particularly its supreme court. Another, broader perspective emerges from a recently published article, "Building a More Perfect Union: Wisconsin and the U.S. Constitution." The article was written by Chief Justice Abrahamson and Elizabeth A. Hartman.[41]

In this article Abrahamson and Hartman review the 143 cases that went from the Wisconsin court system to the United States Supreme Court from territorial days through 1997. Examination of these cases showed that the U.S. Supreme Court affirmed the decisions of the Wisconsin Supreme Court 57 percent of the time and rejected those decisions 43 percent of the time. After calculating the Wisconsin Supreme Court's "batting average," Abrahamson and Hartman turned their attention to the twenty Wisconsin cases that were cited most frequently by "judges writing legal opinions and by lawyers and law professors writing articles about the law."

In reviewing the top twenty cases, the authors found a wide range of subject matter, "including labor, criminal procedure, preemption, tax, the First Amendment, and due process." In these cases the authors could see a "unique historical patina that is Wisconsin's own." There were, for example, important labor cases, which seems natural given Wisconsin's leadership role in the development of labor law, particularly in the areas of workmen's compensation and unemployment compensation law. Likewise, there were significant tax cases, which seems appropriate given Wisconsin's leadership role in the development of tax law through enactment of the nation's first workable income tax.

Additionally, there was an important case related to the freedom of religion, in which the state played a leadership role. In *Wisconsin v. Yoder* (1972) the Wisconsin Supreme Court reversed a conviction of Amish fathers found guilty of violating the Wisconsin compulsory school attendance law for "failing to allow their children to go to school through age sixteen." The supreme court's rationale was that the state's compulsory education law "violated the Amish's right to freely exercise their religion under the First Amendment." The U.S. Supreme Court affirmed the decision of Wisconsin's supreme court, and *Yoder* is the second most frequently cited of the Wisconsin cases that have gone to the U.S. Supreme Court.

In sum, on the basis of the research conducted by Chief Justice Abrahamson and Elizabeth A. Hartman it seems reasonable to conclude that the decisions of Wisconsin's court system have been both visible and important nationally, just as the decisions of its legislature and governor have been.

CHAPTER SIX

Private Interests and Interest Groups

In the power they are perceived to have, two interests, schoolteachers' organizations and general business organizations, far outstrip any other interest in
the fifty states.

> Clive S. Thomas and Ronald J. Hrebenar,
> "Interest Groups in the States," 1996

Wisconsin Manufacturers and Commerce (WMC) is Wisconsin's most powerful
business interest group and perhaps the most important political organization
in the state.

> William De Soto, *The Politics of*
> *Business Organizations*, 1995

In journalistic and scholarly writings about the American economic and political systems, the relationship between the public interest and private interests
is sometimes presented as complementary and at other times as competitive.
The "muckrakers," the investigative journalists who helped to usher in the
Progressive era during the early 1900s, documented the damaging effects that
the unbridled pursuit of narrow economic interests by private corporations
was having on the American economy, public health, and democracy.[1] The
muckrakers' modern journalistic heirs, like some modern scholars, have
generally focused their attention on interest groups rather than on individual
corporations, but the basic concerns about the consequences of private power
and influence in American politics and government remain the same.[2]

Other modern journalists and scholars, however, have a much more
sanguine view of private interests and interest group activity. These scholars

and journalists tend to see the pursuit of public benefits by individuals, business firms, and interest groups as a natural and unremarkable part of American politics. Indeed, they see this type of activity as an essential element of representative democracy.

The two competing views about private interests and interest groups reflect underlying differences in political culture and political philosophy that exist in the national arena and in the states. In Wisconsin, where the moralistic view of politics and government has been the leading view for most of the state's history, there has been a greater sensitivity to the potentially corrosive effects of private interests than there has been in states where the individualistic or traditionalistic political culture is dominant. There has also been a more active attempt in Wisconsin than in many other states to limit the influence that private interests and interest groups have in politics and government.

This chapter begins with a historical perspective of the tension between public and private interests in Wisconsin's politics and government. Wisconsin's historical experience is then compared with that of other states. Next, additional background is provided concerning the competing views scholars hold of the role played by interest groups in American democracy. A brief description of the types of interest groups that operate in Wisconsin and other states comes thereafter, followed by data on contemporary interest group activity in Wisconsin. The final section contains short case studies of interest group influence in the legislative process.

HISTORICAL PERSPECTIVE—THE
POWER OF PRIVATE INTERESTS

As noted in chapter 2, Wisconsin's constitutional framers were worried about the influence that private interests could exert in state politics and on state government. Less than thirty years after Wisconsin became a state, these concerns were reiterated by Wisconsin Supreme Court Chief Justice Edward G. Ryan. In his 1873 commencement address at the University of Wisconsin Law School, Ryan said: "The enterprises of the country are aggregating vast corporate combinations of unexampled capital, boldly marching, not for economic conquest only, but for political power. For the first time, really, in our politics money is taking the field as an organized power. . . . Already, here at home, one great corporation has trifled with sovereign power, and insulted the state. There is grave fear that it, and its great rival, have confederated to make partition of the state and share it as spoils."[3]

As it happened, a young man named Robert La Follette was sitting in the audience listening to these words.[4] In June of 1873 La Follette was only eighteen years old, and his own graduation from the University of Wisconsin was still six years away. Yet Chief Justice Ryan's speech seems to have made a lasting impression on him. Although the chief justice did not name the corporation that had "trifled with" and "insulted" the state, he was talking about the Chicago, Milwaukee, and St. Paul railroad. Ryan's fear was that this railroad would combine with its principal competitor, the Chicago and Northwestern Railroad, and treat the state as "spoils." This was no idle fear for those who understood the situation.

The 1873 commencement address was not the first time that Edward G. Ryan had voiced his concerns about the ways in which corporations could adversely affect the state and its people. He had publicly articulated this concern twenty-seven years earlier, during the 1846 constitutional convention. In fact, Ryan was the leading figure in the Progressive Democrats' efforts to place provisions in the state constitution that would protect the state and its people from the overarching power of private interests.

Although the railroads were not a major economic power in 1846, the economic transformation that took place during the next two decades put the railroads at the center of economic activity. During that period, agricultural and industrial development was occurring rapidly in Wisconsin, and railroads, rather than rivers, became the principal means by which goods were moved from farm and factory to market. Furthermore, during the 1850s and 1860s the railroads became tightly intertwined with another of the state's fastest growing industries—lumber. The pairing of two large, complementary private interests made a powerful economic and political force.

When Edward Ryan spoke at the law school graduation ceremonies in 1873 he had ample evidence of the tactics the railroads were using to get what they wanted from the state. In 1856, only ten years after statehood, the president of the La Crosse and Milwaukee Railroad, Byron Kilbourne, was accused of bribing the governor, the lieutenant governor, and members of the legislature in order to secure land grants from the state. In his defense, Kilbourne argued that he was only using the tactics employed by his major competitor, the president of the Chicago, St. Paul, and Fond du Lac Railroad.[5]

Despite the legislative investigation that uncovered this scandal, and despite the press coverage of it, the railroad's economic power and its influence over state government decision making continued to grow. Among the keys to the growth in profits and political influence was the land the railroads were given by the state; the other was the fact that the timber companies were made up largely of railroad men.[6] A substantial portion of the land given to the railroad companies was sold to the timber companies for a profit. Then the timber companies harvested the lumber for a profit. After it was harvested, the timber companies sold the land for farming or other development and thus made still further profit on that transaction.[7]

By the early 1870s the railroad-timber machine had become dominant in the state, and those who wanted to run for office in the Republican Party needed its blessing. The national and regional recession of the mid-1870s, however, gave an organization of farmers known as the Grangers, and their gubernatorial candidate, William R. Taylor, an opportunity to challenge the railroads. Dissatisfaction with railroad practices was high among farmers, as it was in the Wisconsin cities and villages that had lost in the recession large amounts of money that they had borrowed to help build rail lines to their communities.

The railroad companies were able to demand from municipalities and farmers a large part of the financial capital they needed to construct rail lines. This was accomplished through what, in one view, might be considered economic blackmail, or, in another view, apt use of economic incentives. Local communities grew or declined on the basis of whether they were connected to other locations by railroad tracks. Freight prices for farm goods also depended, in part, on the proximity of the rail line. Consequently the railroads could simply threaten to put their lines elsewhere if a community or a group of farmers did not want to "invest" in the construction of the rail line.

Taylor won the 1874 election, and one of his first initiatives was to press the legislature for a law that would provide for state regulation of the railroads. The key element of the Potter Law, as it was called, was the establishment of a railroad commission that would have the authority to regulate the rates charged for the movement of people and goods. With the support of other Grangers who were elected to the legislature in 1874, Taylor got the legislation passed in 1875.

Even before the Potter law was passed, however, the railroads let it be known that they would not be bound by it. Immediately after the law was passed, the railroads challenged it in court. Their challenge failed when Wisconsin's supreme court voted to uphold the law, and, in his 1874 justification of the court's decision, Chief Justice Ryan articulated the general principle that corporations must be subordinate to the state.[8]

Defeated in court, the railroads switched tactics. Free railroad passes were distributed to legislators, all new construction of railroad lines was stopped, and service to some areas was discontinued.[9] The interruption of what had become an essential service created a backlash. The backlash was fueled by press coverage of the situation and press attacks on Governor Taylor.[10] Taylor and other reformers were thrown out of office in the next election. In 1877 the Potter Law was repealed.

From 1877 until the early 1900s, railroads in the state remained largely unregulated. Then, in an interesting twist of fate, the task of establishing railroad regulation fell upon Robert M. La Follette. In 1905, during his third term as governor, La Follette finally succeeded in getting a bill through the legislature that authorized railroad regulation. As might be expected, however, the new law was just the first round in a continuing battle between the state and the railroads. The battle was joined in the electoral arena, in the legislature, in the administrative arena where the railroad commission was attempting to implement the law, and in the courts.

Although progress in regulating the railroads was sometimes slow, the 1905 legislation did provide the essential foundation for establishing some limits on a corporate power that before had been largely untouchable. Unfortunately Edward G. Ryan did not live to see La Follette and his Progressive supporters achieve this milestone.

COMPARING WISCONSIN'S EXPERIENCE
WITH THAT OF OTHER STATES

Wisconsin was not the only American state in which the railroads were able to control state government during the latter part of the nineteenth and early twentieth centuries. This situation happened throughout the country. Furthermore, the phenomenon of a large private interest gaining control of state government is not restricted to the railroads. According to Clive Thomas and Ronald Hrebenar, "all states have gone through eras in which one or a handful of interests dominated state politics to the extent that they could determine what a state did, and often of equal or more importance, what it did not do."[11]

Thus, while not unique, Wisconsin's experience seems to provide a number of important lessons about the relationship between public and private interests. First, it illustrates the way in which large business interests can capture state governmental institutions and then use them to secure large public subsidies for private gain. Second, the case shows how these private interests can use public institutions to block the efforts of reformers who want to eliminate these public subsidies and reduce the influence these interests have over public policy. Third, the Wisconsin case underscores the fact that economic change and development can lead to rapid and dramatic new concentrations of economic power. This concentration of private economic power can be used to neutralize, and then capture, the institutions of government.

Several other lessons about politics, government, and the influence of private interests can also be gleaned from Wisconsin's experience. For example, the railroad-lumber case shows that private interests can gain control of public policy decision making through the election of people who are partisans for that interest, through legislative lobbying, lobbying of administrative agencies, and/or through the courts. Second, the railroad-lumber case shows that private business interests may closely align themselves with a particular party, as was the situation with the railroad-lumber industry and the Republican Party in Wisconsin during the late 1800s and early 1900s.

Finally, the case highlights the important role the press can play in both elections and public policy decision making. It is worth noting that press coverage of the benefits or subsidies a particular interest is getting from government may provide temporary support for the "reformers." Yet as the costs of the reforms are reported by the press, the coverage may contribute to a backlash against reform. While these lessons are abstracted from a case study of events more than one hundred years ago, in large part they are still applicable in modern times.

Contemporary Circumstances

What, then, are the circumstances surrounding special interests today? Is Wisconsin state government dominated by a few large, complementary private interests? Are the governmental institutions of other states dominated or controlled by such interests? In Wisconsin the answer to the question is no, and the same answer seems appropriate for most other states. One of the main reasons Wisconsin is no longer dominated by a single company or industry is that the state's economy has evolved and changed over the past hundred years. The economies of other states have likewise changed and diversified.

In most states the power of the railroad companies peaked and waned between 1900 and 1930. During the next thirty years (1930–60), the power of the old-line manufacturing, agricultural, mining, and forestry corporations similarly grew and subsequently declined. During the 1960s and 1970s the principal business interests that engaged in attempts to influence public policy in the states were what scholars tend to call the "traditional" interests of business: labor, agriculture, education, and local government.[12] Then, during the 1980s and 1990s, the number and range of interests bent upon influencing public policy rose dramatically.[13]

This evolutionary cycle or process effectively represents Wisconsin's experience. While economic change and diversification seems to be the single most important factor associated with this process, it is not the only one. Scholars also maintain that the expansion of state governmental activity has been very influential in the growth of both the number and type of organized interests that attempt to shape state government activity and policy.

Some states, however, still have what Thomas and Hrebenar call a "prominent interest." States in this category include Nevada, with its gaming industry; Delaware, with the Dupont Company; and Michigan, with the auto manufacturers and unions.[14] Additionally, some areas of the country have more powerful interest group systems than others. Thomas and Hrebenar identify the South as the region where the interest group system is the most powerful and the Northeast the least.[15]

Despite this assessment of conditions in the southern states, Thomas and Hrebenar have concluded that the "days of states being dominated by one or a few interests are likely gone forever."[16] Among the principal reasons the two scholars give for this view is that the number and variety of interests represented in state capitols has grown dramatically over the past thirty years.[17] They also note that political parties, professionalized bureaucracies, the press, and lobbying rules have also had an important role in containing the influence of special interests.

However reassuring this viewpoint might be, even Thomas and Hrebenar concede that "interest groups are still major forces shaping state politics and determining what government does and does not do."[18] They also note that while most interest groups cloak their objectives in public interest terms, most of what they attempt to do is to influence public policy for private gain, whether through tax breaks, exemptions from regulation, or procurement of a budget appropriation.[19]

Nevertheless, neither these two scholars nor many other scholars who study American government see anything wrong with the pursuit of private gain in the policy process by interests or interest groups. Many scholars emphasize the value of having "interests" aggregated and represented in this manner. The underlying presumption here is that the pursuit of self-interest by groups is a natural part of a "pluralistic" democracy.

SCHOLARLY PERSPECTIVES OF PLURALISM
AND INTEREST GROUP INFLUENCE

The pluralist model of American democracy seems to be built on the assumption that there will be plural interests present within society that serve as countervailing powers. Thus, as conceptualized in the early 1950s by political scientist Earl Latham, legislators need only serve as scorekeepers who ratify and record the balance of power among contending groups.[20] Public laws are, then, essentially records of this balance of power at any given point in time, and, according to Latham, they reflect surrenders, compromises, and conquests.[21]

A more recent version of this model has been articulated by a number of scholars, among them David Truman, Robert Dahl, and Charles Lindblom.[22] In their shared concept of group, or pluralist, theory, public policy emerges as a set of compromises among competing interests. The competitors are willing to settle for something less than they might want in order to avoid a zero-sum game. Thus an equilibrium in the policy system is presumed to develop that is relatively acceptable to all of the relevant interest groups. The equilibrium is further presumed to be sustained in part because each interest accepts the notion that competition among groups will operate largely at the margins of existing policy.

But the "flaw in the pluralist heaven," as E. E. Schattschneider and other scholars have defined it, is that the competition among interests is seldom equal, and the competition may not exist in a variety of important areas.[23] Schattschneider and others have identified a heavy bias in the system, and they conclude that the policy process often bears little resemblance to the policy system described by the pluralist model. As Schattschneider puts it, the American political system "sings" with a strong business and upper-class voice.[24] Likewise, in some of his most recent work, Lindblom provides support for this view. Specifically, Lindblom and his co-author, Edward Woodhouse, provide a powerful portrait of the ways in which business interests can affect and distort the policy process.[25]

On the basis of these perspectives, a number of questions relevant to the study of private interests and interest groups in Wisconsin arise:

- What do these groups look like in Wisconsin today?
- Is there an ongoing and equal competition among groups for influence in the policy process?
- Do governors and legislators merely ratify and record the existing balance

of power in a no-holds-barred, zero-sum contest, or do they work to ensure fair competition among groups?

• Do they attempt to find compromise solutions to policy issues that all interested parties can live with, or are they more likely to act as partisans for one interest or another?

TYPES OF INTEREST GROUPS

What is the contemporary lineup of interest groups in Wisconsin? In order to develop a useful answer, "interest group" must be defined. Interest groups are groups of people—associations of individuals, private business firms, or other organizations—that attempt to influence public policy. The primary goal of many interest groups is either to secure economic benefits from government or to avoid regulatory costs. Some interest groups, however, are concerned about things other than money. For example, interest groups that oppose abortion attempt to block or stop abortions for religious or other reasons, not for economic gain.

Often referred to as "special interests" or "pressure groups," interest groups attempt to influence decisions made by members of the legislature, the executive branch, and the courts. More particularly, interest groups attempt to shape the content of state statutes, define the standards used in administrative rules and regulations, and get courts to block—or sometimes to uphold—legislative and administrative decisions. They also play a role in state government elections through campaign contributions to political parties and candidates, direct mail and telephone efforts aimed at mobilizing a block of voters, and through political action committees (PACs) that deliver independent television and radio advertisements.

The type of interest group found most frequently in Wisconsin and most other states today is one that represents private businesses. The business trade group is probably the most ubiquitous type of interest group, with associations that represent paper companies, tobacco companies, liquor companies and wholesalers, restaurants, and many others. Generally speaking, these types of business interest groups have relatively narrowly focused interests, such as the avoidance of regulation. In contrast some business interest groups, like the state Chamber of Commerce, may have broader policy interests.[26]

Professional associations, like those that represent lawyers and doctors, also serve as interest groups. The prevalence of professional and trade associations among Wisconsin's interest groups is noted by scholar David

Wegge. In his study of 1989 interest group activity, Wegge found that trade and professional associations accounted for 49.5 percent of interest groups in the state, while individual businesses accounted for 36 percent; "other" types of interest groups made up 12.5 percent, while interest groups representing individuals made up 2 percent.[27]

The "other" category noted above contains a wide variety of interest group types, including labor unions, which represent employees in both the public and private sectors. Among the oldest type of interest groups are those that represent farmers; among the newest groups in Wisconsin and other states are the "public interest" organizations, which might be focused on environmental protection, natural resource conservation, or consumer protection. Still another type of interest group is the one that represents local governments, such as municipalities or counties.

INTEREST GROUP ACTIVITY

Is there competition among interest groups? Is this competition relatively equal, or do some interests have a significant financial advantage? In order to answer these questions, it is essential to develop a portrait of interest group activity in a state. One way to do so is to look at lobbying expenditures.

In some states it is very difficult to secure this data because the state either does not regulate interest group activity or the regulations are loosely configured and are not administered by a public agency. In Wisconsin, where attempts to regulate private interests began in the 1870s, there are clearly defined rules governing lobbying activities. Among them is the requirement that all organizations or groups that intend to lobby legislators or other public officials register with the Wisconsin Ethics Board. A second rule requires an annual report on lobbying activities. Likewise, interest groups that donate funds to candidates for state office must report their contributions to the Wisconsin Elections Commission.

The Wisconsin Ethics Board produces a report on lobbying activities. This report gives students of interest group activity in Wisconsin data on the amount of money spent by each private interest or interest group. It also provides data on the number of hours spent lobbying. Additionally, the 1999–2000 report contains a summary of the ten legislative bills that were the focus of the most lobbying.

Data on lobbying activity for the 1999–2000 legislative session is provided in the following section. These data are supplemented by data from other legislative sessions, particularly that of 1997–98.

Scope and Scale of Lobbying Activity

During the 1999–2000 legislative session in Wisconsin, 629 organizations were registered to lobby for their interests. These organizations invested an estimated 425,834 hours lobbying legislators or administrative agencies, and they spent a total of almost $44.4 million on this activity.[28] To put these data in comparative perspective, 607 organizations were registered to lobby in 1997–98, 567 were registered in 1989, and 450 were registered in 1985.[29] In short, lobbying has been a growth industry in Wisconsin in recent decades. Scholars have identified similar patterns in other states and in Washington DC.[30]

Simply on the basis of the number of interests registered to lobby in Wisconsin, one might assume that lobbying is ubiquitous. This assumption is borne out by additional data from the 1999–2000 legislative session. During that session, 74 percent of all legislative proposals introduced were lobbied.[31] The data also show that some bills attracted much more interest group activity than did others. Specifically, "28 legislative proposals (2 percent of all legislative proposals) represented 47 percent of all lobbying expended on legislative proposals."[32]

The twenty-six organizations that invested the most in lobbying during the 1999–2000 legislative session are listed in table 6. This list is provided for several reasons. First, the names of the top twenty-six lobbying organizations give body and substance to the seemingly abstract discussion about interest groups. Second, the data in table 6 provide a snapshot of the types of interest groups that were active during a specific legislative session. Third, the data also show, in dollar terms, the level of activity of each interest group.

The data in table 6 show that the state's largest business association, Wisconsin Manufacturers and Commerce (WMC), was the biggest spender on lobbying during the 1999–2000 legislative session. The WMC was created in 1976 when the Wisconsin Manufacturers Association and the state Chamber of Commerce were merged into one organization.[33] In addition to looking after the interests of manufacturers, this association also focuses attention on the overall business climate in the state.

A public utility, Wisconsin Energy Corporation (formerly Wisconsin Electric Company), was the second largest spender, followed by a business association, Wisconsin Merchant's Federation. The telephone and communications company, AT&T Corporation, was the fourth largest spender, followed by another business association, Wisconsin Independent Businesses, Inc.

Table 6.   Top Lobbying Organizations, 1999–2000 Legislative Session
(expenditures for lobbying-related activities)

Rank / Organization	Expenditures
1 Wisconsin Manufacturers & Commerce	$1,214,995
2 Wisconsin Energy Corporation	1,035,257
3 Wisconsin Merchants Federation	960,757
4 AT&T Corporation	911,060
5 Wisconsin Independent Businesses, Inc.	740,174
6 Wisconsin Counties Association	690,086
7 Wisconsin Education Association Council	578,182
8 Green Bay Packers, Inc.	569,248
9 Wisconsin Farm Bureau Federation	558,375
10 Philip Morris Incorporated	516,641
11 Wisconsin Towns Association	493,516
12 Midwest Express Airlines	465,277
13 Wisconsin Health and Hospital Association	453,172
14 State Bar of Wisconsin	428,874
15 Customers First! Coalition	414,712
16 Wisconsin Alliance of Cities	376,298
17 Energize Wisconsin	371,342
18 Distilled Spirits Council of the United States	369,964
19 Wisconsin Association of School Boards	366,719
20 Wisconsin Bankers Association	354,542
21 Ameritech	353,460
22 Milwaukee County	350,909
23 Miller Brewing Company	349,974
24 Wisconsin State Telecommunications Assoc.	333,963
25 Alliant	329,951
26 City of Milwaukee	329,624
Subtotal of top lobbyist organizations	$13,917,072
Balance of organizations whose total expenditures were less than twice the standard deviation of the mean	$30,488,798
TOTAL LOBBYIST EXPENDITURES, 1999–2000	$44,405,870

Source: Wisconsin Ethics Board, "1999–2000 Legislative Session, Total Lobbying Expenditures"

The Wisconsin Counties Association, representing Wisconsin's seventy-two counties, was sixth, followed by the Wisconsin Education Association Council, representing elementary and secondary teachers. A professional football organization, The Green Bay Packers, Inc.—the only publicly owned football team in the National Football League, it may be noted—was the eighth largest spender, followed by an association of farmers, the Wisconsin Farm Bureau Federation, and a tobacco company, Philip Morris, Inc.

Top Ten Organizations and Top Ten
Bills—Competition among Interests

When the list of the ten largest spenders is compared with the ten bills that were most heavily lobbied during the 1999–2000 legislative session, one can see a close but not perfect correspondence. For example, Senate Bill 91 was the most heavily lobbied bill. This bill addressed "access service rates charged to certain telecommunications providers."[34] AT&T, the number-four company on the top-ten list, certainly had an interest in this bill, and it is likely that other telecommunications companies, and other types of private corporations and business associations, did, as well.

The intensity of the lobbying on this bill seems to indicate that a variety of private interests and interest groups believed that this legislation could have a significant impact on their financial condition. The level of activity also indicates that individual corporations and business interest groups sometimes compete with each other to shape the contents of legislation. In short, the data seem to provide support for the pluralist contention that there is competition among the interests, including private sector interests.

The third and fourth most heavily lobbied bills (Assembly Bill 389 and Senate Bill 196, respectively) dealt with energy matters, including control and ownership of transmission facilities, and ownership of nonutility assets.[35] Thus it is not surprising that Wisconsin Energy Corporation was the second largest spender on lobbying activities during the 1999–2000 legislative session. Likewise, the WMC may also have had an interest in such a bill because energy costs are an important part of a manufacturing firm's costs.

Here again the amount of funds spent on lobbying seems to indicate that the financial stakes associated with this legislation were high. The level of spending also suggests that there was significant competition between various public utilities to shape the bill in a manner most closely suited to their self-interest. Other business interests may have been active, too.

Unfortunately what is missing from the picture of lobbying on Assembly Bill 389 and Senate Bills 196 and 91 is qualitative information about the type of competition that occurred and who actually won the most. The expenditure data provided by the Wisconsin Ethics Board give a quantitative snapshot of the lobbying activity, but these data do not provide any clues about the ways in which the interests and interest groups involved in this lobbying viewed the lobbying activity.

Taking Senate Bill 91 as an example, we might consider the following question: Did some public utilities, private corporations, or consumer groups see the competition to shape Senate Bill 91 as a zero-sum game, or were all of the participants committed to finding compromise solutions acceptable to all of the interests that had a stake in the bill? To answer this question, the findings from a case study of this bill are needed. Unfortunately, no such findings were available; we are thus left to speculate about answers to this important question.

Another important question that cannot be answered without an intensive investigation of each of the three pieces of legislation (Assembly Bill 389, and Senate Bills 196 and 91) is whether, in their final form, they recorded what scholar Earl Latham would have expected: surrenders, compromises, or conquests. Again, to make such a determination, an intensive study of the legislation would be required. Since no published studies are available, this key question also must remain unanswered.

Finally, there is one other item that may be of interest here to the many Green Bay Packer fans inside and outside of Wisconsin. The presence of The Green Bay Packers, Inc., on the top-ten spending list for the 1999–2000 legislative session is related to that company's desire to have public funding for a substantial part of stadium renovation costs. The legislation required for this financing arrangement was not among the ten most heavily lobbied bills.

This circumstance may be explained largely by the fact that there was little opposition from other private corporations, business associations, or other types of interest groups to what the Packers wanted. The Green Bay Packers, Inc., nevertheless spent money to lobby legislators in order to ensure that they got what they wanted.

Changes in Interest Group Activity over Time

One might expect that the relative rankings on the top-ten or even the top-twenty-five list would change somewhat from legislative session to legislative session, as the issue agenda of the legislature changes. This presumption is borne out, as shown by a comparison between the 1999–2000 legislative session and the 1997–98 session. In the 1997–98 legislative session, a mining company, Nicolet Minerals, rather than Wisconsin Manufacturers and Commerce, was the biggest spender on lobbying activity.

The fact that Nicolet Minerals was the largest spender for the 1997–98 legislative session was not a random occurrence. One of the top legislative items was statutory guidelines for mine reclamation that would apply to a new mine that Nicolet Minerals wanted to open in southwestern Wisconsin.

These statutory guidelines, and the cost of implementing them, could make the new mine profitable or unprofitable. At the same time, such guidelines were essential for groundwater protection and the protection of local and state government from large costs associated with the remediation of environmental problems caused by mining.

It is also noteworthy that the Wisconsin Counties Association was the second largest spender during the 1997–98 legislative session. In third position was Wisconsin Manufacturers and Commerce, followed by Philip Morris, Inc., Wisconsin Merchants Federation, and Wisconsin Independent Businesses, Inc. Next came Wisconsin Electric Power, the Wisconsin Education Association Council, the State Bar of Wisconsin, and AT&T.

Of these ten interests, only two, Nicolet Minerals and the State Bar of Wisconsin, were not on the top-ten list for the 1999–2000 legislative session. Yet there are differences in the relative "rankings" among the eight that were among the top-ten spenders during the two sessions. The two organizations that made the list in 1999–2000 but not in 1997–98 were The Green Bay Packers, Inc., and the Wisconsin Farm Bureau Federation.

Comparing the Top Ten and the Top Fifty Spenders

In the 1997–98 legislative session the top ten organizations in terms of lobbying expenses consisted of three private corporations, three business associations, one public utility, one association representing lawyers, one association representing local (county) governments, and one association representing public schoolteachers. This profile of organizational types was nearly identical to that for the 1999–2000 legislative session, where the top ten consisted of three private corporations, three business associations, one public utility, one association representing local (county) governments, one association representing public schoolteachers, and one representing farmers.

This pattern or clustering in the top ten is similar to what we find in the organizations comprising the top fifty in terms of lobbying expenditures. For example, during the 1997–98 legislative session nineteen of the top fifty (38 percent) organizations were business associations, and eleven (22 percent) were individual corporations. In other words, thirty of the top fifty organizations, or 60 percent, were focused on private business activity. This is not surprising given that so many businesses are either regulated by the state, do business with the state, or both.

After business-related organizations, the next largest cluster of lobbying

organizations in the top fifty was the one representing local units of government. There were four such organizations, accounting for 8 percent of the top
fifty. Also in the top fifty were three utilities, three organizations representing
farmers, three local governmental units pursuing their own interests, and
three public employee unions. Each of these clusters represents 6 percent of
the top fifty.

THE CONCENTRATION OF LOBBYING
EXPENDITURES AND INFLUENCE

In addition to thinking about lobbying in terms of clusters or groupings,
some additional perspective on private interest and interest group activities
can be gained by further review of lobbying expenditures. The lobbying
expenditures of the top fifty organizations during the 1997–98 legislative
session amounted to $19,856,886, or 47.3 percent of the $42 million dollars
spent by all 601 organizations registered to lobby during that legislative
session. Thus these fifty organizations, which constituted less than 10 percent
of the organizations registered to lobby, accounted for almost half of all
lobbying expenditures.

As we move up the pyramid, we see that the top twenty-five organizations
account for $14,519,756, or 34.5 percent of total lobbying expenditures,
and the top ten organizations account for $8,927,424, or 21.2 percent of
all expenditures. These data underscore the fact that most of the financial
capacity for large-scale, sustained lobbying was limited to a small subset of
the 601 organizations engaged in lobbying during the 1997–98 legislative
session.

The data for the 1999–2000 legislative session show a similar pattern;
most of the capacity for large-scale, sustained lobbying was limited to a
small "elite." This finding is not unique to Wisconsin; similar findings have
been reported from other states. This fact alone might cast some doubt on
the pluralist presumption that there is a relatively equal competition among
various interests in the public policy process.

Limitations of Working with Expenditure Data

While the use of expenditure data provides a relatively concrete measure of
interest group activity, the influence of interest groups is much more difficult
to measure. The fact that so many interest groups are willing to spend money

on lobbying seems to indicate that the leaders and members of these groups believe that their financial investments do have an important payoff. Indeed, it would be highly irrational for organizations (or individual businesses) to continue these activities if there were no benefits.

Yet lobbyists themselves sometimes point out that the interest groups they work for are spending money to gain access to legislators, and access does not guarantee a particular legislative outcome. Thus, while there may be a relationship between spending and influence, the correlation is not perfect. As already noted, there may be times when various private corporations or business interest groups spend a lot of money on lobbying activities as they compete with each other to shape the content of a particular piece of legislation. In these cases it sometimes happens that one corporation, or one type of business association (or one industry), "wins" at the expense of others that "lose."

Legislators' Perceptions of Interest Group Influence

Given the fact that the correlation between expenditures and interest group influence is less than perfect, scholars and journalists have used several alternative measures in their efforts to define interest group influence. Among the most common of such measures is legislative perception. Through interviews with legislators, or through survey questionnaires, journalists and scholars attempt to learn which interest groups legislators believe are the most influential.

In his 1995 study of business lobbying in Wisconsin, William De Soto interviewed thirty-seven legislators to find out what associations they perceived to have the most influence in the state's politics. The top five included: the Wisconsin Education Association Council (WEAC), Wisconsin Manufacturers and Commerce (WMC), the state AFL-CIO, the Wisconsin Realtors Association, and Wisconsin Right to Life.[36] With the exception of the WMC, this list of influential groups is quite different from the influence implied in the list of interest group expenditures.

What factors contributed to legislators' perceptions? An example may be useful. De Soto gives four reasons for the perceived influence of WEAC: longevity at the Capitol, size of staff, size of budget, and size of expenditures in state election campaigns. Each of these factors, as well as the number of members in the association, has been identified as an important variable by scholars who study interest groups.

In WEAC's case, for example, the organization was established in 1853; thus it has had a long-standing presence in the state Capitol. At the time of the study, WEAC had a staff of 165 and a budget of more than $8 million. WEAC's PAC contributions to legislative candidates totaled more than $150,000 in 1994.[37] One might also add that, as the representative of primary and secondary teachers in the state, WEAC's membership was very large, and size of membership can also be an important factor in a legislator's perceptions of an organization's influence. WEAC members, it may be noted, also vote.

Yet perceived influence and actual influence are not perfectly correlated. Some legislators, for example, considered WEAC a "juggernaut," and "its enemies" regarded its power as overwhelming."[38] Indeed, some legislators assumed that WEAC would win any head-to-head contest with the leading business association, the WMC.[39] Not long before these perceptions were recorded, however, WEAC suffered a couple of highly visible setbacks at the hands of the WMC.

The first setback for WEAC occurred in 1992 when the WMC organized and led the opposition to a constitutional amendment on property taxes desired by WEAC. The amendment was defeated at the polls. In 1993 WEAC suffered a significant loss in the legislative arena, when the WMC led the effort to set statewide limits on the growth of property taxes. Such limits, from WEAC's point of view, were undesirable because they made it very difficult to raise teachers' salaries.

Comparative Perspective on Interest Group Influence

As noted above, legislative perception—like expenditures on lobbying—has its limitations as a measure of interest group influence. Yet comparative studies from other states seem to correspond quite closely with the rankings of Wisconsin's interest groups as reported on the basis of expenditure data and legislative perception. Schoolteachers' organizations, like WEAC, and general business organizations, like the WMC, were listed as the two most effective organizations in a study conducted by Thomas and Hrebenar.[40] Indeed, the scholars report that in the influence the two types of organizations "are perceived to have," they "far outstrip any other interest in the fifty states."[41]

Thomas and Hrebenar also list utility companies and lawyers among their top ten in terms of influence. Both interests appeared on the top-ten spending list in Wisconsin for the 1999–2000 legislative sessions. Further, they identify general local government organizations, farm organizations, and realtor organizations among their top twenty.[42] All three appeared on either the top-ten expenditure list or the top-five ranking vis-à-vis perceived interest.

Other organizations on the Thomas and Hrebenar top-twenty-five list include labor unions, physicians and state medical associations, insurance associations and companies, bankers associations and banks, state and local government employees, and health care organizations.[43] All of these types of interests or interest groups also show up among the Wisconsin organizations spending the largest amount of money on lobbying. These comparative data thus support the findings reported here about Wisconsin, and they underscore the fact that neither expenditure data nor legislative perception of influence should be forsaken or ignored. That said, and as Thomas and Hrebenar point out, the two measures must be employed with some care.[44]

INTERESTS, INTEREST GROUPS, LEGISLATORS, AND GOVERNORS

To this point in the chapter, the contemporary lineup of private interests and interest groups in Wisconsin has been described, and the scale and structure of interest group lobbying has been explored. An attempt has also been made to examine the question of whether competition exists among these interests and whether this competition takes a zero-sum form. As already noted, the ability to address the latter question is limited by lack of formal studies of lobbying in Wisconsin.

Of the four questions raised earlier in the chapter, one remains to be considered: Do legislators and governors attempt to constrain interest group conflict by working to find solutions to problems that all parties can agree upon, or do they choose sides when interests collide and act as a partisan for one interest or another?

Undoubtedly there are conflicts among interests and interest groups that legislative leaders and governors attempt to contain or constrain. It is also the case, however, that governors, legislators, and legislative leaders are sometimes advocates for a particular interest, even when the competition between interests might be viewed as a zero-sum game. This type of support can be illustrated symbolically by access; it can also be demonstrated in practical terms through action.

Under Governor Anthony Earl (1982–86), a Democrat, WEAC had good access to the state's chief executive, but it got a comparatively cold shoulder from Republican Governor Tommy Thompson (1986–2001). Friends of WEAC argue that Thompson made a concerted effort to block and reduce its influence. Thompson himself sometimes seemed to acknowledge that this limiting of WEAC's influence was one of his objectives.

In contrast, the WMC's influence in the executive office was limited while Earl was governor, but it was very strong under Thompson. During the fourteen years that Thompson was governor, the WMC not only had access to the chief executive but also to his staff and to executive branch department secretaries and their staffs.[45] Access of this type is a bit unusual, and it could, by itself, enhance an association's perceived influence.

In the case of the WMC and the Thompson administration, however, the relationship went well beyond the symbolic. As a result of his study of business groups in Wisconsin, De Soto concluded that the "WMC and Governor Thompson share a belief that what is best for business is best for Wisconsin."[46] Others at the State Capitol held the view that the WMC's agenda was the Thompson administration's agenda.

Legislators and legislative leaders can also be highly visible partisans for an interest or a cause—including one that is not a popular one within the legislative institution. For example, beginning in March 1963, Senator Fred Risser initiated efforts to block the sale of cigarettes to children under the age of sixteen. Risser took this action nine months before the U.S. Surgeon General's Advisory Committee on Smoking and Health released its report on the health risks associated with smoking. It was a time when the political climate related to smoking was vastly different than it is now.

In historical terms, neither legislators nor legislative leaders in Wisconsin had opposed smoking or the tobacco interests. This was partly a function of the fact that the tobacco interests were well organized and well funded and partly a function of local (state) agricultural patterns. Some farmers in Wisconsin did (and still do) grow tobacco.

Throughout the 1960s, Risser's battle with the tobacco interests was a lonely and frustrating one, as others within the legislature acceded to the tobacco interests and quietly but effectively blocked his initiatives. In the early 1970s, however, Risser, who had become senate president, expanded his efforts to regulate the use of tobacco products by focusing on second-hand smoke, and he introduced legislation in 1973 to ban smoking in enclosed areas of buildings that were open to the public.

As revelations continued to emerge throughout the 1970s about smoking's terrible effects on health, Risser's campaign to ban smoking from public buildings gained momentum. After a decade of struggle he finally got the Clean Indoor Air Act through the legislature and signed into law by Governor

Earl in 1984. Yet the struggle was by no means over. In at least one election after the law was signed, tobacco interests were the chief financiers of his election opponent. Risser survived the election contest, however, and his battle with the tobacco interests continues.

There are also cases where a legislative leader or a governor is, in a very public way, a partisan for one interest or interest group and, at the same time, another legislative leader is publicly committed to a competing interest. Such alignments are sometimes associated with the two main political parties. For example, over the past thirty years interest groups opposed to abortion have generally had close working relationships with Republicans, while interest groups supporting a woman's right to choose to have an abortion have typically been tied to Democrats.

A similar situation has often been at play with regard to the National Rifle Association (NRA). Over the past couple of decades this interest group has usually been more closely aligned with Republicans than with Democrats. This general alignment played out in Wisconsin during the 1980s in a most remarkable way. In this contest, Republican Governor Tommy Thompson and Republican legislative leaders were generally acknowledged as supporters of the NRA, while Assembly Speaker Tom Loftus, Democrat, was the principal opponent.

Ironically, the initial skirmishes in this pitched battle were events that occurred in Illinois and California, not Wisconsin. In 1987, crimes committed with handguns led the community of Morton Grove, Illinois, to establish a ban on the possession of these weapons. Then, in 1989, kids were gunned down in a Stockton, California, schoolyard by an assailant with an assault rifle. This horrific event led to a national discussion about a ban on assault rifles.

The leaders of the NRA's Washington headquarters used both events to energize NRA members. The headquarters' strategy was to push hard to secure a "right-to-bear-arms" amendment to state constitutions, and was apparently built on the presumption that these amendments could be used in the courts to strike down state and local government gun regulations and to prohibit these governments from establishing new regulations.

In Wisconsin the struggle over the NRA's initiative was a hard-fought battle and one that the press helped to make highly visible.[47] It was also a struggle that had important implications for the upcoming elections in which these elected officials and their parties would be competing. Assembly Speaker Loftus believed that stripping state and local governments of their ability to ban guns from school buses, public buildings, and courthouses was bad public policy.[48] During the 1987–88 and 1989–90 legislative sessions, Loftus was able to mobilize enough support within the legislature to stop the NRA's initiatives.

Winning the first battle, however, did not guarantee that Loftus would win the war. In fact, in 1990 he gave up his assembly seat to run for governor against Thompson. The contest was an uneven one, pitting a well-known and popular governor who had a highly unified party and large campaign war chest against a candidate who was not well known statewide, who did not have a strong and unified party behind him, and who did not have access to a large campaign fund. The result was a lopsided victory for Thompson.

With Loftus gone from the legislature, there was no one to lead the opposition to the NRA's campaign. There was no organized group or interest to present the other side of the issue to legislators or to the public. Consequently, with the support of Governor Thompson and the Republican leadership, the National Rifle Association (NRA) was able to put through two consecutive sessions of the legislature the "right-to-bear-arms" language they wanted as an amendment to the constitution. That amendment was ratified by the voters in 1997.[49]

IN SUMMARY

Data contained in this chapter show that large numbers of interests are busy lobbying legislators in Wisconsin's Capitol. The data also show that only a small percentage of these interests, approximately 10 percent, have the financial and staff resources for extended and intensive lobbying. It does appear that competition among these interests takes place, including competition between private corporations and business interest groups. Yet it is difficult to determine whether this competition takes the form of a zero-sum contest or a less brutal competition designed to find compromises that all or most of the interested parties could accept.

It seems reasonable to think that there are times when governors and legislative leaders attempt to contain levels of conflict between interests by fashioning compromise solutions within legislation. Some scholars have suggested that there are also cases in which legislators and governors simply ratify the results of the competition between various interests. In such cases, state statutes serve as records of victories, conquests, and surrenders.

Finally, it is also clear that elected officials sometimes become partisans for one group or another. At least in some of instances these struggles do take the form of a zero-sum game. That is, one side will be the victor in the contest, while the other side will be vanquished. Whether or to what extent the competition among interests—and the reaction of elected officials to that competition—serves the public interest remains, however, an open and very important question.

CHAPTER SEVEN

Political Parties and Elections

Competition for office in and of itself is assumed virtually without question to be an essential in making popular choice meaningful, and competition between parties is the distinctively modern form which it is . . . thought that competition must take.

Leon Epstein, Politics in Wisconsin, 1958

Political organizations, of course, operate in Wisconsin, but the political culture and legal climate are not conducive to cohesive organizations capable of controlling nominations, mobilizing voters, or dispensing patronage.

John Bibby, "Political Parties and Elections in Wisconsin," 1991

Freely contested elections are essential for democratic politics, and political parties are generally regarded as the vehicles through which electoral competition is organized.[1] At a minimum, political parties are supposed to give voters the opportunity to choose between the "ins" of one party and the "outs" of another.[2] A more elevated view holds that competition between parties allows voters to express their policy preferences and to hold elected officials accountable for their actions. Identified as the "responsible party" model in political science circles, this conception of the role of parties in elections holds an important place in twentieth century scholarship.

In the responsible party model, political parties are presumed to play a key role in recruiting candidates for office, providing financial support for their campaigns, developing a common platform for policy positions, and getting the party faithful to the polls.[3] Ironically enough, it may have been during the "machine" era in Wisconsin's political history (the 1870s to 1890s)

Table 7.   Voter Turnout in Presidential Elections (% of voting-age population)

	1980	1984	1988	1992	1996	2000
U.S. Total	52.8	53.3	50.3	55.1	49.0	52.0
Wisconsin	67.4	63.5	61.6	68.9	57.4	66.9

Source: *Statistical Abstracts of the United States*, 1995, 1996, 1999, 2000, 2001, U.S. Department of Commerce, U.S. Census Bureau

that a party apparatus came closest to performing all of these functions. After the election of 1900, however, Robert La Follette and the Progressive Republicans in the legislature enacted reforms that were designed to severely limit the capabilities and influence of political parties in the state.

In this chapter we will look at whether, or to what extent, the two major political parties have played the role in Wisconsin politics they are often presumed to play. We will also look at the extent to which Wisconsin's electoral politics have been characterized by two-party competition and the extent to which its elections have been dominated by a single party. The two questions are related in important ways. The chapter begins with a brief overview of some of the distinctive features of Wisconsin's elections.

OVERVIEW OF ELECTIONS IN WISCONSIN

Wisconsin's elections have several distinctive or even unique features when compared with those of other states. Perhaps the most important is that more of Wisconsin's citizens tend to participate in elections than is the case in the majority of other states. In the 2000 presidential election, for example, almost 67 percent of the voting-age population in Wisconsin voted, while only 52 percent participated nationally.

As the data in table 7 show, the 15-percent difference between voter participation in Wisconsin and the nation in 2000 was not an aberration or a one-time event. In the 1980 presidential election the difference in participation rates between Wisconsin and the nation was almost identical. Furthermore, as the data in the table show, the smallest gap between Wisconsin voter-participation rates and national rates in the five presidential elections between 1980 and 2000 was 11.3 percent.

In addition to presidential elections, Wisconsin voters also participate in the off-year congressional elections at higher rates than do voters nationally. In the 1998 elections 44.2 percent of Wisconsin's voting-age population voted, while only 33.2 percent did so nationally, a difference of 11 percent.

Table 8.   Voter Turnout in Nonpresidential Elections (% of voting-age population)

	1978	1982	1986	1990	1994	1998
U.S. Total	34.9	38.0	33.5	33.1	36.0	33.2
Wisconsin	45.6	46.0	43.4	37.4	40.7	44.2

Source: Statistical Abstracts of the United States, 1995, 1996, 1999, 2000, 2001, U.S. Department of Commerce, U.S. Census Bureau

   The data in table 8 provide an opportunity to look backward twenty years from 1998 to the 1978 congressional off-year elections. In that election we see a gap similar to the 1998 level. In 1978 Wisconsin's participation rates were 10.7 percent higher than were the national figures. There was, however, one election (1990) in which Wisconsin's voter participation rate fell from the standard range of the mid-40 percentile to the mid-30s, and thus was only 1.6 percent higher than the national participation rate. There is no obvious explanation for what happened in Wisconsin that year, but it is fascinating to see that voter participation rates did return to a more "normal" level for Wisconsin after that election.

   A second way in which Wisconsin's elections are distinctive is that they tend to be issue-oriented rather than patronage-based. Like high participation rates the issue orientation in Wisconsin elections can be explained primarily by Wisconsin's moralistic political culture, as Daniel Elazar's research has shown.[4] The lack of patronage is also a function of the early development of civil service laws in Wisconsin.

   In two other areas where Wisconsin elections have distinctive or unique features, the state's political history has also been at least as important a cause as has its political culture. For example, Wisconsin's "open primary" law emerged in the early 1900s after Robert M. La Follette Sr. and the Progressive Republicans finally wrested control of the Republican Party's gubernatorial nomination from the Stalwarts. La Follette and the Progressive Republicans also made an effort to strengthen Wisconsin's campaign finance laws, which were originally put into place during the 1880s by reformers who were determined to limit the power of private corporations and wealthy individuals.

TWO-PARTY COMPETITION AND THE WISCONSIN EXPERIENCE

Within the Anglo-American tradition there is a strong preference for two-party competition over multiparty competition or single-party politics. Multiparty competition, practiced in some European countries, has often been associated with unstable governments and unstable public policy. Single-party politics has been associated with either a high degree of factionalism (within the party) or an absence of accountability and voter choice. Both patterns can produce ineffective or damaging consequences.

V. O. Key's research on the states of the old South, conducted during the late 1940s and early 1950s, documented the dysfunctional effects that can occur in a state when two-party politics is absent.[5] Spurred by Key's work, other scholars began to investigate the extent to which two-party competition existed in states outside of the South. Two of these scholars, Austin Ranney and Wilmoore Kendall, developed a threefold classification scheme for the states.[6] The states were identified as one-party states, two-party states, or modified one-party states.

Wisconsin as a Modified One-Party State

The data used by Ranney and Kendall were drawn from the years 1914 through 1952. In their study they identified many states of the North as modified one-party systems. In contrast to the states of the South, where the Democratic party was dominant, the Republican party was dominant in the states of the North. The patterns for both areas of the country were largely historical vestiges of the Civil War.

Ranney and Kendall labeled Wisconsin a two-party state, even though Wisconsin, like many other states of the North and Midwest, showed Republican dominance in most elections between 1914 and 1952. The two-party label was challenged by Leon D. Epstein, however, in his 1958 book *Politics in Wisconsin*. Epstein was sensitive to the consequences the Progressives' departure from the Republican Party in 1934 had on electoral competition. According to Epstein, Ranney and Kendall labeled the state as a two-party state "only because they included (not unreasonably) the victories of third-party Progressives in their count of second-party victories."[7]

Given this circumstance Epstein argued that Wisconsin was probably more appropriately placed as a modified one-party state in Ranney and Kendall's scheme. With the exception of normal two-party voting patterns for president, Epstein maintained, Republican dominance in all other forms of partisan elections was complete. At the same time, Epstein also noted that during the latter part of the period from 1914 to 1952, and particularly in the post–World War II era, Wisconsin was moving toward a two-party pattern.[8]

From a Two-Party to a One-Party State—and Back (1840–1958)

The movement toward two-party competition in the 1950s could be viewed as an aberration from a long-standing historical pattern. Alternatively it could be viewed as a movement back to the type of politics that existed in Wisconsin during its latter days as a territory and its early years of statehood. Indeed, as noted in chapter 2 ("The Constitution"), two-party competition played an important and highly visible role in Wisconsin politics and elections even before it became a state.

The struggle over the state's constitution during 1846, 1847, and 1848 arose from conflicting views held by members of the Democratic and Whig parties. The parties split over the propriety of economic rights for women and farmers, voting rights for black Americans, whether judges ought to be appointed or elected, and whether the state ought to be allowed to borrow money to make infrastructure improvements.

From the 1860s through the end of the century, however, a single political party dominated Wisconsin's elections and politics. As noted in chapter 1 ("The Character of the State"), the rapid rise of the Republican Party in Wisconsin began after its founding in Ripon in 1854. The Civil War established the Republican Party as the party of the patriotic and respectable elements of society, as was discussed in chapter 3 ("The Legislature"). This made it very difficult for the Democratic Party to mobilize enough voters to win elections.

Indeed, during the forty-year period from 1860 to 1900 Democratic candidates won the governorship on only two occasions. Each of these occasions was preceded by highly visible and specific expressions of grievances by those outside of the Republican Party, especially recent immigrants. These grievances were sparked by such actions of the Republican administration as their attempt to ban the sale of alcohol on Sundays, and to require English language instruction in all public schools.[9]

During the first thirty years of Republican dominance, from the mid-1860s through the late 1880s, competition within the party steadily declined as the party bosses consolidated control. Beginning in the early 1890s, however, and continuing through the early 1930s, there was ferocious competition for control of the party. The contestants were the party bosses, or Stalwarts, who sometimes attempted to buy elections and took a machine-style approach to politics, and the Progressive faction, who were determined to return control of elections and government to the state's citizens.

Robert M. La Follette Sr. made two unsuccessful attempts to win the Republican Party's gubernatorial nomination during the primary elections in 1896 and 1898. During the latter election party bosses maintained control of the Republican Party nomination through dubious means. During the gubernatorial primary of 1900, however, La Follette and the Progressives finally won the party nomination for governor. Shortly thereafter La Follette won the general election for governor.

Although the struggle between the Progressives and the Stalwarts for control of the Republican Party continued for the next four years, by 1904 La Follette was in command. The Progressives would maintain control of the party and the state for most of the next thirty years. In the early 1930s, however, the Stalwarts regained control of the party.[10] As a result, the Progressive cohort left the Republican Party and formed their own. The Progressive Party remained in existence until 1946, when it was disbanded by its leaders. Interestingly, the demise of the Progressive Party coincided with the revitalization of the Democratic Party in the state and its realignment with the national party.[11] These circumstances are clearly visible in the data contained in figure 1, which displays the number of seats various parties held in the state assembly from 1885 through 2003.

Although the revitalization of the Democratic Party after World War II was led by men who would eventually become key officeholders in the state, including William Proxmire, Gaylord Nelson, and Patrick Lucey, a competitive two-party system seemed more like a remote possibility than a sure thing to many people in the latter half of the 1950s. In *Politics in Wisconsin* Leon Epstein was reluctant to make the prediction that Wisconsin would again become a fully competitive two-party state in the future. Epstein's caution should not be surprising, given the fact that the Democrats had won only one important statewide office between 1948 and 1957, and Proxmire's 1957 victory in his campaign for the U.S. Senate could be called something of an aberration.[12]

In this case, as in many others, actual events outpaced expectations and predictions. In November 1958 Democrat Gaylord Nelson captured the governorship, and the Democrats captured a majority of the seats in the state assembly. That event is clearly visible in figure 1.

Since 1958, Wisconsin has been a two-party state. Close electoral competition between the Democratic and Republican parties is now considered a "hallmark" of contemporary state politics.[13] Data on party competition for the state senate is provided in figure 2.

Fig. 1. Party Composition of the Wisconsin State Assembly, 1885–2003 (*Credit:* Wisconsin Legislative Reference Bureau)

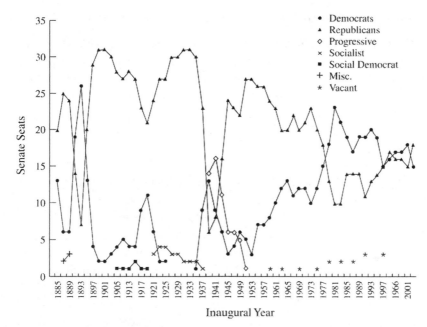

Fig. 2. Party Composition of Wisconsin State Senate, 1885–2003 (*Credit:* Wisconsin Legislative Reference Bureau)

Two-Party Competition between 1960 and 1999

The extent to which Wisconsin has been a two-party state is highlighted by the ongoing ebb and flow of party fortunes in state legislative races since the late 1950s. The state's two-party status can also be documented by the fortunes of two-party competition for the governorship. In the forty years from 1960 through 1999, the Democratic and Republican parties held the governorship for almost the same number of years, despite the fact that Tommy Thompson held the position for fourteen years.

Another indicator of the closeness of two-party competition over the past forty years is the amount of time the state has had a "divided government." This term is commonly used to refer to a circumstance in which one party holds the governorship and the other party holds one house or both houses of the state legislature. Throughout the four decades from the 1960s through the end of the 1990s, Wisconsin had "divided government" most of the time.

Still another way to think about the closeness of party competition in the state is to look at the offices each party held at the end of the twentieth century. In 1999 Democrats held five congressional seats while the Republicans held four. Democrats and Republicans each held three of the six elective statewide offices. Republicans held the offices of governor, lieutenant governor, and treasurer, while Democrats held the offices of attorney general, secretary of state, and superintendent of education. Finally, Republicans held a modest majority in the state assembly, while Democrats held a one-seat majority in the state senate.

ELECTION LAWS

In contrast to some states, Wisconsin's election laws are articulated in statutes rather than in the state's constitution. Although statutory provisions are more susceptible to change than constitutional provisions, Wisconsin's election law has been stable over the past one hundred years. This stability is an important mark of the strong consensus that has existed within the state about the content and value of these laws.

Perhaps the most important feature of these laws is the bias they contain against any organized political apparatus. Specifically, Robert M. La Follette and the Progressives wanted to make sure that the Stalwarts' political machine could not be rebuilt, and they wanted to be sure that no similar party machine emerged in the future. In order to block such developments, laws were passed to prevent political party bosses or leaders from determining nominations for the general election, manipulating large numbers of votes by the party faithful, controlling the flow of money for political campaigns, and distributing patronage.

The Direct, or Open, Primary

The principal statutory provision designed to block party leaders from controlling nominations and mobilizing the votes of party faithful was the "open primary." Under this provision, the nomination of party candidates for the general election takes place through a direct primary election for all offices, rather than through a party convention or caucus. This state requirement makes it virtually impossible for party bosses to control the nomination process. It also makes it very difficult for party leaders to identify citizens who are committed to their candidate, and consequently makes it difficult for the party apparatuses to mobilize votes on behalf of their respective candidates.

The direct, or open, primary may be Wisconsin's best known and most important electoral innovation. Established in 1903, the direct primary allows voters to decide whether they want to participate in the nomination process in either the Democratic or the Republican Party. This means that when voters go to the polls on Election Day, there are no records to indicate whether they are Republican or Democrat. Rather, the voting lists merely show whether they are registered to vote, and in the privacy of the polling booth voters can choose either the Democratic or the Republican ballot.

The significance of the open primary was noted by Epstein in 1958: "The institution of the open primary in Wisconsin dates from 1906, and by now the political habits associated with it are deeply fixed. To many Wisconsin citizens, it would seem undemocratic to be asked to identify publicly with a party as a prerequisite for primary voting, and to restrict oneself in advance to a given party's ballot would seem a foolish deprivation of the opportunity to vote for (or against) an important personality on another ticket."[14]

Of course members of the national party apparatus for the Democrats and Republicans are likely to have a less charitable view of Wisconsin's open primary law. From their point of view, the open primary is more likely to distort the nomination process than to enhance it. More specifically, members of the national party apparatus are likely to believe that the open primary allows members of the opposition party to insert themselves inappropriately into the party's nomination process. Of particular concern is the belief that members of the opposition party might attempt to ensure that the weakest of the party's candidates is nominated. Yet research would appear to show that these concerns are unfounded.[15]

Local Elections as Nonpartisan Elections

Another part of Wisconsin's election law that was intended to prevent the development of a machine-style political apparatus is the requirement that all elections for municipal offices and school boards be nonpartisan. This requirement not only blocks a political organization's ability to develop control at the grass-roots level but also blocks a party's ability to control local nominations and elections from a state apparatus. One negative side effect of this law, however, is that mayors of large cities, particularly Milwaukee, find it difficult to "use their positions as stepping stones to major state or federal office."[16] This situation stands in contrast to circumstances in some other states, where local elections are partisan contests, and mayors of major cities are more likely to become candidates for the governorship and federal offices.[17]

The timing of elections for municipalities and school boards is another means by which party control of nominations and party mobilization of voters is limited. These local elections are held in the spring rather than in the fall, when statewide and national elections are held. While this is not an unusual requirement among the states today, the separation of local elections from state and national elections adds an additional protection against party control or the simultaneous manipulation of local, state, and national elections.[18]

Eliminating Patronage

In addition to blocking party control of primary-election nominations and limiting a party's ability to mobilize voters, the Progressives' statutory reforms of the early 1900s were designed to eliminate a third key element of machine-style politics—political patronage. The objective was to ensure that political parties did not have the ability to reward big contributors with high-paying jobs or reward campaign workers with employment in state agencies.

Thus, the Progressives established statutory limits on gubernatorial appointments in executive branch agencies, and these appointments were limited to a very small cadre of top-level positions. In addition, the Progressives established a civil service system. This system was designed to protect state employees from job loss due to partisan considerations and to ensure that the hiring of new employees was done on the basis of merit. Leon Epstein described the success achieved by the Progressives this way: "One important respect in which Wisconsin practice differs from that of many states is the very limited role of patronage in the political process. . . . It is impossible for an individual candidate or party to build a political organization based on state patronage appointments or on the prospect of such appointment. Civil service is of such long standing and so taken for granted that a party would run great political risks if it sought to introduce large-scale patronage."[19]

John Bibby described the results of the Progressives' antipatronage efforts this way: "The absence of patronage is believed to be one of the factors contributing to the issue-oriented style of politics which sets Wisconsin apart from such Midwestern states as Indiana, Illinois, and Ohio, where the patronage system flourishes."[20]

Political scientists who study the states know how important the elimination of patronage is to both the quality of politics and the quality of government. Likewise, people who are elected to executive and legislative offices in the states are well aware of the benefits of operating in a patronage-free environment. In Wisconsin, the Progressives' legacy of clean and open politics has stood the test of time for approximately one hundred years.

Indeed, it seems almost ironic that the most important test of the Progressives' antipatronage plan may have occurred at the end of the twentieth century rather than at the beginning. That test occurred when Governor Tommy Thompson was elected to serve a second, third, and fourth term in office. The long tenure gave Thompson an unusual opportunity to engage in patronage-based activities and to attempt to manipulate the civil service system. According to his critics, Thompson engaged in both activities. Thompson's supporters argue that he was simply trying to make the bureaucracy more responsive and that his critics misinterpreted his actions.

It appears that Thompson *did* make an aggressive effort to expand the number of people he could appoint within the executive branch agencies.[21] At least at the upper echelon of the executive branch agencies, however, this initiative was not unusual. During the latter half of the twentieth century, many governors attempted to gain direct appointment power of agency secretaries and their immediate subordinates by eliminating agency boards and commissions. Thompson's critics also noted that he demanded an extraordinarily high degree of loyalty from his cabinet secretaries and other senior political managers of the state's executive branch agencies. Viewed within the larger context of politics and administration in the states, this approach was taken by other governors, as well.

It was Thompson's oft-stated suspicion of the "bureaucracy" and his determination to enforce centralized control over it, however, that made his critics suspicious of his actions. They interpreted his actions as an attempt to manipulate the civil service system for his own benefit and the benefit of his party. Some of his critics argued that he was making an aggressive effort to put his own people into executive branch agencies at levels far below the levels of cabinet secretary and assistant secretary.[22] No hard evidence was ever produced to support this contention, however. One might thus conclude that the legacy of keeping Wisconsin's civil service system separate from party politics and patronage was, in fact, sustained.

Regulating Campaign Finance

Another important heritage of the struggle between the Stalwarts and the Progressives is the state's campaign finance laws. Initially established during the late 1800s and early 1900s, state election laws required disclosure of campaign contributions and a prescribed limit to the size of the contributions that any individual or organization could make to a candidate. Those requirements were still in place fifty years later, when Leon Epstein reported that Wisconsin "does require a fairly detailed reporting of campaign contributions and expenditures by all candidates, committees, and organizations."[23]

These campaign finance regulations and the drive to limit the influence of money in elections and state politics put Wisconsin in the forefront of the reform efforts that have been initiated in both the national and state arenas. Furthermore, since Epstein's study was published, more efforts have been made to strengthen or enhance (as well as to weaken) Wisconsin's campaign finance laws. For the most part these attempts have been aimed at strengthening the state's controls on expenditures by candidates and party organizations, and controls on campaign contributions by a candidate's campaign committee and by the political action committees (PAC's). The objective, of course, was to block or limit the corrupting influence that large campaign contributions can have. Governor Patrick Lucey initiated the campaign finance reform efforts of the 1970s, which culminated in the 1973 revision of campaign finance laws. These statutory changes were augmented by legislative enactments in 1977 and 1979. The 1977 reform was noteworthy in that it contained provisions for publicly funding campaigns for state offices.[24] Wisconsin was one of the first states to take such action.[25]

Additional efforts to regulate campaign financing were made in the 1980s and 1990s.[26]

Even some who support the goals articulated for these campaign finance regulations have questioned their effectiveness. Epstein, for example, writing in the late 1950s, argued that the laws limiting candidate and party spending were largely "ineffective" because they simply pushed spending over to voluntary committees set up on behalf of the candidate or the political party. In the past decade the rise of political action committees (PACs) and the emergence of the so-called issue ads that PACs run on television and radio have underscored the kind of concerns Epstein voiced more than forty-five years ago.

Voter Registration, Ballot Types, and Apportionment

Another area in which there have been recent efforts to amend or improve election laws is voter registration. During the 1970s Wisconsin was a leader among the states in efforts to reduce the number of people disenfranchised by voter-registration requirements. Early in his first term in office, Governor Patrick Lucey appointed a task force of citizens and legislators to study election laws in Wisconsin. Among the task force's recommendations was a proposal to reduce the residency requirement. At the time, a person had to be a resident of the state and the community for six months before he or she could register to vote.

While the law was intended to prevent both fraud and double voting, it was actually disenfranchising thousands of people who were either forced to move as a result of a job transfer or chose to move from one community to another. The task force recommended that the law be changed to require a residency of only one month in the new state or community, and the legislature modified the law as recommended. Additional changes were later made in the law that reduced the residency requirement to one week. The most recent change in the state's registration requirements allows a person to register on election day with proper identification and two registered voters who can confirm that person's place of residence.

Another important element of Wisconsin's election law is the form of the ballot used in the state. Wisconsin uses a "party column"–type ballot in which all of a party's nominees for various offices are arranged in a row or column. This type of ballot allows a citizen to vote a straight party ticket or to select candidates office by office. In contrast to other elements of Wisconsin's election law, which seem designed to reduce the strength of political parties, this arrangement seems to do the opposite. This ballot form has been subject to some criticism.

Finally, in historical terms another important element of Wisconsin's constitutional and statutory law has been the requirement that districts be apportioned on the basis of population. Attempts by state officials to comply with these requirements meant that as early as the 1950s Wisconsin's state legislative districts were reapportioned in ways that did not overrepresent the population of the state's rural areas or underrepresent the population of the state's urban areas. Consequently, Wisconsin avoided what occurred in many other northern states, which was an underrepresentation of urban Democrats. In these states, underrepresentation had the effect of relegating the Democratic Party to minority status in the legislature for several decades.[27]

PARTY STRUCTURE AND OPERATION

Wisconsin's statutes both call for and severely constrain formal party organizations. In order to avoid many of these constraints while still meeting statutory requirements, the Democratic and Republican parties have established voluntary mass membership, dues-based party organizations that are separate from the agencies chartered by state statutes. Members of the Republican Party who opposed the Progressive faction were the first to form a voluntary organization outside of the state statutes. They took the necessary steps in 1925. The voluntary form of the Democratic Party organization was finally established twenty years later.

The nonstatutory organizations of the two parties have comparable structures. Both parties have four key units that are closely connected to their functions: the county unit; the congressional district organization; the state convention; and the state administrative or executive committee. Of these units or parts, it is the local or county unit that serves as the base for both parties. According to John Bibby, the dues-paying members of the county organization "attend a county caucus in odd-numbered years," and "elect county party officers, choose delegates to congressional district caucuses and state conventions, and conduct local campaign activities."[28]

Bibby also emphasizes the fact that these dues-paying members of the party organization are likely to be the "activists" who "tend to feel more keenly about political issues than rank and file party voters."[29] Bibby also notes that Republican Party activists tend to be more conservative than Republican voters, and Democratic Party activists tend to be more liberal than Democratic Party voters. Additionally party activists tend to come from the middle and upper classes. For this reason, Bibby maintains that the most active county organizations tend to be located in suburban areas or urban counties that have a substantial concentration of middle- and upper-class voters.[30]

In both parties, the officers for the congressional district organization are elected by caucuses in the spring of each odd-numbered year. The officers are charged with the responsibility of managing the organization's activities. The Republican officers are automatically members of the state executive committee, but this is not the case for Democrats. Another important difference between the two parties is that the Republican congressional caucuses may endorse a congressional candidate, while the Democratic Party forbids its congressional officers and caucuses from doing so.

State convention activities also differ from party to party. The Republican Party convention can endorse primary candidates who are running for election, but the Democratic Party convention is forbidden from doing so. Both parties' conventions do attempt to develop a party platform and policy resolutions. The Democratic convention also elects a state party chair and state officers; the state executive committee performs this function in the Republican Party.

The State Administrative Committee is the governing body of the state Democratic Party; the State Executive Committee performs a similar role for the Republican Party. In both parties the state committee chair is responsible for selecting the staff for the party office, coordinating activities with county organizations, and for coordinating fundraising activities. Governors have traditionally attempted to establish their influence over the voluntary statewide party by influencing the selection of the party chair. Bibby notes that neither party's constitution specifies a formal role for governors in the selection of party chairs, but this role has evolved as a customary practice.[31]

Perspectives on the Roles of Political Parties in Wisconsin

The extent of party activity and the degree of influence that the party organizations have in elections is a matter that deserves some commentary. Not surprisingly, there are differing perspectives, and these perspectives seem to be shaped by the times in which they were offered and the variables on which the commentator focused. This point will be illustrated by examining comments made by scholars Leon Epstein, John Bibby, and former assembly majority leader, Tom Loftus.

In *Politics in Wisconsin*, Epstein provides some very positive commentary on Wisconsin's parties. He observes that "in their organization, contemporary Wisconsin parties exemplify a kind of political activism previously more familiar in Britain and Continental Europe than in the United States. It is the largely non-patronage organization of a regularized, often dues-paying, mass membership."[32]

Epstein goes on to say that the form of party organization found in Wisconsin was (in the late 1950s) a rare exception in the United States.[33] At that time most state parties were "skeletal," with their "form prescribed by statute," and their membership limited largely to those who aspired to "hold public office or public spoils."[34]

Writing almost forty years later, Bibby and Loftus base their comments on the extent to which the parties were able to provide assistance to candidates in elections, rather than on the fact that the parties have a mass membership, dues-paying, voluntary base. According to Bibby, both parties provide financial and technical support to candidates. Yet he concludes that "no candidate for major office relies primarily on the party organization to get elected."[35] In support of this contention, he provides two explanations commonly cited in existing scholarship. First, he notes that modern candidates for office have their own campaign staff and their own fundraising efforts. Second, he observes that interest groups allied with each party make independent contributions to party candidates.

Like Bibby's, Loftus's assessment of the political parties seems to be focused on the limitations or weaknesses of these organizations rather than on their strengths. Also, like Bibby, Loftus acknowledges the importance of candidate-centered campaigns and interest groups allied with each party. Loftus also adds an additional perspective, however, on the relative focus or emphasis of the parties. According to Loftus, "state parties have a fairly narrow focus."[36] The state organization, he contends, concentrates "on statewide races and the presidential campaign," while "local units of state political parties focus on the county court house, fighting to control the offices of clerk and sheriff and coroner."[37] The result, Loftus holds, is that races "for the state legislature receive scant attention."[38]

The rise of the legislative or caucus campaign committee could be a consequence of the phenomenon Loftus identifies. Alternatively, the rise of the legislative campaign committee could also be a cause of state party inactivity in this area. In any case Loftus notes that the legislative campaign committee, which is headed by the party leaders in each house of the state legislature, has not only become a powerful fundraising entity but also has become the institution that recruits candidates for office and provides technical campaign support for these candidates. Loftus underscores the extent to which the desire to either maintain or secure a majority has been, for each party in both the senate and the assembly, the driving force behind election activity in the state.

In conclusion, Wisconsin seems to have viable and active voluntary party organizations. In addition these parties do play a visible and important role in election campaigns for national and statewide offices. In contrast, however, neither party organization seems particularly effective or active in legislative races. This apparent deficiency in party activity may be the result of party structure and functions related to that structure. It may also be due to other factors, including the very active role that caucus committees and legislative leaders now play in these election campaigns.

VOTING BEHAVIOR AND POLITICAL GEOGRAPHY

Studies of voting behavior are designed to identify patterns in a state or in the nation as a whole. They can also provide information that can help to explain why a particular party—or even a particular candidate—won (or lost) an election. While studies of voting behavior are generally ex post (they provide an explanation for why something happened), they can also provide a baseline from which to analyze ex ante activity (activity that precedes an election). Studies of voting behavior can serve as useful tools in the recruitment of candidates for office and in the development of campaign strategy.

Early studies of voting behavior focused on the relationship between party registration and the results of elections. That is to say, if the Republicans held an edge in voter registration of 60 percent to 40 percent in a legislative district, congressional district, or even statewide, the expected result of elections in those districts or in the statewide contest would be a Republican victory. The principal explanation for a Republican victory would be voter party identification, rather than issues related to the particular candidate or to policy issues.

On the other hand if a Democratic candidate won in a legislative or congressional district, or in a statewide race where 60 percent of the voters were registered Republicans and only 40 percent were registered Democrats, factors other than party registration would have to be considered. In this scenario, low turnout among Republican voters and high turnout among Democrats could be identified as the principal cause of a victory by a

Democratic candidate. At the same time, other factors may have suppressed or encouraged turnout, including the perceived integrity of a candidate or a candidate's position on particular public policy issues. Party-registration figures alone cannot explain the results in these cases.

In the political science literature, discussions of both party affiliation and voting behavior have also considered socioeconomic characteristics of the voters. Scholars have attempted to explain party affiliation and voting behavior on the basis of such factors as ethnicity, religion, income, education, employment, race, and gender. Studies of voting behavior have shown that throughout most of the twentieth century, white male Anglo-Saxon Protestants who were born in the United States, have attained high levels of education, and earn a high level of income have been more likely to be registered as Republicans than as Democrats. They have also been more likely to vote for Republican candidates than for Democratic candidates. Regarding employment, people who fit this profile are also more likely to hold professional or managerial positions than clerical or blue-collar positions.

Conversely, white Catholic immigrants from Southern Europe with modest levels of education and income have been more likely to vote for Democratic candidates than for Republican candidates. These people also tend to have blue-collar jobs. Nonwhites with low levels of education and income who work in unskilled jobs are also more likely to vote for Democratic candidates than for Republican candidates.

As noted earlier in this chapter, the Civil War was the most important causal factor in the voting patterns of Republican dominance in Wisconsin and other states of the North during the post–Civil War period (1865–99) and the first half of the twentieth century (1900–1957). The same factor was the principal cause of the voting patterns of Democratic dominance found in the states that made up the South after the Civil War. Since the late 1950s, however, there has been a remarkable realignment of the Democratic and Republican parties nationally. This change has been accompanied by changes in voting patterns in the states that make up both the North and the South.

Because Wisconsin's voting behavior during the entire twentieth century has been studied by scholars, it is possible to identify some of the factors that either inhibited or contributed to new patterns of voting during the second half of the twentieth century. Epstein's study of voting behavior in Wisconsin shows that the development of manufacturing, urbanization, and unions contributed to the growth of votes for Democratic Party candidates.

At the same time, he shows that the Republican base was sustained in part by the unusually large number of small cities in Wisconsin when compared to other highly industrialized states.

Specifically, for the period from 1948 through 1954, Epstein's data make clear that Republican candidates continued to win the statewide contest for the governorship on the strength of the votes they received in cities with populations of less than 50,000. The Republican percentage grew as city size decreased. The Republican percentage was higher in cities of 10,000 to 25,000 than it was in cities of 25,000 to 50,000, and it was higher still in cities of 5,000 to 10,000 than it was in cities with 10,000 to 25,000. Epstein also notes that throughout most of the state the vote in small villages and rural areas was very heavily Republican, but the Republican percentage did not increase in cities and villages with populations under 5,000.

In contrast, a majority of votes for Democratic gubernatorial candidates could be found in Milwaukee and in the five urban areas or cities with populations that exceeded 50,000. These areas include Madison, Green Bay, (Duluth)-Superior, Racine, and Kenosha. At the same time, the Democrats' rural majorities were generally confined to counties in the northern cutover region and in the marginal areas of the northwest through 1956.[39]

Epstein's explanation for these patterns of voting behavior, which are closely tied to the size of towns and cities, is based on historical and sociological factors: "In many small cities and villages, and to a lesser extent in medium sized places, Republicanism has remained the only approved vehicle for political action. Thus, to become a Democrat is not only to join a minority; it is to become a social deviant. Such a break with tradition, in small cities and villages, must be even harder for potential leaders than for ordinary voters."[40]

Epstein's description of and explanation for voting patterns in Wisconsin not only helps us understand what was happening in the post–World War II period, but also provides a baseline that can be used to examine voting patterns in the latter decades of the twentieth century. On the basis of Epstein's findings, it seems reasonable to predict that as urbanization has increased in the state, the Democrats' chances of winning the governorship (and other statewide races) would similarly increase.

This prediction was supported by subsequent historical evidence. The general pattern of voting behavior Epstein identifies remained in place through the end of the twentieth century. Democrats continued to get a much higher percentage of the vote in large urban areas, and Republicans continued to get the larger share in smaller cities and villages.

Three other factors also affected statewide voting patterns, however, in the years after Epstein completed his work. First, the percentage of the state's population in the rural areas declined, which had a negative effect on Republican candidates. Second, the rapid growth of suburbs, particularly to the north and west of Milwaukee, provided new support for the Republicans. Third, as more cities grew to populations of 50,000 or more, the Democratic share in those cities expanded.

These facts of political geography have been and continue to be the basic building blocks for strategy development used by candidates who are running for statewide offices. The rule of thumb is that Democratic candidates must get more than 60 percent of the general election vote in Milwaukee County and have similar strong showings in other counties with major urban areas—Racine County, Kenosha County, Dane County (Madison), and Douglas County (Duluth-Superior urban area)—in order to win. Republican candidates, on the other hand, need to get 60 percent or more of the vote in the suburban counties to the north and west of Milwaukee and they need "substantial pluralities in the Fox River Valley and other out-state counties in the southern half of the state."[41]

Figure 3 shows all seventy-two counties in Wisconsin and designates key Democratic and Republican strongholds. It should be noted that Brown County is included as part of the key Republican area of the Fox River Valley, even though the county contains the major urban area of Green Bay. The City of Green Bay had a population of more than 100,000 in 2000, but the combined total of the many small cities and villages in Brown County constitutes more than one-half of the county's population.

Gubernatorial Elections

The data for gubernatorial elections between 1970 and 2002 show that these propensities of political geography held in all nine elections. The data are displayed in tables 9 (1970–86) and 10 (1990–2002). Between 1970 and 2002 Democrats won the governorship four times: 1970, 1974, 1982, and 2002. Patrick Lucey won in 1970 and 1974, Anthony Earl won in 1982, and James Doyle won in 2002.

In all four elections, the Democratic candidate won 62 percent or more of the vote in the five key Democratic counties (Dane, Douglas, Kenosha, Milwaukee, and Racine). Lucey and Earl also won more than 46 percent of the vote in the two key Republican areas: the three counties located north and west of Milwaukee County (Ozaukee, Washington, and Waukesha),

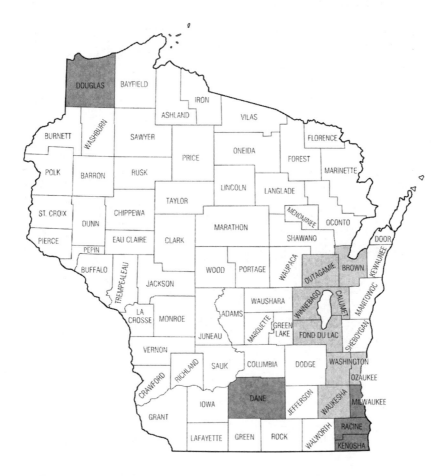

Democratic Counties
Republican Counties

Fig. 3. Key Democratic and Republican Counties in Statewide Elections

Table 9. Gubernatorial Election Data, 1970–1986

Election Year	1970		1974		1978		1982		1986	
Candidates (Dem/Rep.)	Lucey	Olsen	Lucey	Dyke	Schreiber	Dreyfus	Earl	Kohler	Earl	Thompson
Five Key Dem. Counties										
Dane	49,868	38,078	50,648	28,580	54,916	56,631	86,288	34,631	72,204	51,412
Douglas	10,608	4,255	9,275	2,611	8,494	5,504	11,160	3,961	9,063	4,582
Kenosha	22,136	11,944	16,708	8,698	18,976	13,518	24,315	11,015	19,293	12,385
Milwaukee	196,941	110,436	141,383	69,989	168,854	145,363	210,142	98,925	161,149	129,993
Racine	30,086	21,573	23,999	15,215	24,734	26,744	33,079	20,914	24,829	26,575
SUBTOTAL	309,639	186,286	242,013	125,093	275,974	247,760	364,984	169,446	290,538	224,947
Key Rep. Areas N&W of Milwaukee										
Ozaukee	6,830	10,184	8,791	8,393	8,160	17,145	9,852	13,147	8,807	16,973
Washington	9,686	9,636	9,799	7,382	9,951	15,654	12,114	13,505	9,755	16,757
Waukesha	32,969	36,828	33,630	28,030	32,138	62,062	43,128	47,860	36,389	62,387
SUBTOTAL	49,485	56,648	52,220	43,805	50,249	94,861	65,094	74,512	54,951	96,117
Fox River Valley										
Brown	23,869	21,395	21,323	20,591	23,146	31,610	31,375	26,605	27,000	34,762
Calumet	4,295	4,174	4,073	3,945	4,091	5,593	4,953	5,246	3,716	6,492
Fond du Lac	12,434	12,872	9,901	12,105	11,848	16,305	16,302	14,921	9,136	17,248
Outagamie	15,855	17,318	16,494	13,417	16,030	23,544	21,655	18,741	15,701	25,445
Winnebago	17,507	19,286	16,068	17,908	18,137	24,874	24,375	21,649	17,316	25,786
SUBTOTAL	73,960	75,045	67,859	67,966	73,252	101,926	98,660	87,162	72,869	109,733
KEY AREAS TOTAL	433,084	317,979	362,092	236,864	399,475	444,547	528,738	331,120	418,358	430,797
DEM. & REP. TOTALS	728,403	602,617	628,639	497,189	673,813	816,056	896,872	662,738	705,578	805,090

Source: "County Vote for Governor and Lieutenant Governor," Wisconsin Blue Book for 1971, 1975, 1979, 1983–1984, 1987–1988

and the five counties of the Fox River Valley (Brown, Calumet, Fond du Lac, Outagamie, and Winnebago). Doyle won more than 46 percent of the votes in the Fox River Valley, but he won only 39.9 percent in the suburban Milwaukee counties.

In 1970, for example, Patrick Lucey's vote total from the five Democratic counties was almost 123,353 more than Jack Olson's, the incumbent lieutenant governor and Republican candidate. Olson outpolled Lucey in the three Republican counties near Milwaukee, but he won by only 9,500 votes. In the five counties of the Fox River Valley, Olson won by only 1,085 votes. Lucey's vote total for the three areas combined exceeded Olsen's by 115,105. This total was very close to his statewide victory margin of 125,786.

The five Republican gubernatorial victories between 1970 and 2002 occurred in 1978, 1986, 1990, 1994 and 1998. Lee Dreyfus won in 1978, while Tommy Thompson won the other four elections. In all five of these victories, the Republican candidates won 60 percent or more of the vote in both of the key Republican areas, and they won at least 43 percent of the votes in the five key Democratic counties.

In the 1982 election, Dreyfus lost the five Democratic counties by only 28,218 votes, even though his opponent, Martin Schreiber, was from Milwaukee. Dreyfus won the counties north and west of Milwaukee by 44,612 votes; he won the Fox River Valley area by 18,708. The result was that Dreyfus had a net vote margin of 35,106 from the three key areas. The positive margin meant that Dreyfus's victory was almost assured, since Republican gubernatorial candidates tend to get more votes than Democratic candidates from the remainder of the state.

Likewise, when Thompson defeated Earl in the 1986 election, he received more than 63.7 percent of the vote in the three counties north and west of Milwaukee and 60.1 percent of the vote in the counties of the Fox River Valley. He also held Earl below a 60-percent combined margin in the five key Democratic counties. The net result for the three key areas was a margin for Thompson of 12,439 votes.

Thompson's statewide margin in the election was just under 100,000, which indicates that Earl needed to have a net vote margin of at least 100,000 from the three key areas in order to win. In his 1982 victory over Terry Kohler, Earl had a favorable margin from the three key areas of 192,000, almost double the total he needed to win in 1986.

This fact points to the most telling statistic of the pivotal 1986 election: the enormous decline in Governor Earl's Milwaukee County support. In the 1982 election, Earl's initial attempt for the governorship, the voters in the county overwhelmingly chose him. More than 534,000 voters turned out, and Earl got 68.3 percent of the vote. In 1986, however, the turnout was lower, and Earl got only 56.4 percent of the vote.

Earl's 1986 vote total in Milwaukee County was almost 49,993 votes fewer than it was in 1982, and Thompson's was 31,068 votes greater than the total for Terry Kohler, the 1982 Republican candidate. The combined swing in Milwaukee County was a net loss for Earl of more than 80,000 votes. What happened between 1982 and 1986 to bring about this change? Why did Earl's support fade so significantly while the Republican candidate's strength grew?

A local Milwaukee issue was the most important among several factors. Some voters were upset by Earl's decision to use a temporary income tax surcharge to help balance the budget, and Thompson's attack ads criticizing Earl for too much welfare spending probably had an effect, too. Governor Earl's decision to put a prison in Milwaukee, however, was the key, because it generated strong opposition from local citizens and elected officials. For many weeks this story was a headline in the area.

Earl's rationale was straightforward. He believed that it was best for the prisoners to be located near their families, and a substantial part of the state's prison population was from Milwaukee. One potential site for the prison was in a wealthy suburb just north of Milwaukee; another site was near the Milwaukee Brewers' baseball stadium. Strong local opposition to both sites, including the Brewers' threat to leave the state, ultimately forced Earl to abandon the idea. The damage to Earl's reputation and political capital, however, had been done.

After he defeated Earl in 1986, Tommy Thompson's electoral margins grew in 1990 and 1994. This is a testimony to Thompson's incumbency, his strengths, and to the relative weakness of the opposition candidates. Neither Loftus, the 1990 challenger, nor Chvala, the 1994 challenger, had won a statewide race, and neither was well known statewide. In addition, Thompson worked hard during his time as governor to build the Republican Party and public support, particularly in the Milwaukee area.

Thompson, it may be noted, also enjoyed traveling and campaigning, and he had a substantial advantage in the size of his campaign war chest for both elections. Among the most impressive facts about the 1990 and 1994 elections is that Thompson outpolled Loftus in the five key Democratic counties by almost 24,000 votes, and he outpolled Chvala in these counties by more than 128,000 votes.

The data for the 1990 and 1994 gubernatorial elections are shown in table 10, as are the data for the 1998 and 2002 elections.

The data for the 1998 election show that Thompson won the election handily, but there are some other interesting patterns too. Perhaps the most important factor for the future was the resurgence of Democratic strength in the five counties key to Democratic success. Although Thompson won the combined vote total for the third time, his margin was only 10,000 votes. Given the fact that Thompson's Democratic challenger, Ed Garvey, was not well known, had not won a statewide office, and had only modest financial support, this could be considered a successful outcome for Democrats. Thompson won the two key Republican areas by large margins, as he had in the two previous elections, but his statewide margin was smaller than it was in 1994.

With Thompson out of the gubernatorial contest in 2002, and with a Democratic candidate who had won a statewide race for attorney general, Democrats had their best chance of winning the governorship since 1986. It is worth noting that Democrat James Doyle's victory contained the geographic elements required to win. Doyle's vote total in the five key Democratic counties exceeded incumbent Governor Scott McCallum's total by 124,568. That gave Doyle enough votes to overcome the 85,546 vote margin McCallum had in the two key Republican areas. Doyle's net vote advantage from the three key areas was approximately 40,000, a figure that constituted almost 60 percent of his total statewide advantage of 65,736.

Legislative Elections

These facts of political geography also help an observer of Wisconsin politics and elections to understand why Democratic candidates for the legislature are more likely to win in Milwaukee or Madison than are Republicans. An understanding of the state's political geography also provides a basis for understanding why Republican candidates are more likely to win in districts that are principally made up of small towns and villages.

Wisconsin's political geography also provides a basis for understanding and making predictions about state policymaking. Democratic legislators from Milwaukee are likely to vote in blocs and vote in ways that are similar to Democratic legislators from Racine and Kenosha counties. In the struggle over the distribution of shared taxes or school aids, to take one example, these legislators are likely to push for the distribution of state funds on the

Table 10. Gubernatorial Election Data, 1990–2002

Election Year Candidates (Dem/Rep.)	1990		1994		1998		2002	
	Loftus	Thompson	Chavala	Thompson	Garvey	Thompson	Doyle	McCallum
Five Key Dem. Counties								
Dane	66,638	55,998	63,545	71,315	86,234	72,693	97,084	41,810
Douglas	6,140	7,898	4,655	7,921	6,550	5,905	9,291	4,153
Kenosha	12,997	14,750	14,264	24,618	17,011	28,128	21,922	14,833
Milwaukee	108,812	128,835	90,703	176,631	140,666	145,010	150,877	95,015
Racine	18,243	29,318	17,326	38,302	25,803	34,337	27,859	26,654
SUBTOTAL	212,830	236,799	190,493	318,787	276,264	286,073	307,033	182,465
Key Rep. Areas N&W of Milwaukee								
Ozaukee	5,193	16,078	4,765	23,041	7,283	23,716	10,542	20,486
Washington	6,662	15,983	6,109	25,436	9,164	29,102	11,480	25,592
Waukesha	24,679	61,002	21,428	92,484	32,384	98,555	42,327	88,661
SUBTOTAL	36,534	93,063	32,302	140,961	48,831	151,373	64,349	134,739
Fox River Valley								
Brown	26,143	35,561	21,120	42,299	27,302	47,529	29,949	32,368
Calumet	3,151	6,109	2,745	7,706	3,873	9,153	5,528	6,844
Fond du Lac	7,992	16,043	6,480	19,322	7,685	19,682	10,394	17,653
Outagamie	15,010	27,500	12,208	31,036	17,500	32,761	21,158	23,695
Winnebago	14,187	25,972	10,641	30,652	16,436	33,496	22,425	23,110
SUBTOTAL	66,483	111,185	53,194	131,015	72,796	142,621	89,454	103,670
KEY AREAS TOTAL	315,847	441,047	275,989	590,763	397,891	580,067	460,836	420,874
DEM. & REP. TOTALS	576,280	802,321	482,850	1,051,326	548,481	851,108	800,515	734,779

Source: "County Vote for Governor and Lieutenant Governor," *Wisconsin Blue Book* for 1991–1992, 1995–1996, 1999–2000, 2003–2004

basis of need, as defined by the relative property wealth of each district or municipality.

On the other hand, Republican legislators from wealthy suburbs and small cities are more likely to push for distribution of state funds on the basis of origin rather than need. Additionally, these legislators will also try to limit the amount of money in both the shared tax fund and the school aid fund that is redistributed, or set aside for distribution on the basis of property tax wealth or need. The history of the political struggle over these two funds, shared taxes and school aids, shows a very high correspondence to the patterns outlined here.

Of course, voting patterns and policymaking in Wisconsin can also be explained on the basis of factors other than geography and population size. Educational attainment and income, as well as employment and race, can be used to explain voting patterns and make predictions about policy outcomes. These socioeconomic factors can be used in the development of campaign strategy, and they can also be used to make predictions about who will win election contests in specific legislative districts, congressional districts, and even in statewide contests. In sum, studies of voting behavior not only help us understand a state's politics, but also its public policy.

CHAPTER EIGHT

The State Budget and the Budgetary Process

The idea that the budget should be an instrument of policy and control for the governor was part of the efficiency and reform movement of the 1960s.

Anderson, Penniman, and Weidner, *State and Local Governments*, 1968

Actually creating a budget—not just talking about one—is the hardest thing I have ever done. There are literally thousands of decisions that must be made.

Tommy Thompson, *Power to the People*, 1996

A state's budget usually reflects the priorities of its citizens and elected officials, and Wisconsin's Progressive tradition is clearly visible in the amount of money the state spends, the way it spends the money, and in the way it distributes tax burdens. The state's comparatively high level of spending reflects a long-standing commitment to an active governmental role in society, and the large shares of the state budget spent on local government, social welfare, and higher education reflect their special standing. In making tax policy decisions Wisconsin's elected officials have traditionally considered fairness, or ability to pay, to be a guiding principle. While a number of decisions made during the 1980s and 1990s reduced tax progressivity somewhat, Wisconsin's state-local tax system remains among the fairest in the country.[1]

In this chapter, Wisconsin's budget and budgetary process are described and analyzed. The chapter begins with definitions of key terms and a brief comparison of Wisconsin's budget and budgetary process to those of other states. Then the main participants in the process, factors that influence the level of conflict during the process, and factors that shape the outcomes of the process are identified. Next, the structure of the state budget is examined, with emphasis placed on the major sources of revenue and the ten largest areas of state spending. The chapter concludes with a brief discussion of the big budget deficits state officials faced at the beginning of the twenty-first century.

A "budget" is a document that contains estimates of revenues and expenditures for a given period of time. All three parts—document, estimates of revenues and expenditures, and given period of time—of this definition are key to understanding what a budget is.

Wisconsin's budget has dozens of revenue sources and hundreds of expenditure categories. The budget covers a two-year period of time, and thus it is called a "biennial" budget.[2] Each fiscal year of the biennial budget begins on July 1 and ends on June 30.[3]

The budgetary process consists of three basic steps or parts: development, implementation, and audit. Most academic discussion of the budgetary process is focused on budget development, the first stage of the budgetary process. In turn, budget development is usually subdivided into several additional components, which are examined in this chapter.

The process of putting together a state budget involves hundreds of people, and it often has complicated rules. One of the most important rules in Wisconsin, as well as in most other states, is that the state must end the fiscal year with a balanced budget. Consequently, if an economic downturn during the first or second year of the budget's implementation causes state revenues to fall below predicted levels, the governor, agency secretaries, and state legislators may have to reduce spending in order to avoid a budget deficit.

On the other hand, better than expected economic conditions may mean that state revenue estimates can be revised upward during the fiscal year. If spending remains within estimated amounts but revenues exceed estimated amounts, the state could end the fiscal year with a surplus. The expected surplus could be set aside for use in the next fiscal year, put into a Rainy Day Fund, or returned to taxpayers through a one-time tax rebate.

Wisconsin's Budget and Budgetary
Process Compared to Other States

In some very important ways Wisconsin's budget and budgetary process is quite different from the process used in other states.[4] In many states, the processes of creating or modifying legislation are separate from the processes of appropriating money and making decisions about taxes and other revenues.[5] The budget bill, in other words, is handled separately from all other significant bills.

In Wisconsin, however, the budget bill is the central document and the budgetary process is the central vehicle through which existing policy is modified and new policy is made. By statute, no legislation that has an estimated cost of more than $100,000 may be passed before the budget is approved. Furthermore, as soon as the legislature completes its work on the budget it must adjourn.[6]

The highly centralized nature of policy development in Wisconsin has both benefits and limitations. One benefit is the fact that the attention of policymakers is sharply focused on the development of the state budget. Not surprisingly, the attention of those outside of the State Capitol, including interest groups and the press, is also focused on the budgetary process. Thus the budget process is a highly political exercise.[7]

EXECUTIVE BUDGET RECOMMENDATIONS

The last Tuesday in January of every even year is perhaps the most important day in the Wisconsin governmental calendar. On this day, according to statute, the governor must deliver the "Budget Message" to the new session of the Wisconsin Legislature.[8] For the past thirty years governors have presented their budget messages in the Assembly Chamber to a joint session of the legislature. It is a moment much anticipated by legislators, state employees, interest groups, and the press because the Budget Message reveals the governor's view of how much money the state should raise and spend for the two-year budget period. The governor's policy priorities are also outlined in the Budget Message.

With the Budget Message the governor presents written copies of the *State Budget Report* and the biennial budget bill to the legislature. At the governor's request, the budget bill is then introduced for consideration by the Joint Finance Committee of the legislature. This step marks the passage of principal decision-making responsibility from the executive branch to the legislative branch and the midpoint in the twelve- to eighteen-month process of constructing the state budget. Six to nine months of intense activity in the executive branch has preceded this moment, and another six to nine months of activity, largely in the legislative branch, will follow it.

GOVERNMENTAL AND NONGOVERNMENTAL ACTORS IN THE BUDGETARY PROCESS

The governor and state legislators are the final decision-makers in the budgetary process, but many other governmental actors are involved in the process.[9] More than half of those participants are drawn from the eighteen departments and thirteen agencies of the executive branch. The departmental and agency participants include the secretaries, division directors, and members of the budget staffs.

The most visible and important participants in this process from the executive branch work in the Department of Administration, the Department of Revenue, and the Office of the Governor. From the Department of Administration, those involved are the secretary, the budget director, and the analysts in the State Budget Office. In the Department of Revenue, the secretary, the analysts who develop the revenue estimates, and the policy analysts who evaluate proposals for changes in tax laws are the key participants. The governor and senior staff members are the principal actors from the Office of the Governor.

In the legislative branch, the main institutional participants include the Joint Finance Committee, the Legislative Fiscal Bureau, and the Legislative Audit Bureau. The co-chairs and members of the Joint Finance Committee are the most visible of the actors from the legislative branch. The director of the Legislative Fiscal Bureau and the analysts who work in that bureau do most of the technical work on the legislative side of the aisle. The director of the Audit Bureau and the analysts in the organization are also important participants.

The principal nongovernmental participants in the state budgetary process include lobbyists for interest groups, the heads and members of interest groups and organizations, members of the press or media, and individual citizens; lobbyists and members of the media are generally the most important. During the 1980s and 1990s the number and influence of lobbyists grew steadily. Legislators' need for money to support their election campaigns has probably been the primary reason for this development. The number and influence of members of the press also grew during the 1980s and

1990s. Indeed changes in technology, including development of the small, portable minicamera, have made television coverage more immediate and more influential in the budget deliberations.

BUDGET DEVELOPMENT

While the full budgetary process (development, implementation, and audit) usually extends over thirty-six to forty-eight months in Wisconsin, the development phase of the process usually takes only twelve to eighteen months to complete. The budget-development phase can be subdivided into six steps:

- initial revenue estimates
- governor/budget office instructions to the agencies
- agency requests
- executive review and recommendation
- legislative review and appropriation, and
- executive signature or veto

The budget-development process in Wisconsin begins with an initial estimate of revenues expected for the biennium. This estimate is generated by the Department of Revenue, and the governor and the State Budget Office use it to develop a budget strategy. After the budget strategy is developed, the State Budget Office prepares instructions for the executive branch agencies and delivers them to the agency secretaries.

For example, if revenues are expected to grow by 5 percent over the biennium, agencies may be allowed to ask for increases of up to 4 percent of their base budgets. Or, if revenues are expected to stay flat the State Budget Office might instruct agencies to submit requests that are 95 percent or 98 percent of their existing base budget. It is also possible that agencies will be instructed to submit requests that are below their existing base budgets even when revenues are expected to grow substantially during the biennium.

It is worth noting that this was the scenario that happened repeatedly in Wisconsin under Governor Tommy Thompson (1986–2001).[10] It also occurred under some of Thompson's predecessors, including Governor Patrick Lucey during the 1970s. This scenario usually occurs when the governor decides to use all of the estimated new revenue and some of the state's existing expenditures to fund a new program or policy initiative with a big price tag. Governor Tommy Thompson's school-aid initiative is a classic example.

Agency Requests

The next stage in the budget-development process is referred to as the "agency-request" stage. Traditionally, this is the point at which the department secretaries request the funding needed to implement the programs and laws assigned to their agencies. Agency staff have data about the costs of existing programs as well as the expertise necessary to determine how much it will cost to continue those programs in the upcoming biennium. This is the principal rationale for giving agency secretaries the opportunity to define their budget "needs."

In addition to the data they have and their expertise, however, agency staff may also be "advocates" for the programs they administer. That is to say, their calculation of budget "needs" may be designed to provide maximum, rather than minimum, support for program activities. Of course agency staff are often pressured by the interest groups that benefit from these programs to expand or improve them.

Typically, each division in an executive branch agency prepares a budget request and submits the request to the departmental budget office. With the support of the departmental budget office, the secretary will construct a departmental request. In historical terms, Wisconsin's budget documents show that departmental secretaries usually ask for an incremental increase to their "base budget." During the past thirty years, however, and particularly under Governor Thompson, many agency secretaries were not given the opportunity to request an increase in their base budgets.

If an agency secretary is allowed to request new funds, the size of the "increment" requested depends on a number of factors. Some of these factors are tied to the programs themselves, such as the need to adequately fund programs that are underfunded or programs that are just beginning. Other factors may be primarily political, such as the nature of the relationship between the departmental secretary and the governor, the agency's standing with the legislature, and the influence of the interest groups that support the agency and its programs. Once completed, the agency or department request is forwarded to the State Budget Office for review.

Executive Review and Recommendation

The State Budget Office has the role of guardian of the state treasury, and the director and analysts in the office are likely to be skeptical of agency requests. Indeed, even when agencies are allowed to request increases above their base budgets, the agency requests may be trimmed substantially during the State Budget Office review. The extent of the trimming is dependent on many variables, not least among them the amount of new revenues forecast for the biennium.

Generally speaking, the larger the size of the forecasted increase in revenues, the more flexible the budget office is likely to be in granting requests for new funds. Other factors that come into play include the state budget director's calculation of the way an agency's request will be treated by the governor and the legislature, and the budget analyst's assessment of a program or a department's need for additional money.

After the review of agency requests is completed and a government-wide spending plan is matched with estimated revenues, budget recommendations are forwarded to the governor. The State Budget Office's recommendations are reviewed by the governor and his or her staff, and initial decisions are made. If an agency request that is known to have the strong backing of the departmental secretary is rejected, that secretary may be invited to the Office of the Governor to make the case for the funding request. Whether such an invitation is offered may depend on whether the departmental secretary is an appointee of the governor. There is no formal requirement for such an agency "appeals process," but most governors have used a process of this type since at least the early 1970s.

After the agency appeals process is complete, the State Budget Office recalculates total expenditure requests and compares them to estimated revenues. Should estimated expenditures exceed estimated revenues, the governor may need to make some additional reductions in agency requests— no governor wants to submit a budget that is not in balance to the legislature. When the final reconciliation of expenditures and revenues is finished, the State Budget Office develops the Executive Budget document and oversees the development of the budget bill. The governor's staff then works with the State Budget Office and other agencies to prepare the Budget Message.

Legislative Review and Appropriation

After the governor's recommendations are forwarded to the legislature, the members of the Joint Finance Committee and the Legislative Fiscal Bureau take center stage. The Joint Finance Committee includes sixteen legislators, eight from the senate and eight from the assembly. The committee is responsible for making decisions about both the revenue and expenditure sides of the budget, but the expenditure side is likely to get much more attention. The Joint Finance Committee and the two legislative houses operate with time constraints: the fiscal year ends on June 30.

While many in government prefer to begin the new fiscal year with a new budget in effect, the legislative review and appropriation phase usually runs into July or August. In years when budget issues have been particularly contentious—such as 1973, 1975, and more recently in 1995 and 1999—this phase has continued into September and October. In order to keep state programs and the executive branch agencies functioning in the new fiscal year, the legislature and the governor have to extend the spending authority granted in the previous fiscal year's budget or they must formulate an alternative approach. The preferred and most expedient route is a continuing resolution.

The Joint Finance Committee is supported in its work by the Legislative Fiscal Bureau. The bureau's role in support of the committee is similar to the role the State Budget Office plays for the governor. The analysts in the Legislative Fiscal Bureau attempt to evaluate the merits of the governor's recommendations, and the director of the Legislative Fiscal Bureau has to consider the overall package of tax and expenditure recommendations. In one respect, however, the role of the Legislative Fiscal Bureau is more complicated and more difficult than that of its executive branch counterpart. It must respond to sixteen bosses on the Joint Finance Committee, and then respond to all 132 legislators when each house considers the bill recommended by the Joint Finance Committee. The State Budget Office, by contrast, only has to serve the governor.

The Joint Finance Committee holds hearings on the governor's recommendations and then begins deliberations. Lobbyists, citizens, and sometimes managers from the executive branch departments testify at these hearings. Many lobbyists also have direct access to individual committee members. This kind of access is highly prized by private sector organizations and interest groups, and many of these organizations and groups are willing to pay substantial amounts of money in the form of election campaign contributions to get it.

After the Joint Finance Committee completes its work, the newly revised budget bill is considered by each house of the legislature. If the senate and the assembly pass different versions of the budget bill, which they usually do, a conference committee is required to reconcile the differences. Once it has been passed by the legislature, the budget bill is sent to the governor for his signature.

Executive Signature or Veto

Upon receipt, the governor must either sign or veto the budget bill. Since Wisconsin's governor has partial-veto power, a veto of the whole bill is highly unlikely. The partial veto gives a governor the power to select specific parts of the bill for veto while still signing the bill itself. As was noted in chapter 2, the question of whether there are any limits to what the governor can do with the partial veto was the subject of intense political controversy during the latter half of the 1980s and the 1990s. Limits to the partial veto were established during that period of time through constitutional amendment and judicial decision making. Nevertheless the partial veto remains a formidable weapon in the governor's arsenal.

BUDGET IMPLEMENTATION AND AUDIT

The implementation phase of the budget cycle officially begins once the budget bill has been signed by the governor. Departmental secretaries, top-level managers, and the civil servants in the executive branch agencies or departments take center stage during this phase. The appropriations contained in the budget bill establish the resource base within which these managers must work.

Although politicians and critics of government activity like to complain that bureaucrats have more resources than they need, chronic underfunding of programs may be just as common as overfunding. Despite their role in establishing these resource constraints, however, legislators and governors may simply assume that it is up to managers and employees of the agencies to make sure that the programs are fully and effectively implemented. This is sometimes an assumption of convenience, however, rather than a presumption rooted on a factual basis.

The final phase of the budgetary process is the audit, which determines whether the money spent by the executive branch departments was spent properly and efficiently. Generally speaking, this phase of the budgetary cycle begins after the end of the fiscal year covered by the current budget. Audits, however, can be conducted any time during the year, or even some years after the fiscal year is complete. Since the 1980s, the key agency in this phase of the budget cycle has been the Legislative Audit Bureau.

Because the implementation stage of the budgetary process begins after the budget is signed and the audit stage usually begins in the following fiscal year, the full budgetary cycle usually runs for thirty-six to forty-eight months.

This means that elements of the budgetary process from one fiscal year may overlap with other fiscal years. The audit stage for the FY 2002 budget may be underway in fiscal year 2003, at the same time the implementation phase for FY 2003 is underway and agency requests for FY 2004 and FY 2005 are being prepared. This overlap adds to the complexity of a process that is difficult to follow and often arduous to oversee in any single budgetary year.

FACTORS THAT AFFECT BUDGET
DEVELOPMENT AND BUDGETARY OUTCOMES

There are a number of factors that can have a significant effect on the way the budget development process in Wisconsin, as well as in other states, is conducted. Specifically, these factors can affect the level of conflict involved in the process, the length of time needed to complete the process, and the final results. Factors can include: the condition of the national, regional, and state economies; partisan control of the legislature; the policy preferences of governors and legislators; the influence of particular interest groups; decisions made by other levels of government, including the courts; and the budget format used in the state.

In any given year, the condition of the national, regional, and state economies is likely to be the most important factor that determines the level of conflict, the length of time needed to complete the budget deliberations, and the outcomes of those deliberations.[11] The severe national recession that officially began in January of 1980 and continued through November of 1982 had a significant impact on budget decision making in most states. In the Midwest, where the effects of the national recession were particularly harsh, Wisconsin, Michigan, Iowa, and other states faced large gaps between expenditure requests and the level of estimated revenues.

The governors and legislators in those states faced a set of very difficult decisions. Their principal courses of action were to raise taxes, cut expenditures, or pursue some combination of the two. Additional options sometimes employed to deal with prospective or emerging budget deficits include engaging in "creative bookkeeping," such as pushing school aids or other large payments forward into the next fiscal year, or budget redefinition, where certain types of expenditures are moved "off-budget."

In Wisconsin, the Dreyfus administration adopted a strategy for the 1980–82 biennial budget that has been described by one scholar as "toughing it out."[12] Spending was cut and state payments to schools and local governments were pushed forward into future fiscal years. Through this combination of actions, the budget appeared to be balanced. This approach to the state's fiscal problems resulted, however, in the accumulation of a very large state deficit that was left for Governor Anthony Earl to deal with after he took office on January 1, 1982.

When governors and legislators in Wisconsin and other states are faced with prospective budget deficits, the level of conflict in the budgetary process is likely to be high, the negotiations lengthy, and the results may include significant reductions in state programs. In contrast, during periods of steady economic growth state decision-makers may be able to hand out incremental increases in expenditures without raising taxes. This type of incremental budgetary process is more likely to proceed smoothly, to be completed on time, and to result in modest increases in spending rates.

The political party or partisan lineup in the legislature can also have a significant effect on the state budgetary process and its outcomes. For example, if the governor is a Republican, and both houses of the legislature are controlled by the Democratic Party, the level of conflict might be high, and the process might be very lengthy. If the governor's party controls one or both legislative chambers, the budgetary process will probably proceed more smoothly and quickly.

The policy preferences of the governor and legislative leaders can also contribute to the level of conflict in a budgetary process. Conflict is likely to be pronounced when governors attempt to make significant changes in tax or expenditure policy. Such changes inevitably affect the distribution of benefits and burdens in the state, and the potential losers are likely to mobilize to stop the change. The stakes in these battles are particularly high when one party controls the governor's office and the other party controls one or both houses of the legislature.

Examples of these circumstances include, but are not limited to, the 1971–73 and 1995–97 budget processes. In his 1971–73 budget, Democratic governor Patrick Lucey proposed significant changes in tax and expenditure policies at a time when Republicans controlled the state senate. Likewise, Republican Tommy Thompson's 1995–97 budget proposals included significant tax and expenditures changes at a time when Democrats controlled the senate. (These two scenarios are described in some detail in chapters 9 and 11.) It is noteworthy that a high degree of conflict during the budgetary process in Wisconsin usually means that the process will extend beyond the summer and into the fall. As a result, the budget-development process may not be completed until several months into the new fiscal year.

A fourth factor that plays a key role in budgetary decision making is the influence of interest groups or individual corporations; business groups tend to have more influence than do other groups. Manufacturing companies, insurance companies, banks, and telecommunications companies are all represented by high-profile lobbyists. Private sector companies may have their own agendas, and they may hire lobbyists to represent their specific interests. For private sector corporations, the tax side of the budget may be as important, or even more important, than the expenditure side.

Decisions made by the national government and the courts can also have a significant effect on the budget and budgetary process. As part of the Omnibus Reconciliation Act of 1981, for example, grants to states and local governments were cut back sharply in a number of areas, especially in social services.[13] Consequently, state decision-makers had to decide whether to find the lost money elsewhere or to scale back social services programs.

Most states elected to scale back social services, but some attempted to fill the void with their own resources. Wisconsin, under Democratic Governor Anthony Earl (1982–86), sustained and even expanded its support for social services. One of Earl's key initiatives, however, was an expansion of efforts to move AFDC recipients off of the welfare rolls through job-training programs.

Court decisions can also force states to put more money into specific programs or functional areas. Overcrowding in prisons has led to court demands for the reduction of prison populations or the construction of new facilities. For many legislators, neither option is attractive, so the process of deciding what to do can be very difficult, indeed. It is worth noting that Wisconsin's budget has not, to this point, been affected by court decisions of this type.

One additional factor that may have an effect on the budgetary process is the budget format used in a state. The line-item, program, and organizational-unit formats each require and present different kinds of information, and they emphasize different values. Since budgetary deliberations tend to focus on the information provided to decision-makers, the decision-making processes and the outcomes of that process are likely to vary with the type of format used. In line-item formats, the focus tends to be on the details of departmental expenditures, rather than on program goals or achievements.

In Wisconsin, a program format is used for budgetary decision making. Data is presented in a format that provides information about programs within executive branch agencies, so the focus tends to be on program objectives and achievements.

Academic discussions of budgeting often begin and end with the budgetary process. While it is important to understand this process, it is only one of the elements needed to understand state budgeting. Other critical aspects that must be understood are the size, structure, and content of the state budget. Wisconsin's FY 2001–3 budget contained almost $60 billion in estimated revenues and expenditures. In order to report on the structure and content of this biennial budget, it is helpful to break the biennial budget into annual budgets and then to look at the sources and uses of revenue for a single fiscal year. In this case, FY 2003, the second year of the 2001–3 biennial budget will be used.

The first thing a student of the Wisconsin budget discovers through examining the sources of state revenue is that there are two budgets contained within the state budget: the general purpose revenue budget and the operating budget.[14]

General Purpose Revenue and the GPR Budget

The General Purpose Revenue (GPR) budget is the main focus of executive and legislative decision making during the state budgetary process. More specifically, the revenue and appropriation decision items that are the focus of attention for both the governor and the legislature fall within the GPR budget. The principal source of funds for the GPR budget is state taxes that are not earmarked. These taxes include: the individual income tax; sales and use tax; excise tax; corporate franchise and income tax; inheritance, gift, and estate taxes; public utility taxes; and miscellaneous taxes. Department revenue makes up the only other important source of revenue for the GPR budget.

In FY 2003, the GPR budget consisted of almost $10.2 billion in tax revenue. The breakdown of the tax collections is shown in figure 4. It may be pointed out that more than one-half of the state tax revenue in the GPR budget comes from the individual income tax.

Operating Budget Revenue and the Operating Budget

The GPR budget is part of the larger operating budget. Operating budget revenue consists of the general purpose revenues and the program revenues that are deposited in the General Fund. The 2003 State of Wisconsin Annual Fiscal Report shows that program revenue, which consists primarily of In-

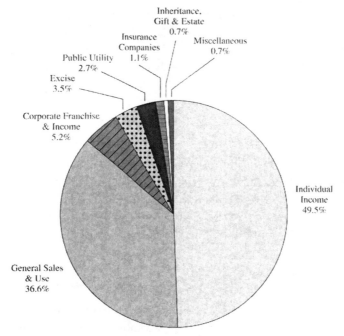

Fig. 4. Sources of Fiscal Year 2003 General Purpose Revenue (State Taxes) (*Source: 2003 State of Wisconsin Annual Fiscal Report*, Wisconsin Department of Administration)

tergovernmental Revenue ($6.7 billion) and Charges for Goods and Services ($2.0 billion), was $10.1 billion. Thus program revenue was only slightly smaller than general purpose revenue ($10.6 billion). Also included in the operating budget are the Transportation Fund ($2.2 billion), Conservation Fund (.2 billion), and some funds in the "other" category, including bonds and notes. In short, the operating budget consists of all state funds except Pension and Retirement Funds and Trust and Agency Funds. Operating budget revenue for FY 2003 totaled $25.9 billion; almost 2.5 times the amount of general purpose revenue.[15]

Pension Contributions and Investment Income and Trust and Agency Funds

Pension contributions made by state employees and the income generated from these pension funds are statutorily excluded from the operating budget. In FY 2003, revenues from these sources totaled $4.1 billion.[16] Trust and Agency Funds, the other revenue sources excluded from the operating budget, consist of funds that are deposited into the state treasury but do not belong to the state. Examples include the College Saving Program Trust, Lottery, Patients Compensation Fund, Veterans Mortgage Repayment, and University Trust Principal and Income. Trust and Agency revenue in FY 2003 was $2.2 billion.

All State Revenues (All Sources)

When the streams of revenue that are not included in the operating budget are added to operating budget revenue, we discover that total state revenue for FY 2003 was $31.3 billion. Of this total, state tax revenue made up 36.2 percent; nontax revenue made up 63.8 percent.[17] Even for those who know something about budgeting, the relatively small percentage that state taxes make up of total state revenue in Wisconsin's budget may be a bit of a surprise.

Budget Decision Making and the GPR Budget

Why is the focus of executive and legislative decision making on the GPR budget, when it makes up less than one-half the total of the operating budget? The answer is simple: general purpose revenue can be spent for any purpose the governor and legislature desire, while the other revenues in the operating budget are earmarked for specific expenditures. In other words, the uses of general purpose revenue are discretionary, while the uses of most other revenues are nondiscretionary.

Two examples may be useful to illustrate the point. In FY 2003 approximately $7.5 billion, or 27.4 percent of revenues in the operating budget, were monies from the national government.[18] Most of this money must be used for purposes determined by the national government. Thus, neither the governor nor the legislature can decide to use transportation funds for environmental protection or social service funds for road building.

Likewise, revenues from specific bond funds are earmarked for specific building (capital) projects. The State Building Commission makes decisions about what these building projects will be, and the decisions are made in a process that is independent of the state budgetary process. The commission members include the governor and members of the legislative leadership. There is consequently no need for additional scrutiny of these decisions, even though the results of the State Building Commission's decisions are formally recorded in the state budget bill.

In summary, we can say that by examining state revenues, a student of Wisconsin's budgetary process discovers that the state budget actually contains two budgets, the GPR budget and the operating budget, and that the GPR budget is the focus of decision making during the budgetary process because the revenues are discretionary.

USES OF STATE REVENUES (EXPENDITURES)

By looking at the uses of state revenues or at state expenditures, we not only learn more about state budgeting but also about the principal activities of Wisconsin state government. To illustrate, although there are hundreds of expenditure accounts in the GPR budget, most of the revenue in the GPR budget was used for eleven major programs during the 1970s and 1980s.[19] These programs were: School Aids; the University of Wisconsin System; Medical Assistance; Corrections; Individual Property Tax Credits; Shared Revenue; Community Aids; Wisconsin Works; Income Maintenance; Vocational, Technical, and Adult Education (VTAE) Aids; and Environmental Aids. Indeed, it is notable that the budgets submitted by five governors from both political parties during the period from FY 1977 through FY 1990 proposed spending between eighty-eight and ninety cents of every GPR budget dollar on these eleven programs.

Decisions made by the Thompson administration and the Wisconsin legislature during the 1990s resulted in changes in the names and content of some of these eleven expenditure programs. Nevertheless, 85 percent of state expenditures were still funneled through the ten largest programs in the FY 1999 GPR budget; for FY 2003 the figure was 84 percent.[20] Data on these ten programs in FY 2003 are listed in table 11.

School Aids, the single largest expenditure in the FY 2003 GPR budget, is state revenue that is sent to school districts. "Approximately 88 percent of school aids are general aids, distributed by a formula designed to equalize each school district's property tax base per student, and aids to support Milwaukee County's voluntary desegregation program."[21] The remaining 12 percent are categorical aids.

Expenditures for the University of Wisconsin System, with its twenty-six campuses and 145,000 students, ranked second in the use of FY 2003 GPR revenues. Medical Assistance, the third-largest GPR expenditure in FY 2003, is money that goes directly to individuals who qualify for this program. These funds constitute the state's share of the national government program

Table 11.   Top Ten Programs in General Purpose Revenue Budget Expenditures,
Fiscal Year 2003

	$ in millions	Percentage of GPR Budget
School Aids	4,756.1	43.1
University of Wisconsin System	1,063.8	9.6
Medical Assistance	1,038.6	9.4
Corrections & Related	852.9	7.7
Property Tax Credits	469.3	4.3
Shared Revenue	430.9*	3.9
Community Aids	180.9	1.6
Property Tax Relief to Individuals	159.5	1.4
Wisconsin Works	131.1	1.2
Supplemental Security Income	128.3	1.2
All others	1,821.2	16.5
SUBTOTAL	11,032.6	100.0

*Reflects use of $598.5 million of proceeds from securitization of tobacco settlement revenues to replace GPR for shared revenue.

Source: 2003 State of Wisconsin Annual Fiscal Report, Wisconsin Department of Administration

designed to provide health care to low-income families and individuals. The fourth-ranked program is Corrections. Expenditures in this program are used to run the state prison system and for related purposes. Individual Property Tax Credits is the fifth-ranked program. Through this program, state funds are sent to local governments for the purpose of reducing property taxes. These funds are literally shown as credits (reductions) on the local government property tax bill sent to each property taxpayer.

Shared Revenue, the sixth-largest use of GPR in FY 2003, had traditionally been the second-largest GPR expenditure program, but the state's severe budget problems in the 2001–3 biennial budget significantly affected its status. In FY 2003, only $430.9 million of GPR was used for Shared Revenue, even though a total of more than $1 billion actually flowed through this account. The remaining $598.5 million in FY 2003 was money generated through the securitization of tobacco settlement revenue.[22] The Shared Revenue appropriation consists of state-collected revenues that state government sends to counties and municipalities. The Shared Revenue funds can be used as the local governments want to use them.

Community Aids, the seventh-largest GPR program in FY 2003, are state expenditures that go directly to local governments to fund various human services programs. Wisconsin Works is the eighth-largest GPR expenditure in the FY 2003 budget; it consists of funds used to provide assistance to welfare recipients or former welfare recipients in the form of training, transportation, and day care. Wisconsin Works is a work-based program designed to help families achieve self-sufficiency.

Income Maintenance, administered through Supplemental Security Income, the ninth-largest expenditure in the FY 2003 budget, is the state's share of the national government program for people who are aged, blind, or disabled. The tenth- and eleventh-largest GPR expenditures are VTAE Aids and Environmental Aids, respectively, and these are followed by a host of smaller accounts that traverse the entire spectrum of state governmental administration.

Uses of Revenue in the Operating Budget

As in the GPR budget, the principal uses of revenue in the operating budget can be found in a relatively small number of programs. Approximately 68 percent of the FY 2003 operating budget revenue was used for the ten largest expenditure programs. Seven of the ten were included in the list of the top ten GPR programs; three were not part of that list. The top ten programs in the operating budget are listed in table 12.

The relative rankings of these ten programs underscore the differences between the GPR and operating budgets. As noted earlier in this chapter, the operating budget contains a larger and more diverse set of revenues. Nevertheless, as in the GPR budget, the principal use of revenue in the FY 2003 operating budget is for School Aids. It is also worth noting that the expenditure figure for School Aids is larger than it was in the GPR budget, as nearly $360 million of state and federal program revenues were added to the GPR total.

The second-largest use of revenues in the operating budget is for Medical Assistance. The expenditure amount for Medical Assistance in the operating budget is 3.6 times the amount in the GPR budget.[23] The difference in the amount spent in the two budgets largely reflects the addition of revenue from the national government to state Medical Assistance program expenditures.

The University of Wisconsin System uses or spends the third-largest amount of revenue in the operating budget.[24] It should be noted that the University of Wisconsin System expenditures in the operating budget are more than three times their size in the GPR budget. Or, to put it in a different context, GPR is the source of only one-third of the revenue for University of Wisconsin System expenditures in the operating budget; the sources of the other two-thirds include: tuition paid by students in the University of

Table 12. Top Ten Programs in Operating Budget Expenditures, Fiscal Year 2003

	$ in millions	Percentage of GPR Budget
School Aids	5,115.5	19.7
Medical Assistance	3,756.9	14.5
University of Wisconsin System	3,269.7	12.6
Highway Improvement/ Maintenance	1,218.4	4.7
Shared Revenue	1,029.4	4.0
Corrections	1,004.3	3.9
Transportation Aids	795.7	3.1
Debt Service/Bonding	705.5	2.7
Property Tax Credits	469.3	1.8
Community Aids	266.5	1.0
All Other	8,303.2	32.0
SUBTOTAL	25,934.4	100.0

Sources: 2003 State of Wisconsin Annual Fiscal Report, Wisconsin Department of Administration; 2003 State of Wisconsin Annual Fiscal Report (Budgetary Basis) Appendix, Wisconsin Department of Administration

Wisconsin System; research grants and contracts; gifts; donations, bequests, and endowments; auxiliary enterprises (such as dormitories); federal appropriations; and state grants and contracts.[25]

Highway Improvement and Maintenance is the fourth-ranked program in the operating budget, but it did not appear on the list of the top ten GPR expenditure programs.[26] The explanation is simple. Most of the revenue for Highway Improvement and Maintenance comes from gasoline taxes collected by the state and national governments. Because most of the state's gasoline tax is earmarked for highway improvement and maintenance, and because the federal gasoline tax revenue flows into the state as an intergovernmental transfer, these revenues are not included in the GPR budget. Likewise, the other primary source for Highway expenditures, debt service–bonding, is not part of the GPR budget.

Shared Revenue is the fifth-ranked program in the FY 2003 operating budget by size of expenditure, but it was ranked sixth in the GPR budget. As the data in table 12 show, the amount spent for Shared Revenue is much larger in the operating budget than it was in the GPR budget. The key here is the addition of the $589.5 million of revenue raised through the securitization of tobacco settlement revenue. Ordinarily, Shared Revenue expenditures consist exclusively of GPR funds. In the FY 2003 budget, however, Wisconsin's legislators used the tobacco funds as a way to avoid steep cuts in the amount of money flowing from the state to cities, villages, towns, and counties.

Corrections ranks sixth in the operating budget list; as noted above, it was ranked fourth in the GPR budget.[27] It may be instructive for students of Wisconsin state government to note that most of the money used to fund state corrections functions is state-raised tax revenue. Only 18 percent of the Corrections funds used for expenditures are from national government revenue or other sources.

Transportation Aids is the seventh-ranked program in the FY 2003 operating budget.[28] Like Highway Improvement and Maintenance, Transportation Aids is not in the top ten GPR expenditure list. Most of the revenue used for Transportation Aids comes from gasoline taxes and other fees that are not part of the GPR budget. Debt Service/Bonding is the eighth-ranked expenditure program in the operating budget. Expenditures in this category are used to repay money borrowed for state purposes and to pay interest costs on that money.[29]

Individual Property Tax Credits ranks ninth in the operating budget, three spots lower than its location on the GPR list. All of the money spent for Individual Property Tax Credits is general purpose revenue. Also on the top-ten list in the operating budget is Community Aids. Nearly $87 million in non-GPR revenue, most of which is federal funds, was added to this expenditure program in the operating budget.[30]

Other programs that figure prominently in GPR budget also do so in the operating budget, if on a smaller scale: Environmental Aids, Wisconsin Works, Children and Family Services (Community Aids), Income Maintenance, and VTAE Aids. These six operating budget programs account for almost 5 percent of operating expenditures. In short, nearly three-quarters of all state operating expenditures flow through the programs detailed in this section.

STABILITY AND CHANGE IN THE STATE GPR BUDGET

The fact that 85 to 90 percent of Wisconsin's GPR budget spending has been funneled through ten or eleven programs since the 1970s shows a high degree of budget stability. Among the reasons for this stability is that the "base" appropriation for a particular program is usually accepted. Thus budgetary decision-makers tend to focus on incremental additions to, or reductions from, the base.

In the political science literature on budgeting, many reasons are offered for this phenomenon. Among the most important is the political dimension of the process. The state agencies, local governments, private sector organizations, nonprofit organizations, citizen groups, and individuals who benefit from state spending are likely to object strongly to any attempt to reduce that spending. These organizations may also lobby for incremental increases in their programs.

Despite the relative stability in the expenditure patterns as a whole, however, significant changes can and do occur within the state budget over time. These changes may include the rise or fall of a given program within the top-ten list, and they may include a shift in the way funds within a top-ten program are distributed. Changes of these types sometimes emerge from highly controversial budgetary decisions. At other times, changes emerge from relatively modest short-term adjustments that grow in importance over time. (In chapter 11, "State-Local Relations," we will examine both types of changes.)

One example of a large-scale, hotly contested change in the way School Aids was distributed is drawn from the 1970s. In this case, the principal author of the change was Governor Patrick Lucey (1970–77). The second case is taken from the 1990s, wherein the state legislature mandated dramatic change in the size of School Aids, but the way in which Governor Thompson chose to implement the change apparently turned out to be a bit of a surprise to some legislators. The legislature's decision and the governor's strategy had very important short-term and long-term consequences for the state, including the creation of a structural budget deficit that became visible during the recession that began in March of 2001.

WISCONSIN'S FY 2001–2003 AND FY 2003–2005 BUDGET DEFICITS

Wisconsin's 2001–3 budget deficit was estimated to be $2.4 billion. Almost half of the deficit was identified by Governor Scott McCallum (Republican), Tommy Thompson's successor in the executive office in February of 2001, as the result of a structural imbalance between revenues and expenditures that was passed forward from the 1999–2001 budget.[31] The recession, with its negative effect on state tax revenue, was identified as the cause for the other half of the deficit.

The large size of the 2001–3 budget deficit put Wisconsin among the states with the most serious fiscal problems in 2001.[32] Those problems were exacerbated by the fact that the state did not have any money in its Rainy

Day Fund. The state's elected officials responded to the deficit by cutting spending and by selling future income from the tobacco settlement. Less than six months after the budget was passed, however, the governor and the legislature had to engage in more cutting of state expenditures and more borrowing against future tobacco proceeds in order to close an additional $1.4 billion gap between estimated revenues and expenditures.

Despite all of these efforts, the deficit for the 2003–5 budget was estimated to be as large as $4 billion. Both Governor McCallum and his Democratic challenger in the 2002 gubernatorial election, Attorney General James Doyle, made a pledge not to increase the state's general taxes. This meant that whoever won the election would have to make additional deep cuts in spending and search for ways to generate additional revenue from sources other than state taxes.

Doyle won the 2002 gubernatorial contest in a close election, and he immediately took a hard-nosed approach to the deficit. Indeed, his first efforts were aimed at reducing the projected size of the current fiscal year (2003) deficit by submitting the Governor's Deficit Reduction Bill in January of 2003. His stated goal was to reduce the FY 2003 projected deficit from $454 million to $292 million through spending cuts and other means.[33]

In February of 2003 Doyle submitted his FY 2003–5 executive budget recommendations to the legislature. The principal goals he articulated for 2003–5 included balancing the budget without tax increases and reducing the state's structural deficit.[34] The deficit for 2003–5 was projected to be $3.2 billion, even after the addition of $1.6 billion in anticipated revenue growth forecast for the biennium. Of the $3.2 billion deficit, $1.1 billion, or approximately one-third, was estimated to be a structural imbalance between recurring revenues and recurring expenditures.[35]

Doyle's 2003–5 budget deficit reduction plan called for substantial cuts in state spending, including a $250 million reduction is support for the University of Wisconsin system.[36] Other cuts included a 10-percent cut in state agency operations each year of the biennium, and a reduction of the state work force by 2,900 positions.[37] Additionally, his plan called for expanding revenue the state could use to pay for GPR expenditures in the 2003–5 budget by tapping federal intergovernmental revenues; using the patients' compensation fund balance for medical assistance provider payments; transferring revenue from the transportation fund; and increasing revenues from the expansion of tribal gaming.[38]

The Republican-controlled legislature charted a somewhat different course for the 2003–5 budget and the budget bill, and a contentious struggle between the governor and the legislature was soon underway. The legislature and the governor differed over how much the state should spend, how the state should spend the money, how much revenue from nonGPR sources the state should transfer into the GPR budget, and how that money should be raised. Major points of contention were whether new revenue should be generated from expanded Indian Gaming, whether the Medical Assistance surpluses should be used for health care, and whether the Transportation Fund should be tapped to support education and health care needs.

The legislature completed its work and sent the governor a budget bill on June 24, 2003. On July 24, 2003, Governor Doyle signed the bill into law, but he did so after he had used his item-veto power 131 times to modify the bill's content. The governor reported that the item vetoes included a reduction of over $315 million from the legislature's appropriations.[39] Further, he reported a $258 million reduction in the structural deficit included in the legislature's budget ($923 million to $665 million).[40] At least one press report noted that, among other changes, the item vetoes "pruned and reshuffled $168 million in spending."[41]

Although none of Governor Doyle's item vetoes were overridden by the legislature, the executive-legislative struggle continued as the legislature challenged the governor's new Indian gaming compact in court. In May of 2004, the Wisconsin Supreme Court rejected the compact in a 4–3 decision. According to the court, the governor had "overstepped his authority in ne- gotiating an expansive gaming compact with the Forest County Potawatomi tribe."[42] One of the ways in which he had done so was by "improperly cutting the legislature out of the decision."[43]

The court's decision, as some observers interpreted it, seemed to raise "thorny questions without any clear-cut answers."[44] In any case, the potential loss of revenue from the new compact was estimated at $200 million for the biennium, which, it was reported at the time, would doubtless put "a new hole in a precariously balanced state budget."[45] As of this writing (May 2005), both the legal issues the court raised and the potential budgetary shortfall that could result from the decision had yet to be resolved.

CHAPTER NINE

Social Welfare Policy

Wisconsin's pioneering efforts in social welfare before the New Deal are well known. They became the models for many of the new federal aid programs that were often drawn so as to minimize the dislocation to that state's established programs.

Daniel Elazar, *American Federalism: A View from the States*, 1984

Concerns were expressed (during the early 1980s) that Wisconsin had become a "magnet" for poor families who were drawn by the state's welfare generosity.

Thomas Corbett, "Welfare Reform in Wisconsin:
The Rhetoric and the Reality," 1995

Since the early 1900s Wisconsin has had a national reputation for being a leader in the development of social welfare policy and administration. The list of major social welfare innovations that Wisconsin initiated during the early 1900s, 1930s, 1960s, and 1970s shows that this reputation is well deserved. Most of these innovations, like those pioneered by the state in other areas of public policy and administration, were adopted in whole or in part by the national government and other states. For this reason, elected officials, scholars, and members of the press have often described Wisconsin as a "laboratory of democracy."

During the 1980s and 1990s Wisconsin again enjoyed national celebrity as an innovator in the area of social welfare policy and administration. Among the innovations that received national attention were "Learnfare" (1987), "Bridefare" (1992), the Two-Tiered Demonstration Project (1992), "Workfare" (1992), and the legislative act in 1993 that terminated the antipoverty program known as Aid to Families with Dependent Children

(AFDC) as of January 1, 1998.[1] At least a dozen other innovations in social welfare policy and administration were initiated between 1979 and 1996, and virtually all of these experiments influenced national and state policy development.[2]

This chapter begins with some historical background on social welfare policy development in Wisconsin and the nation; the remainder is focused on recent policy innovations and the political processes from which they emerged. During the 1980s the rising costs of the state's social welfare programs became an important issue in state politics. Tommy Thompson's upset victory over incumbent Anthony Earl in the 1986 gubernatorial election has been attributed, in part, to the way Thompson used the welfare issue to attack Earl.[3]

Thompson's campaign themes included the charge that welfare costs were out of control. He identified Wisconsin's high AFDC benefits and the migration of people into the state for those benefits as the causes of the problem, and he promised to cut benefits and stop welfare related in-migration. After his election victory in November of 1986, Governor Thompson made welfare programs a central focus of his policy initiatives, and welfare reform remained a priority throughout his four terms in office. Data contained in this chapter show that welfare caseloads declined dramatically between 1986 and 2000, but these reductions were not achieved by simply pushing people off the rolls. As befitting the state's Progressive heritage, the caseload reduction was achieved with substantial state investment in job training, child care support, and health care.

A HISTORICAL OVERVIEW OF SOCIAL WELFARE POLICY DEVELOPMENT

Concerns about the economic and social conditions of Wisconsin's citizens have been a central part of the state's history and policy development. As described in chapter 2 ("The Constitution"), Progressive Democrats attending the 1846 constitutional convention wanted to protect the state's citizens against some of the arbitrariness and excesses of the economic marketplace. One result is the constitutional protection of a citizen's homestead in case of bankruptcy.

When Wisconsin's constitution was written, farming was the occupation of nearly 90 percent of the people in the state and in the nation. Farming was (and still is) a high-risk business. Drought, floods, and insects could and can quickly destroy a season's crops. Even if the farmer survived these risks posed by nature, changing economic conditions could also depress crop prices and reduce or eliminate a farmer's income. Loss of income could result in bank foreclosure on loans, and banks would take everything if they could. The constitutional protection of homesteads prevented this from happening.

While the economic conditions of the farmers remained a concern during the late 1800s and early 1900s, Progressives like Robert La Follette, Francis McGovern, and James O. Davidson attempted to address new problems that were arising as the nation moved from an agricultural to an industrial economy. The Progressives were particularly concerned with the plight of industrial workers, their families, and the growing numbers of poor who lived in urban areas. University of Wisconsin faculty shared these concerns.

State officials and university faculty joined together to address these problems, and their working partnership was a key part of what became known as the "Wisconsin Idea." The Wisconsin Idea was defined by its originator and founder of Wisconsin's Legislative Reference Bureau, Charles McCarthy, as the "willingness to experiment to meet the needs of a changing economic order."[4] Through the partnership between faculty members, including economist John R. Commons, and the state's elected and administrative officials, Wisconsin developed the first workmen's compensation program (1911) and innovative workplace protections for women and children (1913). Workmen's compensation provided temporary income support to workers who were injured on the job. The legislation designed to protect women and children established maximum hours of labor for women, a minimum age for the employment of children, and minimum wage requirements for the employment of women and children.

At the same time that Wisconsin's Progressives began to construct the state's social welfare policy, they established a state income tax (1911). This new tax was designed to provide the revenue needed to support state initiatives in a variety of areas, including social welfare policy and regulatory activities. Up to that point Wisconsin, like other states, depended primarily on the same source of revenue that local governments relied upon—the property tax. Reliance on the property tax alone meant that the state's revenues would remain relatively modest. Such limited state revenues constrained what the state could do to address the economic plight of many of its people.

Not long after Wisconsin took these first pioneering steps in the way of both social welfare and tax policy, the national government and some of the states followed Wisconsin's lead. The national government's action was something that Wisconsin's elected officials and university faculty worked hard to secure. Having a national policy framework for social welfare not only provided protection for the state's social welfare policy innovations but also reduced some of the risks associated with these policies.

Among those risks was the ability of Progressive governors and legislators to win reelection in the face of opposition to these policies. Some of the Progressives' critics labeled the new tax and social welfare policies radical and antibusiness. If these claims came to be regarded as true by the voting public, the Progressives could be turned out of office. Additionally, if business owners accepted this negative view of the social welfare policy innovations, they might move their companies to other states that were perceived to have a more hospitable economic and political climate.

That these policies posed risks for Wisconsin's Progressives proved to be true when the Progressive candidate for governor was defeated in the Republican primary by Emanuel L. Philipp in 1914. In his election campaign, Philipp criticized the Progressives for creating heavy tax burdens and government programs that interfered with business.[5] Furthermore, the newly elected governor described his election victory as a "complete repudiation of the much heralded Wisconsin Idea."[6] Despite the rhetoric, however, Philipp made little effort during his six years in office to overturn the key policy changes initiated by the Progressives.

In 1932 Wisconsin's elected officials again passed new social welfare policy intiatives that would later be adopted nationwide. This time the policy innovation was the establishment of an unemployment compensation system.[7] Once again the state's elected leaders, administrative officials, and university faculty, John R. Commons and Harold Groves among them, worked together and won passage of legislation that would protect workers from the fluctuations of the marketplace.[8] Specifically, the unemployment compensation system was designed to give temporary income to workers who lost their jobs through no fault of their own. This income was meant to protect workers and their families from severe economic hardships or bankruptcy and to support them until the breadwinner could find another job.

Like the critics of Wisconsin's earlier social welfare policy innovations, critics of the workmen's compensation act regarded it as unnecessary regulation and antibusiness. Wisconsin's leaders during the 1930s, like their predecessors in the early 1900s, recognized the importance of nationwide adoption of this policy innovation. Without it, Wisconsin would be at risk in the competition among the states for businesses.

In 1934 President Roosevelt established the Committee on Economic Security. Professor Edwin Witte, a student of John R. Commons, was appointed executive director of the committee. Witte selected a young graduate of the University of Wisconsin's economics department named Wilbur Cohen to serve as his research assistant.[9] The committee's work paved the way for the passage in 1935 of the Social Security Act.

Although the 1935 act is best known for the establishment of Old Age and Survivors benefits, it also established a national framework for unemployment compensation.[10] One of the notable minor provisions of the 1935 act was a program to provide temporary income assistance to children who lived in single-parent households with little or no income. This program would become known as Aid to Families with Dependent Children (AFDC).

Both the aged and children were the focus of the next major wave of innovation in social welfare policy in the 1960s. One of the most interesting social welfare policy innovations that occurred in Wisconsin during the early 1960s was the passage of the Wisconsin Homestead Tax Credit in 1963. Drafted by University of Wisconsin economist Harold Groves, the act was designed to ensure that elderly persons with low income did not pay more than a certain percentage of their income in property taxes. Specifically, the act provided an income tax credit for 50 percent of property taxes paid in excess of 5 percent of income. If the credit exceeded the income tax due, the state was required to send a check for the balance.[11]

Individual Wisconsinites, too, were playing important roles at the national level in the development of social welfare policy. Robert Lampman, a student of Edwin Witte's, authored *The Low Income Population and Economic Growth* (1959). Professor Lampman and his faculty colleague at the University of Wisconsin, Burton Weisbrod, thereafter contributed a pivotal chapter to the 1964 *Economic Report of the President*. The chapter helped to put poverty back on the public policy agenda, and its content influenced the way people thought about both the causes of poverty and solutions for it. Some of this thinking is evident in the major national legislation of the time, the Economic Opportunity Act of 1964. Lampman was to gain additional national visibility as an advocate for the Negative Income Tax, an expanded version of what Wisconsin was already doing in a modest way for the elderly under the Homestead Tax Relief Act.

WELFARE AND WELFARE REFORM
IN THE LATE 1970S AND EARLY 1980S

The Economic Opportunity Act of 1964 was part of the "War on Poverty" initiated by Lyndon Johnson and a Democratically controlled Congress. During the 1970s Democratic legislators followed Johnson's lead by identifying poverty, hunger, and other social conditions that accompanied lack of income as important national problems. Throughout the 1960s and 1970s the states were fiscal and administrative partners with the national government in the social welfare policy system. In this partnership, the national government established the minimum standards for benefit eligibility and minimum benefit levels. The states had to accept these minimum standards to participate in the national welfare programs, but they were allowed to provide higher benefit payments if they desired. The costs of the social welfare programs were borne in roughly equal shares by the national and state governments.

Throughout the 1970s the national-state social welfare system consisted of four principal programs: Aid to Families with Dependent Children (AFDC), Food Stamps, Medical Assistance (Medicaid), and Housing Assistance. These programs were directed to three groups of people whose incomes fell below the poverty line: the elderly, the disabled, and children. One problem with this system was that each program was directed by a different agency at the national level. The same was true in most states. Prospective beneficiaries thus often had to go to four different agencies and fill out four different application forms to apply for benefits.

A solution to this problem was developed in Wisconsin during the mid-1970s, under Governor Patrick Lucey, whereby prospective clients were offered a consolidated form that covered AFDC, Food Stamps, and Medicaid.[12] This form reduced administrative complexity and costs, and it gave clients better access to program benefits. The single application form was adopted by a number of other states.

In the 1980s, however, the focus of elected officials in Washington DC and in some state capitals began to shift from simplifying administrative systems, lowering administrative costs, and serving clients to controlling the costs of entitlements. The catalyzing event in this change at the national level was Ronald Reagan's election to the presidency in 1980. In sharp contrast to the prevailing Democratic and liberal philosophy of the time, Reagan took the position that "Government is not the solution to our problems. Government is our problem."[13] Given this ideological starting point, as well as the electoral gains Republicans made in Congress with Reagan's election, it is not surprising that a different set of presumptions about what constituted desirable social welfare policy rapidly gained visibility and strength in the policymaking system.

Reagan's accession to the White House also resulted in other important fiscal and administrative changes. Specifically, Reagan sponsored huge tax cuts and a rapid build-up in defense spending.[14] This combination of large tax cuts and large increases in defense spending predictably created large annual deficits and a rapid growth of the national debt. At the same time, Reagan launched his "New Federalism" program, which was intended to reduce national government expenditures for social welfare and to return more fiscal responsibility for these programs to the states.[15] Reagan's political ideology provided the baseline for this change. The huge annual deficits he created provided a powerful impetus for constraining national government spending, including spending on social welfare programs.

WELFARE AS A POLICY PROBLEM AND
A POLITICAL ISSUE IN WISCONSIN

Public concerns about welfare were building in Wisconsin before Ronald Reagan's election. Those concerns prompted the Wisconsin legislature to establish the Welfare Reform Advisory Committee in 1978. Acting Governor Martin Schreiber appointed the chair and members of the committee. Robert Haveman, nationally recognized as a leading scholar in the field of welfare and welfare reform, served as the chair. Haveman was a University of Wisconsin faculty member and former director of the university's Institute for Research on Poverty. The committee generated a report in less than a year, which included proposals for "radical changes in existing welfare rules and the creation of new nonwelfare programs."[16]

Whether Acting Governor Martin Schreiber would have actively pushed for the radical changes recommended by this welfare reform committee will remain a matter of speculation. The Acting Governor was defeated in the 1978 election by Republican challenger Lee Dreyfus. The key to Dreyfus's upset victory, as most observers saw it, was a budgetary issue, not the cost of welfare. The Republican candidate made the budgetary surplus forecast for FY 1978 the principal issue of the election campaign.

Dreyfus proposed giving all of the state's surplus back to taxpayers, and with this single bold stroke he put Schreiber on the defensive. After some delay, Schreiber responded to Dreyfus's pledge by offering to send part of the surplus back to taxpayers, while holding the remainder in reserve to cushion the effects of a future recession. This response showed that Schreiber was a prudent fiscal manager, but it did not serve as an effective political response. By taking the offensive, Dreyfus had made Schreiber look stingy with "taxpayers money." Schreiber never recovered from this blow.

After his inauguration in 1979, Dreyfus seemed to be reading from

Schreiber's script about welfare when he said that the "state was prepared to undertake fundamental reform."[17] In fact, however, the Dreyfus administration did not propose wholesale changes. Instead, a series of more modest initiatives, most of which had been proposed by the legislature's Welfare Reform Advisory Committee, were pursued.

Between 1979 and 1982 the state legislature passed an earned income tax credit (EITC) to ease the burdens on the working poor, alternative approaches to assisting the medically uninsured were explored, and pilot programs to stimulate demand for low-skilled workers were established.[18] Perhaps the most important innovation, however, was made in the area of child support, where the possibilities for reducing AFDC costs seemed greatest.[19]

In November of 1982 Anthony Earl, a Democrat, was elected governor in a race against Republican Terry Kohler (the incumbent, Lee Dreyfus, had chosen not to run for reelection). As he took office in January of 1983, Governor Earl was faced with a rapidly growing budget deficit inherited from the Dreyfus administration.

In order to balance the budget, Earl proposed substantial reductions in state spending. He could have used this situation to reduce state support for social welfare programs, but he did not do so. In fact, the new governor actually proposed a modest increase in AFDC benefits for 1984. As the budgetary pressures continued into 1985, however, "a sense of crisis" emerged within state government over the growing costs of the state's social welfare programs.[20] Elected and administrative officials identified several factors contributing to the growth in the AFDC caseload: the sharp drop in job-training funds the national government had once provided to help AFDC recipients move from welfare to work; unpaid child support; Wisconsin's generous AFDC benefits; and the migration of poor people into the state solely to secure these generous welfare benefits.

Governor Earl worked with legislators and administrators to develop responses to each of these concerns; University of Wisconsin faculty and staff were also involved. For example, Assembly Speaker Tom Loftus, Representative John Antaramian, staff from the Department of Health and Social Services, and Professor Irv Garfinkel and Tom Corbett from the Institute for Research on Poverty at the University of Wisconsin–Madison contributed to the development of the Work Experience and Job Training Program in 1986. This legislation established work and training requirements for AFDC recipients, and it provided money for the training programs. Governor Earl also pushed to expand the collection of child support payments from absent parents, and he responded to concerns about whether Wisconsin had become a "welfare magnet" by forming a commission to study the matter.[21]

The members of Governor Earl's commission reported that some people were migrating into the state to secure Wisconsin's generous welfare payments, but they concluded that the number of such immigrants was too small to justify the costs of a policy response.[22] As might be expected, this conclusion was widely debated even within Democratic circles. Additionally, it could hardly have seemed a credible conclusion to a public that had been reading press reports about the "welfare-magnet" problem.

The suspicion persisted both inside and outside of state government that the commission had underestimated the extent of the welfare-magnet problem and the extent to which it was contributing to rising welfare costs. Indeed, even within the Democratic Party growing concerns were voiced about the matter. Democratic officeholders Joseph Stohl and Joseph Andrea, both from Kenosha County, which was considered a gateway for in-migration from Chicago, introduced bills in the Wisconsin Senate to establish work requirements for welfare recipients and to reduce welfare benefits.[23]

Governor Earl's focus, however, seemed to be on the substantive, rather than the symbolic and political, dimensions of the problem. The fact that caseloads were dropping during the year, and ultimately did drop by 5 percent for the full year (1986), may have provided reinforcement for this focus.[24] Nevertheless, concentrating on the substance of the matter put the governor in a vulnerable position.

One could draw a parallel between Earl's vulnerability and what had happened to Martin Schreiber just a few years earlier when the Acting Governor failed to effectively manage the political dimensions of the projected state budget surplus.[25] That said, Governor Earl did not take some of the steps he might have taken to inoculate himself from attack by a political opponent. Perhaps the most important of these steps would have been the proposal of (at least) a modest reduction in welfare benefits.

Governor Earl's challenger in the 1986 election, Republican Tommy Thompson, exploited the opportunity the incumbent had given him. Among Thompson's central campaign themes was the contention that welfare costs were out of control. Among the explanations Thompson offered for this "problem" was the familiar one: that Wisconsin had become a welfare-magnet. Candidate Thompson regularly mentioned the welfare problem in personal appearances, and it was a central part of his media attacks on Earl.

Political scientist Murray Edelman has pointed out that the type of claims

Thompson was making can have a powerful effect on voters.[26] Such claims can feed voters' fears about wasteful state spending and undermine the credibility of the incumbent chief executive. The latter occurs because voters assume that the chief executive can prevent such problems from arising through proper management of state affairs and finances.

What remains a puzzle to some observers is why Governor Earl remained largely silent on the matter during most of the election campaign.[27] Even when he finally did respond to Thompson's charges, he did not attempt to defend his record. The governor could have reported on the ambitious initiatives he had undertaken to recover child support payments from absent parents and to move people off of welfare through employment and training programs.[28] He could also have claimed credit for a reduction in the AFDC caseload. But it is possible that even if he had responded in this way, it may have been too late to repair the political damage done by Thompson's attack ads.

TRENDS IN WELFARE CASELOADS AND COSTS (MID-1960S TO MID-1980S)

As just described, both welfare caseloads and costs rose to the top of the political and institutional agenda in Wisconsin during the early 1980s and were a potent issue in Wisconsin's 1986 gubernatorial race. Tommy Thompson successfully used the welfare issue to unseat his Democratic opponent, Anthony Earl, but this occurred at the very time AFDC caseloads were actually declining. Indeed caseloads declined by 5 percent during 1986, as shown in figure 5.

Given these circumstances, it seems worthwhile to take a close look at the policy "problem" itself. Specifically, three questions deserve consideration:

- Were welfare costs out of control in 1986, as Thompson claimed they were?
- What role did Wisconsin's generous welfare benefits play in the growth of welfare caseloads and costs? (Did these benefits make the state a "welfare-magnet," and, if so, was the effect big enough to make a significant difference in AFDC caseloads and costs?) and
- What did Wisconsin's welfare generosity buy?

In response to the first question, it is clear that Wisconsin's social welfare expenditures did rise sharply during the first half of the 1980s. Between 1982 and 1986, for example, the nominal cost of AFDC increased by 27.7 percent. Furthermore, the data show that Wisconsin's costs were rising much faster

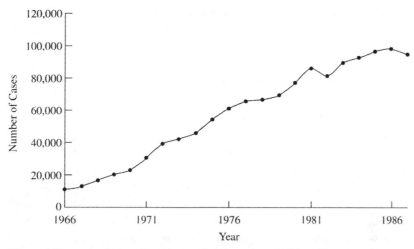

Fig. 5. Wisconsin Aid to Families with Dependent Children Cases, 1966–1987 (*Source*: Thomas J. Corbett, "Welfare Reform in Wisconsin: The Rhetoric and the Reality," Institute for Research on Poverty Reprint Series, University of Wisconsin–Madison)

than those of other states. The average increase in welfare costs on a national basis was only 8.2 percent, or about one-third of the increase Wisconsin experienced.[29]

What factors contributed to the rise in costs? One factor was the modest increase in benefits passed in 1984. Second, high AFDC benefit levels may have provided an economic rationale to collect welfare, rather than to work. Third, it appears that changing economic circumstances contributed significantly to the growing costs.

Historical data show that as unemployment goes up, so, too, does the AFDC caseload. Because the two recessions that ran from January 1980 to July 1980 and from July 1981 to November 1982 hit Wisconsin and other Midwestern states harder than they did the rest of the country, unemployment was considerably higher in Wisconsin during the early 1980s than it was for most other states. Not surprisingly, growth in AFDC caseloads was also proportionately higher for Wisconsin than it was for the nation as a whole.

The recessionary period that extended through the years 1980–82 not only had a particularly harsh effect on Wisconsin's manufacturing employment but also may have accelerated a long-term trend toward higher AFDC caseloads. For example, census data show that Wisconsin moved from a good position vis-à-vis other states in the 1960s to a poor position in the 1980s. In 1960 less than 1 percent of Wisconsin's population received AFDC, while the U.S. average was 1.6 percent. By the mid-1980s the situation was reversed: the U.S. average was 4.6 percent, while the percentage of the population receiving AFDC in Wisconsin was 6 percent.[30]

As already noted, Governor Earl's 1985 study commission reported that Wisconsin's high benefit levels, and the in-migration associated with them, were contributing to the increasing size of the welfare rolls. While there are studies that both support and cast doubt on the finding that in-migration was a significant factor in Wisconsin and elsewhere, there is no doubt about the growing generosity of Wisconsin's AFDC payments over this twenty-year period of time.[31] In FY 1964–65 Wisconsin's per capita welfare expenditures were 11 percent below the U.S. average. Twenty years later, in the mid-1980s, Wisconsin's per capita expenditures were 29 percent above the U.S. average.[32] By 1986 Wisconsin offered the fifth highest AFDC benefit level in the country.[33]

Lest the state spending on welfare be viewed simply as wasteful, however, it is important the note that the state's generosity to its poorest citizens did have some significant benefits. Specifically, AFDC, coupled with food stamps and Medicaid, reduced economic and health hardships for families headed by a single parent (usually female) that had experienced a sharp, temporary reduction in income.[34] These temporary circumstances were often caused by a separation from the spouse; divorce; job loss; a serious illness experienced by the single parent; a serious illness of a child; loss of assistance from their parents or extended families; and related circumstances. A substantial percentage of the single parents in these households typically left the AFDC rolls within one year.

For those whose stay on the welfare rolls extended beyond a year, AFDC also filled in at least "part of the gap between family income and expenditures needed to live at nonpoverty levels."[35] Included among these poorest families were women who possessed few or no job skills, had abusive partners, suffered serious illness, had children with serious illnesses, or dealt with other circumstances that limited their employment prospects.

Data and the Political Dimensions of the Welfare Issue

If the data that showed the dramatic rise in AFDC caseloads and costs was in the hands of Governor Earl, his staff members, or other members of his administration, an objective observer might ask why the administration did not craft a strategy to protect the governor against an attack by a campaign opponent. Even a commitment to make modest reductions in benefit levels and caseloads might have served the purpose. Perhaps Governor Earl assumed that an improving economy and the efforts he already had underway to reduce caseloads were sufficient. Or perhaps he was more concerned about the circumstances of poor children than he was about criticism from a political rival. The welfare of the children would seem to be an appropriate concern for a governor in the Progressive tradition.

WELFARE REFORM INITIATIVES FROM 1987 TO 1990

On January 5, 1987, Tommy Thompson became Wisconsin's forty-third governor. Although he won a four-year term, he wasted little time in attacking the welfare problem he had worked so hard to publicize in his election campaign. In fact, shortly after his election he invited legislative leaders to work with him to identify ways to deal with welfare costs. A few weeks after his inauguration, Governor Thompson offered his initial solution to the problem of rising welfare caseloads and costs in his *1987–89 Executive Budget Recommendations* for the state.

Thompson's welfare reform package had three basic parts: a 6-percent reduction in AFDC benefits; an expansion of the Work Experience and Job Training program initiated by Governor Earl and passed by the legislature in 1986; and several initiatives or experiments that required waivers from the national government.

Of the experiments that required a waiver, "Learnfare" was the centerpiece, and it generated a good deal of national publicity for the new governor.[36] The Learnfare program was aimed at teenagers (13–18) in AFDC households. Specifically, AFDC benefits would be reduced if teenagers of dependent mothers did not attend school. Likewise, teenagers who themselves had children and were receiving AFDC payments would be penalized if they failed to attend school. The Thompson administration argued that the proposal would help to break the cycle of welfare dependency by keeping teens in school. Critics of the plan viewed it as a radical and punitive measure.

Another proposed change that required a waiver involved work requirements for the heads of AFDC households. Thompson wanted to expand the program initiated by Governor Earl that required AFDC recipients to register for work or job-training programs. Under national guidelines, women with children six years of age or under were not required to participate in these programs. Thompson wanted to remove this exemption.

The two other Thompson proposals that required national government waivers actually expanded welfare benefits. The first was an expansion of Medical Assistance coverage to include families that were making the transition from welfare to work. The second was an effort to prevent the cutoff of aid to needy two-parent families if one of the parents worked one hundred hours per month—essentially a part-time job of twenty-five hours per week. The rule that welfare be terminated if one parent worked one hundred hours was part of the national government's welfare requirements.

While these proposed changes were generating interest in Washington DC and elsewhere, Thompson still had to get them approved by a Wisconsin legislature that had Democratic majorities in both houses. The legislature took a cautious but deliberate approach to Governor Thompson's proposed changes in social welfare policy. For example, it approved changes that resulted in a 1-percent increase in AFDC benefits, approved an expansion of the employment training program, and provided support for a more narrowly defined Learnfare program; the latter was focused only on teen mothers who did not attend school.[37] Finally, after months of negotiation and compromise over changes in social welfare policy and other items contained in the budget, the legislature passed the budget bill (Wisconsin Act 27) in August of 1987.

The last word on nearly all social welfare policy matters, however, belonged to Governor Thompson. After the budget bill (Wisconsin Act 27) was passed by the legislature, Thompson employed Wisconsin's unique partial veto 290 times to substantially overhaul the legislature's work.[38] For instance, the legislature had set the AFDC benefit level at 84.04 percent of the "standard of need." By crossing out two numbers, however, Governor Thompson changed this figure to 80 percent. Additionally, he changed the 1-percent benefit increase authorized by the legislature to a 5-percent reduction.[39] He also modified the legislature's approach to Learnfare. Through careful use of the partial veto, Thompson ended up with the more comprehensive version of this plan.

Democrats in the legislature responded with an attempt to curtail the governor's partial-veto power. Legislative leaders from both parties joined together to file a suit in court alleging that Thompson had violated the Wisconsin Constitution by his excessive use of the partial veto.[40] Among the concerns cited in the suit was that the governor had singlehandedly changed or even subverted the intention of the legislature. The Wisconsin Supreme Court, however, upheld Thompson's action in a 4–3 decision.[41]

In October of 1987 the waivers requested by the state were approved by the national government. Thus, the implementation of Learnfare, changes in work requirements for heads of households, medical assistance coverage for families moving from welfare to work, and protection of benefits for families with one parent working 100 hours per month could begin. Yet implementation of these experiments, particularly Learnfare, turned out to be much more difficult for the Thompson administration than getting authorizing language for the programs from the legislature or the waivers from the national government.

As described by one analyst, the initial attempt to implement Learnfare resulted in "chaos."[42] This should not be surprising since new administrative routines had to be established in two executive branch agencies (Health and Social Services and Education), in welfare offices in seventy-two counties and in more than four hundred school districts. It is no wonder that it took the Thompson administration several years to create the working routines required to support the program's objectives.

Like Learnfare, the expansion of the Work Experience and Job Training (WEJT) program from five to fourteen counties also required a large administrative initiative. Here, too, the implementation process was rocky. Although the state had already had the opportunity to test the program in several counties, documentation of program-design requirements was in short supply and evaluation of results even more difficult to find.

Fortunately for the Thompson administration, the third leg of the welfare reform initiatives, the 6-percent reduction in AFDC benefits, could be completed relatively simply and quickly by the Department of Health and Social Services. Here, at least, the administration's new policy could be initiated with relative ease.

WELFARE REFORM INITIATIVES FROM 1991 TO 1994

Having decisively defeated his Democratic opponent, Assembly Speaker Tom Loftus, in the November 1990 general election, Tommy Thompson began his second, four-year term as governor of Wisconsin in January of 1991. Approximately a year later, he put forward a second wave of welfare reform initiatives. Similar to the first set of proposals, the 1992 proposals had three parts: a continued freeze on AFDC benefit levels; an expansion of job-training and job-placement activities; and some new experiments that required national government waivers.

"Bridefare" was one of the new experiments. Formally designated the Parental and Family Responsibility Initiative (PFRI), Bridefare, like its predecessor Learnfare in 1987, generated substantial national publicity for Governor Thompson and Wisconsin's welfare "experiments." One reason for this visibility was that Bridefare was announced in a White House Rose Garden press conference in March of 1992.[43] Bridefare resembled Learnfare in another way, too; it contained provisions that were at odds with existing national policy. Consequently, a waiver from the national government was required before the new policy could be implemented.

Bridefare was aimed at welfare applicants under the age of twenty and their spouses—or the adjudicated fathers of their children. The program was designed to "encourage family formation, discourage subsequent births for those on assistance, and provide income support."[44] The carrots or incentives used to promote the first and third objectives included liberalized AFDC eligibility requirements and liberalized treatment of earnings and benefits. The second objective, discouraging subsequent births for those on assistance, was to be pursued with a stick, that is, by creating strong disincentives. Specifically, benefits would grow only a very small amount for subsequent births. The state's waiver request for Bridefare was approved by the national government in 1992, and in 1994 a pilot project began in four Wisconsin counties.

The second major initiative put forward by the Thompson administration in 1992 was the "Two-Tiered Demonstration" project. Despite the freeze in AFDC benefits already in effect for four years, legislative and public concerns persisted that Wisconsin remained a welfare-magnet. The principal focus of these concerns was on the flow of low-income Chicago residents out of that city and across Wisconsin's southeastern border. Stories written by journalists, data on the number of new welfare applicants moving to Wisconsin from out of state, and public housing records showed these concerns had a basis in fact.

There is, it seems, a bit of irony here. After all, Tommy Thompson had used the welfare-magnet problem very effectively to attack his opponent, Anthony Earl, in the 1986 campaign. He had also promised to fix the problem. Nevertheless, Thompson was now confronted with the very same problem. Unlike his predecessor, however, Thompson was too savvy to allow such public concerns to continue without a response. Thompson needed to take action, and he did.

In the two-tiered system proposed by Governor Thompson, welfare applicants who had just moved to Wisconsin from another state were limited to the benefit levels paid in the state from which they came for six months. The program was identified as a demonstration project for two reasons. First, because it violated existing provisions in national welfare policy—a waiver granting permission to run such an experiment was needed. Second, the Two-Tiered Demonstration project was to be tested in just four Wisconsin counties.

A waiver request for the Two-Tier Demonstration project was filed with the U.S. Department of Health and Human Services, and, in 1993, the permission was granted. Implementation of the demonstration project began in four southeastern Wisconsin counties—Milwaukee, Racine, Kenosha, and Rock—in 1994. All four counties are directly north of Chicago, Illinois.

The Thompson administration offered a third set of initiatives in the area of social welfare in 1993. The centerpiece of the third wave was "Workfare." Formally titled Work Not Welfare (WNW), the program was dubbed "Workfare" because it made participation in work or job-training programs a condition of AFDC benefits. It also limited AFDC benefits to twenty-four months within any forty-eight-month period.

Workfare was widely regarded as Tommy Thompson's attempt to create a time-limited welfare system before President Bill Clinton did so at the national level.[45] Like its two predecessors, Learnfare and Bridefare, Workfare received considerable attention in the state and national press. Workfare, like the Thompson administration's other welfare policy experiments, also required a waiver from the national government.

In contrast to what one might believe on the basis of press reports about Workfare, however, the initiative was not a proposal to overhaul the entire state welfare system. Rather, it was a carefully targeted pilot project, limited to two counties. In the fall of 1993 the national government provided the waiver for the Workfare program. The test did not begin, however, until 1995. Fond du Lac and Pierce counties were the two counties where the pilot project took place, and the number of participants was limited to one thousand.

Partisan Politics and the End of AFDC

Between 1987 and 1992 Governor Thompson had the benefit of working with two Republican presidents, Ronald Reagan and George H. W. Bush, as he requested waivers for his welfare policy experiments. He is reported to have had a good working relationship with Reagan and a genuine friendship with President Bush. In 1993, however, Thompson had to submit his request for Workfare, perhaps the most controversial of his welfare initiatives, to President Bill Clinton, a Democrat. Thompson, a Republican, might have anticipated some difficulties in getting a waiver-request approved.

Ironically, the partisan political struggle that Governor Thompson did encounter occurred in his own state capital, Madison, rather than in Washington DC. A number of Democratic legislators in the state had "apparently tired of reacting to (and generally accepting) Governor Thompson's welfare initiatives."[46] These legislators contended that Workfare was simply another attempt to "tinker with a welfare system that needed to be replaced, rather than reformed."[47] Thus, when Thompson asked the legislature to provide formal authorization for Workfare, the Democrats added something very important to the Thompson administration's bill: a requirement that AFDC be terminated by December 31, 1998, and replaced by a whole new system. The task of drafting the new plan was assigned to the Department of Health and Social Services.

In addition to the demand that the existing welfare system be replaced, Democrats in the legislature provided the governor some guidelines on how he should proceed. Among these were stipulations that the new system "1) guarantee income support to needy persons who could not work; 2) guarantee employment to those who could work but could not find jobs; and 3) assure low-income persons 'affordable child care' and 'affordable health care.' "[48] Despite the Democrats' best efforts, however, this part of their plan did not succeed.

Once again, Governor Thompson used his partial-veto power (since the legislative language was part of the budget bill) to rid himself of these restrictions. When he had finished "rewriting" the sections of the FY 1993–95 budget bill that dealt with welfare policy, all that remained of the new policy was the requirement that a new welfare system be proposed by the Department of Health and Social Services by December 1, 1995.

By formalizing their demand for a new welfare system in statutory law, Democratic legislators presented Governor Thompson with a tremendous challenge and a remarkable opportunity. Up to that point, the governor had offered a series of initiatives that affected various parts of the social welfare system, but he had not offered a proposal for wholesale change. With the exception of a reduction in benefit levels, three of the four most significant changes Thompson proposed (Bridefare, the Two-Tiered Demonstration project, and Workfare) had been limited to experiments in a few counties.

WISCONSIN WORKS (W-2) AND THE
BIRTH OF A NEW "WELFARE" SYSTEM

In November of 1994 Thompson was elected to a third term as governor by a very comfortable margin. At about the same time, planning began for the new welfare system, Wisconsin Works (nicknamed "W-2"). Although little information about the planning process was released by the Thompson administration, some key facts are known. For example, the planning group was relatively small, consisting of fewer than ten people. Among the participants were the Secretary of the Department of Health and Social Services and four other members of the department, two of whom had worked in the George H. W. Bush administration. Two members of the Hudson Institute, a conservative think tank, also participated. Financial support for the planning activities was provided by the Hudson Institute, the Bradley Foundation, of Milwaukee, Wisconsin; the Annie E. Casey Foundation, of Baltimore; and the Steward Mott Foundation.[49]

The philosophy and goals the planners developed for W-2 are listed in the *Wisconsin Works (W-2) Manual.*[50] Key principles that can be excerpted from the statement of philosophy and goals include:

1. Parents without a disability should work and should obtain no entitlement to cash assistance in the absence of work.
2. Expectations for success in the labor market should be high.
3. All cash benefits should be time-limited.

4. Government programs should provide child care and health care assistance to the working poor, not just to public assistance recipients.

5. Those who receive grants should face the conditions that affect the working poor.

6. Administration of public assistance programs need not be handled exclusively by state or local governments; private sector organizations can be used in program administration.[51]

In the spring of 1995 the planning group had a proposal ready for the governor's review. After several months of review, Governor Thompson formally announced w-2 in August of 1995. In October of 1995 the plan was drafted into bill form and introduced in the Wisconsin legislature as Assembly Bill 591.

Ironically, even though w-2 was far more ambitious than any of Thompson's former welfare initiatives, the proposal received little attention outside of the state. At least two explanations can be offered for this turn of events: the media's attention to welfare reform had shifted from the state to the national level, where Congress and President Bill Clinton were floating proposals; and welfare reform in Wisconsin had been undertaken so often that it was no longer news.

After a lengthy six-month review process, the Wisconsin legislature passed a version of Thompson's w-2 plan in mid-March of 1995. Although the legislature left most of the major provisions intact, lawmakers incorporated some important modifications.[52] Local governments, as well as some Republicans in the legislature, played a role in making these modifications. The legislation called for implementation of w-2 by September of 1997. Like all of the other Wisconsin welfare experiments, however, legislative authorization for w-2 was only one of the requirements that had to be met in order to proceed. The other requirement was a waiver from the national government.

Less than a year after w-2 was passed by the legislature, the initiative gained national visibility when it was praised publicly by President Bill Clinton. At the time, Clinton was locked in a struggle with congressional Republicans over welfare reform. The President praised w-2 as a "bold welfare reform plan," and he challenged Congress to pass welfare reform legislation that incorporated provisions included in state welfare reform plans like w-2.[53] Among the provisions that President Clinton wanted were a requirement that welfare recipients work, a time limit for welfare benefits, and stronger child support enforcement.[54]

At the same time, President Clinton invited the Thompson administration to submit the waiver request for w-2. This was a surprise for many members of the Thompson administration, who had come to the conclusion that national government action on welfare reform, and particularly the waivers they requested for w-2, would have to wait until after the presidential election.[55] President Clinton's invitation sent Thompson's staff scurrying to develop a waiver proposal. When the proposal was completed, Governor Thompson delivered it to the U.S. Department of Health and Social Services himself.[56]

The Clinton administration did act relatively quickly on the Thompson waiver request in 1996, and it also got a prize it had been seeking. Late in 1996 Congress passed a national "welfare reform" bill, the Personal Responsibility and Work Opportunity Reconciliation Act (PRWORA), and President Clinton signed it into law. The bill followed Wisconsin's lead in several significant areas. Most importantly, it terminated Aid to Families with Dependent Children (AFDC), set a time limit on benefits, incorporated work requirements for those receiving assistance. The bill also established a block grant system called Temporary Assistance for Needy Families (TANF) to fund state welfare programs. The block grant system gave the states much more flexibility in determining how to use their welfare resources than they had under previous legislation.

At the time PRWORA became law, Wisconsin had adopted a newly designed welfare system, but it had not yet been implemented. The passage of PRWORA was advantageous for the Thompson administration. In addition to incorporating important provisions contained in w-2, the national government's welfare reform initiative also reinforced and supported Thompson's attempt to create a new welfare system.

The Structure of w-2

w-2, as noted above, replaced cash-assistance guarantees or entitlements that were provided under the Aid to Families with Dependent Children (AFDC) program with a system that provided temporary cash assistance only for work or work-like activities. Low-income parents with children twelve weeks of age or older had to meet program requirements to qualify for any assistance.

w-2 was designed to have four tiers of support for adults with children seeking state assistance. Those who met eligibility standards were assigned to a Financial and Employment Planner (FEP), who directed the applicant to one of the tiers in the "self-sufficiency" ladder. The top rung on the ladder, "unsubsidized employment," was for people deemed capable of moving directly into this type of employment. The second rung, "trial job," was for applicants who needed subsidized jobs in private or public organizations. The third tier, "community service job," was for persons "who need[ed] to practice the work habits and skills necessary to be hired by a private sector business."[57] The bottom rung, "w-2 transition," was for those who were "legitimately unable to perform independent self-sustaining work even in a community service job."[58]

A basic income package was defined for each tier of the self-sufficiency ladder. The package included food stamps and the Earned Income Tax Credit for the first two tiers but only food stamps for the third and fourth tiers. The ladder also defined the number of hours recipients were required to work each week, set limits on the amount of time a participant could stay in that rung of the ladder, and specified the amount of co-payment required for child care support.[59] In short, an effort was made to set clear expectations for w-2 participants.

POLICY CHANGES AND THEIR EFFECTS
ON WELFARE CASELOADS AND COSTS

Several questions arise regarding the effects of these social welfare policy changes. First, did welfare (AFDC) caseloads and costs decline during the latter half of the 1980s and throughout the 1990s? If so, were the state's policy initiatives—and particularly Governor Thompson's highly publicized welfare policy experiments—significant causal factors in the decline? The answer to the second question may seem obvious. If the data show that caseloads and costs went down, is it not reasonable to assume that the policy changes of the Thompson administration must have been the cause?

In fact, however, the answer is not so obvious. Many important problems that state policymakers face may arise from economic, social, or cultural causes or trends that have international, national, or regional causes.[60] Thus, even concerted efforts by state policymakers to address these problems may only result in a slight amelioration of the problems. Indeed, the historical relationship between national and regional economic conditions and the size of the AFDC caseload is well documented.

On this basis, we might hypothesize that the best results that Wisconsin policymakers could have achieved would be only modestly better than the results achieved nationally or within the Midwest region.

The AFDC Caseload from 1987 to 1994

The data for the period from December 1986 to December 1994 are included in table 13. The data show that for the period AFDC caseloads in Wisconsin declined from just under 98,307 to 78,507, a drop of 20.1 percent.[61] During this period, AFDC caseloads grew nationally by almost 35 percent.[62] This is a remarkable divergence between the state and nation. It does not support the hypothesis.

The factor that is usually offered to explain the increase in the national AFDC caseload is the recession that officially ran from July 1990 to March 1991. In contrast to the recession a decade earlier, Midwestern states in general, and Wisconsin in particular, fared better than most other states during this downturn. This factor alone, however, cannot account for the sharp divergence between Wisconsin and the nation as a whole in the AFDC caseload figures. What factors beyond regional economic performance contributed to this divergence?

Scholars and analysts who have studied what happened in Wisconsin offer different explanations. Michael Wiseman argues that the AFDC caseload drop that occurred between December of 1986 and December of 1994 was largely the result of three factors: Wisconsin's fast-growing economy, reductions in AFDC benefits, and the job-placement and job-training program.[63] It is also notable, however, that the job-placement and job-training program seems to be identified as the primary explanatory factor in this analysis.

In his study, Wiseman reports that the job-placement and job-training program was established under Governor Earl in 1986, expanded during Governor Thompson's first term in office, and supported through the national government's JOBS program that was part of the Family Assistance Act of 1988. Wiseman also points out that by 1993, the state had 31 percent of adult welfare recipients who were not exempted from work in welfare-to-work efforts.[64] The national standard for that year was only 11 percent.[65] In short, Wisconsin was far ahead of other states in job placement and job training.

Wiseman, who at the time was on the faculty at the University of Wisconsin–Madison, also takes the position that Governor Thompson's highly publicized experimental policy initiatives played a role in caseload declines only at the margins.[66] He points out that most of the decline in the AFDC caseload took place before the end of Governor Thompson's first term (1991), and only Learnfare was in effect by that time.[67] Indeed, Bridefare

Table 13. Wisconsin and U.S. Aid to Families with Dependent Children/
Temporary Assistance for Needy Families

Month/Day/Year	Wisconsin Cases	U.S. Cases (in millions)
Jan. 1, 1966	11,200	1.127
1967	13,167	1.297
1968	16,887	1.522
1969	20,440	1.875
1970	23,248	1.909
1971	38,889	2.532
1972	39,418	2.918
1973	42,390	3.123
1974	46,246	3.170
1975	54,662	3.342
1976	61,360	3.561
1977	65,787	3.575
1978	66,883	3.528
1979	69,670	3.493
1980	77,316	3.642
1981	86,402	3.871
1982	81,523	3.569
1983	98,808	3.651
1984	92,973	3.725
1985	96,575	3.692
1986	98,307	3.747
1987	94,872	3.784
1988	87,269	3.748
1989	80,756	3.771
1990	79,274	3.974
1991	81,068	4.375
1992	81,700	4.769
1993	79,585	4.997
1994	78,507	5.053
1995	73,962	4.963
1996	65,368	4.628
1997	45,586	4.114
1998	13,860	3.305
1999	13,211	2.734
June 1, 2000	16,410	2.208
Jan. 1, 2001	17,012	2.145
2002	19,159	2.095
June 1, 2003	20,871	2.032

Sources: Data for 1966–1992: Thomas J. Corbett, "Welfare Reform in Wisconsin: The Rhetoric and the Reality," Institute for Research on Poverty Reprint Series, University of Wisconsin–Madison; data for 1993–2002: "Change in TANF Caseloads," U.S. Department of Health and Human Services; data for 2003: "TANF Caseloads Reported as of 12/02/03," U.S. Department of Health and Human Services

and the Two-Tier Demonstration project were not passed until 1992, and implementation of these programs did not begin until 1994. Workfare was not passed until 1993, and implementation did not begin until 1995. Furthermore, in all three of these experiments, implementation was begun in only a limited number of Wisconsin counties.

Another scholar, Larry Mead, a political scientist from New York University, takes a position quite different from Wiseman's. Mead argues that the aggressive antiwelfare rhetoric, part of the Thompson administration's launching of programs like Learnfare and Bridefare, contributed to the caseload decline.[68] Even more important, according to Mead, was the establishment of mandatory work requirements.[69] These requirements were originally established in 1986 under Governor Earl in the five counties where the job-placement and job-training program was first established. When Thompson took office in 1987 he persuaded the legislature to increase the number of counties in this program from five to fourteen.

Mead does not ignore the role that economic growth or job-placement and job-training programs played in the caseload decline.[70] Rather, he emphasizes factors that other analysts have minimized or ignored.

Welfare Caseloads (1995–1998)

Between 1995 and 1998 welfare caseloads in Wisconsin declined even more rapidly than they did between December of 1986 and December of 1994. Data assembled in figure 6 show that AFDC/welfare caseloads dropped from approximately 78,000 at the end of 1994 to less than 20,000 in 1998, a 75-percent reduction, before rising again in 2000 (about which, see the next section). Institute for Research on Poverty scholar Thomas Kaplan, however, reports that 15,000 of the cases removed from the rolls were placed into an income-support program specifically designed for disabled adults or adults providing kinship care.[71] Thus, the net caseload reduction overall was actually closer to 55 percent, still a very large reduction.

Nationally, AFDC/welfare caseloads also declined across the country during this period of time. The rate of decline was approximately 26 percent, not nearly as dramatic as the decline in Wisconsin. The fact that caseloads declined across the nation during this period can be attributed to several factors, including strong economic growth and national legislation in late 1996 in the form of PRWORA, which recast the AFDC program as Temporary Assistance to Needy Families (TANF).

The national drop in caseloads was also the result of macroeconomic pat-

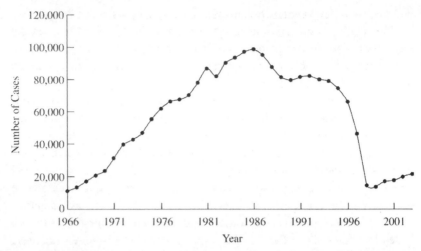

Fig. 6. Wisconsin Aid to Families with Dependent Children/Temporary Assistance for Needy Families Cases, 1966–2003 (*Sources*: Data for 1966–92: Thomas J. Corbett, "Welfare Reform in Wisconsin: The Rhetoric and Reality," Institute for Research on Poverty Reprint Series, University of Wisconsin–Madison; data for 1993–2002: Change in TANF Caseloads," U.S. Department of Health and Human Services; data for 2003: "TANF Caseloads Reported as of 12/02/03," U.S. Department of Health and Human Services

terns of the 1990s. As noted by University of Wisconsin–Madison Economics and Public Affairs Professor Robert H. Haveman and his coauthor Jonathan Schwabish, the economic growth of the 1970s and early 1980s did not lift people out of poverty in the way that it had during the 1950 and 1960s.[72] By the later 1980s, however, and certainly by the early 1990s, economic growth once again became a powerful engine generating employment and income for those at the bottom of the economic scale.[73] One consequence of this macroeconomic trend was a reduction in AFDC caseloads.

As important as both the rate and type of economic growth might have been during the 1990s in both Wisconsin and the nation, it is still necessary to explain why the decline in Wisconsin's welfare caseload was so much more dramatic than elsewhere. Larry Mead maintains that the gap between Wisconsin and other states can be explained by the fact that Wisconsin had both the *will* to make *radical* changes in its welfare programs and the *capacity* within its governmental system to bring about these changes.

Mead says that the will to make radical changes was the result of a unique political climate. Mead reports that in designing the new approach to welfare (W-2) Republicans showed "moderation" and Democrats showed a "willingness to criticize the old system."[74] Additionally, outside groups, "such as black leaders, welfare advocates, and academics, who elsewhere block reform," were also moderate in their protests, and "business groups were supportive."[75] Finally, Mead notes that Wisconsin's "masterful government," the "product of its Progressive past," provided the *capacity* to deliver the changes that the politicians wanted.[76]

No other explanation as comprehensive as Mead's has been offered, and perhaps none is needed. Yet some critics of the welfare changes do not share Mead's view because they hold a different view of what the rapid decline in welfare caseloads really represents. These critics of Wisconsin's welfare reform emphasize the human costs that have been part of welfare reform.

Caseload Reductions and Welfare Program Costs

To whatever causes people attribute the remarkable decline in Wisconsin's welfare caseload, the fact remains that a dramatic decline did occur. With fewer families on the welfare rolls the state's costs for benefit payments declined. This led to substantial savings for the state.

Yet, while the cost of Wisconsin's welfare programs declined in constant dollars, the actual costs did not decline at the same rate as caseloads. There are substantial costs associated with 1) running a large employment and training program for those on welfare, 2) the various experiments attempted by the Thompson administration, and, more recently, 3) the development of an entirely new welfare system (w-2).

There is an important lesson here for those who see Wisconsin as leading the way for other states in social welfare policy. Although part of the attempt to reduce welfare caseloads and costs involved a reduction in benefits, Wisconsin did not attempt to beat other states to the bottom in terms of costs. Rather, the state's elected officials acknowledged the substantial financial requirements needed to support its initiatives, and they provided funding for them.

For example, in the six years between 1988 and 1994, administrative costs for each AFDC case doubled in Wisconsin. Nationally, the increase during this period was only 5 percent.[77] The increased costs were largely the result of more intensive case services and increased services for clients. Also, in the area of employment and training outlays, Wisconsin's investment rose from approximately $14 million in 1986 to $81 million in 1995.[78] Child care expenses rose, too. When Governor Thompson took office in 1987, child care expenditures were only $12 million. At one point, planners put the estimated costs of child care for 1998 at $180 million.[79] To the great relief of state officials, the actual child care costs fell below much more conservative estimates for 1998. The lower costs were due in part to the sharp reductions in caseloads that took place during 1995, 1996, 1997, and 1998.

Another social welfare cost, that of Medicaid, did not decrease at the rate that caseloads decreased. Among the reasons for this is that Thompson's welfare initiatives included an expansion of health insurance coverage to the working poor in a program called Badger Care. This was an important benefit for the working poor, and it came with a price tag.

Simply cutting benefits is a much quicker and easier way to reduce welfare costs than attempting to develop a welfare-to-work system, but Governor Thompson and Wisconsin's legislators chose the latter strategy. For his forthrightness in letting other governors know that a welfare-to-work strategy may cost more than the old welfare system (AFDC), Governor Thompson won praise from *Washington Post* and syndicated columnist E. J. Dionne Jr.—surely a surprise to conservatives, who tended to dismiss Dionne for being a liberal. It was all the more important, however, because Dionne had publicly expressed concerns about the negative effects that welfare reform initiatives might have on the health and lives of poor children.[80]

LOOKING FORWARD (1998–2001)

The success that Governor Thompson and the Wisconsin legislature enjoyed in reducing welfare caseloads has been appropriately acknowledged and publicized. As the evolution of Wisconsin's social welfare policy during the 1980s and 1990s shows, however, policy innovations considered a success during one time period might yield unexpected long-term results or be viewed unfavorably in another context. Changing circumstances and perceptions sometimes precipitate a drive for policy change.

Consequently, it seems useful to use 1998 as a base year and look forward to the 2001 recession and beyond to see whether important hints about future circumstances can be discerned. As shown in figure 6, the number of TANF cases reached a low point of 13,211 on January 1, 1999. Over the next twenty-four months, however—between January 1, 1999, and January 1, 2001—caseloads grew to 17,012, an increase of 3,199, or 28.8 percent. The increase seems a bit surprising given the favorable economic conditions that existed during most of that period. One possible explanation is that the Wisconsin caseload number recorded on January 1, 1999, was below what might be considered a sustainable figure even during good economic times. Other explanations may be discovered through systematic research of the caseload growth.

The data in figure 6 also show that the TANF caseload continued to grow throughout 2001, 2002, and into the first six months of 2003. Indeed, caseloads grew 12.6 percent in the twelve months between January 1, 2001, and January 1, 2002. Yet growth during this period is not surprising, given the fact that the recession of 2001 officially began in March of that year. Employment opportunities are restricted by recession, which makes the welfare-to-work process more difficult.

Although the 2001 recession officially ended in October, TANF caseloads continued to rise in Wisconsin through June of 2003. While welfare caseloads have traditionally declined after a recovery has begun, the national economic recovery of 2002 and 2003 has been called a "jobless" recovery. This circumstance may largely explain the continued caseload growth in Wisconsin through 2002 and into 2003.

The 2001 recession and its aftermath provide an important early test of Wisconsin's most recent welfare reform initiatives. The fact that TANF caseload growth did not spike above prerecession rates during the recession may be an indicator of the continuing success of W-2, or it could be the result of other factors. The picture may become clearer when the Department of Health and Human Services finally releases caseload data for the last six months of 2003 and that for 2004. These data are essential for determining how long after the end of the recession caseloads continued to rise and at what rate; they are also key in determining whether TANF caseloads finally leveled off and began to decline. Careful research will be required, of course, to illuminate why caseloads increased sharply in Wisconsin before the recession began, why the growth did not spike during the recession, and why the numbers continued to grow for so many months after the recession was over.

Shrinking labor market opportunities for TANF/W-2 recipients, however, are not the only threat that the 2001 economic recession and its aftermath posed for Wisconsin's W-2 success story. The state fiscal crisis that began in FY 2001 and continued through the time of this writing (May 2005) may make the high cost of support for the welfare-to-work programs problematic. The 2001 recession not only created a drop in state revenues but also uncovered an underlying structural budget deficit. The causes of the structural deficit can be found in the 1990s, when Wisconsin's policymakers rapidly increased spending and made large cuts in taxes.

The structural deficit that remained visible in Wisconsin's FY 2002, 2003, and 2004 budgets shows that this approach to financial management was unsound. Given the fact that there is now within Wisconsin's political system a strong presumption against new taxes, sizable spending cuts are required to balance the budget. Even programs that support Wisconsin's successful welfare-to-work strategy may be vulnerable in these difficult economic and financial circumstances.

CHAPTER TEN

Local Government

Much has been written about the impact of (Wisconsin's) Progressive reform on national and state government, but the effects were also felt in local government.

> Susan Paddock, "The Changing World of
> Wisconsin Local Government," 1997

[T]he constitutional unitary character of the states proclaimed by the courts (often in the face of clear expressions of the public will to the contrary) sets certain very definite legal limits to local power.

> Daniel Elazar, *The American Mosaic*, 1994

The preceding nine chapters of this book have dealt primarily with the institutions and operations of Wisconsin's state government and the public policy developed through those institutions. This chapter focuses on local governments. As noted in chapter 1, "The Character of the State," local governments in Wisconsin play a key role in supporting the special quality of life that most state residents enjoy. Indeed, local governments provide many of the most visible and important public services, including: police and fire protection, primary and secondary public education, road construction and maintenance, recreation, public welfare, and water and sewer services. In order to deliver these services, Wisconsin's local governments employ more than 200,000 people, approximately three times the number employed by state government.[1]

The chapter begins with a brief overview of the constitutional and legal position local governments have within the American governmental system and in Wisconsin. Then, the development of local government within the state is detailed. Next, the four basic types of local governments that exist within the state are identified, and some of their structural attributes, principal powers, and functions are outlined. Finally, local relationships, including cooperation, competition, and conflict among local governments are examined. The relationship between the Wisconsin state and local governments is touched upon briefly here and taken up more comprehensively in the following chapter, "State-Local Relations."

LOCAL GOVERNMENT IN THE AMERICAN GOVERNMENTAL SYSTEM AND IN WISCONSIN

Many people would be surprised to know that the U.S. Constitution does not even mention local government. In the Constitution power is divided between the national government and the states. It is thus left to the states to create and regulate local governments in the manner they see fit. This is why some political scientists take the position that "local governments may vary in structure, size, power and relation to one another. But in a constitutional sense they are all the same because they all live on power 'borrowed' from the states."[2]

The ways in which the states regard local government vary considerably. Some states, like Virginia, only give to local governments powers that are explicitly articulated in the state constitution or in state statutes.[3] In other states, however, local governments are given much more flexibility to determine which services they will deliver and how they will do it.

Over the past century, advocates of local government have made concerted efforts to extend the principles of federalism to local governments. One manifestation of these efforts has been the campaign to establish "home-rule" provisions in state constitutions or statutes. Particularly during the past two decades, local government officials and their supporters have had considerable success, as home-rule amendments have been added to about half the state constitutions.[4]

Wisconsin is one of a small number of states that has had a home-rule provision in its state constitution for most of the twentieth century. Wisconsin's home-rule provision was incorporated into the state constitution in 1924 as part of the Progressives' drive to improve local government's service-delivery capacity and to give people more direct control over governmental activity. The opening statement of the 1924 home-rule amendment to the Wisconsin Constitution reads: "Cities and villages organized pursuant to state law are hereby empowered, to determine their local affairs and government, subject only to this constitution and to such enactments of the legislature of state-wide concern as shall with uniformity affect every city or village."[5] Although the adoption of this amendment was an important step toward expansion of the discretion and authority of local government officials, it is important to note that the home-rule provision only applied to cities and villages; counties and towns were not included in the language of the 1924 amendment.

Statutory provisions passed in 1925 and 1933 strengthened Wisconsin's home-rule amendment. These two legislative actions substituted "a comprehensive grant of power for the long list of powers enumerated in the original law."[6] Yet even the addition of these statutory provisions did not have the full effect that some supporters of local government in Wisconsin expected them to have. City and village officials did not gain the full range of discretion that some reformers had hoped they would, because the 1924 constitutional amendment stipulated that the state legislature could intervene in local affairs when local governments were dealing with issues of "statewide concern" or when "uniformity" of action across cities and villages was deemed essential. Consequently, it happens from time to time that issues that local officials would like to address and resolve locally are ultimately decided by the state legislature.

This circumstance is not unique to Wisconsin. Local government officials in other states where home-rule provisions have been added to their constitutions, such as Colorado, have also found state legislatures very reluctant to give up the power to intervene in local affairs.[7] These problems notwithstanding, local government officials in Wisconsin and Colorado are still more likely to enjoy greater latitude in the management of their own affairs than are officials in states without home-rule provisions.

EVOLUTION AND TYPES OF LOCAL GOVERNMENT IN WISCONSIN

During the years when Wisconsin was a territory and in the early years following statehood in 1848, Wisconsin had two principal types of local government units: counties and towns. Counties were established when Wisconsin was part of the Michigan territory. In 1818 the land that was to become Wisconsin was divided by the Michigan territorial governor, Lewis Cass, into three counties: Brown, Crawford, and Michilimackinac.[8]

As Wisconsin became a territory, and then a state, these three counties were divided and then subdivided again.

Towns were also authorized during the time Wisconsin was part of the Michigan Territory but not until almost a decade after the three original counties were established.[9] Towns were the designated governing units within geographical subdivisions known as "townships." Townships were units of thirty-six square miles, six miles on each side. These squares were in turn subdivided into thirty-six sections, which were then divided and subdivided twice more. The final subdivided unit was a parcel of forty acres, the basic unit for conveying or selling rural land.[10]

The town structure was particularly well suited to the early Wisconsin settlers who emigrated from New England and New York, where there was a strong tradition of town government. Town government functioned through direct democracy; residents at an annual town meeting made the major decisions. In addition to their preference for conducting political business in this manner, the Yankees found that the town form of government suited them for other reasons, too.

According to historians Robert C. Nesbit and William F. Thompson, the Yankees arriving in Wisconsin "knew the mechanics of public lands surveys and sales, and they often had a line of credit from back home to help them get started. They took possession of the town sites, waterpower (sources) and the best agricultural lands. They became the editors, the preachers, the merchants and the politicians of the territory."[11] Nesbit and Thompson describe these Yankee settlers as "activists," who wanted to connect their "new wilderness home to world markets," and understood the important role that the community and political action would play in this development.[12]

In contrast to the Yankees, settlers emigrating to Wisconsin from southern states preferred the county, as opposed to the municipal (town, village, city) form of government. The differing and sometimes conflicting preferences of the two groups played a role in Wisconsin politics during the first fifty years of statehood.[13] It was not until the late 1880s that the struggle over whether county or municipal (including town) governments would be the primary unit of local government was decided; the municipal form of government prevailed. More than one hundred years later, however, the status and role of counties seems to have been recharged, particularly in some of the more heavily populated areas of southeastern and south-central Wisconsin. As population increased and suburban and town populations expanded in these areas, the perceived value of having the county provide services for multiple municipal units generally increased.

Counties and Towns in the 1848 Constitution

Even though the political formation of counties and towns preceded state-hood, the Wisconsin state constitution of 1848 put them under the control of the state legislature. At the same time, the constitution gave the state legislature the capacity to delegate some powers to these local governments. For example Article IV, section 22, states that "the legislature may confer upon the boards of supervisors of the several counties of the state such power of a local, legislative and administrative character as they shall from time to time prescribe." Language in section 23 of this same article also states that "the legislature shall establish but one system of town and county government, which shall be as nearly uniform as practicable."

The uniformity provision has been amended three times over the past 150 years, as the state legislature has attempted to give county governments the ability to organize and operate in varied circumstances, ranging from modern suburban or metropolitan to relatively isolated and rural. The structure of county government has also been the subject of statutory activity. The uniformity principle has been retained, however, for town government.

Another important dimension of the 1848 constitution was the linking of town government and county government. According to scholars Edward J. Miller and Brett Hawkins, the connection was established by "having the town chairman serve on the county board of supervisors."[14] In addition, each village and each city ward elected one member to the county board of supervisors.[15] This arrangement often gave towns a level of representation and influence in county affairs that was disproportionate to the size of the population living in those towns.

During the 1960s this arrangement ran afoul of the "one man, one vote" principle affirmed by the U.S. Supreme Court in *Baker v. Carr* (1962) and *Reynolds v. Sims* (1964).[16] In these two cases, the Court ruled that the equal protection clause of the Fourteenth Amendment to the U.S. Constitution required that apportionment of seats in both houses of the state legislatures must be based on population. Since the means for establishing representation on Wisconsin's county boards of supervisors were not based on population, the arrangement was challenged in 1965. In that year, the Wisconsin Supreme Court (*State ex rel. Sonneborn v. Sylvester*, 1965) held that apportionment of seats on local policymaking boards must be based on population, and this decision was upheld by the U.S. Supreme Court (*Avery v. Midland County*, 1968).[17]

The Wisconsin legislature responded to these decisions by requiring all counties to "apportion their boards by population and to establish maximum and minimum numbers of members, based on county population."[18] In state statutes, the minimum number of members on county boards was set at seven and the maximum at forty-seven.[19] One very important consequence of the court decisions and the corresponding legislative requirement regarding apportionment was that the towns' influence on the boards of supervisors declined in most counties while the influence of cities grew.

Cities and Villages in the 1848 Constitution

The 1848 constitution also gave the legislature authority, in Article XI, section 3, to provide "for the organization of cities and incorporated villages." The framers of the constitution knew that as the population of the towns grew there would be a need for other forms of municipal government designed for governance in urban rather than rural settings. Indeed, at the time the state constitution was written, there were a dozen villages and only one city—Milwaukee.[20] From 1848 through 1870 the state legislature chartered and controlled cities and villages by special acts.[21] As a result, the structural arrangement and powers granted to local governments varied considerably. The legislature limited its own discretion to create and modify the arrangements of city government somewhat in 1871, when it passed legislation that established classes of cities.[22] Structural arrangements for, and powers granted to, the cities varied by class or type. Then, in 1892, legislation was passed that changed the process through which new cities and villages were created. Consequently, the legislature did not need to pass a special act each time a local unit wanted to be granted the status of a new city or village; such charters could be obtained by following the requirements outlined in statutory law.

Over the years, the state legislature passed a variety of laws that affected cities and villages. As part of the Progressive reforms, state laws affecting villages were codified in 1921. Then, in 1922, laws affecting cities were codified.[23] Of course, the most important of the Progressive actions, as noted earlier, were the 1924 home-rule amendment to the 1848 constitution, and the statutory provisions of 1925 and 1933 designed to strengthen the home-rule provision.

Among the important changes that have occurred in recent years in statutory law relating to municipalities is the expansion of powers given to towns in 1993. In that year, the legislature granted to towns many of the powers previously granted to cities and villages.[24]

School Districts in the 1848 Constitution

Wisconsin was an early pioneer in public education. In 1846, two years before statehood, fourteen thousand children in the Wisconsin territory were already attending public schools.[25] Thus it is not surprising that the 1848 constitution included provisions for public schools. Article X (3) of the 1848 document stipulates that "the legislature shall provide by law for the establishment of district schools, which shall be as nearly uniform as practicable; and such schools shall be free and without charge for tuition to all children between the ages of four and twenty years."[26]

The 1848 constitution also provided two mechanisms to pay for the public schools. One was a state school fund, the monies of which were to come primarily from the sale of state land, with special provision made to allocate 5 percent of the proceeds gained in the sale of the land the state was to gain upon admission to the union. The second mechanism, stated in Article X (4), required each town and city to "raise by tax" the revenue needed to support the public schools.

It is important to note, however, that the constitutional framers did not specify a separate governance structure for school districts. Instead responsibility for governance and administration of the school districts was left to the entities that were responsible for raising revenue for the schools— towns and cities. This was both an efficient and effective mechanism for all of the nineteenth century, since most of Wisconsin's schools were one-room schoolhouses located in rural areas governed by towns. This arrangement did mean, however, that there were a large number of school districts. At the turn of the twentieth century, for example, there were 6,529.[27]

In 1907 the state legislature, through statutory means, provided for the establishment of separate school districts with their own taxing and governing authority.[28] Over the next several decades, most districts were then organized separately from their respective municipal governments. Nevertheless, a small number of school districts remained under the authority and management of a few municipal governments. The state legislature eliminated the option of having school districts operated by municipal governments in 1981.

After the end of World War II, public education seemed to be everyone's concern. Among those calling for changes in the public school system were people who believed that larger schools and larger school districts were better than small schools and small districts. Based in part on the recommendations of the Commission on the Improvement of the Educational System, in 1949 the state legislature began the process of consolidating school districts by giving county school committees the authority to reorganize local districts.[29] Then, in 1959, the state legislature passed an act mandating the inclusion of a high school in every school district.

These legislative actions had a dramatic effect. Between 1952 and 1962 the number of school districts was reduced from 5,298 to 1,752. Between 1962 and 1978 the number dropped further, from 1,752 to 436.[30] By 1992 the number had declined to 428, where it remains today.

THE STRUCTURE AND OPERATION OF CONTEMPORARY LOCAL GOVERNMENT

In many books and articles about local government, the term "local government" is used to mean "general purpose" local governments–local governmental units that provide a wide array of services. Thus articles and books on local government usually focus on counties and municipalities (cities, villages, and towns). It may be noted, however, that local government can include "special purpose" governmental units, which offer a single or a highly specific kind of service. Special purpose local governments include school districts and special districts.

Throughout the rest of this chapter, the term "local government" is used to refer to both general purpose and special purpose local governments. A discussion of the structure and operation of both school districts and special districts is included herein, as well. Wilder Crane and A. Clarke Hagensick, who have studied and written about Wisconsin government and politics during the past thirty years, have characterized the state as having a two-tiered system of local (general purpose) government, with the state divided first into seventy-two counties and then subdivided into cities, villages, and towns.[31] Miller and Hawkins argue that this two-tiered system of government was based on the system used in New York.[32]

Although the two-tiered, or dual, system of local jurisdiction is not unique to Wisconsin, it is important to note that not all states use it. For example, in the rural South, county government has traditionally been the only form of local government.[33] In other parts of the country, New England especially, however, municipal government is the dominant form and counties have only a minimal role. In still other states, such as Virginia, the county may be the principal provider of municipal services within its borders, but independent cities may exist within those borders that deliver their own services.[34]

As of January 1, 2000, Wisconsin's local governments included 72 counties, 190 cities, 395 villages, 1265 towns, 426 school districts, 16 technical college districts, and 626 special districts.[35] The counties varied in size from 1,545 square miles (Marathon County) to 232 square miles (Ozaukee County). Data also show that the counties varied considerably in population and population density. Milwaukee County had the largest population, with a 2000 population of 940,164; Menominee County had the smallest population, with 4,562. Milwaukee County also had the greatest number of persons per square mile, with 3,891, while Iron County had the fewest, with only 9.1 persons per square mile.

The 2000 census data show that 56 percent of the state's population lives in the state's cities, 12.8 percent lives in villages, and 31.2 percent lives in towns. Seventy-three municipalities had populations of 10,000 or more. Milwaukee, with a population of 596,974 as recorded in the 2000 census, was the largest of these cities, and Madison, with a population of 208,054 was second. Merrill, with a population of 10,146 was the smallest of the cities with populations of 10,000 or more.[36]

Counties

The legislative body in all Wisconsin counties is the county board of supervisors. As noted earlier the size of the board is determined by population, with a minimum of seven members required. Counties with populations of more than 100,000 can have up to 47 supervisors; 39 is the maximum number permitted for counties with populations between 50,000 and 99,999. The maximum for counties with 25,000 to 49,999 is 31, and for counties with fewer than 25,000 residents the number is 21.

Sixteen counties (26 percent of the total) operate with boards that are at their legal maximum, and twenty-five counties (36 percent) operate with 80 percent or more of the maximum.[37] No county has fewer than 50 percent of the maximum, and only five have less than 60 percent (Brown, Florence, Kenosha, Pepin, and Pierce). The members of these county boards are elected for two-year terms, with the exception of Milwaukee, where the term is four years. These supervisors are selected in nonpartisan elections held during the spring of odd-numbered years. A person holding a county board seat can expect to put in extensive amounts of time, but the only financial reimbursement most supervisors receive is for expenses related to the job.

The lead executive official in county government is either an elected county executive, an administrator appointed by the county board of supervisors, or an administrative coordinator. The elected county executive has the most formal power of the three types. The elected executive serves a four-year term, has the power to veto ordinances passed by the county board, and can appoint the heads of administrative departments that are not supervised by an independently elected administrator.[38] Nine of Wisconsin's seventy-two counties have an elected executive: Brown, Dane, Fond du Lac, Kenosha, Milwaukee, Outagamie, Racine, Waukesha, and Winnebago.

The county administrator serves at the pleasure of the county board. Although the administrator does not have veto authority, he or she does have the power to appoint, with board confirmation, the heads of administrative departments that do not have an independently elected executive.[39] Six counties—Burnett, Jefferson, Marathon, Marinette, Menominee, and Rock—have a county administrator. Counties that do not have an elected county executive or county administrator are required by statutory law established in 1987 to have an administrative coordinator. The administrative coordinator can either be elected or appointed by the board, but this official has very little power independent of the board. The county board chairperson is often selected for this post.[40] Fifty-seven counties have an administrative coordinator.

There are a number of factors that explain why the majority of Wisconsin counties have selected the weakest form of executive management. The original state constitution did not clearly demarcate executive functions from legislative functions, and no amendment was passed until 1960 to help clarify the situation. There has been a long tradition of legislative (county board) dominance in both legislative and administrative matters. There has also been a preference among many county supervisors for retaining the county board's strong influence in administrative matters.

Another key structural arrangement in county government established in the 1848 constitution is the election of a variety of executive branch or administrative officers. The independently elected members of the executive branch include a clerk, clerk of circuit court, district attorney, register of deeds, sheriff, and treasurer. The coroner or medical examiner is also elected in many counties. Elections for these officials are held in November of every other even year; their term of office is two years. Action to remove these officials can be taken by the county board for cause, except in the case of the clerk of circuit court. Removal of that official must be undertaken by the circuit judge.

Counties had their own courts until 1977, when a constitutional amendment abolished them. The amendment was designed to establish a unified state court system, and sixty-nine circuit courts were created. Sixty-six of the state's seventy-two counties have at least one circuit court, while three pairs of counties—Buffalo-Pepin, Florence-Forest, and Menominee-Shawano—share a circuit court. There is more than one circuit court in thirty-seven counties. Circuit court justices are elected for six-year terms in elections held in April. They are officially nonpartisan.

The movement toward a state-supported court system began with state legislative actions taken in the 1950s and continued in the 1960s. The drive for a unified state court system came in the 1970s through the initiative of Governor Patrick Lucey. Lucey maintained that the property tax was an inappropriate means for financing county courts and circuit courts.[41] He also contended that unified administration would improve the operation of the courts. The legislature eventually accepted Lucey's proposal for a state-funded, unified court system. Two successive legislatures passed the language needed for an amendment to be included on the ballot. In 1977 the people of Wisconsin approved the amendment. Today the "state pays for the salaries of circuit judges and court reporters," and "some of the expenses for interpreters, guardians ad litem, judicial assistants, court-appointed witnesses and jury per diems," but counties still pay a portion of the operating expenses.[42]

Towns

Towns generally serve small, rural populations, but some are located within or are contiguous to large urban areas. Towns are generally referred to as "unincorporated" units of local government. That is to say, they are not formally incorporated by the state, as cities and villages are. The state constitution requires that towns have as uniform a structure as possible—a requirement established in the 1848 constitution. In the mid-1970s the legislature twice approved the language of a constitutional amendment designed to give towns more flexibility to determine their structure, but the constitutional amendment required to implement this change was defeated at the polls in 1978.[43]

State statutes essentially make the town's voting-age population the legislative body through the requirement that the town budget be approved by voters at an annual meeting. Thus it is often said that towns offer the best prospect for citizens to participate in direct democracy. In this context, the town board is an executive body, overseeing the daily implementation of policy decisions.

The town board consists of three members, elected in April of odd-numbered years; elections are nonpartisan, and board members serve two-year terms. A board chair is selected who presides at board meetings and at annual meetings. Towns also have several other elected officials or employees, including an assessor, clerk, treasurer, constable, and municipal justice. Some of the larger towns also have a police chief, highway superintendent, health officer, park and sanitary district commissioners, and zoning commissioners.

Among the most difficult and important issues that those in towns and town governments have faced over the years is the fact that incorporated local units of government—villages and cities—have the right, "subject to court determination, review by the state, and a referendum of the affected inhabitants, to take adjacent land from unincorporated towns."[44] Approval of the residents living in the parts of the town that are not annexed is not needed. The annexation process is sometimes initiated by town residents who want access to a higher level of municipal services provided by a village or city. A city council may also initiate the annexation process. Indeed the city council's desire to expand its area and its tax base has often been the motivation behind annexation. Among the rules governing annexation in Wisconsin is the "rule of reason"—it must make sense and be in the public interest.[45]

Cities

The term "city" is sometimes assumed to be synonymous with a densely populated metropolitan area like New York, Los Angeles, Chicago, Miami, or Detroit. In Wisconsin, however, a city can consist of as few as 1,001 residents. Leon Epstein, a thoughtful observer of Wisconsin government and politics, reported during the 1950s that Wisconsin's pattern of urbanization had "one distinctive feature." According to Epstein, "more of Wisconsin's urban population is in small and medium sized cities . . . than is usually the case in large industrialized states."[46] Epstein's observation remains true today.

Wisconsin's cities are arranged into first-, second-, third-, and fourth-class on the basis of size. The distinction among the classes is based primarily on population, rather than on legal differences.[47] First-class cities have a population of more than 150,000. Second-, third-, and fourth-class cities have populations of more than 39,000, 10,000, and 1,000, respectively. It is important to note, however, that cities do not have to change from one class to another just because they meet population requirements. The decision is entirely in the hands of the city government. For example, the city of Madison, with a population of more than 200,000, has chosen to remain a city of the second class because the statutes governing first-class cities were written for Milwaukee. Another relevant factor is that cities do not lose their status once achieved, even if they lose population. For instance the population of Bayfield (in Bayfield County) fell below 1,000, but the city did not lose its fourth-class city status.

By statute, all cities must have a government structured in one of three forms: mayor-council; council-manager; or commission. Almost all Wisconsin cities use the mayor-council form; only 10 of the 189 cities currently use the council-manager form. The commission form of organization has not been used by any Wisconsin city since 1957.[48]

In both the mayor-council and council-manager forms of city government, city council members are generally elected for two-year terms, but cities can establish terms of up to four years. Elections for city council are held in the spring of odd-numbered years, and they are officially nonpartisan. Although the home-rule provision in the state constitution gives cities the option of using an at-large or district form of representation, most Wisconsin cities use the district form.

The number of members a city council can have is based on population. On average, most city councils have between six and ten members. The largest city council, that of Madison, has thirty-two members. In all cities except Milwaukee, city council members serve on a part-time basis, with most activity conducted during the evenings. City councils are required by statute to meet at least once per month, but many need to meet much more frequently to deal with the press of demands. Most city council members receive only nominal pay for their work.

The mayor is elected at the same time as are city council members. Although the mayor is the designated chief executive in city government, he or she is also a member of the city council. The mayor presides over council meetings, and in cases of a tie vote, the mayor can cast the tiebreaker. It is the council's responsibility to pass city ordinances, but mayors do have veto power over council actions. It is the mayor's principal responsibility to ensure that city ordinances are carried out.

By statute, cities must also have an attorney, clerk, chief of police, fire chief, health commissioner and/or board of public health, treasurer, and weed commissioner. Cities may combine or consolidate these positions. Cities must also have an assessor, board of public works, constable, engineer, and street commissioner. These positions may either be elected or appointed.

Villages

In order to be classified as a village, a local governmental unit must have more than 150 people; village status may, however, be pursued by a town that has more than 150 people. Wisconsin villages are usually smaller than cities, but some villages with populations in excess of 10,000 have retained village status. Among these villages are three in Milwaukee County: Menomonee Falls, Shorewood, and Whitefish Bay.

Just as villages are usually smaller than cities, their structures are also simpler. Most villages have a board of six trustees.[49] The trustees are elected at-large for two-year terms. Half of the trustee positions are up for election in even-numbered years and the other half in odd-numbered years. Elections for the office of village trustee are held in the spring and are officially nonpartisan.

The executive officer in the village is the village president. The president is entitled to vote, however, on all matters before the trustees. Unlike a city mayor, however, a village president does not have veto power over board of trustee actions. Members of the village also elect an assessor, clerk, marshal or constable, and treasurer, unless the trustees have designated that these offices be filled by appointment.

School Districts

Wisconsin's school districts are divided into four types: common school districts, unified districts, union high school districts, and first-class city districts. Districts may differ in terms of grades served, organization, and control. For example, common school districts may be either elementary districts operating grades K–8 or districts operating grades K–12. Union high school districts provide 9–12 only, with a separate district providing elementary education. Yet both common and union school districts operate similarly. Both are governed by a school board, and both have an annual meeting at which voters have an opportunity to ask questions and, most importantly, to approve the tax levy for the upcoming year. Thus, governance is very similar to that of towns, with boards and annual meetings.[50]

In contrast, the unified school district is governed by a board of education, and it does not have an annual meeting. Unified school districts may serve either grades K–8 or K–12. The unified school district is the newest type of district; it was created by the state legislature in 1959 to "incorporate the best features of the common and former city school districts."[51] The only city with a first-class city school district is Milwaukee; it is "known as a special charter district because one entire chapter of the state statutes, Chapter 119, is devoted to it."[52]

Most of Wisconsin's 426 school districts are common school districts. Of the 369 common school districts, 323 run K–12 schools and 46 run K–8 schools. Forty-six school districts are unified, and all but one of these school districts run K–12 systems. Ten districts are union high school systems, with schools covering grades 9–12. As noted above the only first-class city school district is that of Milwaukee.

During the 1990s the Milwaukee school system received a good deal of public and press attention as a result of a program initiated by Governor Thompson called Milwaukee Parental Choice. Passed by the state legislature in 1989 and put into operation in 1990, the program allowed a limited number of low-income parents in Milwaukee to send their children to private schools—at public expense. The "school choice" program was the first of its type in America. It was updated by legislation in 1995 that expanded the program in several ways, the most important of which was to include parochial schools. Opponents of the latter provision petitioned the court to block implementation of the legislation on constitutional grounds, but the Wisconsin Supreme Court affirmed the constitutionality of the expanded program in 1998.

In all school districts, school board members are elected at-large for staggered three-year terms. Like other local government officials, school board members are chosen during the spring in nonpartisan elections, but their three-year term puts them on a different election cycle than other elected officials. Among the school boards' most important duties is the selection of the school district superintendent. The superintendent is usually the person responsible for the daily operation of the school district.

Technical College Districts

Like school districts for elementary and secondary education, technical college districts are special purpose local government units. They have the power to levy taxes, spend money, and buy property. Because they are special purpose districts, however, the presumption is that the funds these districts raise and spend will be used specifically for the purpose of providing vocational-technical education to Wisconsin students.

There are sixteen technical college districts in the state of Wisconsin. Within these districts there are forty-seven main and satellite campuses as of 2001.[53] Each of these districts has a citizen board of nine members, who serve three-year staggered terms. The governor appoints all members of the board. Among the board's principal responsibilities is the selection of a district superintendent. The district superintendent is responsible for overseeing the vocational-technical school or schools in that area. In FY 2000–2001 the sixteen technical college districts served 451,271 part-time and full-time students.[54] On a full-time equivalent (FTE) basis, the total number of students served was 63,783.[55]

Local vocational-technical instructional activities are coordinated through a state agency.[56] Until 1994 that agency was the State Board of Vocational Training and Adult Education (VTAE).[57] Since then, the state agency has been called the Wisconsin Technical College System Board. State and national government funding for vocational-technical education is passed through this board to the local vocational-technical school districts. Federal funding is commonly in the range of 8 to 10 percent in a given year, while state funds commonly support another 70 percent of a local district's activity, with the result that local districts may have to raise only 20 percent of their operating budget through property taxes. Although the local board can determine the tax levy, the state board does attempt to limit and coordinate tax levies across districts.

It is critical to note that technical college districts in Wisconsin do not have to compete for funds with junior colleges. Wisconsin does have two-year colleges, but all of these colleges are a part of the University of Wisconsin system. Because the University of Wisconsin system is supported with state tax revenue and user fees, the local vocational district does not have to compete with the two-year colleges for property tax revenue.

Special Districts

In 1997 there were 684 special districts in Wisconsin. Special districts may be created for projects that are "strictly local in nature but may require cooperation across municipal boundaries."[58] Most special districts are established to solve a single problem or to perform a single or specific function. Special districts are set up as corporate bodies that can levy taxes and establish special assessments, spend money, acquire property, sue or be sued, and borrow money in the bond market.[59] Most special districts are established as permanent entities; others are temporary. Among the most common types of special districts are: water authorities; metropolitan sewerage districts; county drainage boards; natural resource districts, such as lake protection and rehabilitation districts; and housing and community development authorities.[60]

Generally, the fact that most of these local governmental bodies are created for a single function means that their structure is relatively simple, their size is relatively small, and their operations are straightforward. Yet because special districts often do perform functions that cross municipal boundaries, the politics of structuring and managing them can be very complicated. Indeed, boards and managers of special districts may get caught in the crossfire of competing preferences held by elected officials in the municipalities served by these districts.

Wisconsin's largest special district, the Milwaukee Metropolitan Sewerage District (MMSD), is exemplary in this respect. The MMSD was established in 1921 to provide a unified sewer system for Milwaukee and its nearby suburbs. The MMSD commission has eleven members: seven appointed by Milwaukee's mayor and four by suburbs in Milwaukee County. The operating budget is based on user fees and is uncontroversial. In contrast, the district's capital budget is financed on the basis of a municipality's relative share of the total property value within the district. This financing method has been a major point of conflict.[61]

In recent years the number of special districts in Wisconsin has grown quite rapidly, increasing from 399 districts in 1992 to 696 in 1997. In 2002 the number was slightly smaller, 684.[62] A variety of factors have contributed to the proliferation of special districts, including the belief that they can carry out a specific task more efficiently and effectively than a general purpose government. Another reason is that municipal and county officials sometimes prefer to transfer or delegate certain functions to special districts because the charges for services delivered are handled by the special districts themselves. Thus, the services and the charges for those functions do not increase municipal property tax rates, costs, or employment.

FUNCTIONS OF WISCONSIN'S LOCAL GOVERNMENTS

The functions of local government can be described in several ways. Among the most interesting and useful methods is to examine expenditure and employment data. The expenditure data provide a means to compare the relative emphasis each type of general purpose local government (county, town, village, or city) gives to a particular function. The employment data provide an aggregate picture of activity across all of Wisconsin's local governments, including school districts and special districts.

One of the most striking patterns that can be discerned from the expenditure data, shown in table 14, is that town and county spending is concentrated on a particular, albeit different, function. In 2001 towns spent 42.9 percent of their total expenditures on transportation, and counties spent 40.3 percent on health and human services. For those who have some understanding of the role that towns and counties play in Wisconsin's state-local governmental system, the use of funds for these purposes makes perfect sense.

Most towns are located in rural areas, and the rural town roads are essential for getting farm products to markets and for the commute to work in the city or the suburbs. The county is the unit of local government that the state employs to deliver health and social services. Included in these services are many health programs, including drug abuse and mental health programs, services for the aged and for veterans, and social service programs, including income maintenance and general relief programs.[63]

The expenditure data show that cities and villages spend their money across functions in a more balanced way than do towns and counties. Again this underscores the fact that cities and villages provide a broader range of services to local residents than do towns or counties. Nevertheless, it is worth noting that the number-one function, expressed through expenditures for both cities and villages, is public safety. This function consumes 21.5 percent of the cities' resources and 19.3 percent of village resources.

Payment of principal and interest on debt is the second largest expense for both cities and villages, accounting for 15.7 percent of city expenditures and 17.8 percent of village spending. Transportation and sanitation are the third and fourth most important functions for villages, comprising 17.4 percent and 15.2 percent of spending, respectively. Next on the list for villages is the operation of electric, gas, and water utilities. For cities, transportation is third, accounting for 15.2 percent. Operating electric, gas, and water utilities is fourth for cities, followed by sanitation. These functions account for 11.3 percent and 9.7 percent of total city expenditures, respectively.

Functions across All Local Governments

Employment data provide an alternative method for examining the functions of local government. This information provides a more complete portrait

Table 14. 2001 Expenditures of Municipalities and Counties

	Towns			Villages		
	Amount	Per Capita	Percent	Amount	Per Capita	Percent
General Administration	$103,565,745	$61	14.3	$73,928,384	$107	7.7
Public Safety	123,474,742	73	17.1	185,492,295	267	19.3
Health and Human Services	2,878,851	2	0.4	3,582,912	5	0.4
Transportation	310,436,215	184	42.9	166,746,868	241	17.4
Sanitation	56,863,032	34	7.9	146,300,969	211	15.2
Recreation and Education	17,846,197	11	2.5	68,178,605	98	7.1
Conservation and Development	15,043,284	9	2.1	39,456,828	57	4.1
Principal and Interest	71,719,154	43	9.9	170,761,075	246	17.8
Electric, Gas, and Water Utilities	7,710,735	4	1.1	97,376,557	140	10.2
Other	13,120,384	8	1.8	7,334,067	11	0.8
TOTAL	$722,658,339	$429	100.0	$959,158,560	$1,383	100.0

	Cities			Counties		
	Amount	Per Capita	Percent	Amount	Per Capita	Percent
General Administration	$357,210,125	$118	6.8	$547,178,991	$101	9.7
Public Safety	1,134,798,782	375	21.5	741,050,375	137	13.1
Health and Human Services	86,464,932	29	1.6	2,280,287,317	422	40.3
Transportation	802,870,942	266	15.2	845,301,009	157	14.9
Sanitation	515,195,618	170	9.7	62,862,183	12	1.1
Recreation and Education	467,550,929	155	8.8	298,598,160	55	5.3
Conservation and Development	345,518,341	114	6.5	123,830,726	23	2.2
Principal and Interest	827,643,398	274	15.7	370,717,877	69	6.6
Electric, Gas, and Water Utilities	596,708,944	197	11.3	25,111,076	5	0.4
Other	155,683,321	51	2.9	363,798,429	67	6.4
TOTAL	$5,289,645,332	$1,749	100.0	$5,658,736,143	$1,048	100.0

Source: "Municipal and County Finance," Wisconsin Legislative Fiscal Bureau

of local government activities than can be gleaned from expenditure data alone because it includes K–12 school districts, vocational-technical college districts (labeled "Higher Ed. Insruct. in the table), and special districts. Additionally, the functional categories associated with employment data are more detailed than they are for expenditure data. The 2001 employment data for all local governments in Wisconsin are provided in table 15.

Public education for kindergarten through twelfth grade is the primary task of local government, according to full-time equivalent employment data. The number employed in K–12 public school instruction is 91,273; the number employed in public school administration and support is 28,214. Altogether, school districts' FTE employment is 119,487, or 54.6 percent of all local government employees.

As defined by employment, police protection is the second-largest function of local government. The FTE employment total for the two police categories is 14,783, or 6.8 percent of all local government employment. When police and firefighters are added together the data show that 19,321, or 8.8 percent of local government employees, work in the field of public safety. If employees who work in corrections are added to the public safety total, the number rises to 23,641 and the percentage rises to 10.8 percent of local government employment.

As defined by employment, public welfare is the third most important task of local government. FTE employment in this area is 13,604, or 6.2 percent of the local government total. As noted earlier, the counties are the state and national government's principal agent in the delivery of income support and health care (Medicaid) for the poor. In the past five years, these county offices have also had primary responsibility for finding employment for those who are seeking income support.

Streets and highways, which category includes both construction and maintenance, is local government's fourth-largest function. The number of FTE employees in this function is 9,388, or 4.3 percent of local government employment. Given the fact that roads are essential to the modern economy and social activity, it is not surprising that transportation continues to be an important local government function.

For local government, higher education comes next, followed by: public health, central administration, fire protection, corrections; judicial-legal, parks and recreation, financial administration, local libraries, sewerage, and transit. A total of 9,388 full-time equivalents are employed in higher education (instruction and other); 6,008 are employed in health care; 5,078

Table 15. Local Government Employment in Wisconsin, March 2001

Government Functions	Wisconsin Employees	Wisconsin FTE/ 10,000 pop.	U.S. Avg. FTE/ 10,000 pop.
Financial Administration	3,035	5.7	7.6
Central Administration	5,078	9.5	7.6
Judicial & Legal	3,684	6.9	8.7
Police-Arrest	11,195	20.9	21.3
Police-Other	3,588	6.7	6.5
Firefighters	4,538	8.5	9.8
Other	356	0.7	0.8
Corrections	4,320	8.0	8.3
Streets & Highways	9,388	17.5	10.7
Airports	391	0.7	1.4
Water Transport	28	0.1	0.3
Public Welfare	13,604	23.4	10.0
Health	6,008	11.2	8.9
Hospitals	1,825	3.4	18.2
Solid Waste	1,804	3.4	4.0
Sewage Disposal	2,532	4.7	4.4
Parks & Recreation	3,619	6.8	7.7
Housing & Comm. Devel.	1,145	2.1	4.1
Natural Resources	1,021	1.9	1.4
Water Supply	2,212	4.1	5.6
Electric Power	660	1.2	2.6
Gas Supply	0	0.0	0.4
Transit	2,342	4.4	6.7
Elem. & Sec. Instruction	91,273	170.2	151.8
Elem. & Sec. Other	28,214	52.6	64.9
Higher Ed. Instruction	4,285	8.0	4.6
Higher Ed. Other	4,804	9.0	6.3
Local Libraries	2,717	5.1	9.6
All Other	5,158	9.6	9.3
TOTAL	218,824	408.0	398.2

Source: "2001 Employment Data, Local Governments," U.S. Department of Commerce, U.S. Census Bureau

in central administration; 4,538 in fire protection; 4,320 in corrections; 3,619 in parks and recreation; 2,717 in local libraries; 2,532 in sewerage; 2,342 in transit; and 2,212 in water supply. Of these functions, sewerage and water are usually provided by special purpose units of government (special districts) while the rest are usually provided by general purpose governments (counties and municipalities).

Comparing Wisconsin's Local Governments
to Local Governments in Other States

The employment data contained in table 15 provide a means for comparing the functions of Wisconsin's local governments to local governments in other states. Of particular interest in this regard is the relative level of "investment" (as defined by employees) Wisconsin's local governments make in comparison to local governments in other states. The data show some important similarities. First, as in Wisconsin, providing elementary and secondary education is the function that employs the most people. Across the nation, the average number of FTE employees (with the combination of both instruction and other categories) per 10,000 population is 216.7, while it is almost 222.8 in Wisconsin. Likewise, police protection is the second most important function, as defined by employment, with 27.8 FTE per 10,000 population across the United States and 27.6 in Wisconsin.

At the same time, the data show some important differences between the U.S. and Wisconsin averages in the relative emphasis given to various functions. For example, in primary and secondary education, Wisconsin has a higher number of people involved in teaching and a lower number involved in "other" than is the case across the country as a whole. Even more dramatic are the differences in the number of employees in public welfare, hospitals, streets and highways, and higher education (vocational-technical education). Wisconsin's local governments have more than two times the average number of FTE employed per 10,000 in public welfare, and more than one and a half times the number employed in both streets and highways and higher education. Yet Wisconsin has only one-quarter the number usually employed in hospitals across the nation. The latter shows that local governments run very few hospitals in Wisconsin; most hospitals in the state are private.

CURRENT AND FUTURE CHALLENGES FOR
LOCAL GOVERNMENTS AND THEIR OFFICIALS

Perhaps the central theme that emerges from the previous two sections of this chapter is that Wisconsin's local governments differ dramatically in their structure, operation, and function. The economic, social, and ecological environments of each type of local government can also vary tremendously. For example, the types of problems that elected officials and administrators face in cities that are relatively close to Chicago—like Racine, Kenosha, and Milwaukee—are quite different from the challenges that face their counterparts in small cities in the central part of the state, like Horicon, Ripon, or Wausau. Likewise, the circumstances in prosperous suburban villages along Lake Michigan—like Shorewood, Whitefish Bay, or Fox Point—may be very different from those of villages in rural northwestern Wisconsin.

The economic challenges to local governments take three forms. The first might be considered a constant: demands for services will always exceed the supply. The fact that demands on government—and especially local government—continue to grow and grow rapidly is a common theme in literature about government. The rapid growth in the size and complexity of the problems local governments face, the proliferation of interest groups, and the increased sophistication of their lobbying efforts are often cited as reasons for the increased demand.

A second economic challenge for many local governments is the changes taking place in the structure of the economy. One scholar of local government, Beverly Cigler, has noted that "technological and economic changes render the economic foundations of some communities obsolete and create boom-town economies for others."[64] To cope with boom times may not be as difficult as coping with the hardships of rapid economic decline, but it does present its own set of challenges for local officials.

A third economic challenge to local government is the cyclical nature of the economy. Sometimes referred to as the "boom-and-bust cycle," the shift from a growing national or regional economy to a no-growth or recessionary economy presents many problems for local officials. Not the least of the problems is that revenue growth from their own sources, particularly the local property tax, may slow, even stop growing or turn negative, while the need for services increases. This circumstance can be exacerbated by reductions in intergovernmental transfers from national and state governments. Those two levels of government may also attempt to cope with a recession by cutting their expenditures, to the detriment of local governments.

The most recent episode of the boom-and-bust cycle included an eight-year long economic expansion from 1993 through 2000 followed by the recession that officially began in March of 2001. Both the length and amplitude of the boom part of this cycle were unusual and may have created the illusion that recessions were no longer a problem for local governments. The severity of the recession that began in March of 2001, however, shattered that illusion. Furthermore, the budgetary problems local governments faced during the recession as unemployment rose, demands for services grew, and local revenue growth stalled were exacerbated by a lack of national government assistance and by state budgetary cutbacks (see chapter 8, "The State Budget and the Budgetary Process").

The recession that began in March of 2001 marked the third time in two decades that the bust phase of the boom-and-bust cycle had settled in. At the beginning of the 1980s and 1990s many state and local governments were also reeling from economic recession. The pressure to add programs or services during good economic times makes it more difficult for local government officials to cope with periods of recession. Because 75 to 80 percent of local government expenditure is in the form of salaries, wages, and benefits, cutting employees yields the largest short-term savings. Cutbacks in the workforce, however, usually affect the quantity and quality of public services.

Another set of challenges that local governments face are sociocultural, as well as economic, in nature. These challenges include the ready availability of illegal drugs and alcohol, homelessness, out-of-wedlock births, adolescent violence, crime, and the growing number of children with special needs. Although these problems are usually associated with large urban areas, they can and do also affect suburban and rural communities.

There is vigorous debate about what factors contribute to or cause these problems, but local governments have little or no ability to influence most factors usually listed in these debates. For example, some researchers argue that the constant barrage of alcohol advertisements on television is a contributing factor in underage drinking and violence. Others point to the increased level of violence and sex shown on television and in movies as causal factors in adolescent violence, crime, and out-of-wedlock births. Researchers have also identified the trend toward having dual wage-earning families or single-parent households as causal factors of some of these problems. With no adults at home to supervise the children, some researchers argue, we have become a society in which children raise children.[65]

School districts, like municipalities, may face many of these types of problems. Some researchers have identified the trend toward more time spent each day watching television as a factor that contributes to poor performance in school, which may, in turn, lead to troublesome behavior. Additionally, school districts may have to respond to growing populations of children with special needs and the need for remedial education. Standardized testing has made the need for remedial education, particularly in reading and writing, more visible. Of course, there are other causes for these types of challenges, too, including the growing number of immigrant students in K–12 schools who do not speak English. Particularly in poor urban school districts, this puts extra strain on an already inadequate resource base.

Policy and political factors have also contributed to the difficult challenges many local governments currently face and are likely to face in the future. Local governments have long struggled with the burden created by what are commonly called "unfunded mandates." The term usually refers to national government laws that require state governments to take specific actions but provide insufficient funding to pay for these actions. State governments can pass these unfunded mandates on to local governments. Local governments cannot pass them further, and they must comply. School districts, for example, must meet a wide range of mandates related to children with special needs but receive only partial funding to comply with these mandates. These mandates originate at both the national and state levels.

In addition, policy that defines the national-local relationship has changed over the years in ways that some scholars contend have made circumstances for local governments more difficult. John Shannon and others have argued that the "cooperative federalism" of the 1970s gave way to a "fend-for-yourself federalism" in the 1980s.[66] During the Reagan era, the flow of money from the national government to state and local governments was dramatically scaled back; many local governments received no federal funds during this time.[67] In 1988 federal aid again began to rise, but this change may not have been visible in local government budgets. The basis by which much of that federal aid was distributed had shifted from local government, or "place," functions to "person" functions, namely, welfare and health.[68]

The challenges identified here are by no means a comprehensive list of problems local governments in Wisconsin face. Nor are they problems that are peculiar or unique to Wisconsin. Local governments in most of the states confront similar challenges. Since many of the challenges Wisconsin's local governments face do not originate within the borders of their town, village, city, or school districts, they are not easily ameliorated or even addressed by the governing body. Interlocal cooperation may help in efforts to address these challenges, but national-local and state-local cooperation is also likely to be an important ingredient. In this regard, particularly in the area of financial assistance, Wisconsin state government has been particularly helpful and generous. The way in which the state provides support to local governments is the topic of the next chapter.

CHAPTER ELEVEN

State-Local Relations

The key element in Governor Lucey's claim that he had "revolutionized" the state-local finance system was the effort to substitute state tax revenues for property taxes. Specifically, Lucey wanted to finance a greater portion of local costs for services like education and welfare with state funds.

James K. Conant, *Executive Decision Making in the State*, 1983

During the (1986) campaign, I promised to increase the state's share of local education funding to 50 percent, up from the existing level of 46 percent. The theory was, if the share of state aid to schools was increased, local property taxes would go down, because state aid would replace school funding provided by the property tax.

Tommy Thompson, *Power to the People*, 1996

In both historical and contemporary terms, state and local government in Wisconsin have been closely linked as partners. Local officials appropriately say that they serve on the front lines when it comes to service delivery, and this fact has traditionally been understood and accepted in the State Capitol. Indeed, a distinctive feature of the state-local relationship in Wisconsin is the remarkable financial support state officials have provided for local governments. In the 1999–2001 state budget, more than 60 percent of state-raised revenues were returned to local governments. Only the state of Michigan shared more of its state-raised revenues with its local governments during that time period.

This extraordinary commitment to local government seems fitting for a state with a strong moralistic culture. After all, how could the good of the community as a whole be served if the state's local governments were weak? This chapter on the state-local relationship in Wisconsin extends and links together material covered in the chapters on the legislature, governor, political parties and elections, budget, and local government. The chapter's content shows that the state-local relationship has been a central hinge around which state politics, state elections, state policy, and state budgets pivoted during the latter half of the twentieth century and the opening years of the twenty-first century.

The chapter begins with some discussion of the central tenets that have served as historical guideposts for the development of the state-local relationship in Wisconsin. Then the focus shifts to the post–World War II period, the 1960s, and particularly the 1970s, because it is one of the four main periods of policy innovation in Wisconsin. The ongoing development of the state-local relationship during the 1980s and 1990s comes next, followed by a discussion of the way in which the tax and expenditure decisions made in the 1990s, coupled with the national economic recession that officially began in March of 2001, put Wisconsin's highly developed state-local relationship at risk.

THE GUIDING TENETS OF WISCONSIN'S STATE-LOCAL RELATIONSHIP

The 1848 constitution, with its path-breaking commitment to public education, set the direction and tone for the state-local relationship. The Education Article, Article X, gives local governments responsibility "for the establishment of district schools, which shall be as nearly uniform as practicable," and it says that "such schools shall be free and without charge for tuition to all children between the ages of 4 and 20 years." Article X, section 2, stipulates that the state is to establish a fund for the support of all public schools and libraries. Article X, section 3, states that the monies from the state school fund will be distributed "in just proportion to the number of children and youth resident therein." Finally, Article X, section 5, states that the money for the state school fund is to come from the sale of state land and the interest earned on those monies.

In short, the 1848 constitution established several important tenets that remained a central part of the state-local finance system in Wisconsin during the state's first fifty years. First, the state was to be a partner with local government in the delivery of public K–12 education. Second, the source of state funds to be used for education would be explicitly identified. Third, the distribution of these funds would be "fair," that is, based on the number of children in a district or on a per capita basis.

The 1848 constitution also contained some important provisions for the tax or revenue side of the state-local relationship. In the Finance Article (VIII), section 1, the constitutional framers stated that "the rule of taxation shall be uniform, and taxes shall be levied upon such property as the legislature shall prescribe." Progressive Democrats considered this provision one of the most important in the constitutional document. It was inserted, constitutional convention delegate John Rountree reported, in the hope of avoiding "partiality" and "favoritism" that tended to be extended "to certain kinds of property"; delegates also wanted "to promote social, political and economic equality" in taxation.[1]

The provision assumed that taxation of property was to be the principal basis for public tax revenues for both state and local governments. One important effect of this provision was that a constitutional amendment had to be passed in the early 1900s in order to give the state the authority required to establish an income tax. Another was that both state and local governments were expected to treat all types of property in the same manner. This provision has been an important constraint for groups that have petitioned for relief from taxes on particular forms of property and for legislators and governors who have been sympathetic to such demands.

The Progressive Era: A New Model for Financing State and Local Government

At the beginning of the 1900s the basic expenditure and revenue provisions of the state-local relationship established in the 1848 constitution were still in place. The property tax remained the primary source of revenue for both state and local governments, and state financial assistance to local governments was essentially limited to providing school districts a portion of the funds they needed to operate.

In the early 1900s Wisconsin's Progressives produced a fundamental shift in the state-local relationship by winning public support for two major changes in the 1848 constitution. One of these changes was the creation of the state income tax; the other was the establishment of "home rule" for cities and villages. The income tax amendment was approved by voters in 1908, and the enabling statutory law was passed in 1911. The home-rule amendment was approved in 1923.

The Progressives of 1911 had two objectives for the income tax. First, they wanted to improve the equity of the state-local tax system by shifting part of the state and local tax burden from property to income. Of particular concern to the Progressives and others within the state was the fact that income and property were no longer directly connected as they once had been. Their concerns were articulated in the 1898 report of the state Tax Commission, which argued that "the property tax system exploited the poor, especially farmers, because most of their property was tangible and in plain sight, unlike much of the property of the rich."[2]

Second, the Progressives wanted to give local governments greater capacity to respond to local needs. State policymakers did so by giving local governments their own revenue source (the property tax) and by sharing a part of the new income tax and other state revenues with local governments. Passed into law in 1911 this state distribution system became known as the shared tax system.

In the years that followed the establishment of the income tax, the state ceded almost all of the property tax to local governments. The small levy the state retained on property was used primarily to support the school fund.[3] Thus, state services were financed primarily through the income tax, and local services were financed primarily through the property tax. Of course the state's school fund and the shared tax fund provided an important supplement to the revenues local governments raised through the property tax.

In sum, the central tenets the Progressives used to build Wisconsin's state-local relationship during the twentieth century were essentially the same as the tenets established by the constitutional framers during the nineteenth century. The two main ideas were: the determination to have strong local governments, and the determination to have an equitable state-local tax system. By establishing the income tax, the Progressives developed a mechanism to supply state financial support to municipalities and counties, as well as schools. In addition, they did so with a tax source that provided a fairer means of generating state revenue than did the property tax.

The State-Local Relationship in the Post–World War II Era

During the 1930s through the mid-1940s the state-local finance system changed little. The state continued to employ just two principal mechanisms to provide financial support and property tax relief for local governments: the shared tax system and the school fund. Furthermore, only relatively minor modifications were made to these two distribution systems.

During the 1946–47 school year, however, state lawmakers increased the amount of money in the school fund. Then, in 1949, they changed the way in which the money was distributed.[4] The drive to expand the school fund was largely the result of growing enrollments in schools, which put greater pressure on the property tax. The main goal in changing the distribution system was to reduce the large inequities in the resources school districts could provide for their students.

In the early 1950s business and industrial interests began to demand relief from taxes on "personal" property, such as merchants' inventories and manufacturers' stock, finished products, and equipment. Farmers also demanded relief from personal property taxes on livestock and farm equipment and machinery. All three groups complained that the personal property tax put them at a competitive disadvantage in the marketplace. Additionally, local government officials began to demand additional financial assistance from state government, because interest groups and citizens were demanding expanded services and reduced property taxes.

The 1950s and Early 1960s: Governor Nelson and the Sales Tax

The business and industrial interests, faculty at the University of Wisconsin, and the Division of Industrial Development, all of whom were pushing for personal property tax credits, recommended that a sales tax be established to fund this property tax relief.[5] Governor Gaylord Nelson, however, who, in the 1958 elections became the first Democrat elected governor since 1934, was reluctant to support either the business tax credits or a sales tax. Indeed, part of the turmoil over the issue apparently revolved around Governor Nelson's attempt to come to terms with both the political risks and substantive dimensions of the issue.

In the fall of 1959 Governor Nelson announced that he would support a bill that provided a tax credit for personal property, as long as it was phased in over time.[6] In 1960, however, his concerns about the costs of the initiative and the undesirability of a sales tax were played out publicly as his Advisory Tax Commission first supported and then opposed the property tax credits for business.[7] The commission was concerned about the pressure such a program would put on the state budget and the regressive nature of the sales tax.

Pressure on Governor Nelson continued to build, however. In April of 1961, voters approved a constitutional change that allowed nonuniform taxation of personal property. Finally, in the 1961 legislative session the legislature passed a bill that provided a 50-percent tax credit on the personal property (inventory) of merchants, manufacturers, and (inventory and equipment of) farmers, and a general property tax relief program for municipalities. To pay for these programs, the bill also included a 3-percent limited sales tax and changes in income tax rates and brackets.[8]

Governor Reynolds and the Homestead Property Tax Credit for the Elderly

When Democrat John Reynolds was elected governor in 1962, there was a good deal of talk about the effects the property tax had on the elderly. Many senior citizens lived on modest, fixed incomes, and the property tax added to the financial pressures these people faced. During his term in office, Governor Reynolds won legislative support for a program designed to reduce the pressure on the elderly.

Drafted by University of Wisconsin economist Harold Groves, the legislation established a credit against income taxes of 50 percent of property taxes paid if the property tax exceeded 5 percent of the taxpayer's income and the taxpayer's income was below $3,000.[9] The size of the credit, however, was limited to $300.[10] With this act the state continued to expand efforts to support local governments and to reduce the negative effects of the property tax.

The Mid-1960s: Governor Knowles Faces a Budget Gap

In the 1964 gubernatorial election, Governor Reynolds was defeated by Republican challenger Warren Knowles. During Knowles's first two terms as governor, things went fairly smoothly. During his third term in office, however, Knowles's political fortunes became entangled by budget problems and issues related to state-local finance.

As Governor Knowles attempted to put together his 1969–71 executive budget recommendations, he faced two important problems. The first was a gap between state agency expenditure requests and expected revenues of more than $600 million.[11] With a General Purpose Revenue (GPR) budget base of only $1 billion, this $600 million "gap" was very large. Although the governor decided to fund only $400 of this $600 million, he had to raise taxes to do so. The tax he decided to employ to generate additional state revenue was the sales tax. Knowles proposed raising the rate from 3 percent to 4 percent and making the tax a general sales tax.

The second problem was the mounting criticism of the way in which the state distributed funds to local governments in its shared tax system. Under this system, the state returned to local governments a fixed percentage of all income taxes collected from people who lived within those jurisdictions. A fixed percentage of sales taxes and license fees were returned the same way. The result was that governments in wealthy suburban areas got more shared taxes than governments in urban and rural areas.

On the recommendation of his Task Force on Local Government Affairs, known, after its chairman, as the Tarr Task Force, Governor Knowles asked legislative leaders to introduce a bill that redistributed some of the shared tax money to property-poor communities. The proposal created a split within the Republican Party. In addition, the proposed sales tax increase gave Democrats in the state legislature an opportunity to paint Governor Knowles and the Republicans as big taxers and big spenders.

Knowles did secure the increase in the sales tax he sought, and, with the additional tax revenues from this source, he was able to balance the state budget. The bitterness of the conflicts that occurred during the 1968–70 legislative session, however, was sufficiently great that Governor Knowles decided not to run for a fourth term. He was tired, Knowles said, of "living in a fishbowl."[12] Indeed, he decided to leave politics altogether.

THE 1970S: GOVERNOR LUCEY MAKES CHANGES IN THE STATE-LOCAL FINANCE SYSTEM

In 1970 Democrat Patrick Lucey was elected governor by defeating Republican Jack Olson, the incumbent lieutenant governor. During the election campaign, Lucey argued that the Republicans had misdirected tax policy by relying too heavily on the regressive sales and property taxes. Lucey offered a seven-point program to improve the fairness of Wisconsin's tax system and to provide tax relief.[13] The program included: increasing the state share of school costs from 26 percent to 40 percent, expanding the homestead tax for the elderly and extending it to the poor, expanding personal property tax relief, redistributing shared taxes, and eliminating the sales tax on necessities of life.

Like other chief executives who have been elected with an apparent mandate for change, however, Lucey had to confront an economic, fiscal, and political reality that was not particularly conducive to either an immediate or a dramatic shift in government policy. His party (Democrats) had a majority in the assembly, but they were the minority in the senate. Furthermore, Lucey faced a large gap between state agency expenditure requests and anticipated revenues as he began to put together the 1971–73 executive budget.

The fiscal circumstance left many in Lucey's own party—as well as many in the opposition party—wondering how he could balance the budget and put a significant amount of new money into property tax relief programs. He did it with a combination of expenditure reductions and income tax rate increases for upper-income individuals and corporations. He also proposed $100 million of new money for school aids, shared taxes, and other property tax relief programs.[14]

It was Lucey's proposal for redistributing shared taxes, however, that became the focal point for legislative deliberations. Lucey's proposal expanded on what his predecessor, Warren Knowles, had tried to do, but his tactics were different. Lucey included the changes he wanted in the budget bill, rather than in a separate bill. Additionally, Lucey recommended that new money be put into the shared tax account in order to "hold harmless" many of the cities, villages, and towns that otherwise would have received less money under the new distribution scheme.[15]

Neither these tactics nor the fact that 1,400 of the 1,843 municipal tax districts would gain under Governor Lucey's shared tax plan, however, were sufficient to prevent a long and bitter partisan struggle over the proposal.[16] Republicans were united in their opposition to Lucey's shared tax plan and other reform provisions in the budget. They were similarly united in opposing Lucey's efforts to put a major policy change into the state budget.

Lucey also had to deal with potential splits within his own party. His proposed reduction of nine hundred state positions alienated an important segment of his Democratic constituency.[17] Furthermore, there were few supporters in either party of his proposal to merge the University of Wisconsin system with the State University system; there were, however, many energetic opponents. Still, Lucey maintained that both actions were necessary to reduce state spending.

The partisan struggle over Lucey's budget proposals dragged on until mid-October, when a group of moderate Republicans in the Wisconsin Senate agreed to a compromise version of the budget plan. The Republican Assembly Minority Leader Harold Froelich had harsh words for his fellow party members in the senate, calling their move a "surrender."[18] That description of events seems a bit too severe, however, since the compromise agreement significantly reduced the redistributional effects of Lucey's shared tax reform initiative.

An Opportunity to "Revolutionize" State-Local Finance

In the 1973–75 executive budget, Governor Lucey expanded his campaign to reduce and redistribute property tax burdens. Both the number and scale of changes proposed in this budget were much larger than those proposed in the previous budget. A revenue windfall was the principal factor that made this possible. Initially estimated at approximately $500 million, the windfall ultimately totaled approximately $800 million, or 41 percent of the state's $1.95 billion General Purpose expenditure base budget. The $800 million included $464 million in new revenue, a $139 million surplus from 1972, and $170 million in a one-time double shot of federal revenue-sharing funds.[19]

The governor also employed a "conservative" fiscal strategy to ensure that the new revenues could be used for property tax relief. Although the agencies requested $816 million in additional funding, he put strict limits on the amount of new money allocated for state agencies and state programs in the executive budget. He justified this "austerity" program on the basis of a report by the American Center on International Relations (ACIR) showing that Wisconsin's state and local tax burden was the highest among all states in FY 1969–70.[20] Additionally, he used U.S. Census Bureau data, which showed that property tax increases in Wisconsin were the highest in the nation during 1968, 1969, and 1970.[21]

All together, Lucey's executive budget included $490 million of new spending for state aid and property tax relief; $30.8 million was allocated for income and sales tax relief.[22] Lucey's first priority was expanding the state's share of *total* school costs from 31 percent to 40 percent. By adding $274 million to the school aids fund, he expected to achieve this goal. He also proposed significant changes in the way the school aid money was distributed. The changes included a "power-equalized" formula and a "radical" proposal called "negative aids." The negative-aids provision required wealthy school districts with high rates of spending to make a modest contribution to the state school aid fund for redistribution to property-poor districts. The impetus for the changes came from the California Supreme Court's *Serrano* decision; the Doyle Commission provided the blueprint for the changes.[23]

Lucey also wanted to add state money to several other property tax relief programs, including $12.8 million for vocational, technical, and adult education aids, $75 million for General Property Tax Relief, and $34.5 million for Homestead Tax Relief. He also proposed an expansion of the personal property tax credit from 65 percent to 70 percent, but no new state money was required for this purpose.

Lucey's 1973–75 executive budget also included a state takeover of all county costs for Supplemental Security Income, Medical Assistance, and Aid to Families with Dependent Children. Additionally, Lucey recommended that the state pay 75 percent, rather than 55 percent, of county and local government costs for most other mental health, welfare, and social services.[24] The additional state responsibility for these latter programs was to be phased in over time. The 1973–75 price tag for these changes was $85.5 million, with substantial future costs, but Lucey believed that the property tax was not an appropriate vehicle for financing these types of services.

Finally, the 1973–75 executive budget recommendations included levy limits on municipalities and cost controls for school districts. Governor Lucey maintained that these controls were necessary in order to ensure that the new money invested in school aids, other state aid, and property tax relief initiatives would result in lower property tax burdens. As might be expected, however, many local government officials found these proposals objectionable.

The legislative struggle over the 1973–75 executive budget was another bitter partisan contest. Many of the Republicans in the legislature represented suburban districts that would be losers under Lucey's school aid plan, and they worked hard to defeat it. They argued that Lucey was collecting state tax dollars that he did not need and using them to reward big spenders like Milwaukee. Furthermore, they effectively mobilized large numbers of people from their districts to attend a large rally in Madison to demonstrate against Lucey's proposal.

The Wisconsin Assembly, in which the Democrats had nearly a two-to-one majority, quickly passed a budget bill that contained most of what the governor wanted. The Wisconsin Senate, on the other hand, which still had a slim Republican majority, passed its own version of a state budget. This set the stage for a conference committee between the two houses of the legislature. As part of his efforts to break the logjam in the conference committee, Governor Lucey offered to expand the amount of money in the budget aimed at business tax relief. The key element of his proposal was an exemption for manufacturers' equipment and inventory. The cost for this program was estimated to be $51.1 million dollars in 1974.

Even with this "sweetener," however, senate Republicans refused to approve a budget bill unless Lucey's school aid proposals were modified substantially. The compromise that was worked out between Governor Lucey and senate Republicans watered down Lucey's proposed changes. A final glitch in getting the budget approved was created by members of Governor Lucey's own party. Senate Democrats refused to sign the bill, because they believed they had been left out of the final negotiations.[25] They wanted a large role in the future, and only agreed to vote for the budget after they extracted a promise from Governor Lucey that a study committee would be appointed to look into the issue.

Sustaining the "Revolution" in the Face of (Another) Large Budget Gap

In November of 1974 Patrick Lucey was elected to a second four-year term as governor of Wisconsin. As part of his reelection campaign, Lucey had promised that there would be no increase in state taxes, and he had further promised to continue his efforts to reduce and redistribute property taxes. Despite these commitments, however, some members of the opposition party and of the press had doubts about Lucey's capacity to deliver on his promises. As it turned out, there were some very good reasons for these doubts.

In January of 1975, only two months after Lucey was reelected, the governor's secretary of revenue, David Adamany, held a press conference to announce that the state faced a $1 billion gap between the agencies' general purpose expenditure requests and anticipated revenues. Adverse economic conditions were identified as key causes of the problem. High rates of inflation were pushing up state costs at the same time that revenue growth was slowing as the national, regional, and state economies moved into a recession.

An equally important cause of the budget problems, however, was the decision to dramatically expand the state contribution to school aids and other property tax relief programs during the 1973–75 biennium. Specifically Governor Lucey and the state legislature had committed themselves to more than $600 million in new spending, even though nearly one-half of the revenue used to pay for it was one-time money.[26]

This huge budget gap meant that Governor Lucey was faced with a set of unpleasant choices. He could attempt to close the gap by raising taxes; rejecting all or most of the state agency requests for new funds *and* cutting existing expenditures; or some combination of tax increases and expenditure reductions. Lucey ruled out the first and third options, because he had made a pledge during his reelection campaign that he would not recommend or permit an increase in state taxes. Consequently, he not only rejected most agency requests for new funds but also cut some agencies' budgets below their FY 1974–75 bases. In fact, Lucey ultimately proposed a total base budget for FY 1975–76 that was $9 million below the FY 1974–75 base.

Through this tactic, Lucey was able to recommend that almost all of the estimated new revenue in the 1975–77 budget be used to expand state aid to local governments and to provide property tax relief. Specifically, in his executive budget Lucey proposed to add $472 million to state aid and property tax relief programs. Of this total, Lucey proposed that $172 million go into school aids, in order to keep the state share of school costs at 40 percent; $164 million was proposed for the state takeover of county mental health and welfare costs. Most of the remainder of the new funding was to go toward personal property tax relief for business and into the exemption for manufacturers' equipment and inventory.[27] Lucey continued his attempts to modify the shared tax distribution system and the school aids formula in order to get more money into property-poor communities.

The partisan political struggle that took place in the state legislature over Lucey's 1975–77 budget proposals was even more intense than it had been during the previous two budgets. In short, the politics of scarcity turned out to be even more difficult than the politics of redistribution. During this budget cycle, Lucey did not have money to "hold districts harmless" from the changes he wanted to make in the shared tax and school aids formulas. In addition, he did not have extra money to use as a sweetener for Republicans in the senate who were opposed to his budget plan.

In the end, it was the majorities the Democrats had in both houses of the legislature that made it possible for Lucey to secure most of his tax relief and tax redistribution goals. The final 1975–77 budget included $118 million of additional state funding for school aids; $228 million to complete the takeover of county mental health, welfare, and social service costs; and $127 million for other property tax relief programs.[28]

The budget passed by the legislature also included provisions that redistributed part of the money in the shared tax system and in the school aid fund from property-wealthy communities to property-poor communities. In fact, the bill that Governor Lucey signed even contained a provision for negative aids. Less than a year after the budget was passed, however, the Wisconsin Supreme Court declared the negative aids unconstitutional. Consequently, Lucey's victory on this count was taken from him.

Governor Lucey did some additional "pruning" of the state budget before he signed the compromise bill. He used the partial veto sixty-five times to trim out spending provisions that he found objectionable. Some Democrats applauded the governor for having the courage to trim unnecessary spending. Many Republicans, however, complained bitterly about this abuse of the partial-veto power—just as they had previously complained bitterly about Lucey's use of the state budget as a tool for making policy changes. Among the Republicans who voiced the strongest objections was Tommy Thompson. Yet, as will be recalled, when his turn came in the executive office, Thompson used the partial veto much more aggressively than had Lucey.

Assessing Lucey's State-Local Finance Strategy

What were the effects of Governor Lucey's efforts to provide property tax relief and reform? Measured against his stated objectives the results could be considered rather remarkable. For example, the average statewide property tax rate dropped by almost 30 percent in the eight years between 1970 and 1977.[29] In addition, net property taxes per $1,000 of personal income fell from $56.60 to $43.70 during that time, a reduction of 23 percent.[30]

In order to fully comprehend the effects of the governor's initiative, it is essential to understand how property taxes are billed and how property tax rates affect what a homeowner (or owner of commercial property) might pay. The two principal components of a homeowner's property tax bill are the municipal tax and the school tax. In both cases, property tax rates are set or stated in "mills." A mill is one-tenth of a cent per dollar, so a municipal property tax rate of 20 mills means a tax of 2.0 cents per dollar of assessed property value. For example, if a house was assessed at $50,000 in 1970, a municipal property tax rate of 20 mills would mean a municipal property tax bill of $1,000 for the year. If the school mill rate in the same year was 30 mills, the homeowner would owe $1,500 for school property taxes. Together, the municipal and school property taxes total $2,500. To this amount must be added the county property tax and the property tax for the Vocational, Technical, and Adult Education district in the area. While the property taxes assessed for these two jurisdictions would be substantially less than either the municipal or school amount, these two jurisdictions might add $300 to $700 to the property tax bill, depending on the county in which the home was located. Thus, the total bill on the $50,000 house could be as much as $3,200. The homeowner would receive this property tax bill by mail. Both the visibility and the size of the property tax tend to make homeowners sensitive to property tax increases.

Governor Lucey's initiatives also had a dramatic effect on municipal and school district tax rates. Before Lucey took office, the number of municipalities with high tax rates was growing very rapidly. In 1966, 46 percent had tax rates of 25 mills or higher, but the figure grew to 76 percent in 1971. In 1977, however, after the effects of Lucey's property tax initiatives were in place, only 2 percent of municipalities had property tax rates of 25 mills or more.[31]

Lucey's initiatives also reversed the trend toward higher property tax rates for school districts. In 1966 only 7 percent of school districts had tax rates in excess of 20 mills. By 1970, 55 percent had property tax rates in excess of 20 mills. By 1977, however, less than 1 percent of municipalities had tax rates in excess of 20 mills.[32]

The fact that the rates for so many municipalities and school districts fell so dramatically underscores the powerful redistributional effect Lucey's shared tax and school aids initiatives had. Most of the municipalities and school districts whose tax rates were growing the most rapidly were either older cities, where property values were declining, or rural areas, which had little residential, commercial, or manufacturing property. In short, the primary beneficiaries of Governor Lucey's property tax relief and reform initiatives were the property-poor districts and the people who lived in them.

THE 1980S: ECONOMIC RECESSION AND
THE LIMITS OF STATE CAPACITY

Republican Lee Sherman Dreyfus was the upset winner over Acting Governor Martin Schreiber in the 1978 gubernatorial election. Dreyfus won the election by promising to return to taxpayers all of the state's rapidly growing surplus, which ultimately reached almost $300 million. Dreyfus contended that the surplus existed only because the state was collecting money it did not need. In fact, the surplus was a product of two factors: economic growth and inflation that yielded unusually high rates of revenue growth; and frugal management of state spending by Acting Governor Schreiber and the legislature. Ironically, the temporary surplus cost Martin Schreiber the election.

In any case, the 1978 election underscored the way in which the business, or "boom-and-bust," cycle of the economy once again had a powerful effect on Wisconsin's electoral politics and budget strategy. Additionally, Dreyfus's promise to return the state surplus marked an important change in gubernatorial strategy toward state-local relations and particularly state-local finance. Unlike Lucey, Dreyfus did not commit the surplus to local assistance programs like school aids or property tax relief.

Not long after his inauguration in January of 1979, Dreyfus decided to return some of the surplus with a 12-percent income tax credit for 1978 taxes. The credit replaced the income tax deduction for property taxes paid, and it was to be paid quickly—by April 15, 1979. The estimated cost of this program for the FY 1978 budget was $115 million.[33]

Of course, the device Governor Dreyfus used to return the surplus to taxpayers also had some hidden costs. It reduced the amount of money the governor and the legislature had to fund state operations, state aid, and property tax relief programs in the FY 1979–81 executive budget. Since a substantial constituency expected increases in each of these areas, one might have predicted that the politics of the next budget would be somewhat difficult. Furthermore, Dreyfus's income tax credit committed the state to a new, ongoing expenditure, and the size of this expenditure would continue to grow. This, too, would cut into the capacity the governor and legislature had to respond to constituencies looking for an increase in state funding.

Although Governor Dreyfus managed to get through the 1979–81 executive budget process without extraordinary difficulty, the troubles that might have been anticipated by veteran observers of the budgetary process set in during the subsequent 1981–83 budgetary process. As that process began, a national recession started to take hold. The harshest effects of that recession were felt in the upper Midwest.

Democrats in the legislature were suspicious of the revenue estimates used by the Dreyfus administration for the 1981–83 executive budget. Some Democrats believed that slowing revenues and increasing demands for state services had to mean that the budget could not be balanced without a tax increase or expenditure reductions. Those suspicions were strengthened when Dreyfus decided not to run for reelection in 1982. Yet the full picture of just how bad the state's fiscal circumstances were in 1982 was not fully known until 1983.

Governor Earl Confronts a Large Budget Deficit

When the newly elected Democratic Governor, Anthony Earl, attempted to put together the 1983–85 executive budget, he discovered that he had to deal with an emerging deficit for the current fiscal year (FY 1982–83) before he could put together the executive budget recommendations for 1983–85. Earl responded to the crisis by cutting spending for FY 1982–83 and by putting a surcharge of 5 percent on the income tax state taxpayers owed for 1982.

A second consequence of the deficit became clear during the process of assembling the 1983–85 executive budget recommendations. That is when Governor Earl and his advisors realized that they could not carry on the property tax relief program Patrick Lucey pursued so aggressively during his seven years in office. Their calculations showed that they would need a large amount of new money to sustain the state's commitments to local governments and to property tax relief programs. Their calculations also showed that they would not have the money to do so.

In addition, Governor Earl decided to make the reduction of state taxes, rather than property taxes, his first priority. In particular, he wanted to reduce income tax burdens, so he proposed a reduction in the number of income tax brackets and income tax rates. He further proposed the indexing of income tax brackets to inflation. By doing so, Earl removed the automatic growth in state income taxes that inflation had produced. Thus, in addition to reducing state tax burdens for individuals, the governor also reduced the revenue stream that state officials needed to support state aid and property tax relief programs.

Despite the fact that Governor Earl effectively guided the state through a fiscal crisis in his first two years in office and then reduced state taxes in his third year, he was defeated in his bid for reelection in 1986 by Republican challenger Tommy Thompson. Among the promises Thompson made during that campaign was that he would not increase state taxes, would cut state spending, and would increase state aid for schools to 50 percent of costs. Like his predecessors in the executive office, Thompson attempted to follow through on those promises after he took office in January of 1987. The difficulty of meeting these potentially conflicting objectives, however, really began to show in the early 1990s.

THE 1990S: EXPANDING SCHOOL AID AND CUTTING TAXES

In contrast to his predecessor, Anthony Earl, Tommy Thompson began his term as governor (in 1987) with favorable economic and fiscal circumstances. Yet Thompson's budget strategy was similar to Patrick Lucey's; he planned to squeeze the state agencies in order to generate the money he needed to pursue his political and policy objectives, of which increasing the state's share of school costs to 50 percent was particularly important because Thompson had pledged to do so during his 1986 campaign.[34]

Thompson added money to the school aids fund in his 1987–89 and 1989–91 executive budget recommendations. The revenue required to support these actions was generated from cutting state agency budgets and from strong economic growth. The 1991–93 executive budget, however, was being developed just as the recession that officially began in July of 1990 was setting in. Nevertheless, Thompson proposed and secured an additional $122 million for the school aid fund.[35]

The 1991–93 school aids recommendation was accompanied, however, by an expression of frustration. Thompson noted that despite the additional money he put into school aids in the 1989–91 biennial budget, property taxes were going up by 8 to 10 percent a year, rather than down.[36] Indeed, Thompson expressed misgivings about whether state revenue sharing could work the way he wanted it to work. Thompson summed up his doubts this way: "the history of the prior property tax cut efforts in Wisconsin demonstrate that 'robbing Peter to pay Paul' had never lowered either Peter or Paul's taxes."[37] The Peter in this tale was state government, and Paul was local government.

This insight might have led Thompson to make a fundamental shift in budgetary strategy, but it did not work out that way. In the 1991–93 budget Thompson pursued a method for controlling property taxes first employed by Patrick Lucey in the 1970s: cost controls for schools and levy limits for municipalities. In 1991, however, Democrats controlled the state senate, and they were reluctant to give Thompson any additional power to manage the state's affairs. Consequently he had to wait for two years to win legislative approval for cost controls and levy limits.

In the meantime, Thompson's frustration continued. "By 1993," he noted, "I had increased state aid to local schools by more than $1 billion, but the schools were spending the extra money and getting more from property taxes at the local level."[38] In short, the results did not fit Thompson's theory about the state-local financial relationship. Thompson presumed that "if the share of state aid to schools was increased, local property taxes would go down, because state aid would replace school spending funded by the property tax."[39] He was not the first governor to employ this theory or the first to question its validity. Governors Nelson, Reynolds, Knowles, and Acting Governor Schreiber each subscribed to it to some degree, and Governor Lucey was its major advocate; governors Dreyfus and Earl had their doubts.

Ironically, at the time when Tommy Thompson's misgivings about state revenue sharing seem to have reached their peak, he became a champion for dramatically expanding it. Policy proposals and partisan politics in Michigan and Wisconsin were key causal factors. Michigan's governor, John Engler, proposed the elimination of the property tax as a source for funding K–12 schools, and the proposal was soon echoed by voices in Wisconsin. According to Thompson, "Wisconsin Democrats introduced legislation to remove school spending from the property tax completely and fund it entirely at the state level."[40]

The Democrats' proposal was probably spawned by a mixture of motives, including a genuine desire to see a more equitable method for funding K–12 education. At the same time, Democrats also knew that Thompson planned to run for reelection, and it may have appeared that an increase in state taxes would be required to fund the higher levels of school aid. If that were the case, Thompson might be forced to advocate a tax increase during his run for reelection in 1994.

In any case, the ultimate result of the legislative struggle over the school funding proposal was a conference committee compromise "plan to remove two-thirds of school spending from the property tax."[41] The estimated price tag for the plan was $1.2 billion, and the legislation called for implementation in FY 1995–96. The legislation did not specify a method for funding the higher level of school aid.

The governor acknowledged that absorbing "$1.2 billion in new spending in a budget . . . was not an easy task."[42] Further, he had promised to fund the new proposal without an increase in state taxes. Whatever his private thoughts about the position the Democrats had apparently put him in, Tommy Thompson's public posture on the matter appeared to be upbeat throughout the 1994 election campaign.

In November of 1994 Thompson was elected to a third term as governor. As he prepared his 1995–97 executive budget plan, Thompson knew that he could count on approximately $400 million in new revenue for the school aid initiative, because the state's economy was growing at a rapid rate. He also knew that he would need another $800 million to cover the full cost of the initiative, and this money would have to come from cutting expenditures.

"The bulk of the spending cuts," Thompson recalled, "came from reducing the budgets of state agencies."[43] He began the budget process by asking all agencies to cut 5 percent from their 1994–95 base budget for 1995–96 and 10 percent for 1996–97.[44] In addition, Thompson generated additional expenditure reductions by "restructuring twenty-one agencies, eliminating twelve others, and phasing out 170 government boards and commissions."[45]

In short, Thompson's budget plan included an increase of more than $1 billion in school aids, but it did not include an increase in state taxes.

The 1997–1999 and 1999–2001 Executive Budgets

The requirement that the state fund two-thirds of school costs continued to drive spending up through the 1997–99 and 1999–2001 executive budgets. Both budgets also included important policy decisions on the tax or revenue side. Specifically, both included tax cuts. The combination of rapid spending increases and large tax cuts included in these budgets would soon make it difficult for the state to balance its budget.

During the 1997–99 biennium, a strong economy helped to generate $819 million of new general purpose tax revenue. Of this total, $332 million, or more than 40 percent, was put into school aids.[46] Nearly every penny of the remainder was committed to other expenditures. It is notable that despite the large growth in tax revenues, the Thompson administration acknowledged that "balancing the 1997–99 budget was almost as great a challenge as balancing the 1995–97 budget when the state reached two-thirds funding of schools without a general tax increase."[47]

This fact notwithstanding, the Thompson administration was an active participant in the development of the 1997–99 tax cuts that would make balancing future budgets more difficult. In its final form, the 1997–99 executive budget included a one-time sales tax rebate of almost $700 million that was scheduled for FY 2000.[48] Additionally, a permanent income tax rate reduction, as well as other reductions, was scheduled to take effect during FY 2001. The estimated cost of these changes for FY 2001 alone was $1.059 billion.[49]

During the 1999–2001 biennium, the net total of new General Purpose tax revenue available was only $413 million, less than one-half of the amount of new revenue generated in the 1997–99 biennium. Tax revenues actually grew by $998 million, or 10 percent, in FY 2000, but nearly $700 million of that revenue was spent to pay for the one-time sales tax rebate.[50] In FY 2001, tax revenues actually fell by $883 million, or 8.1 percent.[51] Thus, the impact of the income tax cuts included in the 1997–99 executive budget was highly visible in the revenue results for the year and the biennium.

Despite the modest amount of new revenue available to spend in the 1999–2001 biennium, an additional $313.6 million of general purpose revenue was put into the school aids fund in FY 2000, and $239.9 million was added in FY 2001.[52] Thus, the total school aids commitment during the biennium was

$553.5 million, more than 1.3 times the net amount of new tax revenue collected during the 1999–2001 biennium.

Results Achieved by Increasing School
Aids and Revenue Sharing Funds

In the early 1990s Governor Thompson expressed frustration over the fact that property taxes in the state were going up, even though he had put more than $1 billion of new state money into the school aids fund. By 1997, however, frustration had turned to celebration. The *State of Wisconsin Budget in Brief 1997–1999*, for example, contains the following statement: "In 1996–1997, Wisconsin citizens experienced the largest increase in state financial support of public schools and the largest decrease in property taxes in the state's history." The text continued, "State school aids and tax credits increased by just over $1 billion in 1996–1997, while state school property taxes decreased by nearly 24 percent."[53]

Of course, school property taxes are not the only type of property taxes in Wisconsin. Property taxes are also used as the primary revenue source for municipalities, counties, and technical colleges. Thus, in order to see the results as a voter in the state might have seen them, it is important to define how much total property tax relief was achieved during the 1990s. In short, a measure that combines all forms of property taxes must be used.

Perhaps the best measure to use is the amount of property taxes per $1,000 of personal income. A graph in the *1997–1999 Budget in Brief* shows that net property taxes per $1,000 of personal income reached a high point in 1994, and then began declining in 1995. The decline continued in 1996 and was projected to continue through 1997 and 1998. This result was labeled an "historic" achievement in the *1997–1999 Budget in Brief* on the grounds that the state had "never before had a period of sustained property tax relief without a significant general increase in the personal income tax or the sales tax."[54] This important statement is factually correct, as the materials contained in this chapter show.

THE TWENTY-FIRST CENTURY, ECONOMIC
RECESSION, AND BIG BUDGET DEFICITS

Governor Thompson resigned his position in February of 2001 to become secretary of the U.S. Department of Health and Human Services in the George W. Bush administration. One month later, in March of 2001, the official announcement was made that a national recession was underway. For Thompson, the chance to leave the state came at an opportune time. For Scott McCallum, who became governor upon Thompson' departure, the timing was unlucky.

The combination of spending increases and tax cuts enacted during the 1990s created an underlying structural deficit that was temporarily hidden from view during the latter part of the decade by unusually strong economic growth and the fact that the large tax cuts had been phased in over time. The recession, however, unmasked the structural deficit—the gap between recurring revenues and recurring expenditures. The recession also created a cyclical deficit. As it turned out, Wisconsin's FY 2002 deficit was almost 15 percent of its revenue, one of the largest deficits in the nation. The deficit problems continued into the 2003–2004 executive budget.[55]

Governor McCallum Attempts to Deal with a $3.7 Billion Deficit

According to budget documents produced by the Wisconsin Department of Administration, the 2001–3 budget deficit was at least $2.4 billion. Of this total, $1.1 billion was described as a structural deficit inherited from the 1999–2001 budget; $1.3 billion was attributed to the falling revenues caused by the recession. Governor McCallum promised not to increase state general taxes to balance the budget, which meant that he had to rely on spending cuts and whatever one-time revenues he could find.

One of the cuts McCallum proposed was the phasing out of the shared revenue fund over the course of the biennium. The legislature elected to use one-time revenue—the state's tobacco settlement money—instead of eliminating the shared revenue fund. Nevertheless, it was a narrow, and perhaps temporary, escape for the local governments. Shared taxes made up 25 percent of the revenue stream for most of the state's municipal governments, and loss of these funds would have a devastating effect on local budgets, employment, and services.

McCallum and the legislature ultimately passed a 2001–3 budget that relied heavily on the tobacco settlement funds and on spending reductions. Although the budget was designed to rectify the $2.4 billion deficit, only a few months after its passage McCallum acknowledged that the deficit had grown by an additional $1.4 billion. The governor and the legislature engaged in more cutting to address the problem, and they used up more of the state's tobacco settlement money.

Governor Doyle Faces a $3.5 Billion Budget Shortfall

In November of 2002 Democrat James Doyle defeated McCallum in the gubernatorial election. During the election campaign Doyle maintained that the size of the state's deficit was as much as $4 billion dollars. Like McCallum, Doyle promised that he would not raise taxes to fix the deficit.

After his election, Doyle faced a 2003–5 projected deficit that was similar in size to the one McCallum had faced. Doyle's circumstances, however, were even worse than McCallum's because nearly all of the state's tobacco settlement money was used to close the deficit for 2001–3. Thus, Doyle's election victory simply meant that large cuts in state spending were forthcoming.

Doyle's proposed remedies for the $3.5 billion budget shortfall included spending cuts, freezing the state's contribution to school aids, and making selective reductions in other local assistance programs. Most of the cutbacks fell, however, on state agencies and state programs, and included a plan to lay off three thousand state employees.

Reflections on Incremental and Nonincremental Change

During the latter half of the twentieth century, Wisconsin's governors and legislators made many incremental changes in the way the state provided financial support to local governments, the way the state provided direct property tax relief, and in the amount of money it provided for both. There were also two multiyear periods when governors and legislators made dramatic changes in the state-local finance system.

The first period was between 1971 and 1977, when Governor Patrick Lucey substantially expanded the state's commitment to share state-raised revenues with local governments and to provide direct property tax relief to taxpayers. Lucey, for example, proposed large increases in school aids, shared taxes, and the Homestead Tax Relief program, and he persuaded the legislature to take over county costs for a host of social service programs. He also pushed through the legislature changes in the way school aids and shared taxes were distributed to school districts and municipalities. Finally, in order to make possible the expansion of state revenue sharing and property tax relief, Lucey increased state income taxes.

The second period of major change was between 1993 and 1997. In 1993 the legislature enacted the requirement that the state pay for two-thirds of school costs. The estimated cost of this law was $1.2 billion for FY 1995–96, the year the law had to be implemented. Additional state costs of at least 200 million to 300 million per year were also projected for the future. In response to this legislative mandate, Governor Thompson put forward a 1995–97 executive budget designed to meet the new school aids requirement without raising state taxes. It was, as Thompson himself admitted, a very difficult thing to do.

Then, in 1997, as part of the 1997–99 budget, Thompson and the legislature passed a one-time, $700 million sales tax rebate and made permanent cuts in state tax revenue of approximately $1 billion per fiscal year. Despite the recurring demand for a substantial amount of new revenue needed to meet the new commitment to pay for two-thirds of school costs, the governor and the legislature made a dramatic reduction in the state's revenue stream.

On the face of it, the two major policy and budget changes of the 1990s, large tax cuts and a sizable increase in expenditures, seemed incompatible. The deficit state lawmakers had to confront in the 2001–3 executive budget showed that they were, in fact, incompatible. Furthermore, even though Governor McCallum and the legislature took action in 2001 and 2002 to address a $3.7 billion deficit, their actions were not sufficient to fix the fiscal problem. In 2003 Governor Doyle and the legislature faced a projected budget shortfall of $3.5 billion, and they had to resort to additional steep cuts in state programs and state spending in order to try to bring the budget back into balance.

IN SUMMARY

Wisconsin's commitment to sharing state-raised revenues with school districts was established in the state constitution, and its commitment to sharing state-raised revenues with municipalities and counties was made in the early 1900s by the Progressives. Indeed, the Progressives passed an income tax to make this support possible. Over time, commitments to local governments grew and demands for property tax relief also grew. In 1961 a limited sales tax was added to pay for the expansion of state revenue-sharing and property tax relief programs. In less than a decade, the sales tax was expanded to a general, rather than a limited, tax, and the rate was raised. Incremental expansion of state commitments continued throughout the 1960s.

Much of the material in this chapter has focused on the 1970s and 1990s, two periods in which major innovations in the state-local finance system occurred. The material has shown that the two governors who did the most to expand the sharing of state-raised revenues with local governments, Lucey and Thompson, wanted to strengthen local governments' capacity to deliver services while, at the same time, reducing property tax burdens.

It seems reasonable to conclude that neither these governors nor the legislatures that served during their terms in office envisioned a circumstance in which state government's capacity to implement laws and deliver programs would be jeopardized by the financial support they were committing to local governments and to property tax relief. There were warning signs during the 1970s and 1980s that this could happen, and it is difficult to escape the conclusion that this is, in fact, precisely what did occur in the 1990s. The combination of a huge increase in funding for school aids and large cuts in state taxes created a structural deficit, which the first two governors and legislatures of the twenty-first century had to address. It was an unenviable assignment.

Perhaps Wisconsin's century-long experience with state revenue sharing, and particularly its experience in the 1990s, underscores some of the more general lessons that have been offered by scholars about American politics and public policymaking. These include the view that making public choices often involves making trade-offs among desirable objectives, that it is possible to have too much of a good thing, and that nonincremental change may spark intense conflict and yield unexpected and undesirable consequences.[56]

At the same time, Wisconsin's experience also highlights the remarkably vibrant democracy that has existed in the state. For more than 150 years, the state's elected officials have continuously attempted to respond to the preferences and desires of local officials and state citizens. Those preferences have included a desire for a high level of service provision, for strong local governments, and for control of property taxes. Unfortunately, the policy decisions state lawmakers made in the 1990s engendered a multiyear state budget crisis. That crisis forced cutbacks not only in state programs but also in the state's support for local governments and property tax relief. How severe the retrenchment becomes remains to be seen.

CHAPTER TWELVE

Wisconsin in the Federal System

[I]t was not until Robert M. La Follette defeated the regular Wisconsin political machine in 1900 that Progressivism in the states really got started.

Arthur A. Ekirch Jr., *Progressivism in America*, 1974

Among the states that became notable for progressive reforms were California, Oregon, and Wisconsin. Wisconsin perhaps offered the most striking example of the reforms and innovations that characterized progressivism. . . . These reforms, in turn, served as models that were copied, in whole or in part, by many other states and by the national government.

Robert S. Maxwell, *La Follette and the*
Rise of the Progressives in Wisconsin, 1956

In this chapter, Wisconsin's government and politics are examined within the context of the American federal and intergovernmental system. As noted in previous chapters, Wisconsin's institutional and policy experiments throughout the twentieth century made the state an important "laboratory of democracy." This point is underscored by the fact that the twentieth century opened with President Theodore Roosevelt praising Wisconsin as a model that other states and the national government would do well to follow; the century closed with President William Jefferson Clinton voicing similar praise.

Wisconsin's relationship with the national government is the focus of this chapter, but interstate relationships are also considered. Specific topics examined include the degree of cooperation and conflict in the national-state relationship, the diffusion of Wisconsin's institutional and policy innovations to the national government and to other states, and the ways in which Wisconsin benefits from national government policies. Also examined are the economic and political risks Wisconsin has run as a result of its Progressive tax and social welfare policies, the constraints that national government policy imposes on Wisconsin's lawmakers, and the ways in which some national policy has adversely affected Wisconsin's citizens. The chapter concludes with a look at the unique circumstances of the American Indian in Wisconsin and the federal system.

CONFLICT AND COOPERATION IN THE
NATIONAL-STATE RELATIONSHIP

In the American federal system, power and responsibility (government functions) are divided between the national government and the fifty state governments. The ongoing attempt to define the proper balance of power and responsibility between the two levels has been a central dynamic of the American governmental system and a source of both conflict and cooperation.

Geography, historical experience, and political culture are three factors that have traditionally determined whether the relationship between the national and state governments is characterized by cooperation or conflict. For example, Wisconsin's relationship with the national government, like that of most states of the North, has traditionally been one of respect and cooperation. In contrast, the relationship between the national government and the states of the South has tended to be one of conflict.

A notable exception to Wisconsin's cooperative relationship with the national government, however, occurred in 1854, when the state openly defied the Fugitive Slave Act of 1850. Specifically, the Wisconsin Supreme Court broke ranks with the national government when it agreed to free from jail an abolitionist named William Booth. Mr. Booth had been jailed because U.S. Attorney John Sharpstein brought charges against him and several others for obstructing enforcement of the Fugitive Slave Act of 1850. The "obstruction" occurred when Booth and other abolitionists helped free Joshua Glover, a runaway slave, from a Racine jail where he was being held for return to Missouri.[1]

In other areas, such as land use and management, geography and history have also been key factors in the level of cooperation or conflict between the national and state governments. In particular, the national government's ownership of, and control over, large parts of the land areas of states located in the Southwest and West has been a source of tension. For example, 87 percent of the land area in Nevada is owned by the U.S. government and is managed by the U.S. Forest Service and by the U.S. Bureau of Lands Management.[2] Additionally, the national government owns and manages 43 percent of the land in Arizona; 45 percent in California; 43 percent in New Mexico; 66 percent in Utah; 29 percent in Washington; and 48 percent in Wyoming.[3] Influential private interests in all of these states have demanded expanded use of these lands for grazing, mining, drilling, and timber harvest.

In Wisconsin, however, the national government owns and manages less than 5 percent of the state's land area, and state officials have consistently supported national government policy in the areas of natural-resource conservation. As a result, Wisconsin has enjoyed a good working relationship with the national government officials. This constructive atmosphere has been facilitated in part because private interests in the state have accepted the national government's objectives for these lands.

Like its geography and history, a state's political culture can have an important effect on the extent to which its relationship with the national government is marked by conflict or cooperation. As Daniel Elazar has noted, "Every state has certain dominant traditions about what constitutes proper government action, and every state is generally predisposed toward the federal programs it can accept as consistent with those traditions."[4] In fact, the type of political culture a state has is likely to be closely related to its regional setting, and thus it is likely to reinforce or amplify the types of national-state relationships already described in this chapter.

Since Wisconsin's dominant political culture is moralistic, the national government's historical trajectory during the twentieth century toward more active engagement in efforts aimed at the betterment of the community as a whole, rather than an elite few, has been strongly supported within the state. It is also important to recall that many of the social welfare programs the national government established during the twentieth century were first developed in Wisconsin.

In contrast, elected officials and citizens in the states of the South—where the political culture is traditionalistic—have been more likely to view an activist national government as overbearing or intrusive, rather than as a partner. This sentiment is illustrated in a variety of ways in Diane D. Blair and Jay Barth's *Arkansas Government and Politics*.[5] Blair and Barth point out that running against the national government or national government programs is a commonly used and widely accepted part of electoral politics in that state. For much of the twentieth century, in fact, many in the South have pictured the national government as an oppressor rather than as a partner.[6]

Support for an activist national government has sometimes been shown by the votes of Wisconsin's congressional delegation; at other times it has been articulated by the state's elected officials. Sometimes the support for the national government's efforts to help its citizens has been shown by the way the majority have voted for a particular presidential candidate, and at other times the testimonial has come in the form of the close working relationship between Wisconsin's administrative officials and those of the national government.

In the early 1900s, for example, Wisconsin's elected officials and administrative officials not only supported but also actively pushed national legislation to protect children and to protect workers' health and safety.[7] In the 1930s elected and administrative officials from Wisconsin actively participated in and provided support for Franklin Roosevelt's New Deal.[8] Of special importance here were the efforts to provide assistance to those who did not have employment, food, or shelter—and, it may be added, to conserve natural resources.

During the 1950s some of the state's elected and administrative officials worked on or provided support for the development of the interstate highway system. In the 1960s Wisconsinites contributed to the development of Kennedy's New Frontier and Lyndon Johnson's Great Society, and many of the state's elected officials actively supported national programs that emerged from these two administrations.[9] During the 1970s state officials and the majority of the state's citizens supported the national government's efforts to reduce air and water pollution.[10] Finally, during the 1980s the state actively cooperated with the national government in efforts designed to reduce the risks that hazardous wastes posed for human health.[11]

WISCONSIN AS AN INSTITUTIONAL AND POLICY PIONEER

When Wisconsin rose to national prominence as an institutional and policy pioneer in the early 1900s, profound changes were occurring in the social and economic fabric of American life. The economy was being transformed from an agricultural into an industrial economy, and economic wealth and power were being concentrated into the hands of a small number of corporations and business executives.[12] Hundreds of thousands of people were forced to leave the farm and seek a livelihood in the cities. Immigrants were flooding into the country, many destined for tenements in New York, Chicago, and other urban areas.[13] Factory workers—including women and children—worked from dawn to dusk in dark, dangerous factories. Many were maimed or killed in industrial accidents; many others—particularly those who were unable to find employment in the new industrial economy—suffered from hunger and succumbed to disease.[14]

Political conditions at the turn of the century were also far from ideal. In the early 1900s most American states, like most American cities, were controlled by political machines. These machines were usually corrupt, and served as the "medium through which dishonest businessmen obtained franchises and contracts from government."[15] Special interests, especially those in the financial and industrial sectors, were often able to use state and local governments to enrich themselves at the expense of the majority. The rapacious exploitation of a state's natural resources was one source of their enrichment; the exploitation of workers was another.

Wisconsin's emergence as a model for other states and the nation as a whole was due to the development of a robust Progressivism. The goals of that movement were to put the machinery of government under the direct control of the people, remove corrupt influences from government, expand government in order to curb the power of special interests, and promote the economic and social well-being of the individual citizen.[16] To achieve these objectives, Wisconsin's Progressives inaugurated "a comprehensive program of political, economic, and social reforms that affected the lives of every person in the state."[17]

Although Progressive reform movements developed in approximately one-half of the states, the achievements of Wisconsin's Progressives were, in many respects, broader, more durable, and more visible than those in other states that had strong Progressive movements, including California and Oregon.[18] Robert M. La Follette's leadership within the state was an essential ingredient in the remarkable success achieved by Wisconsin's Progressives. Likewise his efforts as a U.S. senator and candidate for the Progressive Party's presidential nomination in 1912 gave Wisconsin's institutional and policy innovations additional visibility.

Of course, La Follette's success was dependent on a set of variables not found in many other states, including Wisconsin's geography (particularly its regional setting); frontier experience; population (particularly its settlement patterns, which included large numbers of Germans and Scandinavians); historical experience; moralistic political culture; and economic development. The success La Follette and the Wisconsin Progressives enjoyed was also a function of the remarkable institutional connection that evolved during the late 1800s and early 1900s between the state and the university. "Wisconsin's Progressive reforms," argues Arthur A. Ekirch Jr., "owed much to the unique alliance between the state government and the state university."[19] He adds that "in Wisconsin the state and the university joined in advancing social democracy, and 'the Wisconsin Idea' became a term to describe the application of scholarship and theory to the needs of the people."[20]

Still another factor that contributed to both the form and durability of Wisconsin's Progressive reform movement was the (creative) tension that existed between the state's Progressives and Stalwarts. Some of the more "radical" institutional changes sponsored by Progressives in other states, such as initiative and referendum, were opposed by Wisconsin's Stalwarts and rejected by the state's voters.[21] One consequence is that politics and policymaking in Wisconsin has been much more stable than in some of the states where initiative and referendum were adopted, such as California and Oregon.[22]

The success enjoyed by La Follette and Wisconsin's Progressives in the early 1900s was also affected by factors outside of the state. For example, President Theodore Roosevelt helped to set the social and political climate that Wisconsin's Progressives needed to pass their reforms.[23] Roosevelt's much-publicized efforts at trust-busting and railroad regulation, his agitation over the mass poverty he saw in the country, and his determination to root out corruption wherever he found it in government not only highlighted serious problems but also demonstrated that these problems could be addressed by government.[24]

Likewise, the work of the Muckrakers "was closely bound up with the progressive movement for reform."[25] In popular magazines such as the Atlantic Monthly, Arena, Colliers, Cosmopolitan, Ladies Home Journal, Mc-Clure's, Harper's, Scribner's, The Century, and the Nation, the Muckrakers documented some of the awful consequences that unrestrained corporate interests could have on the health, safety, and economic well-being of the vast majority of Americans.[26] They also identified the ways in which these corporate interests spawned corruption in government.[27] In sum, if Wisconsin state government had existed alone, outside of the U.S. federal system, these important factors would not have come into play with the force or prominence they did in the state's politics and policymaking.

Examples of Policy and Institutional Reforms

During the early 1900s Wisconsin's Progressives pioneered a number of important institutional innovations. Perhaps the best-known and most widely copied of these innovations was the Legislative Reference Bureau (1901).[28]

The bureau provided bill-drafting, library, and research services for legislators. Charles McCarthy, who had just completed his Ph.D. at the University of Wisconsin, was appointed the first director of Wisconsin's Legislative Reference Bureau. Over the next two decades, McCarthy was a "passionate advocate of the legislature as an institution," and he made the Legislative Reference Bureau "a powerful tool" for the development of Progressive reform legislation that could pass constitutional muster.[29] The institutional model that McCarthy helped to pioneer was eventually adopted by the national government and many other states.

Closely related to the development of the Legislative Reference Bureau, and equally important to Wisconsin's Progressive reforms, was another institutional innovation that served as a model for other states. This innovation was the remarkable collaboration between the University of Wisconsin–Madison and the state government. One scholar has described the university's role during the early decades of the 1900s as that of "a fourth department of government, cooperating with legislative, executive, and judicial branches."[30]

Among the faculty at the University of Wisconsin whose work contributed to the development of new institutional and policy forms was economist Richard Ely.[31] His views on the role the state should play in society were reflected in the statement of principles adopted by the American Economics Association he helped to found in 1885. The opening sentence read: "We regard the state as an agency whose positive assistance is one of the indispensable conditions of human progress."[32] The belief that the state could play a positive role in society for the betterment of all people was strongly held by many of the Progressives in Wisconsin and elsewhere in the country.

In 1905 Wisconsin moved into the vanguard of state institutional initiatives in two other areas: 1) a civil service, and 2) independent regulatory commissions. The Civil Service Act was requested by Governor Robert M. La Follette and approved by the legislature. The act put Wisconsin among the first states to move from a patronage-based system for hiring administrative personnel to one based on merit. Also in 1905 the legislature approved another La Follette initiative—a commission to regulate railroads. The passage of this legislation marked one of the longest, most bitterly contested, and most important of the Progressive reforms in Wisconsin.

By passing these two acts in the same year, Wisconsin set an important benchmark for the Progressive reform initiatives in other states and at the national level. As reported by M. H. Bernstein, Progressives "believed that regulation would overcome privilege, restore decency, and save industry from its own avarice and self-destruction."[33] Additionally, Progressives believed that if state governments "were to assume a broader range of regulatory functions," the effectiveness of the regulatory agencies "might depend on the development of an impartial corps of public administrators— a bureaucracy of experts and intellectuals removed alike from the corrupting influences of business and politics."[34]

The railroad commission would give Wisconsin's leaders an opportunity to learn about the strengths and weaknesses of various institutional arrangements, and the lessons from this experiment could provide a base for designing other regulatory agencies. At the same time, the Civil Service Act would serve as the vehicle by which a corps of public administrators could be properly trained for the roles and duties they would have to perform within regulatory commissions and other agencies of state government.

Four years after the passage of the Civil Service Act and the establishment of an independent regulatory commission for the railroads, Wisconsin's lawmakers passed legislation that contained another important institutional innovation. In 1909 Wisconsin became the first state to adopt provisions for the continuous revision of its statutes. Among the potential benefits of this step was that the exact form of existing laws would be more clearly defined, and thus attempts to amend or delete existing statutory provisions would be better understood. Another potential benefit of the change was that existing statutory law could be better understood by individuals who were not formally trained in the law. A number of states soon followed Wisconsin's lead, but others were slow to adopt this important innovation.

In more recent times (1947) the state pioneered once more with the establishment of the Legislative Council. The task assigned to the council was to conduct studies on matters affecting the welfare of the state.[35] Then in 1961 the state innovated again with the establishment of the Legislative Fiscal Bureau.[36] The bureau was established to give the state legislature the capacity to analyze the governor's budget, and thus make the legislature a more capable and active participant in the budgetary process. In the 1980s and 1990s the state continued to develop its legislative institutions, particularly through its efforts to employ technology for enhanced communications between legislators and citizens.

Among the best-known examples of Wisconsin's pioneering efforts in public policy is the income tax. Scholar David Nice uses this example to illustrate how policy development often works in the federal system. In *Federalism: The Politics of Intergovernmental Relations*, he notes that "many national government programs were initially adopted at the state or local level. For example, the modern income tax was developed by Wisconsin, spread to other state governments, and finally was adopted by the national government."[37]

The adoption of the income tax in Wisconsin involved a multistep process. In 1905 and 1907 the state's legislature passed the language needed for a vote of the people on a constitutional amendment. Then, in 1908, Wisconsin voters approved an amendment to the state constitution that was needed to establish a tax on both corporate and individual incomes. In 1911 authorizing legislation for the new tax was passed, and the state soon began collecting revenue from this new source.

Among the important consequences of the actions taken by Wisconsin's elected officials and citizens was that the state stopped using the property tax as its primary source of revenue. This, in turn, gave local governments more opportunity to increase the revenue they could raise from the property tax. The added revenue then gave local governments the capacity to expand the services they provided to citizens.

By the end of the decade, seven states had followed Wisconsin's lead in adopting the personal income tax. In addition, eight states followed Wisconsin by adopting the corporate income tax. The states that adopted the personal income tax were: Mississippi (1911); Oklahoma (1915); Massachusetts (1916); Virginia (1916); Delaware (1917); Missouri (1917); New York (1919); and North Dakota (1919).[38] The states adopting the corporate income tax were: Connecticut (1915); Virginia (1915); Missouri (1917); Montana (1917); New York (1917); Massachusetts (1919); and North Dakota (1919).[39]

It is worth noting that this pattern of adoption did not follow one of the common patterns noted by scholars, whereby policy innovation is diffused first to other states within the geographic region, and then followed by diffusion outside of the region.[40] Wisconsin's policy innovation took on somewhat different forms in different states. For example, Wisconsin's income taxes—and particularly its corporate income tax—were considerably more progressive (tax rates increased as incomes increased) than the taxes adopted by other states.[41] Finally, it is important to note that the majority of states did not adopt either the personal or corporate income tax until the 1930s, when the Great Depression made them desperate for revenue.[42]

Another striking dimension to the pattern of adoption of Wisconsin's innovations is that the national government actually adopted both the personal income and corporate income tax in 1913—before most of the other states.[43] Unlike the lead set by Wisconsin and followed by some of the other states, however, the national government's income tax was very narrowly tailored and affected only the top end of the income scale. Scholar John Witte reports that the national government's first income tax affected only 2 percent of the working population between 1913 and 1915.[44] Scholar Susan Hansen notes that as late as 1939 only about 6 percent of U.S. citizens had to pay a federal income tax.[45] As the Roosevelt administration and Congress began to rebuild military capacity in preparation for World War II, however, the need for revenue became paramount and the tax was expanded.

In the same year that the income tax was put into law (1911), Wisconsin also became the first state to pass a workmen's compensation act. This act provided compensation for injuries sustained on the job, and it provided widows benefits in cases where an employee died from the injuries. Given the tremendous number of industrial accidents and injuries that were occurring in the new economy, this was a very important step. One source reports that, during the early 1900s, "five hundred thousand workers were either killed or badly maimed each year" throughout the United States.[46] Wisconsin's initiatives, as well as those taken at the national level, helped to spur reluctant states to take action in this critical area. By 1915 twenty-five states had established workmen's compensation laws.[47]

In 1911 Wisconsin was also among the first states to establish a state life insurance fund and a state teacher's retirement fund. Then, in 1913, the state pioneered in the development of workplace protections and minimum wage requirements for women and children. These initiatives diffused rather quickly to other states and to the national government.

In 1932 these important social welfare initiatives were extended again when Wisconsin developed the first unemployment compensation system. This legislation served as the model for the national government's action in 1935, when a national system for unemployment compensation was established. (More contemporary examples of Wisconsin's social welfare policy innovations are articulated in some detail in chapter 9, "Social Welfare Policy".)

PROGRESSIVE POLICY AND RISK IN THE FEDERAL-COMPETITIVE ECONOMIC SYSTEM

As noted in the previous section, the policy innovations developed by Wisconsin's Progressives during the first three decades of the twentieth century included the income tax (1911) and key elements of what is often called the social safety net (1911, 1913, 1915, 1934, et cetera). While these policies provided important benefits for many of Wisconsin's citizens, they also put the state at some economic risk. After all, the state of Wisconsin is situated within both a federal governmental system and a competitive economic system.

Within the federal system, states compete with each other for businesses and wealthy individuals. Within the competitive economic system, both businesses and wealthy individuals are mobile, and they may respond to state government policies that they view as unfavorable by relocating to another state with a more favorable business or tax climate. Thus, Wisconsin's policymakers were taking a big risk in the early 1900s by putting in place an income tax that had important economic effects on both wealthy individuals and business firms. Similarly, Wisconsin's social welfare policies also set constraints on the behavior of businesses that some firms found objectionable.

One of the reasons that Wisconsin was able to continue the development of its Progressive policies during the 1920s and 1930s was the national government's adoption of the income tax. After it did so—and particularly after the tax was made progressive—the prospects for its diffusion to other states was enhanced. Similarly, after Congress and the president established national standards in the area of social welfare, Wisconsin's policies were more secure than they otherwise would have been if the state had been the only one to take such actions on behalf of its citizens.

Although national policy often sets the minimum, rather than maximum, standards, the fact that the national government did establish prohibitions on child labor, limits on the hours that women could work, disability pay for those injured on the job, and a national system for unemployment compensation reduced some of the risks that the state of Wisconsin faced from other states in the competition for business. The fact that all but a small number of states eventually did adopt the income tax—both on personal and business income—also reduced the risks that Wisconsin faced in the competition for business and wealthy residents.

It should be noted that not all of the states adopted the personal or business income tax, and because Wisconsin's income tax rates were much more progressive than most other states, the tax had a more noticeable effect on both businesses and individuals in Wisconsin than it did elsewhere.[48] Thus, Wisconsin remained vulnerable to losing businesses as well as wealthy residents to states with lower or no income taxes. Particularly in the period from 1970 through 1999, stories about the emigration of wealthy Wisconsinites to Florida, Texas, or Arizona (three states without a personal income tax) circulated broadly. Yet it is also well known that many of these emigrants were likely to spend almost half of the year in Wisconsin, visiting their extended families or residing at their vacation homes.[49]

In spite of the competitive pressure from other states, Wisconsin's elected officials continued to initiate policies intended to promote the economic and social well-being of all of its citizens until the mid-1980s. At that point, a shift in the direction of the state's policy began to emerge. Ronald Reagan's election as president in 1980 set the stage for a revival of conservative forces nationally and the Stalwart forces within the state. The principal cause of the policy shift, however, was the coupling of the deepest national recession since the Great Depression with a severe regional recession in the upper midwest. These two events caused Wisconsin's economic performance to decline, unemployment to rise to more than 11 percent, the state's revenues to decline, the bankruptcy of the state's unemployment fund, and state welfare expenditures to rise steadily.

The remarkable—and even ironic—result is that Wisconsin's visibility within the federal system near the end of the twentieth century emerged primarily from efforts that were designed, at least in part, to alter its progressive policy structure. Arguably, the first of these important policy initiatives occurred in 1985, when Wisconsin's elected officials reduced the number of income tax brackets and lowered the top income tax rate from 10 percent to 7.9 percent.

The 1985 income tax changes were initiated by Democratic governor Anthony Earl, who made the reduction of state taxes his top priority. Earl was sensitive to the bitter complaints that some members of the business community expressed toward Wisconsin's personal income tax rates, and he wanted to improve the business climate by addressing this perceived problem. Earl and members of his administration also wanted to simplify the tax code and thus broaden the income base to which the income tax applied.[50]

The net result of the income tax changes the legislature adopted in 1985 amounted to, in the view of scholar John Witte, "the most radical changes in our [income] tax system since its inception in 1911."[51] Witte's evaluation of the results was generally favorable, in large part because of the extent to which the changes met overall tax reform objectives—particularly tax simplification.

The tax changes did reduce state income tax revenues by an estimated $275 million over the 1985–87 biennium, with $171 million of that total consisting of permanent, ongoing changes.[52] Estimates by the Legislative

Fiscal Bureau also indicated that the principal beneficiaries in the changes were joint filers with (1984) incomes over $100,000, whose (estimated) state income tax liability fell by $23.9 million. Witte notes, however, that this small group of top income-earners, which consisted of just 0.7 percent of all state taxpayers, still paid 9.1 percent of total income taxes compared to 9.8 percent before the tax changes were adopted.[53]

While these changes may seem to be a modest reduction in tax progressivity, they were an important change for the state that had pioneered the progressive income tax. Equally noteworthy is the fact that these changes were proposed by a Democratic governor who considered himself a Progressive in the lineage of La Follette and the other early Progressive reformers. Yet Earl apparently felt compelled by economic and political circumstances to take these steps and he worked actively to ensure their adoption.[54]

A further irony of this 1985 tax policy innovation served as a model for the national government and other states during the 1980s and 1990s. For example, the income tax policy changes made in Wisconsin were carefully studied by the Reagan administration. In 1986 President Reagan proposed "tax reform" legislation that was similar in direction and degree to the Wisconsin approach.[55] Reagan's plan reduced the number of brackets and the rates of the federal income tax, while attempting to simplify the tax code and broaden the income tax base. One consequence was a reduction in the progressivity of the federal income tax. A number of other states soon followed suit.

An even more dramatic shift in the direction of state policy occurred in Wisconsin in 1993. In that year, the state's elected officials decided to terminate its participation in the national program known as Aid to Families with Dependent Children (AFDC). Since no other state had done more to help create this safety net for women and children, this was big news. In fact, the story got a good deal of national press coverage, even a front page headline in the New York Times: "Wisconsin Pledges to Exit U.S. System of Public Welfare."[56]

The state gained additional national attention in 1995 when its new welfare system was launched. In this new system, the primary emphasis was placed on finding work for single parents who were on the welfare rolls, rather than providing cash assistance for children living in households with income below the poverty line. The national government adopted legislation in 1996 that was similar in form to that which created Wisconsin's system—

and thus the entire structure of social welfare policy in the American federal system was changed.

In 1999 an exclamation point was nearly added to the change in policy direction that had taken place in Wisconsin between 1985 and 1995. A third major change in the structure of state policy established by Wisconsin's Progressives was almost made when Wisconsin's business lobby pushed a bill designed to end the corporate income tax through one of the legislative chambers. This extraordinary occurrence was reported by the (Milwaukee) *Journal Sentinel* in a front-page headline, "Big business to escape state taxes."[57]

In the end, however, state legislators and the governor opted for a series of large permanent cuts in the income tax and a large one-time rebate of the sales tax rather than the elimination of the corporate income tax. Yet the fact that this change was ever seriously contemplated illustrates the way in which policymaking in Wisconsin was moving in a direction quite different from the one Robert M. La Follette and the other Progressives charted at the beginning of the twentieth century.

BENEFITS OF NATIONAL GOVERNMENT POLICY

Wisconsin, like the other forty-nine states within the federal system, benefits from its relationship with the national government in a wide variety of ways. Perhaps the most important benefit is that states need not focus a large part of their energy or resources on defending their citizens from foreign threats; the national government has primary responsibility for this task.

The second most important benefit that Wisconsin and the other states gain from the federal system is money. On average, the national government supplies approximately 25 percent of the money that states spend. Yet the national share of Wisconsin's expenditures was closer to 20 percent than 25 percent for most of the period from the 1970s through the 1990s.[58]

Wisconsin consistently finds itself in the unenviable position of being among the states with the lowest amount of funding per capita from the national government. In FY 2001, for example, Wisconsin ranked forty-eighth in that category.[59] These rankings are a continuous source of frustration for Wisconsin's elected representatives and administrative officials, as are the data on the "balance of payments" by states. The balance-of-payments data show that Wisconsin's citizens pay substantially more taxes into the national treasury than the state gets back in federal funds. In other words, Wisconsin's citizens are subsidizing the citizens of other states in the federal system.[60]

Despite this unhappy situation, most Wisconsin officials do understand the importance of the national government funds that flow to the state. Specifically, the funds provide the means for the state to do many things that it could not otherwise do for its citizens. A summary of selected federal grants, just one of the ways in which federal funds flow to a state, is presented in table 16.

Of course, the federal grant funds usually arrive with strings attached. That is to say, they have traditionally come in the form of grants for specific purposes, functions, or categories of activities. In fact, these grants have traditionally been referred to as "categorical grants." While the states may have some discretion in determining how the funds will be used within a program or functional area, such as social services for the poor, the grant funding for social services cannot be used for road building or transportation. Likewise, national government funds for road building cannot be used to support wildlife conservation programs.

At least since the 1960s social welfare has been the functional or programmatic area to which the largest amounts of national government funds have been committed.[61] During the 1970s, 1980s, and early 1990s the national government provided half or more of the funding needed for programs like Aid to Families with Dependent Children (AFDC) and Medicaid. Perhaps even more impressive is the fact that the national government supplied almost *all* of the funding for programs such as food stamps and housing assistance for the poor. Without these funds, Wisconsin would have been very hard-pressed to provide the level of financial assistance it has to people living on incomes below the poverty line.

Transportation and pollution control are other areas where substantial amounts of national government money have flowed to the states. During the 1950s the national government made a huge commitment of resources to the development and maintenance of the Interstate Highway System, and since the 1970s the national government has invested large amounts of money to reduce air pollution and water pollution, as well as to deal with the problems posed by solid and hazardous wastes.

In addition to sending money to the states, the national government has also provided benefits in other ways. Perhaps the most important of these areas is natural-resource conservation, with the establishment of national forests, national parks, and national wildlife refuges. In Wisconsin, the national government owns two large parcels of land that make up approximately 4.3 percent of the state's total acreage: the Chequamegon National Forest, an area of 848,000 acres, and the Nicolet National Forest, comprising

Table 16. Federal Grants to Wisconsin Government by Agency and for Selected
          Programs, Fiscal Year 2000

Department / Agency	$ in Thousands
Agriculture	210,479
Commerce	16,004
Corporation for National & Community Service	7,527
Corporation for Public Broadcasting	5,644
Defense	28,488
Education	471,167
Energy	41,298
Environmental Protection Agency	76,402
Equal Opportunity Employment Commission	1,006
Federal Emergency Management Agency	27,503
Health and Human Services	3,335,114
Housing and Urban Development	113,773
Institute of Museum and Library Services	5,735
Interior	27,193
Justice	56,486
Labor	116,265
National Aeronautics and Space Administration	10,557
National Archives and Records	526
National Endowment for the Arts	868
National Endowment for the Humanities	1,960
National Science Foundation	65,673
Small Business Administration	395
Social Security Administration	894
State	2,244
State Justice Institute	2
Transportation	618,240
Treasury	1,032
Veterans Affairs	10,734
Other	614
TOTAL	5,253,812

Source: The Book of the States 2002, vol. 34, Federal Grants by Agency and for Selected
Programs by State and Territories in FY 2002

651,000 acres.[62] The former is located in the upper northwestern section of
the state; the latter is located in the northeastern section.

Neither the national government's ownership nor its management of this
Wisconsin land has been contentious. In fact, there are good reasons to
believe that most state officials and state residents have been grateful that
the national government has preserved and protected these forests. One of the
most important outcomes of the national government's efforts is that twenty

acres of old-growth pine forest—the type that once covered large parts of Wisconsin—has been preserved in the Chequamegon National Forest. The trees in this section of the forest are 350 to 400 years old.

Another parcel of land owned and managed by the national government is the Horicon Natural Wildlife Refuge.[63] The refuge consists of 20,976 acres, and it makes up the northern two-thirds of the Horicon Marsh. The southern one-third of the marsh, known as the Horicon Marsh Wildlife Area, is owned and managed by the State of Wisconsin.[64] Its land area is approximately 11,000 acres. The two parcels of land are managed through a national-state partnership.

It is a point of pride for many Wisconsinites that the national and state governments co-manage what is now the world's largest cattail marsh.[65] Wisconsinites committed to land and wildlife preservation delight in the fact that each autumn, the Horicon Marsh becomes one of the world's busiest "landing strips" for ducks and geese. It is an extraordinary sight to see—and hear. Besides ducks and geese, 250 other species of birds have been observed in the refuge, including great blue herons, great egrets, pied-billed grebes, and Virginia rails.[66]

CONSTRAINTS AND NEGATIVE EFFECTS OF NATIONAL GOVERNMENT POLICY

While the benefits that Wisconsin gains from national government policy are extensive, not all national government policy has provided opportunities to Wisconsin's lawmakers or unqualified benefits to its citizens. In some cases, national government policy has required state and local governments to fund regulatory or service functions prescribed by Congress. In other cases, decisions made in Washington DC have forced Wisconsin's officials to take actions they did not want to take. Some policies have distributed benefits unevenly across the states, with Wisconsin on the losing side. Finally, a few national government policies have put some of Wisconsin's citizens at a disadvantage within the competitive economic system, making it difficult for them to sustain their livelihoods, their property, and their way of life.

Among the most highly publicized problems with national government policy is that of "unfunded mandates." In the mid-1980s the estimated costs of national government laws requiring state and local governments to take action that were either not funded by the national government or only partially funded was more than $200 billion.[67] The huge national government deficits that emerged during the Reagan years exacerbated the problem, and the unfunded costs to states of these mandates continued to grow throughout the 1980s and the 1990s.[68] The reemergence of large national budget deficits early in the George W. Bush administration seems to indicate that the problem of unfunded mandates to the states will worsen in the future.

In addition to the problem of unfunded mandates, state decision-makers are sometimes forced to take actions they do not support. During the mid-1980s Wisconsin's governor and legislature were very reluctant to accept the nationally mandated drinking age of twenty-one. Despite the state's long-standing efforts to support programs that protect the health and welfare of its citizens, this national government policy was one that collided with important aspects of Wisconsin's ethnic culture.

Many state lawmakers seemed to be more sensitive to the state's large German ethnic population and its long tradition of brewing and consuming beer than they were to the risks associated with drunk driving. Of course, this legislative sensitivity may have been substantially increased by the lobbying efforts of the state's beer industry and the bar and restaurant associations. Had the state's lawmakers not been threatened with the loss of enormous amounts of federal highway funds if they failed to comply with this law, their resistance to the national government's policy surely would have continued for longer than it ultimately did.

Within the area of transportation, Wisconsin has long been among the states disadvantaged in the distribution of highway funds. For most of the 1970s, 1980s, and into the 1990s, Wisconsin received back from the national government less than 90 percent of the gasoline tax funds the state collected and sent to Washington. Other states, however, received amounts that exceeded 100 percent. Wisconsin's governors and legislators have perceived this situation as unfair, since Wisconsin taxpayers are subsidizing road-building and other transportation projects in other states.

Although this situation has annoyed Wisconsin's officials, and particularly its governors, for more than twenty-five years, the state's congressional delegation was unable to bring about a significant change in the allocation of national government funds. Wisconsin's nine-member delegation simply did not have a sufficient number of votes to make changes in the funding formula, and it was unsuccessful in forming a coalition large enough to effect change.[69] Indeed, it was not until the latter part of the 1990s that Wisconsin's position improved. Wisconsin officials, including Governor Thompson, worked hard for the change, but it took a coalition of many similar "losers" in the existing system to make it more equitable.

Even more problematic for the state than the national government's transportation funding system has been the milk price support system. The system is one of the factors that has contributed to the decline of the family farm in Wisconsin. Established by an act of Congress during the Great Depression of the 1930s, the milk price support system puts dairy farmers in the state known as "America's Dairyland" at a huge competitive disadvantage in the sale of fluid milk.[70] The price support system is based on the distance the dairy farmer is from Eau Claire, Wisconsin. The farther a farmer is from Eau Claire, the higher the federal price support. Thus dairy farmers in Wisconsin and Minnesota get the lowest price support in the whole country, while dairy farmers in Southern Florida receive the highest.[71]

How did this policy come about in the first place? Why has this national policy survived for sixty-five years when it so egregiously discriminates against the farmers in the two states that may have natural environments best suited to dairy farming? Why is the national government interfering with the marketplace and promoting the expansion of dairy farming in states like Florida and Texas, where the environment is poorly suited to this type of agriculture?[72]

The origins of the policy were based on good intentions. In the mid-1930s the Roosevelt administration attempted to respond to low dairy product prices caused by an excess of dairy production. The administration was also attempting to find ways to improve public health by providing "incentives" for dairy production in states where there was little milk production at the time. There was no interstate highway system in the 1930s and no huge refrigerated tanker trucks. The combination of inadequate local production and a primitive transportation system meant that the demand for dairy products could not be met and that many urban markets did not have enough milk.

The means of shipping or hauling of milk today are, of course, dramatically different than they were in the mid-1930s. Wisconsin and Minnesota, whose geography, climate, related agriculture, and abundance of fresh water are perfectly suited to dairy operations, produce fluid milk in sufficient quantity to supply a large part of the country, but the dairy farmers in these two states simply cannot compete with farmers in the Northeast, South, Southwest, or West that have very large federal price supports. So in an era of deregulation—and an era where praise for the "efficiency of markets" is loud and vociferous—how, exactly, has this policy survived?

Quite simply, the policy has survived on the basis of congressional arithmetic, rather than economic merit or wisdom. With a total of seventeen votes in the House of Representatives and four in the Senate, Wisconsin and Minnesota do not have the voting muscle needed to change the policy. Furthermore, since many states benefit handsomely from this arrangement, Wisconsin and Minnesota have been unable to put together a coalition large enough to overcome the block of states that benefits from the current policy.

These political "facts of life" were illustrated in dramatic fashion during 1999. A headline in the front section of the *Washington Post* (November 17, 1999) summed it up this way: "GOP Leadership Sour on Milk Reform." The article chronicled the tale of how in 1995 Congress instructed the U.S. Department of Agriculture (USDA) to devise a milk price support system that was more market driven and fairer. After four years of work and countless hours of meetings with dairy farmers and related interests all across the country, the USDA put forward a price system that included some modest reform. Even that modest reform proposal, however, fell victim to a decision made by then Senate Majority Leader Trent Lott (R-MS) and Speaker of the House of Representatives Dennis Hastert (R-IL) based on congressional arithmetic. More state delegations wanted to kill the reforms than wanted to make them the law of the land.[73]

By its actions, the GOP leadership dashed the best hope that Wisconsin's elected officials—and more importantly, its long-suffering dairy farmers— had had in the past fifty years for some reduction in the price discrimination they face. As viewed by members of the Wisconsin and Minnesota delegation, it was a matter of "the whole country ganging up on the Midwest."[74]

The fact that national government policy makes it difficult for farmers in America's Dairyland to stay in business underscores some very important lessons about politics and policy development in Washington DC. National government policy may have quite divergent effects on different parts of the country. When 51 percent of the members of the House and Senate put something in place that benefits citizens in their states, they may care little about the negative effects that policy has on the citizens of other states. Neither arguments about "fairness" nor economic efficiency, nor the problems created by interfering with the marketplace, are likely to matter to members whose states are "winners" in the policy game.

At the same time, it is important to consider the fact that Wisconsin's state government officials have opportunities to deliver services or conduct regulatory activities that they might not otherwise be able to without national government support. Furthermore, it is worth remembering that large numbers of Wisconsin's citizens have benefited in a wide variety of ways from national government programs and resources. On the whole, national government policy during the twentieth century evolved in ways that fit the vision that Wisconsin's elected officials and citizens have held as to what constituted proper government action. Of course, Wisconsin's institutional and policy innovations have often provided the impetus for the development of policy at the national level.

AMERICAN INDIANS IN WISCONSIN AND THE FEDERAL SYSTEM

At the end of the twentieth century, Wisconsin was the home of eleven Indian tribes or bands.[75] During the 1970s and 1980s the difficult plight of American Indians gained visibility and attention within the state and throughout the nation. Factors that contributed to this visibility included the civil rights movement and new literature that was highly critical of the way the U.S. government and European settlers had treated, and continued to treat, the Indians. The Indians themselves also generated media and public interest in their circumstances by pursuing their economic, social, and political interests in the courts and by lobbying national and state policy makers to respond to their needs and aspirations.

In Wisconsin, the tension between state government and the Indian tribes revolved around two issues. The first issue was whether the Chippewa had the right to hunt and fish off of their reservation lands, as they contended. The roots of the issue extended back to treaties the U.S. government had negotiated with the Chippewa during the 1800s, and its outcome was heavily dependent on federal court interpretations of those treaties. The second issue, Indian gaming, is a more recent development, and its outcome was largely determined by changes made in state and national policy during the late 1980s.

The historical record shows that Wisconsin's lawmakers have, from time to time, shown responsiveness to and support for Indian needs and claims. For example, in 1854 the state legislature asked the U.S. Congress to rescind an executive order that President Zachary Taylor issued in 1850 canceling the hunting, fishing, and gathering rights that the Chippewa were granted in an 1842 treaty that ceded Chippewa lands to the United States. That order also decreed that the Chippewa were to leave Wisconsin and the upper peninsula of Michigan and settle on tribal lands in Minnesota.[76] Wisconsin's legislature asked that the treaty rights be respected and that the tribe be given reservations within Wisconsin and Michigan.[77] The request was honored as part of a new treaty signed in 1854, which established Chippewa reservations in Wisconsin, Michigan, and Minnesota, and protected the tribes' hunting and fishing rights in lands ceded to the United States.[78]

More than a century later, however, during the 1970s and 1980s the relationship between the State of Wisconsin and the Chippewa was strained. Ironically, the point of conflict was the state's efforts to conserve its natural resources, including fish and game. Since the early 1900s Wisconsin has been a leader among the states in the area of natural-resource conservation. The opening round of the modern conflict occurred in 1969, when wardens of the Department of Natural Resources, in two separate incidents, arrested six members of the Red Cliff band of the Lake Superior Chippewa and two members of the Bad River band for fishing with gill nets in Lake Superior adjacent to their respective reservations.[79]

The Chippewa contested the arrests in the state court system by arguing that they had the right to hunt and fish on former tribal lands ceded to the United States as part of treaties negotiated during the 1800s. In 1972 a state circuit court ruled that the 1854 treaty granted the Chippewa the right to fish and hunt on their reservation as they pleased, but it did not give them the right to fish in Lake Superior. Upon appeal, however, the ruling was overturned by the Wisconsin Supreme Court.

Wisconsin's Court cited a 1918 decision by the U.S. Supreme Court, *Alaska Pacific Fisheries v. the United States* (248 U.S. 78 [1918]), as the basis for its decision. In that case, the U.S. Supreme Court ruled that fishing rights granted by treaty included the right to fish in Lake Superior.[80] Yet the 1918 decision seems to have contradicted a number of court rulings from the 1800s.[81] It is also notable that in a 1971 decision the Michigan Supreme Court ruled, in a case similar to Wisconsin's, that state game regulations did not apply to Indians protected by the 1854 treaty.[82]

Despite these rulings, however, the conflict over off-reservation hunting and fishing continued throughout the 1970s and 1980s, as many more institutions and people were drawn into the fight, including the state and federal courts, Wisconsin's governor and legislature, the Wisconsin Department of Natural Resources, and various interest groups. At stake were issues related to Indian property rights under various treaties, the authority of the national government, the authority of the state government, race relations, and natural-resource conservation.

Ultimately, the United States Court of Appeals for the Seventh District became the focal point for the resolution of the dispute. In a series of ten decisions on cases running from 1974 through the 1980s, federal district judges James Doyle (father of the James Doyle elected governor in 2002) and Barbara Crabb worked through the question of whether the Chippewa had off-reservation hunting and fishing rights, and, if so, whether the state could establish limits on any of those rights.[83] The tenth and final ruling on the matter was issued in 1991 by Judge Crabb.

The final judgment "recapitulated major findings" of the nine previous rulings. In brief, the findings affirmed the Indians' claims to off-reservation hunting and fishing rights on lands ceded to the U.S. government in treaties made during the 1800s so long as the lands were not privately held and so long as particular considerations of conservation practice were observed. Also affirmed was the right of the Chippewa to hunt and fish on their own reservations as they pleased without state interference.

It is important to note, however, that the state and the various bands of the Chippewa were negotiating while the court decision-making process was taking place, and that the parties already had a series of agreements on natural-resource conservation issues by the time the court's final judgment was put into place. Indeed, Buzz Besadny, the secretary of the Department of Natural Resources at the time, heralded the court's findings and the state-tribe negotiations as the beginning of a new and more constructive relationship between the Chippewa and the state.[84]

Not all of the parties involved in the dispute over off-reservation hunting and fishing rights shared this positive view, however. Those who were opposed to off-reservation rights for the Chippewa mounted and sustained a vigorous campaign against the Indians' claims. The opposition's concerns included fears that Indian off-reservation hunting and fishing would seriously deplete stock, decrease sport angler fishing and tourism in areas used by Indians, and give special privileges to Indians that were not available to other state residents.

The opposition's campaign unfortunately degenerated into physical confrontation at some off-reservation sites where Indians were spear fishing; it further included making demands on state legislators to resist Indian claims: both of these elements made it a very visible issue. In fact, in two polls of Wisconsinites, more than 80 percent reported that they had heard of or read about the issue.[85]

In the Thirty-fourth Assembly District, where opposition to treaty rights was particularly vigorous, a petition to recall the assembly representative, James C. Holperin (Democrat), was initiated, largely because Holperin refused to criticize or attempt to overturn the court's decisions and state negotiations. The recall election for the Thirty-fourth Assembly District was held on March 6, 1990. In that election, Holperin faced a challenger from his own party, Gene C. Ahlborn, as well as a Republican challenger,

Brian Sherrin. Both challengers were opposed to off-reservation hunting and fishing rights. Holperin won the recall election by getting 9,534 votes; Ahlborn received 4,370 and Sherrin 603.[86]

Holperin's victory in the special recall election did not put an end to the matter, however. Six months later, Holperin faced a well-known opponent of off-reservation treaty rights, Dean Crist, in the Democratic primary on September 11, 1990. Holperin won by a margin of nearly two to one. Holperin faced Republican challenger Sherrin in the general election of November 6, 1990. Holperin's vote total was 11,136 to Sherrin's 8,242.[87] Holperin faced Sherrin again in the 1992 election, and Holperin again won with 16,645 votes to Sherrin's 12,088.[88] It seems noteworthy that the share or percentage of the vote Holperin and Sherrin each won remained relatively stable in the 1990 and 1992 general elections. This may indicate that results of the special recall election, the court rulings, and the negotiations between the state and the Chippewa did little to change the minds of those who opposed the Chippewa's off-reservation hunting and fishing rights. Nevertheless, the issue seemed to fade from the statewide media spotlight after the opposition groups failed to win the recall election.

Representative Holperin did not run for reelection in 1994, nor did his three-time opponent Sherrin continue his bid for the seat. Representative Holperin's governmental service did not end, however, with his departure from the legislature. In 2003 Governor James Doyle appointed Holperin secretary of tourism.

Casino Gambling

Before the principal elements of the off-reservation hunting and fishing dispute were resolved, another issue emerged that strained the relationship between the state and the eleven Indian tribes of Wisconsin. The conflict was over Indian casino gambling, or gaming, a new possibility that was a result of a constitutional amendment approved at the state level and new statutes established by the U.S. Congress.

In 1987 Wisconsin's voters approved a constitutional amendment that overturned the state's long-standing prohibition against lotteries. Then, in 1988, Congress passed the Indian Gaming Regulatory Act. The law's stated objectives were to provide economic development and employment opportunities for members of Indian tribes, and the legislation gave Indians the opportunity to engage in the gaming business if state laws permitted. The legislation also specified that the tribes had to establish a compact with the state and that the compact had to be approved by the secretary of the U.S. Department of the Interior.

After the 1987 constitutional amendment won voter approval in Wisconsin, disagreement developed over whether the amendment permitted the legislature to authorize any form of gambling it chose or whether the legislature's options were limited to a state lottery. At the core of the dispute was the interpretation of the term "lottery" used in the state's 1848 constitution. Some took the position that the term should be broadly interpreted as referring to all types of gambling, while others argued that a narrower definition, referring only to games commonly associated with state lotteries, should be used.

There were two questions at the heart of the dispute, and answers to the questions had significant consequences for the Indian tribes in Wisconsin. The first question was whether the legislature could authorize casino gambling as part of its state-run lottery. If so, under the 1988 Indian Gaming Regulatory Act, the state could negotiate compacts with the tribes for casino-style gambling. The second question was whether the legislature could authorize commercial or private casino-run gambling. If this were the case, the Indian tribes would not have exclusive rights to casino-style gaming, and the economic opportunities would be very different than they had hoped.

In the midst of this controversy, two important events occurred. In 1989 the Wisconsin legislature passed Act 196, which authorized the governor to negotiate gaming contracts on behalf of the state; surprisingly Act 196 contained no provision for legislative review of those compacts;[89] and, in late 1989, tentative agreements were reached with several tribes to allow them to operate certain casino games.[90] The negotiations were led by the state's attorney general, Don Hanaway (Republican), at Governor Thompson's request.

Before Governor Thompson could approve the agreements, however, Attorney General Hanaway issued an opinion early in 1990 on the meaning of the term "lottery" and consequences related to that definition. The attorney general used the narrow definition of lottery in his opinion. Nevertheless, he maintained that since the constitutional amendment authorizing a state lottery did not specifically prohibit casino-style gambling, the legislature could "statutorily authorize state or private casino gambling at any time."[91]

The attorney general's opinion was a shock to several tribes because they had already opened casinos in anticipation of an approved compact with the state.[92] In response, the Lac du Flambeau and the Sokaogon (Mole Lake) Chippewa bands sued the state in federal court, arguing that the state had not negotiated with them in good faith. Judge Barbara Crabb issued a ruling in the case in 1990 that the tribes could not operate casinos without signed agreements, but she also held that enforcement authority was strictly in the hands of federal officers.[93]

Then, in 1991, newly elected Attorney General James Doyle (Democrat) offered a new opinion on the meaning of the term "lottery." Doyle took the position that the term should be interpreted broadly to mean gambling, including all games of chance. He also took the position that the legislature could authorize state-operated games of chance, including casino gambling.[94] Not long after this opinion was issued, Judge Crabb, in a second case, cited Doyle's opinion in her decision, and she ruled that the legislature could authorize state-operated casino games.[95]

In August of 1991 the first of the state's gambling compacts with the tribes was completed with the Lac Courte Oreilles Chippewa. In June of 1992 gaming compacts with all eleven tribes were in place and approved by the secretary of the U.S. Department of the Interior. The compacts were to extend for seven years, with automatic five-year extensions unless either party gave formal notice of intention not to renew. In 1998 and 1999 all of the compacts were renewed for five years.[96]

The compacts included a limitation of two full-scale casinos that offered blackjack and electronic games and pulltabs. Off-reservation casinos required consent from the governor, the secretary of the U.S. Department of the Interior, and affected counties, municipalities, and nearby tribes.[97] Other regulations included minimum-age requirements for casino visitors, limits on bets wagered at any time, and payout ratios for games and machines.

To pay for state regulatory costs, and in exchange for the exclusive right of the tribes to conduct certain types of games in the state, the tribes agreed to pay an annual licensing fee of $350,000 prorated among the tribes. When the compacts were renewed in 1988 and 1989 state estimates put other annual payments by the tribes from gambling activities at about $24 million.[98] The tribes' profits from their casinos were estimated at about $300 million per year.

In 2001 the tribes' gambling revenue totaled almost $900 million, but three-quarters of that was earned by only three of the eleven tribes: the Forest County Potawatomi, the Ho-Chunk nation, and the Oneida.[99] Three other tribes—the St. Croix Chippewa, the Stockbridge-Munsee, and the Lac du Flambeau Chippewa—generated a combined total of almost 20 percent of the revenue, while the other five tribes shared the remaining five percent. The distribution of the revenue is shown in table 17.

Table 17.   2001 Casino Revenues

Tribe	2001 Revenue	% of Total
Forest County Potowatomi	$250,459,914	27.93
Ho-Chunk Nation	241,461,664	26.93
Oneida	164,881,515	18.39
St. Croix Chippewa	85,408,253	9.52
Stockbridge-Munsee	53,596,362	5.98
Lac du Flambeau Chippewa	37,214,046	4.15
Menominee	21,460,723	2.39
Lac Courte Oreilles Chippewa	18,763,113	2.09
Bad River Chippewa	13,400,965	1.49
Sokaogon (Mole Lake) Chippewa	7,354,334	0.82
Red Cliff Chippewa	2,781,204	0.31

Source: *Milwaukee Journal Sentinel*, June 2, 2003

It is noteworthy that the principal source of gambling revenue for the tribe with the largest revenues, the Forest County Potawatomi, is its Milwaukee casino. The origins of this casino are interesting, and they show the potential permeability of the state compacts. The Potowatomi did not have any tribal or reservation land in Milwaukee, so the tribe purchased a parcel of land in the city's Menomonee Valley and put the land in trust status. In 1990 the Potowatomi opened a high-stakes bingo operation. Then, in June of 1992, and with the support of the U.S. Department of the Interior, the Potowatomi secured a gaming compact from the state of Wisconsin that included two hundred slot-video games.

City officials argued that their permission had not been secured for this agreement, and they objected to it. Nevertheless, Federal District Court Judge Crabb, in a September 1993 decision, gave the tribe permission to operate the casino under the state compact.[100] The city of Milwaukee did approve an expansion of gaming at the casino in 1999, as part of the amendment and extension of the state compact. For its support, the city secured direct payments, substantial financial support for Indian education, and job training and youth development. Commitments were also made to hire low-income Milwaukee residents and to use disadvantaged businesses for casino-related construction, service, and supply.[101]

The eleven tribes' gambling casinos are dispersed throughout the state. Proximity to large population centers remains a key to casino revenue, and the desire for off-reservation sites near these population centers remains strong with several tribes. For example, one tribe bought land in the Madison area during the mid-1990s and built a casino on the property. At the same time, the tribe pursued the required local and state support for casino gambling on the site. As of this writing (May 2005), neither local nor state support has been provided, however, and the tribe can only offer bingo games at that location. Whether approval will be granted in the future remains an open question. Local governments and the state have clearly stated their preference not to have casino-style gambling in Madison. Tribal lobbying, however, will likely continue, and the financial pressures these governments face will probably keep the issue alive for many years to come.

CHAPTER THIRTEEN

Continuing Traditions
and Emerging Issues

I have sought to show what a democratic people is in our days.

Alexis de Tocqueville, *Democracy in America*, 1838

Thanks to the movement for genuinely democratic government which Senator La Follette led to overwhelming victory in Wisconsin, that state has become literally a laboratory for wise experimental legislation, aiming to secure the social and political betterment of the people as a whole.

Theodore Roosevelt, 1912

In popular culture, Wisconsin is known as America's Dairyland, the Badger State, and the home of the Green Bay Packers. In the study of government and politics, however, Wisconsin is known as The Progressive State and for its role as a laboratory of democracy within the American federal system. Since the early 1900s, when Robert M. La Follette and the Progressives gained control of state government, Wisconsin has been the home of both institutional and policy experiments aimed at improving the political, social, and economic condition of its people. Many of these innovations have been adopted by other states and by the national government.

Wisconsin entered the Union in 1848 as a frontier state at the northwestern edge of the major settlement pattern of the time. The state's frontier experience, its sectional location within the growing United States, and its own internal settlement patterns all contributed to its political development. The state's moralistic political culture, and thus its Progressive foundation, was clearly visible in its 1848 constitution. That document was written by "an assemblage of young Yankee farmers," who were not only industrious and highly educated, but also had a clear conception of the role that government should play in society.[1] They believed that government ought to serve the interests of the people as a whole, rather than the interests of the few.

Wisconsin's historical experience shows, however, that constitutions, as well as democracy itself, can be very fragile. Only twenty-five years after the state entered the Union, narrow economic interests (the railroads and timber industry, particularly) had taken control of Wisconsin's governmental institutions. Through their grip on these institutions the railroad and timber companies were able to gain large economic subsidies for themselves, while, at the same time, the policies they sponsored and the business practices they employed severely damaged the state's environment and the economic well-being of large numbers of its citizens.

If it had not been for Robert La Follette and other Progressives, Wisconsin's modern political history might have been very different, and thus the nation's history might have been very different, too. It is conceivable, of course, that the railroad and timber men who gained control of Wisconsin's governmental institutions during the 1870s and 1880s might eventually have been displaced by other economic interests, rather than by La Follette and the Progressives. History shows that the balance of private power in a state can change dramatically as the structure of a state's economy changes. Yet if one set of powerful private interests had merely been displaced by another, Wisconsin's governmental institutions would likely have remained the captive of the few at the expense of the many.

It is also important to note that the victory that La Follette and the Progressives won over the machine was a close call. The machine's leaders were very capable men, and they were highly adept at managing elections, even if that meant stealing or buying votes. They were also skilled at using bribery to get what they wanted from the state legislature. Fortunately, despite its dominance, the machine was not able to corrupt the electoral process or the legislature so completely that the aspirations and interests of the majority were permanently undermined.

Perhaps the nature of the struggle that La Follette endured, as well as the ferocity of his determination to return control of the state's institutions to its people, was best characterized by Woodrow Wilson in 1912. During the election campaign of that year, Wilson, who would ultimately win the contest and emerge as the country's next president, said:

> Now there arose in Wisconsin that indomitable little figure of Bob La Follette.
> I tell you ladies and gentlemen, I take off my cap to Bob La Follette. He
> has never taken his eye for a single moment from the goal he set out to

reach. He has walked a straight line to it in spite of every temptation to turn aside. . . . I have sometimes thought of Senator La Follette climbing the mountain of privilege . . . taunted, laughed at, called back, going steadily on and not letting himself be deflected for a single moment. . . . I love these lonely figures climbing this ugly mountain of privilege. But they are not so lonely now. I am sorry for my part that I did not come in when they were fewer. There was no credit to come in when I came in. The whole nation had awakened.[2]

Clearly, La Follette was the key figure in the effort to restore both political democracy in Wisconsin and the economic well-being of the state's citizens. Yet it is critical to remember that the moralistic culture was deeply rooted in the state before the political machine took control of state government, and even a leader as determined and capable as La Follette could not have succeeded without broad support. Thus, it should not be surprising that in some of the other states that fell under the influence of the timber and railroad interests in the 1880s and 1890s, the restoration of democratic institutions and processes proceeded much more slowly than it did in Wisconsin—if, that is, it happened at all. Nor, given Wisconsin's experience, should it be difficult to understand why even today states and their public policy can be held hostage by a small number of narrowly focused private interests.

Other Progressive leaders played an important role in the recovery and expansion of Wisconsin's democratic roots. Indeed, La Follette's successors in the executive office, Francis McGovern and James O. Davidson, may have been more successful in their pursuit of the Progressives' legislative agenda than was La Follette. Credit must also be accorded to faculty members at the University of Wisconsin–Madison. They played a critical role in the Progressives' efforts to open up the state's political institutions and in the development of the Progressives' policy innovations. They also helped to secure the passage of Progressive reforms.

Finally, it should be remembered that the establishment of a strong civil service system during La Follette's term as governor was a critical factor in the implementation of the policy innovations that emerged during the Progressive era. Without the expertise of these civil servants, many of the innovations discussed in this book would have floundered. John R. Commons, an early architect of Progressive reforms and a University of Wisconsin faculty member, argued that having strong administrative capacity was the key to successful policy innovation.[3]

In addition to helping us understand how fragile democracy can be, Wisconsin's experience also serves to underscore the significance of the competition that exists in the nation as a whole between what Daniel Elazar has called the "marketplace" and "commonwealth" conceptions of the (proper) political order. According to Elazar, these two political cultures pull toward opposing poles of "Power" and "Justice." These poles, he maintains, "encompass the basic political concerns of all civil societies, namely, 'who gets what, when and how' (Power), on the one hand, and the development of the good society (Justice), on the other hand."[4]

In historical terms, there has been an ebb and flow between these two poles nationally, with one in the ascendancy for a time before it is eventually replaced by the other. The shifts between the two political cultures can have a strong effect on who is elected to national and state offices. In turn, these shifts can profoundly affect the kinds of policies that elected officials produce.

Officials whose candidacy depends on narrow economic or political interests, or who have been socialized in the marketplace culture, are not likely to care much about social justice or the development of the good society unless doing so temporarily provides some political advantage. On the other hand, officials who are rooted in the commonwealth conception of the political order may (mistakenly) think that they can succeed simply on the merits or legitimacy of their policy preferences. They may not, in other words, pay sufficient attention to marketplace forces or the need to accumulate power in order to achieve policy objectives.

Because Wisconsin and the other states exist within a federal system, the ebb and flow between the commonwealth and marketplace cultures can both constrain and benefit those in the state whose approach to politics fits one or the other model. Robert M. La Follette, his successors in the governor's office, Francis McGovern, James O. Davidson, and the early Progressives benefited from the broad national current that was flowing in the direction of the commonwealth model during the early 1900s, and they in turn helped to propel it. They were also lucky to be pursuing their agenda at a time when inhabitants of the White House, like Theodore Roosevelt and Woodrow Wilson, and a sufficient number of congressmen wanted to have the national government adopt many of Wisconsin's institutional and policy innovations.

Later Progressives, including Robert La Follette's son, Philip, were lucky to have Franklin Roosevelt in office at the time they were pursuing their agenda of institutional and policy innovation. In Franklin Roosevelt, of course, Wisconsin's Progressives benefited from an elected chief executive for whom the pursuit of social justice was an impassioned objective. A strong national current of support for social justice also helped Patrick J. Lucey win the governorship in 1970. The commonwealth current also provided a political climate in which Lucey and state legislators could pursue a wide range of policy innovations designed to improve fairness in the distribution of state and local tax burdens as well as fairness in the distribution of expenditure benefits.

In more recent times, such as the 1980s, the national current shifted rather dramatically away from the commonwealth model and toward the marketplace conception of government. No single individual contributed more to this change than Ronald Reagan. At the same time, this shift at the national level not only helped propel Tommy Thompson into the governor's seat in Wisconsin but also provided the political climate in which he could pursue a marketplace-oriented policy agenda.

Like the national political climate, economic change has contributed to the ebb and flow of the two cultures within the nation and Wisconsin. The national economic recessions of the 1880s and 1890s helped the Progressives take office in Wisconsin in the early 1900s. The Great Depression of the late 1920s and early 1930s gave them new life in the state. More recently, during the early and mid-1980s, a national recession, coupled with a deep regional recession, provided an opportunity for candidates who preferred the marketplace vision of the political order, such as Tommy Thompson, to gain office.

Despite the resurgence of the marketplace model in Wisconsin during the last two decades of the twentieth century, Wisconsin still had political processes, governmental institutions, and public policies in place at the time of its Sesquicentennial, in 1998, that, viewed from a moralistic or commonwealth perspective, compared favorably to those of most other states in the nation. Furthermore, particularly in the area of social welfare policy, Wisconsin's national visibility for pioneering was as high as it ever had been.[5] In short, there was much for the people of Wisconsin to celebrate about their Progressive heritage at the time of the state's Sesquicentennial and much for the nation to celebrate, too.

Yet at the very time the Sesquicentennial celebrations were underway in the state, the roots of some important, emerging problems were already in place. Some of these problems or challenges are unique to the state, but others are common across states. The four principal types of problems or challenges include:

- the corrosion of electoral and legislative processes
- the "stretching" of the state constitution
- the power imbalance between the governor and the legislature, and
- the state's fiscal problems

Problems with the electoral and legislative processes were made visible in a rather dramatic way in 2001. Media stories began to appear about the use of legislative party caucus staff in election campaigns. These stories were eventually followed by the revelation that state legislative leaders secretly used hundreds of thousands of dollars of public funds to hire lawyers to defend themselves against charges related to the caucus scandal. Then, in October of 2002, came the news of indictments filed by the Madison and Milwaukee district attorneys against a Democratic party leader in the senate and Republican Party leaders in the assembly. These charges included the use of state employees in election campaigns and for campaign fundraising, as well as the shaking down of lobbyists for campaign donations.[6]

The developments have been shocking for Wisconsin's citizens. The scandals rank as the most serious violations of state ethics and the Progressive tradition in more than a century. Yet for some observers of these events, the culture of denial that seemed to be associated with them is as worrisome as the scandals themselves. Legislative caucus staff members claimed they did not know that working in election campaigns was illegal, and candidates for whom the caucus staff worked claimed that they did not know where their campaign support was coming from. Legislative leaders also seemed to deny responsibility for the scandal, even though they supervised these staff members and apparently assigned them to campaigns or campaign-fundraising activities.[7] Furthermore, legislative leaders apparently attempted to excuse shaking down lobbyists as something they were required to do as part of their job responsibilities and on behalf of their parties.

While a final assessment of these circumstances must await the completion of the legal process, the reported scandals have seriously affected the assumptions Wisconsin's citizens have long held about their state, and they have damaged the state's national reputation. For example, an article that appeared in the *New York Times* contained the following highlight: "The 'laboratory of reform' becomes contaminated."[8] Other unflattering reports about the scandals have also appeared in the *New York Times* and the *Washington Post*. In order to restore public trust in, and national respect for, Wisconsin's legislative institutions, legislators will have to ensure that the practices that led to the caucus scandal and the apparent shaking-down of lobbyists are eliminated.

Unfortunately, as in other states, Wisconsin's electoral and legislative processes have also been corroded in more complex ways. For example, a wild distortion of candidate records now regularly occurs through "issue ads" produced and paid for by interest groups. One consequence is that the voices of the candidates themselves are often drowned out in a sea of accusations and exaggerations that are constantly directed at the electorate through television ads. Another consequence is that narrow economic or political interests can more easily gain an enormous advantage in electoral competition.

An additional source of corrosion is the blurring of the line between legislator and lobbyist. This has happened despite the fact that Wisconsin has very strict lobbying rules and disclosure requirements. There are a number of reasons for this shift. One is that the number of lobbyists who are former legislators continues to grow. Generally speaking, these former legislators have easy access to their former colleagues, and they have a keen understanding of leverage points in the political process. A second reason is that legislators need the support of economic interests or groups that have deep pockets, because election campaign costs have risen rapidly.

A third reason the line between legislator and lobbyist has blurred is that lobbying has become more and more professionalized and specialized. The lobbyists who represent organized interests are likely to have more information about the potential consequences of a given policy than those who are not organized. Thus, the public's interest may get overlooked or lost in the flow of information that legislators get about legislation that is being considered. Finally, as lobbying has become more and more sophisticated, current legislators are increasingly sensitive to the fact that these specialized interests can fund opposition candidates or even *recruit* opposition candidates. Consequently, the "natural instinct" some legislators have to give in to a narrow interest with a strong position on a piece of legislation has become even more pronounced.[9]

The second area in which Wisconsinites face important future challenges is constitutional "stretching." Perhaps the single most important recent example of this stretching is the use of public funds to supply the capital needed by a private corporation—the Milwaukee Brewers. To make a bad situation even worse, the legislature and governor established a special break from the 5-percent state sales tax on Brewers tickets for the economic interests that have the financial resources required to buy luxury skyboxes in the Brewers' new stadium. The rest of the folks who go through the gates of the new stadium, however, have to pay sales tax as part of their ticket price.

The Wisconsin Supreme Court's reluctance to intervene in this stretching of the constitution can be viewed as both surprising and risky. When the protectors of the constitution fail to constrain those who want to ignore existing boundaries, it provides encouragement for others to test constitutional boundaries, as well. It is easy to visualize a variety of new ways in which public funds might be used in the future to provide subsidies to private corporations—despite the constitutional prohibition against it.

A third important challenge for the future is the balance of power between the legislature and the governor. During the 1980s and 1990s the governor became the dominant figure in policymaking and administration, while the legislature's role and power declined. This can be primarily attributed to the long tenure of a governor (Tommy Thompson) who aggressively worked to expand his power—and to use it for his own purposes. The Wisconsin Supreme Court's reluctance to establish limits on the governor's use of the partial veto was a key contributing factor.

Another reason for the power imbalance during the 1980s and 1990s was the failure of legislators themselves to put the interests of their institution above the interests of their party. As one veteran observer of the legislature put it, "Every legislator ought to know that the game of institutional power is a zero-sum game. If one institution gains more, the other has less."[10] One consequence of this circumstance was that Governor Thompson was able to use the partial veto to create new law that the legislature did not pass, did not intend to pass, and had not even considered; still, those vetoes were not overridden by the legislature.

The departure of four-term governor Tommy Thompson for Washington DC has given the legislature an opportunity to recover some of its power. Yet if that power is recovered simply by virtue of an aggressive and destructive partisanship aimed at little more than blocking all gubernatorial initiative, little will be gained. As shown throughout this book and reported in this chapter, this type of destructive partisanship has already been costly for the state, and it could prolong the state's fiscal problems.

The fourth major challenge that Wisconsin's elected officials, administrators, and citizens face is the state's fiscal condition and the tough choices associated with the large deficits that came into view during the 2001 recession. Beginning in the 1960s and 1970s the state's governors and legislators continually expanded the financial assistance provided to local school districts and municipal and county governments. The most recent dramatic expansion of aid occurred in the mid-1990s, when the state's share of school costs was expanded from 48 percent to 66 percent. Yet, in contrast to similar increases in the 1960s, 1970s, and 1980s, there was no increase in state taxes in the mid-1990s to offset this very large, additional commitment of state funds. In fact, rather than raising taxes the governor and the legislature decided to make very large cuts in state taxes.[11]

The permanent imbalance these decisions created between state spending commitments and state revenues was hidden from view until the recession that officially began in March of 2001 pushed the state into a budget crisis. Wisconsin's 2001–3 and 2003–5 budget deficits have been among the largest in the country because the state has had to deal with both a cyclical deficit caused by the recession and a structural deficit caused by tax and spending decisions made in the 1990s.[12] Although substantial cuts in state spending were made in the 2001–3 budget, the size of those cuts was limited because the state borrowed against future tobacco settlement revenues and used the money as a source of temporary revenue.

With most of that one-time money used up, however, the cuts required in the 2003–5 budget were much deeper, and they included the elimination of a large number of state government positions. Nevertheless, the state continues to face severe budgetary pressure that may require additional large expenditure reductions. State support for local governments and for the state's highly regarded welfare reform initiative are among the many places that major cuts could occur, and if large cuts in these areas are made they could entail a whole new set of undesirable consequences. Many other state programs and state employees also remain vulnerable.

In short, the elected officials, administrators, and citizens of the State of Wisconsin seem to be facing a host of difficult challenges at the beginning of the twenty-first century. Regrettably, some of these challenges are reminiscent of the problems Robert M. La Follette and the Progressives faced at the beginning of the twentieth century. Whether a leader of La Follette's quality emerges, and whether legislators who have the values and courage of the early Progressives will step forward, however, is a matter about which we can only speculate. It seems clear, however, that courageous political leadership will be needed if the state's most pressing problems are to be addressed.

CHAPTER FOURTEEN

Studying Wisconsin Politics and Government

A Guide to Resources

Any author who wants to write about Wisconsin has the benefit of an enormous body of source material on most topics. There is wonderful literature on the historical settlement of the state; Wisconsin's geography and climate; the state's economic development; the development of the state's governmental institutions; and its public policy innovations. At the same time, it is worth noting that the amount of contemporary research published on the state constitution, political parties, interest groups, and other important topics would appear to be surprisingly limited. For example, the last comprehensive study of the state constitution was conducted by the Wisconsin State Historical Society in the early 1900s; the most recent comprehensive study of the role that political parties play in state politics dates to the late 1950s; and attempts to systematically examine the role that interest groups play in state politics are also dated. In short, there is plenty of opportunity for those who want to generate new research on Wisconsin politics and government.

GENERAL RESOURCES
Libraries

For most research on Wisconsin, the best place to begin is the library, and Wisconsin has two excellent libraries in the capital city of Madison. The Wisconsin State Historical Society Library is housed in a beautiful marble building on the campus of the University of Wisconsin–Madison. The society was established in 1846 as a private organization, chartered by the state legislature in 1853, and began receiving state funds in 1854. The library contains an enormous collection of primary and secondary materials on the state, and it houses the offices of the Wisconsin State Historical Society.

The second major library in Madison is the Dr. Rupert H. Theobold Legislative Library. The library is part of the Legislative Reference Bureau, established in 1901 as part of the Progressive reform initiatives. Charles McCarthy was the champion of the bureau and the library as well as its first leader. The library is a treasure trove for anyone who is looking for state documents. For most of this century, the Legislative Reference Bureau and the library were located in the State Capitol, but they are now located across the street from the State Capitol on East Main Street.

Another large collection of materials on the state can be found in libraries at the University of Wisconsin–Madison. The Memorial Library, located directly across from the Wisconsin State Historical Society Library, has the university's largest collection. Other libraries that contain valuable primary and secondary sources on the state include the School of Agriculture's library; the Helen C. White Library; the Institute for Research on Poverty's library; the library of the La Follette School of Public Affairs; and the Geography Department's library. The first four of these libraries are located on Observatory Drive, while the Geography library is located in Science Hall, which is situated cater-corner to the Wisconsin Union.

Newspapers

The daily newspapers of Wisconsin's two largest cities, Milwaukee and Madison, have traditionally been superb sources of information about Wisconsin politics and government. For most of the last half of the twentieth century, Milwaukee had two large independent daily newspapers, the *Milwaukee Journal* and the *Milwaukee Sentinel*; the former was an afternoon paper and the latter a morning paper. The two papers had independent staff reporters located in the State Capitol at least part of the year, and they had a somewhat different slant on Wisconsin government and politics. In 1998, however, the two papers were merged into the (Milwaukee) *Journal Sentinel*.

Madison still has two newspapers, the *State Journal* and the *Capital Times*. The former has historically had a more conservative point of view and the latter a more liberal take. At one point, the two papers seemed to be relatively evenly matched competitors. Over the past several decades, however, the *Capital Times*, an afternoon paper, has suffered the fate of most afternoon papers, and its circulation has declined.

Daily newspapers also exist in most of the state's medium-sized cities. In fact, the *Wisconsin Blue Book 1999–2000* lists sixteen daily newspapers. Among the papers that have traditionally had good coverage of state government and politics are the *Green Bay Press Gazette* and the *Appleton Post-Crescent*. Unfortunately, the number of daily newspapers has fallen over time, as has the quality of the coverage given to state politics and government. The latter circumstance is largely the result of having independent daily newspapers swallowed up by large media chains. In addition to daily newspapers, the *Wisconsin Blue Book 1999–2000* lists more than two hundred weekly, biweekly, or monthly newspapers in the state. These newspapers, however, are more likely to stress local than state news.

Journals, Newsletters, and Magazines

The University of Wisconsin–Madison's *Law Review* is an academic journal that regularly includes coverage of court cases and judicial decisions. *Focus*, published three times per year by The Institute for Research on Poverty, contains concise and punchy summaries of articles published in peer-reviewed journals, as well as books, on policy problems in Wisconsin and the nation. The *La Follette Policy Report*, published semiannually by the La Follette School of Public Affairs, contains summaries of research supported by the institute, as well as summaries of academic publications on public policy research. Both *Focus* and the *La Follette Policy Report* are highly regarded by other scholars and by policymakers in Wisconsin and other states. Among the best newsletters for information on state government and state policy is the *Wisconsin Taxpayer*, published by the Wisconsin Taxpayers Alliance.

Magazines that are focused on state topics include the *Wisconsin Magazine of History*, published by the Wisconsin State Historical Society, and the *Wisconsin Academy Review*, published by the Wisconsin Academy of Sciences, Arts, and Letters. Wonderful coverage of the state's natural resources and human interaction with land, water, and wildlife is provided in *Wisconsin Natural Resources*. This magazine is published bimonthly by the Wisconsin Department of Natural Resources. *Milwaukee Magazine* and *Madison Magazine* sometimes publish articles on state government and politics, but the main focus is business, social and cultural life, and local politics. *Wisconsin Trails* has articles about vacation spots, restaurants, and cultural events in Wisconsin. *Midwest Living* covers similar topics, with coverage on Wisconsin and other Midwestern states.

Data Sources

The single most valuable and comprehensive source of data on Wisconsin that is produced by an agency of the State of Wisconsin is the *Wisconsin Blue Book*. The *Blue Book* has been published since 1853. Modern versions of the book have been compiled by the Legislative Reference Bureau, and they typically run more than nine hundred pages. The *Wisconsin Blue Book* includes biographies of Wisconsin's elected representatives in the U.S. Senate and House; state constitutional officers; Wisconsin Supreme Court justices; members of the Wisconsin Senate and Assembly; and key legislative officers. Modern volumes of the *Blue Book* also contain a feature article about a topic of interest, and they contain a copy of the state constitution as amended over time.

Modern editions of the *Blue Book* also contain an overview of Wisconsin state government; a section on the Wisconsin legislature that includes descriptions of the key legislative committees and agencies; an organization chart of the executive branch and a description of all of the executive branch departments and agencies; a section on the state's court system, including the Wisconsin Supreme Court; statistical information about the state; and data about Wisconsin elections.

Other valuable data on Wisconsin are collected and published by the United States Bureau of the Census (U.S. Department of Commerce). The Census Bureau's publications include the *Statistical Abstract of the United States* (various years), and other publications focused on state, local, or state-local finance, including *State Government Finances* (various years), *County Government Finances* (various years), and *City Government Finances* (various years). Still other data on Wisconsin can be found in the *Book of the States* and other publications from the Council on State Governments, located in Lexington, Kentucky, and in publications from the National Council of State Legislatures, located in Denver, Colorado.

Research Bureaus

Most of the state's executive branch departments have divisions or bureaus that collect and publish data and conduct research. The *Wisconsin Blue Book* is probably the most convenient source to use to identify the relevant research bureau within each department. Among the most visible of the state government research entities are the Wisconsin State Budget Office, located in the Department of Administration, and two divisions within the

Department of Revenue, the Research and Analysis Division and the State and Local Finance Division.

The legislative branch also has substantial research capacity in each of the principal legislative agencies. These agencies include the Legislative Council, the Legislative Audit Bureau, the Legislative Fiscal Bureau, and the Legislative Reference Bureau.

The University of Wisconsin–Madison also has a number of units that regularly conduct research on state government and state policy. These units include: the La Follette School of Public Affairs (formerly the La Follette Institute of Public Affairs), The Institute for Research on Poverty, the Government Affairs Unit, the School of Agriculture, and the Department of Agricultural Economics. A number of units within the University of Wisconsin Extension, particularly the agricultural extension unit, also conduct research on the state.

Finally, it is worth noting that there are a host of nonprofit and private sector organizations that conduct research on particular areas of state policy. Of course, some of this research is not intended to be objective in its design or preparation because it is to be used for the purpose of advocacy on specialized public policy issues. One nonprofit organization that generally receives high marks for its research, however, is the Wisconsin Taxpayers Alliance, located only a few blocks from the State Capitol in Madison.

Public Opinion Surveys

The only regularly conducted statewide survey in Wisconsin is a joint product of St. Norbert College, in De Pere, Wisconsin, and the Wisconsin Public Broadcasting Company. The statewide survey is known as the Wisconsin Survey. It is conducted every other year by faculty and staff at St. Norbert College, and survey findings are reported by the college and the Wisconsin Public Broadcasting Company. The survey includes questions about income, employment, and party affiliation, as well as questions about public policy issues.

State Election Data

Voting data for all congressional offices, statewide offices, and legislative offices is contained in the *Wisconsin Blue Book* (various years). Information on the rules governing the financing of election campaigns and data on campaign contributions are published by the Wisconsin Elections Board.

STATE GOVERNMENT DOCUMENTS

Most of the data presented in the "Statistical Section" of the *Wisconsin Blue Book* are based on publications from the national government and state government agencies. The original sources can be found in one or more state depository libraries. These libraries consist of three types: state-level, regional, and select. The complete list of these libraries can be found in the *Wisconsin Blue Book*. The three state-level libraries are the Wisconsin State Historical Society Library, the Reference and Loan Library of the Department of Public Instruction, and the Legislative Reference Library. Among the valuable publications of the Wisconsin State Historical Society is one entitled "Wisconsin Public Documents."

The principal documents related to the ongoing business of the state legislature are the *Bulletin of the Proceedings of the Wisconsin Legislature* and the *Weekly Schedule of Committee Activities*. New statutes passed by the legislature and signed by the governor are published in a prescribed sequence. Session laws are published first in the form of "slip" laws. Then, within ten working days after publication of the slip law, the act's number, title, and original bill number are printed in the (Milwaukee) *Journal Sentinel*, the newspaper currently designated as the official state paper for publication of legal notices. At the end of each biennium, the slip laws are bound into volumes called the *Laws of Wisconsin*. The laws are then placed into the *Wisconsin Statutes* by the Revisor of Statutes Bureau.

TOPICAL BIBLIOGRAPHY
The Essentials

One of the best ways to learn about Wisconsin is through literature about the state and its people. Perhaps the most enduring theme of this literature is the important connection between the people of Wisconsin and their environment. Among the best known and most beloved books about life in Wisconsin when it was a frontier society are Laura Ingalls Wilder's *Little House in the Big Woods*, and Carol Ryrie Brink's *Caddie Woodlawn*, a Newberry Medal award-winner. Both books tell about the adventures of young girls who are growing up in a landscape that is only slowly being settled by people of European descent.

The Wisconsin frontier experience and the relationship between people and their physical environment figured prominently in the writings of two nationally known figures who grew up in Wisconsin. John Muir's family moved from Scotland to a modest homestead near Portage, Wisconsin, in 1849. In *The Story of My Boyhood and Youth* (1913), Muir describes the years he spent growing up on the farm and his years at the University of Wisconsin. Remarkably, Frederick Jackson Turner was born in the city of Portage in 1861 and lived there until he was 18. As a scholar, Turner argued that the frontier was a critical factor in shaping and defining the American democratic experience.

Hamlin Garland's *A Son of the Middle Border* (1917) and Zona Gale's *Friendship Village* (1908), *Mothers to Men* (1911), and *When I Was a Little Girl* (1913) describe life in Wisconsin during the late 1800s and early 1900s. In *A Son of the Middle Border*, Garland says, "I count myself most fortunate in the fact that my boyhood was spent in the middle of a charming landscape and during a certain heroic era of western settlement." Zona Gale's early books tell the stories of humble people growing up in an ordinary (Wisconsin) town. The life of ordinary people in an ordinary town is also the subject of Madison-born author and playwright Thornton Wilder's *Our Town* (1938). The play was apparently based on his memories of growing up in Madison.

Sterling North's *Rascal* (1963), another Newbery Medal award-winning book, is a wonderful autobiographical sketch of a young boy who grows up in southeastern Wisconsin during World War I. With his pet raccoon, Rascal, North goes fishing in the Rock River, swims in Lake Koshkonong, and has a host of other outdoor adventures.

The most comprehensive attempt to record and interpret life in a Wisconsin community can be found in August Derleth's Sac Prairie Saga. The series is focused on Prairie du Sac, a small town located on the Wisconsin River (south of Portage). Among the early titles in the series are *Place of the Hawk* (1935); *Still is the Summer Night* (1937); *Restless is the River* (1939); *Walden West*; and *Return to Walden West* (1970).

The most important of the modern books written about Wisconsin and its environment is Aldo Leopold's *A Sand County Almanac* (1949). Unlike Muir and Frederick Jackson Turner, Leopold did not live in Wisconsin as a child. He moved to the state when he was an adult, but the farm on which he lived was located near Portage and was only a dozen miles or so from the Muir family farm. Leopold's book is a classic statement about the beauty of the natural environment and the need to protect and preserve it.

Perhaps Wallace Stegner's essay "The Sense of Place" contextualizes the special connection between Wisconsinites and their natural environment. Stegner begins the essay with the following quotation from Wendell Berry,

"If you don't know where you are, you don't know who you are." William Cronon, a scholar at the University of Wisconsin–Madison, invokes Stegner at the beginning of a marvelous 1991 essay entitled "Landscape and Home: Environmental Traditions in Wisconsin." "My sense of this place" (Wisconsin), Cronon says, "is mainly that of a child and young adult growing up and coming of age here." In this sense, Cronon's experience corresponds to that of most of the Wisconsin authors mentioned above and most of the main characters in their books.

Cronon describes himself as an inheritor of Wisconsin's special environmental tradition. In his 1991 essay he reports on ways in which he explored the Wisconsin landscape. He then describes the influence that the Wisconsin landscape had on Muir, Turner, and Leopold. Cronon argues that these three men "represent three different strands of Wisconsin's environmental tradition." These three strands can also be found both in the emergence of the American environmental tradition and in its ongoing development. It is also notable that the founding father of Earth Day, the national day of celebration of the natural environment, was Gaylord Nelson, a U.S. senator from Wisconsin.

The Character of the State

Austin, H. Russel. *Wisconsin's Story: The Building of a Vanguard State.* Milwaukee WI: *Milwaukee Journal,* 1964.

Conant, James K. *Executive Decision Making in the State.* Ph.D. Diss. Department of Political Science. University of Wisconsin–Madison, 1983.

Current, Richard. *A History of Wisconsin.* New York: W. W. Norton, 1977.

Elazar, Daniel. *American Federalism: A View from the States.* New York: Harper and Row, 1984.

Finely, Charles. *Wisconsin Geography.* Madison: University of Wisconsin Press, 1976.

"Framework of Government." In *Wisconsin Blue Book 1999–2000,* 201–10. Madison: Joint Committee on Legislative Organization, 1999.

"The Framework of Your Wisconsin Government." 10th ed. Madison WI: Wisconsin Taxpayers Alliance, 1997.

Holand, H. R. *Old Peninsula Days.* Minoqua WI: Heartland Press, 1990.

Howe, Frederick C. *Wisconsin: An Experiment in Democracy.* Madison: n.p., 1912.

Kincaid, John. "Political Cultures and Quality of Life." *Publius* 10, no. 2 (Spring 1980): 1–16.

La Follette, Robert M. *La Follette's Autobiography*. Madison: University of Wisconsin Press, 1960.

Maxwell, Robert S. *Robert M. La Follette and the Rise of the Progressives in Wisconsin*. Madison: Wisconsin State Historical Society, 1956.

McCullough, David G. *The Path Between the Seas: The Creation of the Panama Canal 1870–1914*. New York: Simon and Schuster, 1977.

Nesbit, Robert C., and William F. Thompson. *Wisconsin: A History*, 2d ed. Madison: University of Wisconsin Press, 1989.

Ostergren, Robert C., and Thomas R. Vale. *Wisconsin Land and Life*. Madison: University of Wisconsin Press, 1997.

Paul, Justus F., and Barbara D. Paul, eds. *The Badger State: A Documentary History of Wisconsin*. Grand Rapids MI: William B. Eerdmans, 1979.

Sayre, Wallace. *Robert M. La Follette: A Study in Political Methods*. New York: New York University Press, 1930.

Stark, John O. "Wisconsin Writers." In *Wisconsin Blue Book 1977–1978*, 95–185. Madison: Joint Committee on Legislative Organization, 1977.

Torell, Ellen, ed. *The Political Philosophy of Robert M. La Follette*. Madison: The Robert M. La Follette Co., 1920.

Wisconsin: A Guide to the Badger State. 2d ed. New York: Hastings House, 1954.

Wisconsin Atlas and Gazetteer. Yarmouth ME: DeLorme, 1992.

In addition to these sources, the Wisconsin State Historical Society has an extraordinary series of books on the state's history. These books (given in order of date of publication due to their serial aspect) are:

Smith, Alice E. *The History of Wisconsin I: From Exploration to Statehood*. Madison: Wisconsin State Historical Society, 1973.

Current, Richard N. *The History of Wisconsin II: The Civil War Era 1848–1873*. Madison: Wisconsin State Historical Society, 1976.

Nesbit, Robert C. *The History of Wisconsin III: Urbanization and Industrialization 1873–1893*. Madison: Wisconsin State Historical Society, 1985.

Buenker, John D. *The History of Wisconsin IV: The Progressive Era 1896–1914*. Madison: Wisconsin State Historical Society, 1998.

Glad, Paul W. *The History of Wisconsin V: War, A New Era, and Depression 1914–1940*. Madison: Wisconsin State Historical Society, 1990.

Thompson, William F. *The History of Wisconsin VI: Continuity and Change 1940–1965*. Madison: Wisconsin State Historical Society, 1989.

The Constitution

Abrahamson, Shirley S. "Divided We Stand: State Constitutions in a More Perfect Union." *Hastings Law Quarterly* 18 (1991): 723.

Blair, Diane D., and Jay Barth. "Preface." In *Arkansas Politics and Government*, 2d ed. Lincoln: University of Nebraska Press, 2005.

"Constitution of the State of Wisconsin." *Manual for the Use of the Assembly of the State of Wisconsin, for the Year 1853*. Madison: Brown and Carpenter, 1853.

Elazar, Daniel J. "The States in the Political Setting." In *American Federalism: A View from the States*, 2d ed. New York: Harper and Row, 1984.

———. "Series Introduction." In *Arkansas Politics and Government*, by Diane D. Blair and Jay Barth, xiv–xv. Lincoln: University of Nebraska Press, 1988.

Fine, Michael. "The Constitution." In *Wisconsin Government and Politics*, 5th ed., edited by Wilder Crane and A. Clarke Hagensick, 15–35. Milwaukee: University of Wisconsin–Milwaukee, 1991.

"History of Constitutional Amendments." In *Wisconsin Blue Book 1999–2000*, 192–97. Madison: Joint Committee on Legislative Organization, 1999.

Loftus, Tom. *The Art of Legislative Politics*. Washington DC: CQ Press, 1994.

Kellogg, Louise Phelps. "Admission of Wisconsin to Statehood." In *The Movement for Statehood 1845–1846*, edited by Milo M. Quaife, 18–29. Madison: Wisconsin State Historical Society, 1918.

Paxson, Frederic L. "Wisconsin: A Constitution of Democracy." In *The Struggle Over Ratification 1846–1847*, edited by Milo M. Quaife, 30–38. Madison: Wisconsin State Historical Society, 1920.

Quaife, Milo M., ed. *The Convention of 1846*. Madison: Wisconsin State Historical Society, 1919.

Ranney, Joseph A. *Trusting Nothing to Providence: A History of Wisconsin's Legal System*. Madison: University of Wisconsin Press, 1999.

Smith, Alice E. *The History of Wisconsin: From Exploration to Statehood*. Madison: Wisconsin State Historical Society, 1973.

Thwaites, Reuben G. "Historical Outline of the Admission of Wisconsin to the Union." In *Wisconsin Blue Book 1909*, 17–20. Madison: Democratic Printing, 1909.

"Wisconsin Constitution." In *Wisconsin Blue Book 1999–2000*, 149–91. Madison: Joint Committee on Legislative Organization, 1999.

The Legislature

"Biographies of members of the state senate and assembly." In *Wisconsin Blue Book* (various years). Madison: Joint Committee on Legislative Organization.

Dunn, Delmer. *Public Officials and the Press*. Reading MA: Addison-Wesley, 1969.

"Electoral Success Rates of Incumbents Seeking Reelection in Wisconsin Legislative Elections, 1978–1988." Madison: Wisconsin Legislative Reference Bureau, 1990.

Epstein, Leon D. *Politics in Wisconsin*. Madison: University of Wisconsin Press, 1983.

"Executive Vetoes, 1931–1993 Sessions." In *Wisconsin Blue Book 1995–1996*, 273. Madison: Joint Committee on Legislative Organization, 1995.

The Fifty States and Their Legislatures. Common Cause, 1970.

Hedlund, Ronald. "The Wisconsin Legislature." In *Wisconsin Government and Politics*, 5th ed., edited by Wilder Crane and A. Clarke Hagensick, 117–53. Milwaukee: University of Wisconsin–Milwaukee, 1991.

Key, V. O. *Southern Politics in State and Nation*. New York: Random House, 1949.

"Legislative Branch." In *Wisconsin Blue Book 1995–1996*, 259–318. Madison: Joint Committee on Legislative Organization, 1995.

Loftus, Tom. *The Art of Legislative Politics*. Washington DC: CQ Press, 1994.

"Profile of the 1995 Wisconsin Legislature." Wisconsin Legislative Reference Bureau, January 1995.

Theobold, H. Rupert. "Equal Representation: A Study of Legislative and Congressional Apportionment in Wisconsin." In *Wisconsin Blue Book 1970*, 71–260. Madison: Wisconsin Legislative Reference Bureau, 1970.

Watchke, Gary. "Legislative Turnover in the 1963–1991 Sessions of the Wisconsin Legislature." Madison: Wisconsin Legislative Reference Bureau, 1992.

"Wisconsin Legislative Sessions, 1848–1995." In *Wisconsin Blue Book 1997–1998*, 693–96. Madison: Joint Committee on Legislative Organization, 1997.

The Governor

Bergan, Hal. "The Morning After." *Milwaukee Magazine*, January 1997.

The Book of the States. Lexington KY: Council of State Governments (various years).

Conant, James K. *Executive Decision Making in the State*. Ph.D. Diss. Department of Political Science. University of Wisconsin–Madison, 1983.

———. "Gubernatorial Strategy and Style: Keys to Improving Executive Branch Management." *State Government* 59, no. 2 (July–August 1986): 82–88.

———. "Reorganization and the Bottom Line." *Public Administration Review* 46, no. 1 (January–February 1986): 48–56.

———. "In the Shadow of Wilson and Brownlow: Executive Branch Reorganization in the States 1965 to 1987." *Public Administration Review* 48, no. 4 (July–August 1988): 892–902.

———. "Can Government Organizations Be Excellent, Too?" *State and Local Government Review* 19, no. 2 (Spring 1987): 47–53.

Elling, Richard C. "State Bureaucracies." In *Politics in the American States: A Comparative Analysis*, 4th ed., edited by Virginia Gray, Herbert Jacob, and Kenneth N. Vines, 244–83. Boston: Little, Brown, 1983.

"Executive Branch." In *Wisconsin Blue Book 1999–2000*, 271–514. Madison: Joint Committee on Legislative Organization, 1999.

"It Pays to Know Tommy Thompson." *Milwaukee Journal Sentinel*, November 2, 1997.

"King Tommy and the Turbulent Priest." *Madison Capital Times*, July 14, 1996.

Milfred, Scott. "Portrait in Power," *Madison State Journal*, December 24, 2000.

Miller, Edward J. "The Governorship." In *Wisconsin Government and Politics*, 5th ed., edited by Wilder Crane and A. Clarke Hagensick, 155–83. Milwaukee: University of Wisconsin–Milwaukee, 1991.

Sabato, Larry Sabato. *Good-bye to Good-Time Charlie: The American Governorship Transformed*, 2d ed. Washington DC: CQ Press, 1983.

Thompson, Tommy G. *Power to the People: An American State at Work*. New York: HarperCollins, 1996.

Walters, Stephen. "Thompson's Legacy." *Milwaukee Journal Sentinel*, December 24, 2000.

"The Turmoil over Tommy." *Milwaukee Journal Sentinel*, November 9, 1997.

Walters, Stephen. "Thompson's Legacy," *Milwaukee Journal Sentinel*, December 24, 2000.

Weinberg, Martha. *Managing the State*. Cambridge MA: MIT Press, 1978.

The Courts

Abrahamson, Shirley. "Reincarnation of State Courts." *Southwestern Law Journal* 36 (1982): 951.

———. "Criminal Law and State Constitutions." *Texas Law Review* 63 (1985): 1141.

———. "Divided We Stand: State Constitutions in a More Perfect Union." *Hastings Law Quarterly* 18 (1991): 723.

Abrahamson, Shirley, and Elizabeth A. Hartman. "Building a More Perfect Union: Wisconsin and the U.S. Constitution." *Wisconsin Magazine of History* 85 (Autumn 2001): 16–23.

Abrahamson, Shirley, and Diane S. Gutmann. "The New Federalism: State Constitutions." *Judicature* 71 (August–September 1987): 88–99.

"Biographies of the Supreme Court Justices," 8–10, in *Wisconsin Blue Book 1999–2000*. Madison: Joint Committee on Legislative Organization, 1999.

The Book of the States 1998–1999. Lexington KY: Council of State Government, 1998.

Brennan, William J. Jr. "State Constitutions and the Protection of Individual Rights." *Harvard Law Review* (January 1977): 489–504.

Curran, Barbara, and Clara N. Carson. *Lawyer Statistical Report: The U.S. Legal Profession in the 1990s*. Chicago: American Bar Association, 1994.

Hartmann, Michael E. "The Follie of 'Fully' Publicly Financing State Supreme Court Campaigns." *Wisconsin Interest* 7, no. 1 (Spring–Summer 1998): 51–61.

Jacob, Herbert. "Courts: The Least Visible Branch." In *Politics in the American States: A Comparative Analysis*, 6th ed., edited by Virginia Gray, Herbert Jacob, and Kenneth N. Vines, 253–85. Washington DC: CQ Press, 1996.

"Judicial Branch," 563–98, in *Wisconsin Blue Book 1999–2000*. Madison: Joint Committee on Legislative Organization, 1999.

Kincaid, John. "The New Judicial Federalism." *Journal of State Government* 61 (September–October 1988): 163–69.

Kincaid, John, and Robert F. Williams. "The New Judicial Federalism: States Take the Lead in Rights Protection." *Journal of State Government* 65 (April–June 1992): 50–52.

Thelen, David P. *Robert M. La Follette and the Insurgent Spirit*. Madison: University of Wisconsin Press, 1985.

Thompson V. Jackson, 199 Wis.2d. 715 (1966).

Private Interests and Interest Groups

Bentley, Arthur F. *The Process of Government: A Study of Social Pressures.* Chicago: University of Chicago Press, 1908.

Braybrooke, David, and Charles E. Lindblom. *A Strategy of Decision.* New York: Free Press, 1963.

Broder, David S. "Whose Government is This?" *Washington Post*, July 13, 1999.

Buchwald, Art. "Guns-R-Us," *Washington Post*, 1998.

Dahl, Robert. *Democracy and Its Critics.* New Haven: Yale University Press, 1989.

De Soto, William. *The Politics of Business Organizations: Understanding the Role of the State Chambers of Commerce.* Lanham MD: University Press of America, 1995.

Dunn, Delmer. *Public Officials and the Press.* Reading MA: Addison-Wesley, 1969.

Goldschmidt, William J. *The Legislative Lobby in Wisconsin since 1901.* Ph.D. Diss. University of Wisconsin–Madison, 1912.

Latham, Earl. *The Group Basis of Politics.* Ithaca: Cornell University Press, 1952.

Lindblom, Charles E. "The Science of Muddling Through." *Public Administration Review* 19 (1959): 79–88.

———. *The Intelligence of Democracy: Decision Making through Mutual Adjustment.* New York: Free Press, 1965.

Lindblom, Charles E., and Edward J. Woodhouse. *The Policy-Making Process*, 3d ed. Englewood Cliffs NJ: Prentice Hall, 1993.

"Lobbying Effort in Wisconsin, 1997–1998 Legislative Session." Madison: Wisconsin Ethics Board.

"Lobbying Effort in Wisconsin, 1999–2000 Legislative Session." Madison: Wisconsin Ethics Board.

Loftus, Tom. *The Art of Legislative Politics.* Washington DC: CQ Press, 1994.

Lowi, Theodore J. *The End of Liberalism.* New York: W. W. Norton, 1969.

Riordan, William L. *Plunkitt of Tammany Hall.* New York: Dutton, 1963.

Schattschneider, E. E. *The Semi-Sovereign People.* New York: Holt, Rinehart and Winston, 1960.

Thomas, Clive S., and Ronald J. Hrebenar. "Interest Groups in the States," 122–58, in Virginia Gray, Herbert Jacob, and Kenneth N. Vines, eds. *Politics in the American States: A Comparative Analysis*, 6th ed. Washington DC: CQ Press, 1996.

Truman, David. *The Government Process.* New York: Alfred A. Knopf, 1951.

Wegge, David G. "Interest Groups." In *Wisconsin Government and Politics,* 5th ed., edited by Wilder Crane and A. Clarke Hagensick, 91–116. Milwaukee: University of Wisconsin–Milwaukee, 1991.

Wisconsin: A Guide to the Badger State. New York: Hastings House, 1954.

Zeigler, L. Harmon. "Interest Groups in the States." In *Politics in the American States,* 4th ed., edited by Virginia Gray, Herbert Jacob, and Kenneth N. Vines, 97–131. Boston: Little, Brown, 1983.

Political Parties and Elections

Bibby, John F. "Political Parties and Elections in Wisconsin." In *Crane and Hagensick's Wisconsin Government and Politics,* 6th ed., edited by Ronald E. Weber, 47–75. New York: McGraw Hill, 1996.

Dahl, Robert A., ed. *Political Oppositions in Western Democracies.* New Haven: Yale University Press, 1966.

Elazar, Daniel. *American Federalism: A View from the States.* New York: Harper and Row, 1984.

Epstein, Leon D. *Politics in Wisconsin.* Madison: University of Wisconsin Press, 1958.

Key, V. O. *Southern Politics in State and Nation.* New York: Alfred A. Knopf, 1950.

———. *Politics, Parties, and Pressure Groups.* New York: Thomas Y. Crowell, 1952.

Loftus, Tom. *The Art of Legislative Politics.* Washington DC: CQ Press, 1994.

Ranney, Austin, and Wilmoore Kendall. "The American Party Systems." *American Political Science Review* 48 (June 1954): 477–85.

Wisconsin: A Guide to the Badger State. New York: Hastings House, 1954.

Wisconsin Blue Book (various years). Madison: Joint Committee on Legislative Organization.

The State Budget and the Budgetary Process

Annual Fiscal Report (various years). Madison: Wisconsin Department of Administration.

Appendix, Annual Fiscal Report (various years). Madison: Wisconsin Department of Administration.

Budget in Brief (various years). State Budget Office. Madison: Wisconsin Department of Administration.

Executive Budget Recommendations (various years). State Budget Office. Madison: Wisconsin Department of Administration.

Wisconsin State Budget: Comparative Summary of Budget Provisions (As Enacted) (various years). Madison: Wisconsin Legislative Fiscal Bureau.

Abney, Glenn, and Thomas P. Lauth. "The Line-Item Veto in the States: An Instrument for Fiscal Restraint or for Partisanship?" *Public Administration Review* 85, no. 3 (May–June 1985): 372–77.

Anton, Thomas. *The Politics of State Expenditure in Illinois.* Urbana: University of Illinois Press, 1966.

Clynch, Edward J., and Thomas P. Lauth, eds. *Governors, Legislatures, and Budgets: Diversity Across the American States.* New York: Greenwood Press, 1991.

Conant, James K. *Executive Decision Making in the State.* Ph.D. Diss. Department of Political Science. University of Wisconsin–Madison, 1983.

———. "Budget Making in the States." In *Dollars and Sense: Policy Choices and the Wisconsin Budget,* vol. 1, edited by Robert H. Haveman and Jack Huddleston, 5–12. Madison: The Robert M. La Follette Institute of Public Affairs, 1990.

———. "The Growing Importance of State Government." In *The Handbook of Public Administration,* edited by James Perry, 25–39. San Francisco: Jossey-Bass, 1990.

———. "Winners and Losers in Wisconsin's Tax and Expenditure System." In *Dollars and Sense: Policy Choices and the Wisconsin Budget,* vol. 2, edited by James K. Conant, Robert H. Haveman, and Jack Huddleston, 37–57. Madison: The Robert M. La Follette Institute of Public Affairs, 1991.

———. "Dealing with the Bust Phase of the Boom and Bust Cycle, Again!" *Public Budgeting and Finance* 23, no. 2 (Summer 2003): 1–4.

———. "Wisconsin's Budget Deficit: Size, Causes, Remedies, and Consequences." *Public Budgeting and Finance* 23, no. 2 (Summer 2003): 5–25.

Gosling, James J. "Wisconsin Item-Veto Lessons." *Public Administration Review* 46, no. 4 (July–August 1986): 292–300.

———. *Budgetary Politics in American Governments.* White Plains NY: Longmans, 1992.

Hansen, W. Lee, and Kathryn R. Sell. "The UW System Budget." In *Dollars and Sense: Policy Choices and the Wisconsin Budget,* vol. 2, edited by James K. Conant, Robert H. Haveman, and Jack Huddleston, 83–118. Madison: The Robert M. La Follette Institute of Public Affairs, 1991.

Lauth, Thomas P. "Budgeting during the Recession Phase of the Business Cycle." *Public Budgeting and Finance* 23, no. 2 (Summer 2003): 26–38.

Lee, Robert D., Jr. "Developments in State Budgeting: Trends of Two Decades." *Public Administration Review* 51, no. 3 (May–June 1991): 254–62.

Nichols, Donald A. "The Effect of Recession on the Budget." In *Dollars and Sense: Policy Choices and the Wisconsin Budget*, vol. 2, edited by James K. Conant, Robert H. Haveman, and Jack Huddleston, 61–82. Madison: The Robert M. La Follette Institute of Public Affairs, 1991.

Thompson, Tommy G. *Power to the People: An American State at Work.* New York: HarperCollins, 1996.

Torphy, John. "Wisconsin's Budget." In *Dollars and Sense: Policy Choices and the Wisconsin Budget*, vol. 2, edited by James K. Conant, Robert H. Haveman, and Jack Huddleston, 13–35. Madison: The Robert M. La Follette Institute of Public Affairs, 1991.

Wildavsky, Aaron. *The Politics of the Budgetary Process.* Boston: Little, Brown, 1964.

Social Welfare Policy

Bergan, Hal. "The Morning After." *Milwaukee Magazine*, January 1997.

Corbett, Thomas J. "Welfare Reform in Wisconsin: The Rhetoric and the Reality," in Donald F. Norris and Lyke Thompson, eds. *The Politics of Welfare Reform.* Sage Publications, 1995.

Corbett, Thomas J., Robert H. Haveman, and Michael Wiseman. "Income Support and Welfare Reform." In *Dollars and Sense: Policy Choices and The Wisconsin Budget*, vol. 1, edited by Robert H. Haveman and Jack Huddleston, 19–54. Madison: The Robert M. La Follette School of Public Affairs, 1990.

Dionne, E. J., Jr. "Welfare Reform: The Clues Are In Wisconsin." *Washington Post*, September 23, 1997.

Edelman, Murray. *The Symbolic Uses of Politics.* Urbana: University of Illinois Press, 1964.

———. *Politics as Symbolic Action.* Chicago: Markham, 1971.

Hansen, W. Lee, and James F. Byers, eds. *Unemployment Insurance: The Second Half-Century.* Madison: The University of Wisconsin Press, 1990.

Haveman, Robert H., and Jonathan Schwabish. "Economic Growth and Poverty: A Return to Normalcy?" *Focus* 20, no. 2 (Spring 1999): 1–7.

Kaplan, Thomas. "Wisconsin's W-2 Program: Welfare As We Might Come To Know It." Madison: Institute for Research on Poverty, 1998.

Mead, Lawrence M. "The Decline of Welfare in Wisconsin." Madison: Institute for Research on Poverty, 1998.

———. "Statecraft: The Politics of Welfare Reform in Wisconsin." Madison: Institute for Research on Poverty, 1999.

Thompson, Tommy G. *Power to the People: An American State at Work.* New York: HarperCollins, 1996.

Wiseman, Michael. "State Strategies for Welfare Reform: The Wisconsin Story." *Journal of Policy Analysis and Management* 15, no. 4 (Autumn 1996): 515–46.

———. "Welfare Reform in the United States: A Background Paper." *Housing Policy Debate* 7, no. 4 (1996): 595–648.

Local Government

Burns, James McGregor, J. W. Peltason, Thomas E. Cronin, and David B. Magleby. *State and Local Politics: Government By the People*, 8th ed. Upper Saddle River NJ: Prentice Hall, 1996.

Cigler, Beverly A. "Trends Affecting Local Administrators." In *Handbook of Public Administration*, edited by James L. Perry, 40–53. San Francisco: Jossey-Bass, 1990.

"County Organization and Administration," Wisconsin Taxpayers Alliance. *The Wisconsin Taxpayer* 65, no. 4 (April 1997): 8–9.

Crane, Wilder, and A. Clarke Hagensick. *Wisconsin Government and Politics.* Institute of Government Affairs/University of Wisconsin–Extension, 1976.

Curti, Merle E. "The Making of an American Community: A Case Study of Democracy in a Frontier County." Stanford CA: Stanford University Press, 1959.

Donaghue, James R. "The Local System of Government in Wisconsin." In *Wisconsin Blue Book 1935*, 105–8. Madison: Legislative Reference Bureau.

Elazar, Daniel. *The American Mosaic.* Boulder CO: Westview Press, 1994.

Epstein, Leon D. *Politics in Wisconsin.* Madison: University of Wisconsin Press, 1958.

"Framework of Government." In *Wisconsin Blue Book 1995–1996*, 245–56. Madison: Joint Committee on Legislative Organization, 1995.

Miller, Edward J., and Brett Hawkins. "Local Government." In *Crane and Hagensick's Wisconsin Government and Politics*, 6th ed., edited by Ronald E. Weber, 25–43. New York: McGraw-Hill, 1996.

"Municipal and County Finance." Madison: Wisconsin Legislative Fiscal Bureau, 1997.

Nesbit, Robert C., and William F. Thompson. *Wisconsin: A History*, 2d ed. Madison: University of Wisconsin Press, 1989.

"1997–1999 Biennial Report." Wisconsin Technical College System, October 15, 1999.

1997 Census of Governments. U.S. Department of Commerce, Bureau of the Census. Washington DC: Government Printing Office, 1999. See especially table 3.

Paddock, Susan. "The Changing World of Wisconsin Local Government," 99–172, in *Wisconsin Blue Book 1997–1998*. Madison: Joint Committee on Legislative Organization, 1997.

Rogers, Joel, Wolfgang Streeck, and Eric Parker. "The Wisconsin Training Effort." In *Dollars and Sense: Policy Choices and the Wisconsin Budget*, vol. 2, edited by James K. Conant, Robert H. Haveman, and Jack Huddleston, 119–53. Madison: The Robert M. La Follette Institute of Public Affairs, 1991.

Shannon, John. "The Return to Fend-for-Yourself Federalism: The Reagan Mark." *Intergovernmental Perspective* 13, no. 3 (1987): 34–37.

"Technical Colleges: Old Idea, New Look." Wisconsin Taxpayers Alliance. *The Wisconsin Taxpayer* 65, no. 5 (May 1977): 1.

Thomas, John P. "Perspective on County Government Services and Financing." *State and Local Government Review* 19, no. 3 (1987): 119–21.

Wehrwein, George S. "The Town Government in Wisconsin," in *Wisconsin Blue Book 1935*. Madison: Wisconsin Legislative Reference Bureau, 1935.

State-Local Relations

"An Unusual Approach to State-Local Finance." Wisconsin Taxpayers Alliance. *The Wisconsin Taxpayer* 66, no. 9 (September 1998): 1, 3.

Annual Fiscal Report: Budgetary Basis, State of Wisconsin (various years). Madison: Wisconsin Department of Administration.

Barrows, Richard, and Marvin Johnson, "Education Finance." In *Dollars and Sense: Policy Choices and the Wisconsin Budget*, vol. 2, edited by James K. Conant, Robert H. Haveman, and Jack Huddleston, 155–78. Madison: The Robert M. La Follette Institute of Public Affairs, 1991.

Conant, James K. *Executive Decision Making in the State*. Ph.D. Diss. Department of Political Science. University of Wisconsin–Madison, 1983.

———. "Winners and Losers in Wisconsin's Tax and Expenditure System." In *Dollars and Sense: Policy Choices and the Wisconsin Budget*, vol. 2, edited by James K. Conant, Robert H. Haveman, and Jack Huddleston, 37–57. Madison: The Robert M. La Follette Institute of Public Affairs, 1991.

———. "Dealing with the Bust Phase of the Boom and Bust Cycle, Again!" *Public Budgeting and Finance* 23, no. 2 (Summer 2003): 1–4.

———. "Wisconsin's Budget Deficit: Size, Causes, Remedies, and Consequences," *Public Budgeting and Finance* 23, no. 2 (Summer 2003): 5–25.

Lampman, Robert J., and Timothy D. McBride. "Changes in the Pattern of State and Local Government Revenues and Expenditures in Wisconsin, 1960–1983." In *State Policy Choices: The Wisconsin Experience*, edited by Sheldon Danziger and John F. Witte, 35–69. Madison: University of Wisconsin Press, 1988.

Nice, David C. *Federalism: The Politics of Intergovernmental Relations*. New York: St. Martins Press, 1987.

"Personal Data on Wisconsin Legislators, 1989–1999 Sessions." In *Wisconsin Blue Book 1999–2000*, 224. Madison: Joint Committee on Legislative Organization, 1999.

Stark, Jack. "Property Tax and Property Tax Relief in Wisconsin." In *Wisconsin Blue Book 1991–1992*, 99–164. Madison: Joint Committee on Legislative Organization, 1991.

Thompson, Tommy G. *Power to the People: An American State at Work*. New York: HarperCollins, 1996.

Witte, John F. "Wisconsin Income Tax Reform." In *State Policy Choices: The Wisconsin Experience*, edited by Sheldon Danziger and John F. Witte, 108–29. Madison: University of Wisconsin Press, 1988.

Over the past fifty years a number of blue-ribbon commissions have been appointed by the governor and/or the legislature to study the state-local relationship. These commissions usually became known within the state by the name of their chairs, and they include the Kellett Commission, the Tarr Task Force, The Doyle Commission, and, most recently, the Kettl Commission. Each of those commissions collected publications about the state-local relationship, collected its own data, developed its own publications, and produced a report that contained its principal findings and recommendations.

The best place to begin a search for the publications produced by these blue-ribbon commissions is the Rupert H. Theobold Legislative Library.

Wisconsin in the Federal System

Addams, Jane. *Twenty Years at Hull House*. New York: Macmillan Company, 1910.

Beals, Melba Pattillo. *Warriors Don't Cry*. New York: Washington Square Press, 1994.

Blair, Diane D. and Jay Barth. *Arkansas Government and Politics*, 2d ed. Lincoln: University of Nebraska Press, 2005.

Blum, John. *The Progressive Presidents: Roosevelt, Wilson, Roosevelt, and Johnson*. New York: W. W. Norton, 1980.

Broder, David. *Democracy Derailed: Initiative Campaigns and the Power of Money*. New York: Harcourt, 1999.

Brownlee, Elliot W. *Progressivism and Economic Growth: The Wisconsin Income Tax 1911–1929*. Port Washington NY: Kennikat Press, 1974.

Catton, Bruce. *The Army of the Potomac: Glory Road*. Garden City NY: Doubleday, 1952.

Conant, James K. "The Growing Importance of State Government." In *Handbook of Public Administration*, edited by James L. Perry, 25–39. San Francisco: Jossey-Bass, 1989.

Conant, James K., and Robert K. Evanson. "Federalism in the Russian Federation." *International Journal of Public Administration* 22, nos. 2–3: 1293–1500.

Conlan, Timothy J., Margaret T. Wrightson, and David R. Beam. *Taxing Choices: The Politics of Tax Reform*. Washington DC: CQ Press, 1990.

DeParle, Jason. "Wisconsin Pledges to Exit U.S. System of Public Welfare." *New York Times*, December 14, 1993.

Dionne, E. J., Jr. *They Only Look Dead: Why Progressive Will Dominate the Next Political Era*. New York: Simon and Schuster, 1996.

Duquette, Jerold J. *Regulating the National Pastime: Baseball and Antitrust*. Westport CT: Praeger, 1999.

Ekirch, Arthur A., Jr. *Progressivism in America: A Study of the Era from Theodore Roosevelt to Woodrow Wilson*. New York: New Viewpoints: 1974.

Elazar, Daniel. *The American Mosaic: The Impact of Space, Time, and Culture on American Politics*. Boulder CO: Westview Press, 1994.

Foote, Shelby. *The Civil War: From Fort Sumter to Perryville*. New York: Vintage, 1986.

Grunwald, Michael. "GOP Leadership Sour on Mild Reform." *Washington Post*, November 17, 1999.

Hansen, Susan B. *The Politics of Taxation*. New York: Praeger, 1983.

Hansen, W. Lee, ed. *Academic Freedom on Trial*. Madison: Office of University Publications/University of Wisconsin Press, 1998.

Heberlein, Thomas A. *Social Issues and Wildlife at The Horicon Marsh*. Madison: University of Wisconsin Press, 1987.

Herzberg, Donald O., and Alan Rosenthal. *Strengthening the States*. New York: Doubleday, 1971.

The Jaws of Victory. The Ripon Society. Boston: Little, Brown, 1972.

Kind, Ron. "Michigan Lobsters." *Washington Post*, September 22, 1999.

Lank, Avrum D. "Big Business to Escape State Taxes," *Milwaukee Journal Sentinel*, June 13, 1999.

Lewis, Anthony. *Gideon's Trumpet*. New York: Vintage, 1989.

Lewis, Tom. *Divided Highways: Building the Interstate Highways, Transforming American Life*. New York: Penguin Books, 1997.

Maxwell, Robert S. *La Follette and the Rise of the Progressives in Wisconsin*. Madison: Wisconsin State Historical Society, 1956.

Moore, J. W. "Mandates Without Money." *National Journal* 18, no. 40 (1986): 2366–70.

Morris, Edmund. *The Rise of Teddy Roosevelt*. New York: Coward, McCann, and Geoghagan, 1979.

Mowry, George. *Theodore Roosevelt and the Progressive Movement*. Madison: University of Wisconsin Press, 1946.

Nevin, David. *Dream West*. New York: G. P. Putnam's Sons, 1983.

Nice, David C. *Federalism: The Politics of Intergovernmental Relations*. New York: St. Martin's Press, 1987.

"97011: Dairy Policy Issues," U.S. Congressional Research Service. Washington DC: Government Printing Office, 1999.

Penniman, Clara. *State Income Taxation*. Baltimore: Johns Hopkins University Press, 1980.

Ranney, Joseph A. *Trusting Nothing to Providence: A History of Wisconsin's Legal System*. Madison: University of Wisconsin Law School, 1999.

Regier, C. C. *The Era of the Muckrakers*. Gloucester MA: Peter Smith, 1957.

Riis, Jacob A. *How the Other Half Lives: Studies among the Tenements of New York*. New York: Charles Scribner's Sons, 1890.

Rose, Mark H. *Interstate: Express Highway Politics 1939–1989*. Knoxville: University of Tennessee Press, 1990.

Sinclair, Upton. *The Jungle*. Cambridge MA: Robert Bentley, 1946.

Steffens, Lincoln. "Enemies of the Republic." *McClure's* 22 (March 1904): 587–99.

———. "Rhode Island: A State for Sale." *McClure's* 23 (February 1905): 337–53.

Tarbell, Ida. *The History of the Standard Oil Company*. New York: W. W. Norton, 1969.

Walker, Jack. "The Diffusion of Innovations Among the American States." *American Political Science Review* 63:880–99.

Witte, John. *The Politics and Development of the Federal Income Tax*. Madison: University of Wisconsin Press, 1985.

Wisconsin Atlas and Gazetteer. Yarmouth ME: DeLorme, 1992.

Wisconsin Blue Book 1999. Madison: Wisconsin Legislative Reference Bureau, 1999.

Wright, Deil S. *Understanding Intergovernmental Relations*, 3d ed. Pacific Grove CA: Brooks/Cole, 1988.

Continuing Traditions and Emerging Issues

Conant, James K. "Dealing with the Bust Phase of the Boom and Bust Cycle, Again!" *Public Budgeting and Finance* 23, no. 2 (Summer 2003): 1–4.

———. "Wisconsin's Budget Deficit: Size, Causes, Remedies, and Consequences." *Public Budgeting and Finance* 23, no. 2 (Summer 2003): 5–25.

Elazar, Daniel, *American Federalism: A View from the States*, 3d ed. New York: Harper, 1969.

Feldman, Michael. "Clean State, Dirty Politicians." *New York Times*, October 24, 2003.

La Follette, Robert. *La Follette's Autobiography*. Madison: University of Wisconsin Press, 1960.

Loftus, Tom. *The Art of Follette's Autobiography*. Washington DC: CQ Press, 1994.

Smith, Alice E. *The History of Wisconsin: From Exploration to Statehood*. Madison: Wisconsin State Historical Society, 1973.

Wisconsin: A Guide to the Badger State. New York: Hastings House, 1954.

Notes

INTRODUCTION

1. The close correspondence between Wisconsin and Tocqueville's ideal was first brought to the author's attention by Larry Mead, a scholar at New York University. Mead drew this conclusion after studying Wisconsin politics and government while on sabbatical at the University of Wisconsin–Madison. During a discussion the author had with Dr. Mead, he made a statement that seemed worth recording: "Wisconsin and Minnesota may be the closest living examples of Tocqueville's model democratic polity that exist now—or have existed at any time."

2. This point is made by the distinguished American historian, Henry Steel Commager. See Alexis De Tocqueville, *Democracy In America* (London: Oxford University Press, 1947), "Introduction" by Henry Steele Commager, pp. vii–xx.

3. Daniel Elazar, *American Federalism: A View from the States* (New York: Harper and Row, 1984), pp. 95–98.

4. Richard N. Current, *Pine Logs and Politics: A Life of Philetus Sawyer* (Madison: Wisconsin State Historical Society, 1950), p. 236.

5. Current, *Pine Logs*, pp. 239–40.

6. Current, *Pine Logs*, pp. 213–19.

7. *Outlook Magazine*, 1911.

8. Cited in Ellen Torelle, Albert O. Barton, and Fred. L. Holmes, comps., *The Political Philosophy of Robert M. La Follette as Revealed in His Speeches* (Madison: The Robert M. La Follette Co., 1920), p. 10.

9. Daniel Elazar, *American Federalism*, p. 88.

1. THE CHARACTER OF THE STATE

John O. Stark, "Wisconsin's Writers," *Wisconsin Blue Book 1977–1998* (Madison: Joint Committee on Legislative Organization, 1997), pp. 95–185. The writers

Stark includes in his essay are John Muir, Hamlin Garland, Zona Gale, Aldo Leopold, Horace Gregory, Glenway Wescott, Mark Shorer, August Derleth, and Ben Logan; Stark, *Wisconsin Blue Book 1977–1998*, p. 127.

1. The cities that are likely to make one or another of these rankings during any give year include Appleton, Eau Claire, Kenosha, Neenah/Menasha, Green Bay, Janesville/Beloit, La Crosse, Madison, Milwaukee, Oshkosh, Racine, Sheboygan, and Wausau.

2. For example, in 1995, *USA Today* selected Madison as the number-one city. In 1996, *Money* rated Madison the best place to live in America. These recent ratings are among a long string of such awards. Fifty years before the *Money* survey was published, *Life* published a survey on the best places to live in America. In that 1946 survey, Madison was listed as the number-one city.

3. According to the Wisconsin Department of Tourism, almost half (48 percent) of all people who take vacations in Wisconsin are from out-of-state. The single largest block of vacationers who travel to the state are from Illinois (23 percent) followed by Minnesota (9 percent) and Michigan (4 percent). The remaining 12 percent come from all over the country, with the states of Iowa and Missouri at or near the top of the list. These data were provided by David Scheler, director of research for the department, June 1998.

4. In 1997–98, 9.1 million people visited Wisconsin's state parks, 5.2 million people visited Wisconsin's state forests, 677,000 visited state recreational areas, and 671,000 used state bike trails. These data can be found in the *Wisconsin Blue Book 1997–1998*, p. 619. For a wonderful tour of Wisconsin's scenic roads, see photographs by Robert Rashid, text by Bill Stokes et al., in *Wisconsin's Rustic Roads: A Road Less Traveled* (Boulder Junction WI: Lost River Press, 1995).

5. The remains included wood chips, sawdust, and stumps. A "wild tangle of brush" that grew up in areas that had been clear-cut is cited as a principal source of fuel for the fires by Richard N. Current, *Pine Logs and Politics: A Life of Philetus Sawyer* (Madison: Wisconsin State Historical Society, 1950), p. 277.

6. Background on the Grange movement can be found in Solon J. Buck, *The Granger Movement: A Study of Agricultural Organizaton and Its Political,Economic and Social Manifestations, 1870–1880* (Cambridge, 1913).

7. Richard N. Current, *The History of Wisconsin: The Civil War Era, 1848–1873* (Madison: Wisconsin State Historical Society, 1976), pp. 592–93.

8. A dramatic statement of this condition can be found in Robert Maxwell's *Robert M. La Follette and the Rise of the Progressives in Wisconsin* (Madison: Wisconsin State Historical Society, 1956). On page 6, Maxwell says: "For more than a quarter of a century after the Civil War most of the prominent men in public life in Wisconsin were identified with either the railroads or lumber interests, and the

presidents of the two great systems were important figures that must be consulted before any major decision concerning state policy was made."

9. In 1896 and 1898 La Follette was confident that he had enough votes to win the Republican Party's nomination at the convention. At the last moment, the party bosses apparently used bribes to steal the victory from La Follette. See Richard N. Current, *A History of Wisconsin* (New York: W. W. Norton and Co., 1977), pp. 188–89.

10. The special connection between the University of Wisconsin and the state government is often referred to as "The Wisconsin Idea." For more discussion of the university-state relationship during the era of Progressive reforms, see Robert M. La Follette, *La Follette's Autobiography* (Madison: University of Wisconsin Press, 1960), pp. 13–15; Charles McCarthy, *The Wisconsin Idea* (New York: Macmillan, 1921); Jack Stark, "The Wisconsin Idea: The University Service to the State," *Wisconsin Blue Book 1995–1996*, pp. 101–24; and *Wisconsin: A Guide to the Badger State*, Workers of the Writer's Program of the Works Progress Administration in Wisconsin, comp. (New York: Hastings House, 1954), p. 62.

11. Sources include Richard N. Current, *A History of Wisconsin*, pp. 193–94, and James K. Conant, *Executive Decision Making in the State*, pp. 22–25.

12. Wisconsin's governors have a form of the item-veto power that is unique among governors. The latter allows the governor to line-out, or eliminate, appropriations numbers or language in the budget bill.

13. The author is using the traditional land-based measurement long employed for such comparisons. It is important to acknowledge, however, that a new measurement based on a combination of land and water is now being used by the Bureau of the Census to report the size of the states. The result is that in the 1995 edition of the *U.S. Statistical Abstract* (Washington DC: Bureau of the Census, 1995) Michigan's size was slightly larger than Wisconsin's.

14. Depending on which type of size measurements are used, the state ranks from twenty-first to twenty-fifth.

15. *Wisconsin: A Guide to the Badger State*, p.3.

16. Lawrence Martin is credited with establishing these five regions. The two principal sources employed for this discussion of the regions are *Wisconsin: A Guide to the Badger State*, and Charles Finley, *Wisconsin Geography* (Madison: University of Wisconsin Press, 1976).

17. The cities include Green Bay, Neenah, Menasha, Appleton, Oshkosh, and Fond du Lac.

18. This figure comes from the Wisconsin Department of Natural Resources.

19. Waltraud A. Brinkman, "Challenges of Wisconsin's Weather and Climate," in

Robert C. Ostergren and Thomas R. Vale, eds., *Wisconsin Land and Life* (Madison: University of Wisconsin Press, 1997), p. 49.

20. Brinkman, *Wisconsin Land*, p. 49

21. Brinkman, *Wisconsin Land*, p. 49.

22. *Wisconsin: A Guide to the Badger State*, p. 4.

23. H. R. Holand, *Old Peninsula Days* (Minoqua WI: Heartland Press, 1990), p. 8. For a comprehensive discussion of Native American tribes and life in Wisconsin, see "Wisconsin Indians," by William H. Hodge, in *Wisconsin Blue Book 1975* (Madison: Wisconsin Legislative Reference Bureau, 1975), pp. 98–191.

24. *Wisconsin: A Guide to the Badger State*, p. 32.

25. Holand, *Old Peninsula Days*, pp. 6–8.

26. An account of La Salle's exploration can be found in Holand's *Old Peninsula Days*, chap. 4.

27. *Wisconsin: A Guide to the Badger State*, p. 39.

28. Louise Phelps Kellogg, "The Admission of Wisconsin to Statehood," in Milo M. Quaife, ed., *The Movement for Statehood, 1845–1846* (Madison: Wisconsin State Historical Society, 1918), p. 27.

29. Frederick L. Paxson, "A Constitution of Democracy," in Quaife, *Movement for Statehood*, p. 51.

30. Current, *The History of Wisconsin*, p. 76.

31. Current, *The History of Wisconsin*, p. 76.

32. Current, *The History of Wisconsin*, p. 218.

33. Current, *The History of Wisconsin*, p. 218.

34. Current, *The History of Wisconsin*, p. 218.

35. Current, *The History of Wisconsin*, p. 221.

36. *Wisconsin: A Guide to the Badger State*, p. 42.

37. Historian Shelby Foote tells how the Iron Brigade won its name in a stirring passage about the extraordinary valor these men showed in battle. See Shelby Foote, *The Civil War: From Fort Sumter to Perryville* (New York: Vintage Books, 1986), pp. 625–27.

38. W. D. Hoard and Chester Hazen were key players in the change to dairy farming. See *Wisconsin: A Guide to the Badger State*, pp. 92–93.

39. *Wisconsin: A Guide to the Badger State*, p. 66.

40. *Wisconsin: A Guide to the Badger State*, p. 77.

41. The data from which the job losses were calculated can be found in the *Wisconsin Blue Book 1985–1986* (Madison: Wisconsin Legislative Reference Bureau, 1985), p. 702.

42. There are differences of opinion among economists as to what the multiplier

value of manufacturing jobs really is. Some place the multiplier value for each manufacturing job at something just over one; others place it at two or three.

43. In 1991, service sector employment (546,100) was within one hundred employees of manufacturing (546,200). By 1992, the service sector surged ahead of manufacturing with 570,500 employees compared to 549,600 in manufacturing. These data are from "Employment in Wisconsin by Industry, Annual Average 1990–1994," *Wisconsin Blue Book 1995–1996* (Madison: Joint Committee on Legislative Organization, 1995), p. 661.

44. In 1979, for example, employment for machinery production was 20.4 percent of total manufacturing employment. In 1994, the figure was 17.2 percent. See the *Wisconsin Blue Book 1980–1981*, p. 674, and *Wisconsin Blue Book 1997–1998*, p. 645.

45. In 1995, Wisconsin was third among the states in percentage of earned income from manufacturing. Michigan and Indiana ranked first and second, respectively. See *Wisconsin Blue Book, 1997–1998*, p. 644.

46. *Wisconsin Blue Book, 1997–1998*, p. 587.

47. In the early 1990s, California displaced Wisconsin as the top producer of milk. Among the reasons for this change is the fact that the national government's price supports have favored California and hurt Wisconsin. Price supports are calculated on the basis of proximity to Eau Claire, Wisconsin. The farther away a milk producing establishment is from Eau Claire, the higher the price support.

48. *Statistical Abstract of the U.S.* (Washington DC: U.S. Census Bureau, 2000), table 727. 1999 ranking: *Wisconsin Blue Book 1997–1998*, p. 664; 1999 ranking in comparison to earlier rankings: *Wisconsin Blue Book 1997–1998*, p. 664.

49. *Wisconsin State Journal*, "Jobless Rate a Steady 6%: But Many New Workers Get Part-time, Low-Paying Jobs," July 9,1994.

50. Scott Lautenschlager, "How New Jobs Leave Most Workers Short," *Wisconsin State Journal*, June 21, 1992, p. 1, and Mike Ivey, "Wisconsin Jobs Pay Least in Region," *Capital Times*, October 24, 1996, p. 1.

51. Discussion in the following paragraphs is drawn from Daniel J. Elazar, *American Federalism: A View from the States*, 3d ed. (New York: Harper and Row, 1984). Contrasting conceptions: pp. 84–85, 90–91; "basic political concerns . . .": p. 91; definition of cultural conceptions: p. 93; importation of moralistic culture: pp. 108–9.

52. For a sophisticated examination of the relationship between state fiscal capacity, fiscal need, and fiscal comfort in 1987 and 1994, see Robert Tannenwald and Jonathan Cowan, "Fiscal Capacity, Fiscal Need, and Fiscal Comfort among U.S. States: New Evidence," *Publius: The Journal of Federalism* 27, no. 3 (Summer 1997): 113–25.

53. Current, *Pine Logs*, p. 236.

54. See "It Pays to Know Tommy Thompson," *Journal Sentinel*, Nov. 2, 1997.

55. *Wisconsin Blue Book 1997–1998*, pp. 218–22.

56. In the 1996 election, 62 percent of senate districts had general election contests that featured candidates from both major parties.

57. Phil Brinkman, "Caucuses get new life with Senate Clerk," *Wisconsin State Journal*, January 3, 2002. Although the caucuses were abolished as independent bodies, concerns remain that "shadow caucuses" were created by adding six staff positions for the majority and minority leaders in both houses of the legislature.

58. "Partial veto" is the term used in official Wisconsin state government publications and documents, including the *Wisconsin Blue Book* and Wisconsin Supreme Court decisions. More discussion of the terms "item veto" and "partial veto" is provided in chapter 2.

59. The four principal models of executive branch organization are the secretary-coordinator, cabinet, traditional, and pretraditional models. The first has the highest degree of executive branch consolidation; the latter has the least. For a more complete description of these models and their relevance for understanding a governor's institutional powers, see James K. Conant, "State Reorganization: A New Model?" *State Government* 58, no. 4 (June 1986).

60. *Wisconsin Blue Book 1999–2000*, p. 274. For a description of how Wisconsin's comprehensive reorganization compared to other states during the 1960s, 1970s, and 1980s, see James K. Conant, "In the Shadow of Wilson and Brownlow: Executive Branch Reorganization in the States, 1965–1987," *Public Administration Review* 48, no. 5 (September–October 1988): 892–902.

61. A description of the new judicial federalism can be found in John Kincaid and Robert F. Williams, "The New Judicial Federalism: States Take the Lead in Rights Protection," *Journal of State Government* 65, no. 2 (April–June 1992): 50–52.

62. Leon D. Epstein, *Politics in Wisconsin* (Madison: University of Wisconsin Press, 1958).

63. For example, see John Torphy, "Wisconsin's Budget," in James K. Conant, Robert H. Haveman, and Jack Huddleston, eds., *Dollars and Sense: Policy Choices And The Wisconsin Budget*, vol. 2 (Madison WI: The Robert M. La Follette Institute of Public Affairs, 1991).

64. *State of Wisconsin 2003 Annual Fiscal Report*, Wisconsin Department of Administration, October 10, 2003, p. 9.

65. Governor Patrick J. Lucey began the use of levy limits on municipalities and cost controls on school districts during the early 1970s.

66. David Callender, "Gaming, Campaign Money Linked," *Capital Times* (Madison, Wisconsin), January 13, 1996.

67. Jeff Mayers, "Anti-Gambling Push Resisted," *Wisconsin State Journal*, April 14, 1992, p. 1B.

68. Wisconsin Ethics Board, "Lobbying Effort in Wisconsin, 1999–2000 Legislative Session."

2. THE CONSTITUTION

Milo M. Quaife, "Some General Observations," in Milo M. Quaife, ed., *The Movement for Statehood, 1845–1846* (Madison: Wisconsin State Historical Society, 1918), p. 10; Tom Loftus, *The Art of Legislative Politics* (Washington DC: CQ Press, 1994), p. 62.

1. Daniel Elazar maintains that a state's political culture, sectionalism, and the (continuing) frontier shape the operation of its political system. In this chapter we will show the ways in which Wisconsin's political culture, historical experience, and regional setting shaped the framing of the state's constitution. See Daniel J. Elazar, "The States in the Political Setting," in *American Federalism: A View from the States*, 3d ed. (New York: Harper and Row, 1984).

2. Andrew Jackson was elected president in 1828. His election is sometimes viewed as the beginning of a political revolution against the control of government by the commercial and financial centers of the East and toward popular democracy.

3. Michael Fine, "The Constitution," in *Wisconsin Government and Politics*, 5th ed., ed. Wilder Crane and A. Clarke Hagensick, p. 15 (Milwaukee: University of Wisconsin–Milwaukee, 1991).

4. *Wisconsin Blue Book 1997–1998* (Madison: Joint Committee on Legislative Organization, 1997), pp. 218–22.

5. U.S. Constitution, Article IV, section 4. Daniel Elazar points out this key fact in his discussion of state constitutions. See, "Series Introduction," in Diane D. Blair and Jay Barth, *Arkansas Politics and Government* (Lincoln: University of Nebraska Press, 1988) pp. xiv–xv.

6. This is the standard definition for "republic." See, for example, *Webster's New Ninth Collegiate Dictionary* (Springfield MA: Merriam Webster, 1986), p. 1001.

7. Elazar, "Series Introduction," pp. xiv–xv.

8. The states that emerged from the Northwest Territory were Ohio, Indiana, Michigan, Illinois, Iowa, and Wisconsin.

9. Daniel Elazar, "Series Introduction," pp. xv.

10. These are criteria Elazar defines as key elements of a commonwealth form; see "Series Introduction," pp. xiv–xv.

11. *Wisconsin: A Guide to the Badger State*, Workers of the Writer's Program of the Works Progress Administration in Wisconsin, comp. (New York: Hastings House, 1954), p. 40.

12. Reuben G. Thwaites, "Historical Outline of the Admission of Wisconsin to the Union," *Wisconsin Blue Book 1909* (Madison: Wisconsin State Historical Society, 1909), p. 17.

13. Thwaites, "Historical Outline," p. 17.

14. Thwaites, "Historical Outline," p. 17.

15. *Wisconsin: A Guide to the Badger State*, p. 41.

16. Quaife, "Some General Observations," p. 13.

17. Milo M. Quaife, ed. *The Convention of 1846* (Madison: Wisconsin Historical Society, 1919), p. 800.

18. Thwaites, "Historical Outline," p. 19.

19. Alice E. Smith, *The History of Wisconsin: From Exploration to Statehood* (Madison WI: Wisconsin State Historical Society, 1973), p. 655.

20. Thwaites, "Historical Outline," p. 20; Smith, *History of Wisconsin*, p. 654.

21. Frederic L. Paxson, "Wisconsin: A Constitution of Democracy," in Quaife, *Movement for Statehood*, p. 36.

22. Louise Phelps Kellogg, "Admission of Wisconsin to Statehood," in *The Movement for Statehood 1845–1846*, ed. Milo Quaife, p. 26 (Madison: Wisconsin State Historical Society, 1918), and Paxson, "Wisconsin: A Constitution of Democracy," p. 36.

23. Kellogg, "Admission," p. 26.

24. *Wisconsin: A Guide to the Badger State*, pp. 50–52.

25. *Wisconsin: A Guide to the Badger State*, pp. 50–52.

26. *Wisconsin: A Guide to the Badger State*, pp. 52–53.

27. *Wisconsin: A Guide to the Badger State*, pp. 50–52.

28. Smith, *History of Wisconsin*, p. 664.

29. *Wisconsin: A Guide to the Badger State*, p. 52.

30. *Manual for the Use of the Assembly of the State of Wisconsin, for the Year 1853* (Madison: Brown and Carpenter, 1853), p. 248.

31. Thwaites, "Historical Outline," p. 19.

32. *State of Wisconsin Blue Book 1995–1996*, (Madison: Joint Committee on Legislative Organization, 1995), p. 243.

33. Michael Fine, "The Constitution," p. 15.

34. Fine, "The Constitution," p. 16.

35. "Constitution of the State of Wisconsin" *Assembly [of the State of Wisconsin] Manual*, p. 8.

36. The term "common good" is used in the Wisconsin Constitution; see Article I, section 4.

37. "Wisconsin Constitution," *The Wisconsin Blue Book 1999–2000* (Madison: Joint Committee on Legislative Organization, 1999), pp. 150–99, is the primary source

for the data employed in this section. In some cases, *Wisconsin Blue Books* for other years were used.

38. "The Judicial Branch," *Wisconsin Blue Book 1999–2000*, p. 519.

39. "Wisconsin Constitution," *Wisconsin Blue Book 1999–2000*, p. 192.

40. "Wisconsin Constitution," *Wisconsin Blue Book 1999–2000*, p. 192.

41. "Wisconsin Constitution," *Wisconsin Blue Book 1981–1982* (Madison: Joint Committee on Legislative Operation, 1981), p. 226.

42. Tommy Thompson, *Power to the People: An American State at Work* (New York: HarperCollins, 1996), p. 132.

43. "Wisconsin Constitution," *Wisconsin Blue Book, 1999–2000*, p. 166.

44. In "The Constitution," Michael Fine argues that the general thrust of La Follette and the Progressives was to expand public services to state citizens (p. 29). Although banks were private corporations, there is a correspondence here with the attempt to expand services.

45. "Constitution of the State of Wisconsin," *Assembly [of the State of Wisconsin] Manual.* p. 26.

46. "Wisconsin Constitution," *Wisconsin Blue Book 1995–1996*, p. 225.

47. Opponents of the measure objected to it on procedural grounds. The fact that the amendment was only approved by one legislature, rather than two, made the supreme court decision a relatively straightforward matter.

48. *Wisconsin Blue Book 1995–1996*, p. 239.

49. "Wisconsin Constitution," *Wisconsin Blue Book 1989–1990* (Madison: Department of Administration, 1989), pp. 307–8.

50. "Wisconsin Constitution," *Wisconsin Blue Book 1989–1990*, p. 308.

51. Blair and Barth, *Arkansas Politics and Government*, p. 124.

52. For an interesting discussion of the ways in which constitutions are changed, see James L. Garnett, "Operationalizing the Constitution via Administrative Reorganization: Oilcans, Trends, and Proverbs," *Public Administration Review* [Special Issue] (1997): 35–44.

53. It is worth noting that both WHEDA and its predecessor survived court challenges.

54. *Wisconsin Blue Book 1997–1998*, p. 297. The bonds for this financing were moral obligation rather than general obligation bonds.

55. The vote on the sports lottery was a clear rejection of public financing for the stadium, with 618,377 voting against the amendment and only 334,818 voting affirmatively. See the *Wisconsin Blue Book 1999–2000*, p. 197.

56. *Wisconsin Blue Book 1997–1998*, pp. 296–97.

57. The 1995 Stadium Act provides the legal authority for a new "stadium district" to sell moral obligation bonds. A recent summary of these types of commitments can be found in Sheila S. Kennedy and Mark S. Rosentraub, "Public-Private

Partnerships, Professional Sports Teams, and the Protection of the Public's Interest," *American Review of Public Administration* 30, no. 4 (December 2000): 436–59. An excellent summary of background issues related to use of public money to build stadiums can be found in "Stadium Finance: Government's Role in the 1990s," Wisconsin Legislative Reference Bureau, Informational Bulletin 96–1, January 1996.

58. The sales tax was to be applied only in the five counties that were geographically contiguous to the stadium.

59. "Constitution of the State of Wisconsin," *Assembly [of the State of Wisconsin] Manual*, p. 26.

60. Joint Study: The Legislative Audit Bureau and the Legislative Fiscal Bureau, September 14, 1995, p. 2.

61. Most observers of state politics believe that this challenge was poorly presented and thus a weak one.

62. *Libertarian Party v. State*, 199 Wis.2d. 790 (Wis. 1996).

63. *State ex. rel. State Senate v. Thompson*, 144 Wis.2d. 429 (Wis. 1988).

64. The new law was Act 27 (Assembly Bill 150).

65. *Benson v. Thompson*, 199 Wis.2d. 674 (1996).

66. *Risser v. Klauser*, 207 Wis.2d. 176 (Wis. 1997).

67. *Wisconsin: A Guide to the Badger State*, p. 55.

68. *Wisconsin Blue Book 1909*, p. 861.

3. THE LEGISLATURE

Samuel C. Patterson, "Legislative Politics in the States," in Virginia Gray, Russell L. Hanson, and Herbert Jacob, eds., *Politics in the American States: A Comparative Analysis*, 6th ed. (Washington DC: CQ Press, 1996), p. 181.

1. Wisconsin's upper legislative house, as in all other states, is called the state senate. Wisconsin's lower house, like those in New York and several other states, is called the state assembly. Members of the assembly are called representatives.

2. The governor's office is located on the second floor of the east wing; the Wisconsin Supreme Court is located on the third floor.

3. *Wisconsin Blue Book 1995–1996* (Madison: Joint Committee on Legislative Organization, 1995), pp. 289, 305–306.

4. A fiscal note is an estimate of the cost of the legislation. The note is usually prepared by the executive branch agency that will have responsibility for implementing the proposed law because agency staff have the expertise to make these computations. On the Joint Legislative Committee, see the *Wisconsin Blue Book 1995–1996*, p. 281.

5. In the area of communications, for example, all Wisconsin legislators have toll-free numbers, e-mail, and cellular phones.

6. John D. Buenker, *The History of Wisconsin: The Progressive Era, 1893–1914* (Madison: Wisconsin State Historical Society, 1998) pp. 566–68.

7. *The Fifty States and Their Legislatures* (Common Cause, 1970).

8. Virginia Gray and Peter Eisinger, *American States and Cities*, 2d ed. (New York: Addison-Wesley, 1997), pp. 132–33.

9. Patterson, "Legislative Politics in the States," pp. 159–160, 197.

10. Diane D. Blair and Jay Barth, *Arkansas Politics and Government* (Lincoln: University of Nebraska Press, 1988), chap. 8, and Cole Blease Graham Jr. and William V. Moore, *South Carolina Politics and Government* (Lincoln: University of Nebraska Press, 1994), pp. 119–37.

11. *Wisconsin Blue Book 2001–2002* (Madison: Joint Committee on Legislative Organization, 2001), p. 264.

12. *Baker v. Carr* (396 U.S. 186); *Reynolds v. Sims* (377 U.S. 533).

13. For a comprehensive discussion of redistricting in Wisconsin, see H. Rupert Theobold's "Equal Representation: A Study of Legislative and Congressional Apportionment in Wisconsin," *Wisconsin Blue Book 1970* (Madison: Legislative Reference Bureau, 1970), pp. 71–260.

14. Wilder Crane and A. Clarke Hagensick, *Wisconsin Government and Politics* (Institute of Government Affairs/University of Wisconsin-Extension, 1976), p. 6.3.

15. Crane and Hagensick, *Wisconsin Government and Politics*, p. 6.4.

16. "Electoral Success Rates of Incumbents Seeking Reelection in Wisconsin Legislative Elections, 1978–1988," Legislative Reference Bureau [of the State of Wisconsin].

17. Gray and Eisinger, *American States and Cities*, pp. 131–32.

18. Tom Loftus, *The Art of Legislative Politics* (Washington DC: CQ Press, 1994).

19. Interview with Senator Fred Risser. The three changes in majority control of the senate are described later in this chapter.

20. According to Samuel C. Patterson, about a dozen states provide office staff for members of both houses; see his "Legislative Politics in the States," pp. 189–90.

21. The fact that members of both the upper and lower houses are paid the same is unusual among the states; in most states, members of the upper house are paid more.

22. V. O. Key, *Southern Politics in State and Nation* (New York: Random House, 1949).

23. The twin claims are also reported in William P. Brown and Kenneth VerBurg, *Michigan Politics and Government: Facing Change in a Complex State* (Lincoln:

University of Nebraska Press, 1995) pp. 195. Historians provide support for the claims of both cities, but there is no dispute over which meeting was held first, the fact that the meeting in Ripon resulted in the call for a new party, or that the organizer of the meeting, Alvan E. Bovay, proposed the name "Republican" for the new party.

24. Discussion in the following three paragraphs draws on Leon D. Epstein, *Politics in Wisconsin* (Madison: The University of Wisconsin Press, 1983). Quotations are on pp. 35–37.

25. Like his father, Robert M. La Follette Jr. was an isolationist. For discussion of this and other factors that led to the demise of the Progressive party, see William F. Thompson, *The History of Wisconsin: Continuity and Change 1940–1965* (Madison: Wisconsin State Historical Society, 1988), pp. 404–10.

26. Changes occurred in the elections of 1958, 1960, 1964, 1966, 1970, and 1994.

27. The changes took place as a result of the general election of 1974, three vacancies created in 1992 due to the resignation of incumbents, the special elections held 1993 to fill the vacancies, and the recall election of 1996.

28. In the 1994 election, Peter Barca was defeated by Republican challenger Mark Neumann.

29. Both Democratic senators (Feingold and Barca) had two years remaining in their terms before they needed to run for reelection. The job Thompson offered Marvin Rochelle was in the Division of Buildings and Safety, Department of Industry, Labor, and Human Relations.

30. Ironically, purchasers of the luxury "sky boxes" in the new stadium were given a waiver from the state's general sales tax on the grounds that this tax, which amounted to 5 percent of the sales price, would prevent potential buyers from paying the $75,000 annual lease fee for the boxes.

31. Religion is a factor often considered in demographic profiles, and data from other states show that most legislators are Protestants. Unfortunately data on the religious background of Wisconsin legislators is not collected by the state legislative agency that gathers and reports demographic data.

32. The data listed in table 1 and other data presented in this section of the chapter are compiled from surveys of Wisconsin legislators. The data for each session of the Wisconsin legislature can be found in the *Wisconsin Blue Book* for each of these legislatures.

33. *Wisconsin Blue Book 2001–2002* (Madison: Legislative Reference Bureau, 2001), p. 277.

34. Diana Gordon, "Citizen Legislators—Alive and Well," *State Legislatures* 20, no. 1: 24–27.

35. Gordon, "Citizen Legislators," 24–27.

36. National data used for comparison are from 1992 and 1993 and found in Patterson, "Legislative Politics in the States," p. 177.

37. "Women in State Legislatures 2003," National Conference of State Legislatures, www.ncsl.org/programs/legman/about/women03.htm (January 13, 2004).

38. Patterson, "Legislative Politics in the States," p. 177.

39. "Biography," Pedro A. Colón, Wisconsin Assembly Eighth District, www.legis. state.wi.us/assembly/asm08/news/bio.html (August 5, 2004).

40. It is worth noting, however, that in the 2001–2 legislature the percentage of members with degrees beyond the bachelor's degree was lower than it was in 1975. This circumstance may be explained in part by the apparent reduction in the number of members with law degrees.

41. Although the strength of the party organization and the level of recruitment activity may vary from year to year, the competitive two-party circumstances that currently exist in Wisconsin provide an incentive for party involvement.

42. *Wisconsin Blue Book 2001–2002*, p. 277.

43. Gray and Eisinger, *American States and Cities*, p. 119.

44. "Legislators' Reasons for Not Returning, 1963–2001 Sessions," Legislative Reference Bureau [of the State of Wisconsin].

45. Patterson, "Legislative Politics in the States," p. 199. Patterson cites Todd Donovan and Joseph R. Snipp, "Support for Legislative Term Limitations in California: Group Representation, Partisanship, and Campaign Information," *Journal of Politics* 56:492–501.

46. Alan Rosenthal, *The Third House: Lobbyists and Lobbying in the States* (Washington DC: CQ Press, 1993), p. 42.

47. *U.S Term Limits v. Thornton* (519 U.S. 799).

48. Concerns about the corruption of state politics and state legislatures were a key part of the populist and Progressive roots of initiative and referendum. An especially useful discussion of initiative process in the states is Shaun Bowler and Todd Donovan, "The Initiative Process," in Virginia Gray, Russell L. Hanson, and Herbert Jacob, eds., *Politics in the American States: A Comparative Analysis*, 8th ed. (Washington DC: CQ Press, 2004).

49. For summaries of state term-limit legislation, see the National Conference of State Legislatures, "Summary and Citations of State Term Limits Laws," at www.ncsl.org/programs/legman/about/citations.htm. This source also reports that only fifteen states had term limits for state legislators in 2004, because state supreme courts "voided term-limits provisions in Massachusetts, Oregon, Washington, and Wyoming."

50. "Electoral Success Rates of Incumbents Seeking Reelection in Wisconsin Leg-

islative Elections, 1978–1988," Legislative Reference Bureau [of the State of Wisconsin], October 1990.

51. "Legislator Data and Services," National Conference of State Legislatures, www.ncsl.org/programs/legman/about/legislator_overview.htm (August 4, 2004).

52. "Legislative Term Limits: An Overview," National Conference of State Legislatures, www.ncsl.org/programs/legman/about/termlimit.htm (August 4, 2004).

53. Patterson, "Legislative Politics in the States," pp. 161–62, 179–80.

54. The senate president and the assembly Speaker are the co-chairs of the committee. Members from the senate include the majority and assistant majority leaders as well as the minority and assistant majority leaders. Members from the assembly include the majority and assistant majority leaders as well as the minority and assistant minority leader.

55. For a more comprehensive description of these records, see the *Wisconsin Blue Book 1995–1996*, p. 264.

56. *Wisconsin Blue Book 1995–1996*, p. 269.

57. Some state constitutions have a single subject and clear title rule for bills. Wisconsin's constitution has such a provision, but it applies only to private and special bills.

58. Although both houses have rules that require delay for reconsideration between engrossment and the vote in the house chamber, the rules can be suspended by unanimous consent or a two-thirds vote so that the second and third readings can occur on the same legislative day. During the final days of a legislative session the request for "unanimous consent to suspend the rules" is likely to be a continuous part of floor proceedings.

59. *Wisconsin Blue Book 2001–2002*, pp. 269, 304.

60. *Wisconsin Blue Book 1997–1998* (Madison: Joint Committee on Legislative Organization, 1997), pp. 251, 696.

61. *The Book of the States 2000–2001*, vol. 33 (Lexington: Council of State Governments, 2001), pp. 108–9.

62. Ron Hedlund, "The Wisconsin Legislature," in Wilder Crane and A. Clarke Hagensick, eds., *Wisconsin Government and Politics*, 5th ed. (Milwaukee: University of Wisconsin–Milwaukee, 1991), p. 122.

63. Hedlund, "Wisconsin Legislature," p. 121. Hedlund reports that these perspectives emerged from interviews with the senate president and others.

64. Hedlund, "Wisconsin Legislature," p. 122.

65. Hedlund, "Wisconsin Legislature," pp. 121–22. Hedlund reports that the members of the assembly with only two assignments usually have a seat on the Joint Committee on Finance, where the workload is very high.

66. Prior to 1979 the lieutenant governor served as the presiding officer of the senate.

67. *Wisconsin Blue Book 2003–2004* (Madison: Joint Committee on Legislative Organization, 2003), p. 575.

68. The data on staff numbers for each agency are drawn from the *Wisconsin Blue Book 2003–2004*, pp. 286, 288, 287, 292, and 291, respectively.

69. Mr. Cattanach also held other posts in Wisconsin government. He served as secretary of transportation under Governor Lee Dreyfus.

70. Some scholars consider casework to be part of oversight. See, for example, Gray and Eisinger, *American States and Cities*, pp. 117–49.

71. Gray and Eisinger, *American States and Cities*, p. 139.

72. A classic study of legislative oversight is found in Eugene Bardach, *The Implementation Game: What Happens After a Bill Becomes a Law* (Cambridge MA: MIT Press, 1977).

73. *Wisconsin Blue Book 1999–2000*, p. 242.

74. Richard C. Elling, "The Utility of State Legislative Casework as a Means of Oversight," *Legislative Studies Quarterly* 4 (August 1979): 353–79.

75. This fact was acknowledged by former members of both parties of the legislature. For example, former Democratic senator Tim Cullen told a reporter that Governor Tommy Thompson dominated the policy-making agenda and its outcomes. See Scott Milfred, "Portrait in Power," *Wisconsin State Journal*, December 24, 2000, p. 1.

76. Dee J. Hall, "State Employees Secretly Campaign," *Wisconsin State Journal*, May 20, 2001, p. 1.

77. Michael Feldman, "Clean State, Dirty Politicians," *New York Times*, October 24, 2002, p. 35.

78. David E. Rosenbaum, "Scandal Begins to Tarnish Wisconsin's Political Luster," *New York Times*, July 10, 2002, p. 12. Cost of caucus staff employees, 2001: Hall, "State Employees Secretly Campaign," p. 1.

79. Dennis Chapman, "Agreement ends partisan caucus system," JSOnline, October 11, 2001; *Milwaukee Journal Sentinel*, July 28, 2004, www.jsonline.com/new/state/octo1/caucus121011o1a.asp.

80. Richard P. Jones, "Burke charged with 18 felonies," JSOnline, June 27, 2002. *Milwaukee Journal Sentinel*, July 28, 2004, www.jsonline.com/news/state/jun02/54217.asp.

81. David S. Broder, "Scandals Rocking Wisconsin Politics," *Washington Post*, June 23, 2002, p. 5.

82. Dee J. Hall and Phil Brinkman, "For Jensen, 3 felony counts," madison.com, October 18, 2002; *Wisconsin State Journal*, July 27, 2004, www.madison.com/wisconsinstatejournal/caucus/34429.php.

83. Steve Schultz and Richard P. Jones, "Chvala charged with extortion," JSOnline, October 18, 2002; (Milwaukee) *Journal Sentinel*, July 28, 2004 www.jsonline.com/news/state/oct02/88618.asp.

84. J. R. Ross, "State's top court to tackle caucus appeal," *Capital Times*, June 24, pp. 1, 3.

85. "Editorial: Bad ruling on Capitol corruption," madison.com, June 28, 2004; *Capitol Times*. August 2, 2004, www.madison.com/tct/opinion/editorial/index.php?ntid=5787&ntpid=2.

86. Steven Walters, "Supreme Court to consider lawmakers' roles in caucus scandal," JSOnline, June 22, 2004; *Milwaukee Journal Sentinel*, August 2, 2004, www.jsoline.com/news/state/jun04/238602.asp.

87. Ross, "State's top court to tackle caucus appeal."

88. "Court to hear lawmakers' appeals," *Wisconsin State Journal*, June 23, 2004, p. 3.

89. Walters, "Supreme Court to consider lawmakers' roles in scandal."

90. Rosenbaum, "Scandals Begin to Tarnish Wisconsin's Political Luster."

91. Rosenbaum, "Scandals Begin to Tarnish Wisconsin's Political Luster."

92. Hall, "State Employees Secretly Campaign," p. 6.

93. Hall, "State Employees Secretly Campaign," p. 6.

94. Hall, "State Employees Secretly Campaign," p. 6.

95. Feldman, "Clean State, Dirty Politicians."

96. Hall, "State Employees Secretly Campaign," p. 7.

97. Hall, "State Employees Secretly Campaign," p. 7.

98. Hall, "State Employees Secretly Campaign," p. 7.

99. Broder, "Scandals Rocking Wisconsin Politics." It is worth noting that the day after this circumstance was reported, Charles Chvala did reimburse the state for his expenses. See, Richard P. Jones and Dennis Chapman, "Lawmakers' tabs revealed in Capitol campaign scandal," JSOnline, May 11, 2002; *Milwaukee Journal Sentinel*, July 29, 2004, www.jsonline.com/news/state/may02/42460.asp.

100. Broder, "Scandals Rocking Wisconsin Politics"; Jones and Chapman, "Lawmakers' tabs."

101. Rosenbaum, "Scandals Begin to Tarnish Wisconsin's Political Luster."

4. THE GOVERNOR

1. Thompson's claim to the Progressive heritage can be found in his book, in which he calls his policy reforms part of a new progressive movement. See Tommy G. Thompson, *Power to the People: An American State at Work* (New York: HarperCollins, 1996). Thompson's claim of Progressive lineage was controversial within the state, and it struck a discordant note among some journalists from

outside of the state. E. J. Dionne Jr., who praised Thompson's welfare reforms, found his claim to the Progressive mantle a bit improbable. See E. J. Dionne Jr., "Welfare Reform: The Clues are in Wisconsin," *Washington Post*, 1997.

2. Ellen Torelle, Albert O. Barton, and Fred L. Holmes, eds., *The Political Philosophy of Robert M. La Follette* (Madison: The Robert M. La Follette Co., 1920).

3. In addition to this unattractive reputation, Thompson faced a primary opponent named Jonathan Berry who was telegenic and had earned good marks during his tenure as Dane County Executive.

4. According to former Earl staff member Hal Bergan, this factor may have been the most important of all of the variables. See Hal Bergan, "The Morning After," *Milwaukee Magazine*, January 1997, p. 73.

5. Bergan, "The Morning After," p. 69.

6. Bergan, "The Morning After," p. 107. For example, the author says that "we were speaking in metaphors without knowing it and sending messages which seemed insensitive to the economic distress and social anxiety people were feeling in 1983."

7. See "It Pays to Know Tommy Thompson," *Milwaukee Journal Sentinel*, November 2, 1997, pp. 1, 13.

8. Tommy G. Thompson, *Power to the People: An American State at Work*, p. 145.

9. Even at the end of his term, Thompson's distrust remained strong, as recorded by Stephen Walters in "Thompson's Legacy," *Journal Sentinel*, December 24, 2000, pp. 1, 10. Walters also reported that the "solution" Thompson had for this problem was to "inject . . . people who had his political trust into each (state) agency. He saw it as a way to make state government responsive to the governor. . . . Critics say it replaced Wisconsin's civil service system with Republican-dipped cronyism."

10. The title of "King" was well known to, and employed by, members of the press. See, for example, the large, cartoon-style color drawing of "King Tommy" in the (Milwaukee) *Journal Sentinel*, November 9, 1997, p. 1. The cartoon is located next to an article titled "The Turmoil over Tommy."

11. Knowles won the 1966 contest by a relatively comfortable margin.

12. Up to that point, every other race for governor had occurred during the presidential election.

13. Only one governor, Philip La Follette, attempted to run for a fourth term, and he was defeated. There is some reason to believe that there may have been an informal presumption within the state that no one should serve more than three terms as governor. Edward J. Miller maintains that Governor Walter Kohl's decision not to seek a fourth term was based on this "tradition." See Edward J. Miller, "The Governorship," in Wilder Crane and A. Clarke Hagensick,

eds., *Wisconsin Government and Politics*, 5th ed. (Milwaukee: University of Wisconsin–Milwaukee, 1991).

14. Among the others who played a leadership role in rebuilding the Democratic Party during the late 1940s and 1950s were William Proxmire, who was elected to the U.S. Senate, and James Doyle, who went on to serve as a distinguished federal judge.

15. The individual data for this record are contained in the annual volumes of the *Wisconsin Blue Book*. Data from the *Wisconsin Blue Book* have been compiled and reported by Edward J. Miller for the years 1848–1990 in "The Governorship." See his table VII–1, p. 158. Computations that include data for the years 1991–2002 have been done by the author of the present volume.

16. Miller, "The Governorship," table VII–1, p. 158.

17. Miller, "The Governorship," table VII–1, p. 158.

18. Martin Schreiber received his law degree from Marquette University; Anthony Earl received his law degree from the University of Chicago.

19. Miller, "The Governorship," table VII–2, p.159.

20. Miller, "The Governorship," p. 161.

21. Miller, "The Governorship," pp. 161, 163.

22. *Wisconsin Blue Book 1995–1996*, p. 321.

23. Of these independently elected constitutional officers, it is the attorney general that potentially poses the greatest challenge for a governor, particularly when the attorney general is not from the governor's party. This circumstance is discussed in chapter 5, "The Courts."

24. For example, see Thad Beyle, "The Governors," in Virginia Gray, Russell L. Hanson, and Herbert Jacob, eds., *Politics in the American States: A Comparative Analysis*, 7th ed. (Washington DC: CQ Press, 1999), table 6.5, pp. 210–11.

25. Edward J. Miller lists a variety of reasons why modern governors may not want to play this role. The reasons include the fact that modern gubernatorial candidates may decide to build their own campaign organization and distance themselves from the party and the fact that modern governors have little to hand out to party followers in terms of governmental positions. See Miller, "The Governorship," pp. 177–79.

26. For a discussion of the options available to governors who want to try to manage the executive branch, see James K. Conant, "Gubernatorial Strategy and Style: Keys to Improving Executive Branch Management," *State Government* July–August 1986: 82–88.

27. For a discussion of the differences and similarities in public- and private-sector management, see James K. Conant, "Can Government Organizations Be Excellent, Too?" *State and Local Government Review* 19.2 (spring 1987): 47–53.

28. One governor who attempted to manage the executive branch was Thomas Kean of New Jersey. For a case study focused on his core initiative, see James K. Conant, "Reorganization and the Bottom Line," *Public Administration Review* 46, no. 1 (January–February 1986): 48–56. For a classic case study of Michael Dukakis of Massachusetts, a governor who suffered the frustrations described here, see Martha Weinberg, *Managing the State* (Cambridge MA: MIT Press, 1978).

29. One of Governor Thompson's early moves was to have his chief of staff, Scott Jensen, run for an assembly seat. With the backing of Thompson, Jensen was elected, and he quickly became assembly Speaker.

30. It is worth noting that Reynolds served as attorney general before he was elected governor and went on to be a federal judge after he left the governorship.

31. A more complete biography of Patrick Lucey can be found in James K. Conant, *Executive Decision Making in the State*, Ph.D. diss., Department of Political Science, University of Wisconsin–Madison, 1983.

32. A description of important tax and expenditure policy decisions made by Lucey is given in chapter 11, "State-Local Relations."

33. The company was Sentry Insurance Company, headquartered in Stevens Point, Wisconsin.

34. This information was provided in an interview the author had with former governor Patrick Lucey while Lucey was a visiting instructor at the John F. Kennedy School of Government in 1986.

35. Thompson's preference for the Department of Transportation was reported in the Wisconsin press as well as other media outlets. Some believe that Transportation would have been a better assignment for a man who not only was a great road-builder in his own state but also served as the chairman of Amtrak's Board of Directors and had a passion for high-speed trains. In his post-announcement press conference, Thompson was quite emotional about bidding his state and the governorship farewell.

36. "Government in Molasses," *Washington Post*, June 12, 2001, p. 25.

5. THE COURTS

Herbert Jacob, "Courts," in Virginia Gray, Herbert Jacob, and Kenneth N. Vines, eds., *Politics in the American States: A Comparative Analysis*, 4th ed. (Boston: Little, Brown and Co., 1983), p. 222.

1. Herbert Jacob, "Courts: The Least Visible Branch," in *Politics in the American States: A Comparative Analysis*, 6th ed., ed. Virginia Gray, Russell L. Hanson, and Herbert Jacob, p. 253 (Washington DC: CQ Press, 1996).

2. For example, see John D. Buenker, *The History of Wisconsin, Volume IV: The Progressive Era, 1893–1915* (Madison: Wisconsin State Historical Society, 1998)

pp. 437–38. La Follette's claim was disputed by Philetus Sawyer, the Republican Party boss whom La Follette contends offered the bribe. A dispassionate, systematic examination of this important event is provided in Richard N. Current, *Pine Logs and Politics: A Life of Philetus Sawyer* (Madison: Wisconsin State Historical Society, 1950) pp. 258–69.

3. Buenker, *History of Wisconsin*, p. 437.

4. Buenker, *History of Wisconsin*, p. 404.

5. Joseph A. Ranney, *Trusting Nothing to Providence: A History of Wisconsin's Legal System* (Madison: University of Wisconsin Law School, 1999), p. 360.

6. Alfred H. Kelly and Winfred A. Harbison, *The American Constitution: Its Origins and Development*, 4th ed. (New York: Norton, 1970), pp. 525–26.

7. Buenker, *History of Wisconsin*, pp. 555–58.

8. The primary source employed here is Ranney, *Trusting Nothing to Providence*. Ranney provides a discussion of cases relating to political reforms on pp. 263–68; cases related to civil service reform on pp. 272–74 and 380; cases related to tax reforms on p. 366; and cases related to workmen's compensation on p. 371.

9. Ranney, *Trusting Nothing to Providence*, p. 278. In his assessment of John R. Commons, Ranney says that "Commons put his stamp on most of Wisconsin's Progressive [e]ra legal reforms, and a strong argument can be made that he is the most important person in the history of Wisconsin's legal system. Edward Ryan is the only other person who could seriously contend for that position."

10. Ranney, *Trusting Nothing to Providence*, p. 284; see also pp. 368–74.

11. Ranney, *Trusting Nothing to Providence*, p. 287.

12. Ranney, *Trusting Nothing to Providence*, p. 172.

13. Ranney, *Trusting Nothing to Providence*, p. 175.

14. Jacob, "Courts," in Gray, Jacob, and Vines, *Politics in the American States*, 4th ed., p. 223.

15. Henry R. Glick and Kenneth N. Vines, *State Court Systems* (Englewood Cliffs NJ: Prentice-Hall, 1973), p. 61

16. Jacob, "Courts: The Least Visible Branch," in Gray, Hanson, and Jacob, *Politics in the American States*, 6th ed., p. 278.

17. *Thompson v. Jackson*, 199 Wis.2d 715 (1996).

18. "Municipal Courts," Wisconsin Court System, www.courts.state.wi.us/about/organization/municipal/index (July 19, 2004).

19. "Municipal Courts," Wisconsin Court System, www.courts.state.wi.us/about/organization/municipal/index (July 19, 2004).

20. "Municipal Courts," Wisconsin Court System, www.courts.state.wi.us/about/organization/municipal/index (July 19, 2004).

21. "Municipal Courts," Wisconsin Court System, www.courts.state.wi.us/about/or ganization/municipal/index (July 19, 2004).

22. "Municipal Courts," Wisconsin Court System, www.courts.state.wi.us/about/or ganization/municipal/index (July 19, 2004).

23. *Wisconsin Blue Book 2003–2004*, p. 574.

24. "2002 statewide Wisconsin circuit court caseload," Wisconsin Court System, www.courts.state.wi.us/about/pub/circuit/circuitstats.htm. (July 21, 2004).

25. "Court of Appeal Annual Report—2002," Wisconsin Court System, www.courts. state.wi.us/html/ca/CA_02AR.htm. (July 19, 2004).

26. *The Book of the States, 1998–1999* (Lexington KY: Council of State Governments, 1998), pp. 133–35.

27. Michael E. Hartmann, "The Folly of 'Fully' Publicly Financing State Supreme Court Campaigns," *Wisconsin Interest* 7, no. 1 (Spring–Summer 1998): 51–61.

28. Jacob, "Courts," pp. 271–72.

29. Barbara Curran and Clara N. Carson, *Lawyer Statistical Report: The U S. Legal Profession in the 1990s* (Chicago: American Bar Association, 1994), p. 238.

30. *Wisconsin Blue Book 2001–2002*, pp. 586–87.

31. "Rose Board Under Scrutiny: A Special Report," *Wisconsin State Journal*, March 11, 1999.

32. The U.S. Supreme Court followed suit in the *Zelman* case.

33. Wis.2d. 835 (1998).

34. William J. Brennan Jr., "State Constitutions and the Protection of Individual Rights," *Harvard Law Review*, January 1977: 489–504.

35. 197 Wis.2d. 200 (1995).

36. 392 U.S. 1 (1968).

37. 201 Wis.2d. 383 (1996).

38. 201 Wis.2d. 839 (1996).

39. John Kincaid and Robert F. Williams, "The New Judicial Federalism: States Take the Lead in Rights Protection," *Journal of State Government* 65 (April–June 1992): 50–52. See also John Kincaid, "The New Judicial Federalism," *Journal of State Government* 61 (September–October 1988): 163–69.

40. Examples of her published work on this topic include: Shirley S. Abrahamson, "Reincarnation of State Courts," *South West Law Journal* 36 (1982): 951; "Divided We Stand: State Constitutions in a More Perfect Union," *Hastings Law Quarterly* 18 (1991): 723; "Criminal Law and State Constitutions," *Texas Law Review* 63 (1985): 1141; and Shirley S. Abrahamson and Diane S. Gutmann, "The New Federalism: State Constitutions," *Judicature* 71 (August–September 1987): 88–99. Abrahamson was appointed to the Wisconsin Supreme Court by Governor Patrick Lucey in 1976. She won election to the court in 1979 and

reelection in 1989 and 1999. She has been chief justice since 1996. Prior to her appointment to the court, Abrahamson was in private practice in Madison and was Professor of Law at the University of Wisconsin Law School.

41. Shirley S. Abrahamson and Elizabeth A. Hartman, "Building a More Perfect Union: Wisconsin and the U.S. Constitution," *Wisconsin Magazine of History* 85 (Autumn 2001): 16–23. Quotations in the following discussion appear on pp. 17, 17, 23, 21, and 21, respectively.

6. PRIVATE INTERESTS AND INTEREST GROUPS

This book chapter appears in *Politics in the American States: A Comparative Analysis*, 6th ed., ed. Virginia Gray, Russell L. Hanson, and Herbert Jacob, pp. 122–58 (Washington DC: CQ Press, 1996).

1. The work of the "muckrakers" is more fully described in chapter 12, "Wisconsin in the Federal System."

2. Some of this journalism and scholarship illustrates the extent to which special interests have been able to block legislation or administrative rules that were designed to protect or benefit the public at large. Other work provides documentation on the ways in which individuals and individual business firms secured government subsidies and tax breaks, and they have provided rich documentation of the ways in which interest groups work to secure economic and other tangible benefits for their members. Like journalists and scholars the public is also concerned about the power of special interests, as shown by responses to public opinion surveys. For example, see David S. Broder, "Whose government is This?" *Washington Post*, July 13, 1999, p. 17. Broder highlights some of the findings of a recent public opinion survey in which a majority of respondents reported that they believed government was more likely to respond to special interests than to the peoples' interests.

3. As quoted in *Wisconsin: A Guide to the Badger State* (New York: Hastings House, 1954), p. 57.

4. *Wisconsin: A Guide to the Badger State*, p. 57.

5. *Wisconsin: A Guide to the Badger State*, p. 55.

6. *Wisconsin: A Guide to the Badger State*, p. 55.

7. *Wisconsin: A Guide to the Badger State*, p. 55.

8. *Wisconsin: A Guide to the Badger State*, p. 56.

9. *Wisconsin: A Guide to the Badger State*, p. 56.

10. *Wisconsin: A Guide to the Badger State*, p. 56.

11. Clive S. Thomas and Ronald J. Hrebenar, "Interest Groups in the States," in *Politics in the American States: A Comparative Analysis*, 6th ed., ed. Virginia

Gray, Russell L. Hanson, and Herbert Jacobs, p. 122 (Washington DC: CQ Press, 1996).

12. Thomas and Hrebenar, "Interest Groups in the States," p. 125.
13. Thomas and Hrebenar, "Interest Groups in the States," p. 125.
14. Thomas and Hrebenar, "Interest Groups in the States," p. 123.
15. Thomas and Hrebenar, "Interest Groups in the States," p. 153.
16. Thomas and Hrebenar, "Interest Groups in the States," p. 125.
17. Thomas and Hrebenar, "Interest Groups in the States," p. 125.
18. Thomas and Hrebenar, "Interest Groups in the States," p. 123.
19. Thomas and Hrebenar, "Interest Groups in the States," p. 129.
20. Earl Latham, *The Group Basis of Politics* (Ithaca: Cornell University Press, 1952).
21. Latham, *Group Basis*, pp. 35–36.
22. David Truman, *The Government Process* (New York: Alfred A. Knopf, 1951); Robert Dahl, *Democracy and Its Critics* (New Haven: Yale University Press, 1989); Charles E. Lindblom, "The Science of Muddling Through," *Public Administration Review* 19 (1959); Charles Lindblom, "The Intelligence of Democracy," *American Political Science Review* 1965; and Braybrooke and Lindblom, *A Strategy of Decision* (New York: Free Press, 1963).
23. E. E. Schattschneider, *The Semi-Sovereign People* (New York: Holt, Rinehart and Winston, 1960), p. 35.
24. Schattschneider, *Semi-Sovereign People*, p. 35.
25. Charles E. Lindblom and Edward J. Woodhouse, *The Policy-Making Process*, 3d ed. (Englewood Cliffs NJ: Prentice Hall, 1993).
26. William De Soto, *The Politics of Business Organizations: Understanding the Role of the State Chambers of Commerce* (Lanham MD: University Press of America, 1995), p. 3.
27. David G. Wegge, "Interest Groups," in *Wisconsin Government and Politics*, 5th ed., ed. Wilder Crane and A. Clarke Hagensick, p. 109 (Milwaukee: University of Wisconsin–Milwaukee, 1991).
28. Wisconsin Ethics Board, "Lobbying Effort in Wisconsin, 1999–2000 Legislative Session."
29. The data for 1997–1998 are from the Wisconsin Ethics Board, "Lobbying Effort in Wisconsin, 1997–1998 Legislative Session." The data for 1985 and 1989 are taken from Wegge, "Interest Groups," p. 93.
30. David G. Wegge, "Interest Groups," p. 109. Wegge makes the argument that the "Reagan Revolution" may have been a key factor in this growth. As authority was shifted from the national government to state and local governments, interest group activity grew in parallel with the locus of policy and administrative decision making.

31. Wisconsin Ethics Board, "Lobbying Effort in Wisconsin, 1999–2000 Legislative Session."

32. Wisconsin Ethics Board, "Lobbying Effort in Wisconsin, 1999–2000 Legislative Session."

33. Wisconsin is not the only state with a "merged" organization, but the manufacturers association and the state Chamber of Commerce remain separate in some states. A brief history of the merger in Wisconsin, as well as some of its costs and benefits, can be found in William De Soto, *Politics of Business Organizations*, pp. 92–97.

34. Wisconsin Ethics Board, "1999–2000 Legislative Session: Plotting Bills," p. 2.

35. Wisconsin Ethics Board, "1999–2000 Legislative Session: Plotting Bills," p. 2.

36. De Soto, *Politics of Business Organizations*, p. 102.

37. De Soto, *Politics of Business Organizations*, p. 103.

38. De Soto, *Politics of Business Organizations*, pp. 102, 104.

39. De Soto, *Politics of Business Organizations*, p. 102.

40. Thomas and Hrebenar, "Interest Groups in the States," p. 149.

41. Thomas and Hrebenar, "Interest Groups in the States," p. 148.

42. Thomas and Hrebenar, "Interest Groups in the States," p. 149.

43. Thomas and Hrebenar, "Interest Groups in the States," p. 149.

44. Another measure that holds promise is what can be called a legislative "batting average." Specifically, the objective is to find out what legislative objectives the various interest groups have and then examine the legislative record in an attempt to determine success rates. Of course success for an interest group could mean that certain kinds of bills never appear on the legislative agenda. Success could also mean that tangible benefits, in the form of tax breaks, regulatory relief, or direct subsidies, are provided. In any case this approach also contains some important methodological challenges, too, and it is both expensive and time-consuming.

45. De Soto, *Politics of Business Organizations*, p. 99.

46. De Soto, *Politics of Business Organizations*, p. 107.

47. Unfortunately scholarship on the role of the press in Wisconsin politics and government is in relatively short supply. For a very interesting study that predates this particular struggle but has useful insights that can be used to make sense of it, see Delmer Dunn, *Public Officials and the Press* (Reading MA: Addison-Wesley, 1969). Dunn discusses the way in which the press covers state politics, highlighting the way in which elected officials learn about state politics and policy from the press.

48. Tom Loftus, *The Art of Legislative Politics* (Washington DC: CQ Press, 1994), pp. 87–104. The Loftus perspective on this struggle is articulated in these pages.

49. Other explanations for the amendment's ratification can be offered, of course,

including socioeconomic factors. For example, one might argue that supporters of the amendment were lower-income individuals from rural areas who like to shoot, hunt, and watch movies that feature gun-toting protagonists or villains, while those who prefer some sort of gun regulation are upper-income suburbanites who are, in the main, horrified by these activities.

7. POLITICAL PARTIES AND ELECTIONS

1. Especially in the two decades after the end of World War II, this topic received a good deal of attention in the American political science literature. Among the most important and comprehensive studies of the topic is Robert A. Dahl, ed., *Political Oppositions in Western Democracies* (New Haven: Yale University Press, 1966). Of particular concern for political scientists during the 1950s, 1960, and 1970s was the extent to which elections were merely devices used to legitimize regimes, rather than a means through which citizens could make choices about who represented them in government and what policies these representatives should pursue. Elections were held in Communist countries and voter turnout in those elections was often much higher than it was in Western democracies. The fact that the only candidates from which voters could choose, however, were candidates selected by the Communist Party made many Western observers conclude that these elections were hollow or forced exercises.

2. Leon D. Epstein, *Politics in Wisconsin* (Madison: University of Wisconsin Press, 1958), p. 33.

3. The responsible party model is often associated with British political parties. Although it has been used by some scholars of American political parties as a normative model, other scholars have used it as a baseline for conducting empirical research.

4. Daniel Elazar, *American Federalism: A View from the States* (New York: Harper and Row, 1984).

5. V. O. Key, *Southern Politics in State and Nation* (New York: Alfred A. Knopf, 1950).

6. Austin Ranney and Wilmoore Kendall, "The American Party Systems," *American Political Science Review* 48 (June 1954): 477–85.

7. Epstein, *Politics in Wisconsin*, p. 34.

8. Epstein, *Politics in Wisconsin*, p. 34.

9. *Wisconsin: A Guide to the Badger State* (New York: Hastings House, 1954), p. 54.

10. Among the key reasons the Stalwart Republicans regained control of the party was because they established a "voluntary" organization outside of existing statutory guidelines and restrictions in 1925. By outflanking the Progressive Republicans

in this manner, the Stalwart faction left the Progressives with the difficult choice of either disbanding or forming a new party.

11. Several scholars, including Epstein, see a causal relationship between the demise of the Progressive Party and the rise of the Democratic Party.

12. Proxmire won the election for the Senate seat left open by Joseph McCarthy upon the latter's death. McCarthy, it may be noted, had been totally discredited prior to his death, and Proxmire's election could be viewed as a reaction against McCarthy and the Republican Party rather than an outright victory for the Democratic Party. It is also worth noting that Proxmire was known to state voters because he was the Democratic candidate for governor in 1952, 1954, and 1956. In the latter two races, he lost by relatively small margins.

13. *Wisconsin Blue Book 1999–2000* (Madison: Joint Committee on Legislative Organization, 1999), p. 800.

14. Epstein, *Politics in Wisconsin*, p. 25.

15. John F. Bibby, "Political Parties and Elections in Wisconsin," in *Wisconsin Government and Politics*, 5th ed., ed. Wilder Crane and A. Clarke Hagensick, pp. 67–68 (Milwaukee: University of Wisconsin–Milwaukee, 1991).

16. Bibby, "Political Parties and Elections," p. 57. See also Epstein, *Politics in Wisconsin*, p. 24.

17. For example, mayors of Baltimore, Boston, and Los Angeles have recently run for the governorship of their states.

18. It is important to note, however, that county officers are elected during the fall and are listed on the same ballot as state and national officials.

19. Epstein, *Politics in Wisconsin*, p. 29.

20. Bibby, "Political Parties and Elections," p. 59.

21. One of the principal tactics he employed for this purpose was the reorganization of executive branch agencies. Specifically, his objective was to get rid of the boards and commissions that oversaw several state agencies. By doing so, Thompson gained the ability to appoint the agency secretary and other top managers.

22. The presumption here is that Thompson put his own people or Republican Party faithful into classified positions, or that he created new positions outside of the classified service. In most agencies, the Wisconsin governor nominates the agency secretary, and either the governor or the agency secretary nominates the deputy secretary and assistant secretaries.

23. Epstein, *Politics in Wisconsin*, p. 29.

24. *Wisconsin Blue Book 1981–1982* (Madison: Legislative Reference Bureau, 1981), p. 861.

25. Tom Loftus, *The Art of Legislative Politics* (Washington DC: CQ Press, 1994), p. 29.

26. A description of the 1977 and 1986 reforms can be found in Bibby, "Political Parties and Elections," pp. 65–66.

27. Bibby, "Political Parties and Elections," pp. 57–58.

28. Bibby, "Political Parties and Elections," p. 61.

29. Bibby, "Political Parties and Elections," p. 61.

30. Bibby, "Political Parties and Elections," pp. 60–61.

31. Bibby, "Political Parties and Elections," p. 62.

32. Epstein, *Politics in Wisconsin*, p. 77.

33. Epstein, *Politics in Wisconsin*, p. 77.

34. Epstein, *Politics in Wisconsin*, p. 77.

35. Bibby, "Political Parties and Elections," p. 64.

36. Tom Loftus, *The Art of Legislative Politics* (Washington DC: CQ Press, 1994), p. 37.

37. Loftus, *Art of Legislative Politics*, p. 37.

38. Loftus, *Art of Legislative Politics*, p. 37.

39. Epstein, *Politics in Wisconsin*, p. 54.

40. Epstein, *Politics in Wisconsin*, p. 68. In taking this position, Epstein cites existing work on this topic by several scholars, including V. O. Key and Duncan MacRae. See Epstein, *Politics in Wisconsin*, pp. 68–70, 168.

41. Bibby, "Political Parties and Elections," p. 73.

8. THE STATE BUDGET AND THE BUDGETARY PROCESS

1. In its 1991 study of state-local tax systems, Citizens for Tax Justice rated Wisconsin's tax system the second most progressive system after Minnesota's. The report is titled "A Far Cry From Fair." In a 1996 study by Citizens for Tax Justice and the Institute on Taxation and Economic Policy, Wisconsin's ranking fell several places, which seems to reflect changes in state policy. The 1996 report is titled "Who Pays? A Distributional Analysis of the Tax Systems of All 50 States." Some of the policy decisions that have reduced Wisconsin's tax progressivity are described in chapter 11, "State-Local Relations."

2. In the second year of the biennium, what might be described as a "minibudget" process is run. This process was originally established by statute in the 1960s as an "annual review" process, and it was designed to address technical corrections to the biennial budget. During the 1970s, however, the annual review bill grew to include new policy initiatives, and the statutory authority for the annual review process was withdrawn in the early 1980s. Nevertheless, governors have continued to submit annual review bills to the legislature, and the legislature continues to act on them.

3. Some states use the federal fiscal year, which begins October 1 and ends September 30.

4. There are a number of books and articles that describe and assess budgeting in other states. For an early classic, see Thomas Anton, *The Politics of State Expenditure in Illinois* (Urbana: University of Illinois Press, 1966). More recent books include: Robert D. Lee Jr. and Ronald W. Johnson, *Public Budgeting Systems* (Baltimore: University Park Press, 1983), and Edward J. Clynch and Thomas P. Lauth, eds., *Governors, Legislatures, and Budgets: Diversity Across the American States* (New York: Greenwood Press, 1991).

5. According to James Gosling, Wisconsin gives its elected officials greater flexibility to include policy changes in the state budget than any other state. Gosling reports that some states, including Colorado and Pennsylvania, have constitutional provisions that prohibit the inclusion of substantive policy language in the state budget. Other states, such as New York, Ohio, California, and Oregon, provide decision-makers a good deal of flexibility. See James Gosling, *Budgetary Politics in American Governments* (White Plains NY: Longman Publishing Group, 1992) pp. 103–4.

6. John Torphy, "Wisconsin's Budget," in *Dollars and Sense: Policy Choices and the Wisconsin Budget*, vol. 2, ed. James K. Conant, Robert H. Haveman, and Jack Huddleston, p. 13 (Madison: Robert M. La Follette Institute of Public Affairs, 1991).

7. The scholar that is probably best known for the articulation of this theme in the study of national government budgeting is Aaron Wildavsky, and his *The Politics of the Budgetary Process* (Boston: Little, Brown and Co., 1964) is the classic in the field.

8. The statutory basis for this requirement still stands. On January 6, 1997, however, Senate Joint Resolution 1 extended the deadline to February 12, 1997. On January 14 the assembly concurred in extending the deadline for that year. Since actions of this kind often set precedents, it would not be surprising to again see legislative resolutions that push back this key date.

9. It is conceivable that the courts could intercede in the process, and thus appear to be final decision-makers on appropriations. Even if such intervention occurred, however, governors and legislators would probably have to take some formal steps to finalize or implement court decisions.

10. This topic is discussed in chapter 11," State-Local Relations."

11. For a discussion of how large an impact even relatively modest changes in the national economy can have on Wisconsin, see Donald A. Nichols, "The Effect of Recession on the Budget," in Conant, Haveman, and Huddleston, *Dollars and Sense*, vol. 2, pp. 61–82. For a discussion of the effects economic changes

can have on other states' budgets, see "Budget Making in the States," James K. Conant, in *Dollars and Sense*, vol. 2, pp. 5–6.

12. Nichols, "Effect of Recession on the Budget," pp. 61–82.

13. For more discussion of this topic, see James K. Conant, "The Growing Importance of State Government," in James Perry, ed., *The Handbook of Public Administration* (San Francisco: Jossey-Bass, 1990) pp. 26–28.

14. The operating budget was first described in an academic text on Wisconsin's state budget by John Torphy, who served as state budget director and later as secretary of administration. The method Torphy used to establish the numbers for the FY 1989 operating budget is used here to examine the FY 2003 budget. See Torphy, "Wisconsin's Budget," pp. 13–35.

15. The data used to calculate this total come from the *2003 State of Wisconsin Annual Fiscal Report*, Wisconsin Department of Administration, October 10, 2003, pp. 17–19.

16. *2003 State of Wisconsin Annual Fiscal Report*, p. 19.

17. *2003 State of Wisconsin Annual Fiscal Report*, p. 17.

18. *2003 State of Wisconsin Annual Fiscal Report*, p. 17.

19. Torphy, "Wisconsin's Budget," p. 28.

20. *1999 State of Wisconsin Annual Fiscal Report*, Wisconsin Department of Administration, October 15, 1999, p. 20.

21. *2003 State of Wisconsin Annual Fiscal Report*, p. 9.

22. *2003 State of Wisconsin Annual Fiscal Report*, p. 9.

23. The $3,756.9 million Medical Assistance figure used in table 12 can be found in the *2003 State of Wisconsin Annual Fiscal Report*, p. 10.

24. The $3,269.7 million figure used in table 12 can be found in the *2003 State of Wisconsin Annual Fiscal Report [(Budgetary Basis) Appendix]*, part 1-C.

25. For a superb discussion of the budget of the University of Wisconsin System, see W. Lee Hansen and Kathryn R. Sell, "The UW System Budget," in Conant, Haveman, and Huddleston, *Dollars and Sense*, vol. 2, pp. 83–118.

26. The $1,218.4 million figure in table 12 can be found in the *2003 State of Wisconsin Annual Fiscal Report [(Budgetary Basis) Appendix]*, p. 13.

27. The $1004.3 million figure in table 12 comes can be found in the *2003 State of Wisconsin Annual Fiscal Report [(Budgetary Basis) Appendix]*, p. 14.

28. The $795.7 million figure in table 12 can be found in the *2003 State of Wisconsin Annual Fiscal Report [(Budgetary Basis) Appendix]*, p. 13.

29. The $705.5 million figure in table 12 can be found in the *2003 State of Wisconsin Annual Fiscal Report [(Budgetary Basis) Appendix]*, p. 31.

30. *2003 State of Wisconsin Annual Fiscal Report*, p. 10.

31. Scott McCallum, Governor, "Budget Reform Bill Summary," Division of Ex-

ecutive Budget and Finance, Wisconsin Department of Administration (January 2002), p. 1.

32. A systematic review of the deficit, its size, causes, as well as remedies proposed and taken by state elected officials, can be found in James K. Conant, "Wisconsin's Budget Deficit: Size, Causes, Remedies, and Consequences," *Public Budgeting and Finance* (Summer 2003): 5–38.

33. Jim Doyle, Governor, *2003–2005 Executive Budget Summary*, Wisconsin Department of Administration, Division of Executive Budget and Finance (February 2003), p. 3.

34. Doyle, *2003–2005 Executive Budget Summary*, p. 1.

35. Doyle, *2003–2005 Executive Budget Summary*, p. 5.

36. "2003–05 Budget Update: Governor Signs Budget," University of Wisconsin System, www.wisconsin.edu/budget (July 26, 2004).

37. Doyle, *2003–2005 Executive Budget Summary*, p. 15.

38. Doyle, *2003–2005 Executive Budget Summary*, p. 15. Given the concerns Doyle articulated during his time as attorney general about the risks gambling posed to the state's democratic institutions and practices, his support for expanded gambling seems surprising. It appears that the extraordinarily difficulty fiscal circumstances he faced, combined with his commitment to balance the budget without tax increases, meant that gambling was one of the few options he had for generating additional state revenue.

39. Jim Doyle, Governor, *Restoring Fiscal Responsibility for Wisconsin's Future: 2003–2005 Wisconsin Act 33*, Wisconsin Department of Administration, Division of Executive Budget and Finance (July 2003), p. 4.

40. Doyle, *Restoring Fiscal Responsibility*, p. 9.

41. Steven Walters, "Doyle vetoes property tax cap." JSOnline, *Milwaukee Journal Sentinel*, www.jsonline.com/news/state/jul03/157342.asp (July 26, 2003).

42. Steve Schultze and Stacy Forster, "Court strikes down casino deal." JSOnline, *Milwaukee Journal Sentinel*, www.jsonline.com/news/state/may04/229122asp (May 13, 2004).

43. Schultze and Forster, "Court strikes down."

44. Schultze and Forster, "Court strikes down."

45. Schultze and Forster, "Court strikes down."

9. SOCIAL WELFARE POLICY

1. One example of this national publicity is the front-page article in the *New York Times* of December 14, 1993, titled "Wisconsin Pledges to Exit U.S. System of Public Welfare," which described the 1993 legislative act that set a termination date for AFDC.

2. Thomas J. Corbett, "Welfare Reform in Wisconsin: The Rhetoric and the Reality," pp. 19–54, in Donald F. Norris and Lyke Thompson, eds., *The Politics of Welfare Reform* (Sage Publications, 1995), pp. 19–54 (University of Wisconsin–Madison, Institute for Research on Poverty [IRP] Reprint Series 747).

3. Hal Bergan, "The Morning After," *Milwaukee Magazine*, January 1987, pp. 69, 71; Thomas Kaplan, "Wisconsin's w-2 Program: Welfare As We Might Come To Know It," (Madison: Institute for Research on Poverty, 1998) pp. 10–11.

4. *Wisconsin: A Guide to the Badger State* (New York: Hasting House, 1954), p. 62.

5. *Wisconsin: A Guide to the Badger State*, p. 62.

6. *Wisconsin: A Guide to the Badger State*, p. 62.

7. A history of Wisconsin's unemployment compensation legislation as well as an examination of the performance of the unemployment compensation system at the national and state levels can be found in W. Lee Hansen and James F. Byers, eds., *Unemployment Insurance: The Second Half Century* (Madison: University of Wisconsin Press, 1990).

8. For a description of the passage of the unemployment compensation legislation in Wisconsin, see Raymond Munts, "Unemployment Compensation in Wisconsin: Origins and Performance," in Hansen and Byers, *Unemployment Insurance*.

9. Wilbur Cohen eventually became the head of the Social Security Administration and he served as secretary of the Deparmtent of Health and Human Services under Lyndon Johnson. Professor W. Lee Hansen describes Cohen as a lifelong analyst and champion of the unemployment compensation system. See the preface to Hansen and Byers, *Unemployment Insurance*.

10. One of the minor provisions of the 1935 act was a program set up to provide temporary income assistance to children who lived in single-parent households that had little or no income. This program would become known as Aid to Families with Dependent Children (AFDC), and, during the 1960s and 1970s, both the number of families receiving aid from the program and the costs of the program expanded rapidly. The growing costs of the program, however, ultimately made it the focal point of the debate about welfare reform that took place in Wisconsin and the nation during the 1980s and 1990s.

11. The credit could not exceed $300; see Jack Stark, "A History of the Property Tax and Property Tax Relief in Wisconsin," *Wisconsin Blue Book 1991–1992* (Madison: Joint Committee on Legislative Organization, 1991), p. 137.

12. Corbett, "Welfare Reform in Wisconsin," p. 21.

13. President Ronald Reagan, Inaugural Address, January 1980.

14. Wonderful descriptions of these initiatives can be found in William Grieder, *The Education of David Stockman and Other Americans* (New York: E. P. Dutton,

1981), and in James P. Pfiffner, "The Reagan Budget Juggernaut," in James P. Pfiffner, ed., *The President and Economic Policy* (Philadelphia: ISHI Press, 1986).

15. For a more complete description, see James K. Conant, "The Growing Importance of State Government," in James Perry, ed., *The Handbook of Public Administration* (San Francisco: Jossey-Bass Publishers, 1990), pp. 25–39.

16. Corbett, "Welfare Reform in Wisconsin," p. 32.

17. Corbett, "Welfare Reform in Wisconsin," p. 33.

18. Corbett, "Welfare Reform in Wisconsin," p. 33.

19. Corbett, "Welfare Reform in Wisconsin," pp. 33–34.

20. Corbett, "Welfare Reform in Wisconsin," p. 34.

21. Corbett, "Welfare Reform in Wisconsin," p. 36.

22. Corbett, "Welfare Reform in Wisconsin," p. 36.

23. Corbett, "Welfare Reform in Wisconsin," pp. 34–35.

24. The data for this statement are drawn from Corbett, "Welfare Reform in Wisconsin," p. 39.

25. Additionally, other cases that show the risk incumbents run when they do not respond effectively to perceived crises can be found in the public administration and political science literature. Among the best of these case studies is that written about Governor Francis Sergeant of Massachusetts: see Martha Wagner Weinberg, *Managing the State* (Cambridge MA: MIT Press, 1977).

26. The symbolic dimensions of politics have been eloquently discussed by Murray Edelman in *The Symbolic Uses of Politics* (Urbana: University of Illinois Press, 1964), and *Politics as Symbolic Action* (Chicago: Markham, 1971). These pathbreaking books are highly regarded by political scientists, and they are excellent reading for anyone interested in the study of politics.

27. Kaplan, "Wisconsin's W-2 Program," p. 10.

28. Kaplan, "Wisconsin's W-2 Program," p. 10.

29. Corbett, "Welfare Reform in Wisconsin," p. 33.

30. Corbett, "Welfare Reform in Wisconsin," p. 30.

31. For one perspective on this issue, see Paul Voss, Tom Corbett, and Richard Randell, "Interstate Migration and Public Welfare: The Migration Decision Making of a Low-Income Population," in Patrick Jobes, William Stinner, and John Wardwell, eds., *Community, Society, and Migration* (Lanham MD: University Press of America, 1992), pp. 111–48.

32. Tom Corbett, Robert H. Haveman, and Michael Wiseman, "Income Support and Welfare Reform," in Robert H. Haveman and Jack Huddleston, eds., *Dollars and Sense: Policy Choices and The Wisconsin Budget*, vol. 1 (Madison: Robert M. La Follette School of Public Affairs, 1990), p. 99.

33. Kaplan, "Wisconsin's W-2 Program," p. 10.

34. The cash grant provided by AFDC reduced hardship, but it did not, by itself, lift a family out of poverty. Even at its most generous point, the state's AFDC cash grant was approximately 80 percent of the income a family needed to reach the poverty line. Interestingly, when the percentage of the population below the poverty line was calculated, only the cash benefit was counted. If, however, an AFDC recipient also qualified for "in-kind" support in the form of food stamps and/or housing assistance, which many did, the value of the total aid package (if it was calculated as cash) would have provided an income above the poverty level. In addition, a substantial percentage of the children of AFDC recipients qualified for Medicaid. If the cash value of this benefit was added to the other benefits, the AFDC package would have put recipients well above the poverty line. Indeed, their income-equivalent would have exceeded the income of a large percentage of the "working poor," and this was a key objection lodged against the welfare system as a whole.

35. Corbett, Haveman, and Wiseman, "Income Support and Welfare Reform," p. 100.

36. Corbett, "Welfare Reform in Wisconsin," p. 36.

37. Corbett, "Welfare Reform in Wisconsin," p. 38.

38. Corbett, "Welfare Reform in Wisconsin," p. 38.

39. The "standard of need" was the figure set by each state to determine the economic requirements of low-income people. Thus, when the legislature set the figure at 84.04 percent, it was setting the baseline figure for an AFDC recipient.

40. The petitioners included Senator Fred Risser, Senator Brian Burke, Representative David Travis, and Sheila R. Mooney. The respondents were James R. Klauser and Tommy G. Thompson.

41. *State ex. rel. State Senate v. Thompson* 144, Wis.2d. 429, 424 N.W.2d 385, 386, n.3 (1988).

42. Thomas Corbett, "Welfare Reform in Wisconsin," p. 39–40.

43. Michael Wiseman, "State Strategies for Welfare Reform: The Wisconsin Story," *Journal of Policy Analysis and Management* 15, no. 4 (Fall 1996): 515–46 (University of Wisconsin–Madison, Institute for Research on Poverty [IRP] Reprint Series 753).

44. Corbett, "Welfare Reform in Wisconsin," p. 25.

45. Kaplan, "Wisconsin's w-2 Program," p. 12.

46. Kaplan, "Wisconsin's w-2 Program," p. 12.

47. Kaplan, "Wisconsin's w-2 Program," p. 12.

48. Wiseman, "State Strategies for Welfare Reform," p. 532.

49. Kaplan, "Wisconsin's w-2 Program," p. 13.

50. *Wisconsin Works (w-2) Manual*, Wisconsin Department of Workforce Development, January 1, 1998, pp. 1–2.

51. Kaplan, "Wisconsin's w-2 Program," pp. 3–4.

52. Kaplan, "Wisconsin's w-2 Program," pp. 14–18.

53. Wiseman, "Welfare Reform in the United States: A Background Paper," *Housing Policy Debate* 7, no. 4 (1996): 635 (University of Wisconsin–Madison, Institute for Research on Poverty [IRP] Reprint Series 755).

54. Wiseman, "Welfare Reform in the United States," p. 635.

55. Wiseman, "Welfare Reform in the United States," p. 635.

56. Wiseman, "Welfare Reform in the United States," p. 635.

57. Wiseman, "State Strategies for Welfare Reform," p. 533.

58. Wiseman, "State Strategies for Welfare Reform," p. 533.

59. The four tiers and the assistance provided in each is concisely summarized in tabular form in Kaplan, "Wisconsin's w-2 Program," p. 2.

60. For example, state policymakers do not control the distribution of income across segments of the population in the country or even their own state. National government policy and economic conditions are the key factors here, one result of which is that the top 20 percent of the population earns approximately 40 percent of the income generated in a given year, while the bottom 20 percent earns less than 5 percent of the income. Furthermore, during the 1980s and first part of the 1990s national government policy tended to widen, rather than shrink, this disparity in income.

61. Wiseman uses the figure 22.5 percent for this period, but he used data from December of 1994 rather than January of 1994. See his "State Strategies for Welfare Reform," p. 528.

62. This figure is for the period 1987–1994. The data are found in Kaplan, "Wisconsin's w-2 Program," fig. 1.

63. Wiseman, "State Strategies for Welfare Reform," pp. 528–29.

64. Wiseman, "Welfare Reform: The Wisconsin Story," pp. 529–30.

65. Wiseman, "Welfare Reform: The Wisconsin Story," p. 530.

66. Wiseman, "Welfare Reform: The Wisconsin Story," p. 531.

67. Wiseman, "Welfare Reform: The Wisconsin Story," p. 528.

68. Lawrence M. Mead, *The Decline of Welfare in Wisconsin* (Madison: Institute for Research on Poverty, 1998), p. 12.

69. Mead, *Decline of Welfare*, pp. 12 and 29.

70. Mead, *Decline of Welfare*, p. 29.

71. Kaplan, "Wisconsin's w-2 Program," pp. 22–23.

72. Robert H. Haveman and Jonathan Schwabish, "Economic Growth and Poverty: A Return to Normalcy?" *Focus* 20, no. 2 (Spring 1999): 1, 6.

73. Haveman and Schwabish, "Economic growth and poverty," p. 6.

74. Lawrence M. Mead, "Statecraft: The Politics of Welfare Reform in Wisconsin" (Madison: Institute for Research on Poverty, 1999), abstract.

75. Mead, "Statecraft" (abstract).

76. Mead, "Statecraft" (abstract).

77. Wiseman, "State Strategies for Welfare Reform," p. 530.

78. Wiseman, "State Strategies for Welfare Reform," p. 530, fig. 4.

79. Kaplan, "Wisconsin's w-2 Program," p. 27.

80. E. J. Dionne Jr. "Welfare Reform: The Clues Are In Wisconsin," *Washington Post*, September 17, 1997, p. A17.

10. LOCAL GOVERNMENT

1. This statement is based on data for 1997, which are presented on p. 675 of the *Wisconsin Blue Book 1999–2000* (Madison WI: Joint Committee on Legislative Organization, 1999). The data are stated in terms of FTE (full-time equivalent employees), rather than in terms of individual employees or people. The exact number of FTE listed for local government in 1997 is 201,633; for state government the number is 64,709.

2. James McGregor Burns, J. W. Peltason, Thomas E. Cronin, and David B. Magleby, eds., *State and Local Politics: Government By the People*, 8th ed. (Upper Saddle River NJ: Prentice Hall, 1996), p. 171.

3. Virginia is referred to as a "Dillon Rule" state, in which local governments only have the powers the state has specifically delegated to them by constitution or statute. Efforts to change this situation have intensified in recent years as Northern Virginia's populous counties have asked for, lobbied for, or even demanded more flexibility to address their needs and circumstances. The response from Richmond, the state's capitol, however, has not been encouraging.

4. Burns et al., *State and Local Politics*, p. 172.

5. *Wisconsin Blue Book 1997–1998* (Madison WI: Joint Committee on Legislative Organization, 1997), p. 210.

6. Susan Paddock, "The Changing World of Wisconsin Local Government," *Wisconsin Blue Book 1997–1998*, p. 107.

7. Daniel Elazar, *The American Mosaic* (Boulder, Westview Press, 1994), p. 287.

8. Susan Paddock, "Changing World," p. 109.

9. Susan Paddock, "Changing World," p. 115.

10. For a complete description of governmental units in Wisconsin, see Wilder Crane and A. Clarke Hagensick, eds., *Wisconsin Government and Politics*, 5th ed. (Milwaukee: University of Wisconsin–Milwaukee, 1991), p. 3.5.

11. Robert C. Nesbit and William F. Thompson, *Wisconsin: A History*, 2d ed. (Madison: University of Wisconsin Press, 1989), p. 152.

12. Nesbit and Thompson, *Wisconsin: A History*, p. 152.

13. Nesbit and Thompson, *Wisconsin: A History*, pp. 152–55.

14. Edward J. Miller and Brett Hawkins, "Local Government," pp. 25–44, in Ronald E. Weber, ed., *Crane and Hagensick's Wisconsin Government and Politics*, 6th ed. (New York: McGraw-Hill, 1996); quotation on p. 28.

15. Miller and Hawkins, "Local Government," p. 28.

16. Miller and Hawkins, "Local Government," p. 28.

17. Miller and Hawkins, "Local Government," p. 28.

18. Miller and Hawkins, "Local Government," p. 28.

19. Miller and Hawkins cite Wisconsin Statute 59.03(3)(a) as the location where the maximum number of board members is defined by the legislature.

20. Paddock, "Changing World," p. 115.

21. Paddock, "Changing World," p. 106.

22. Paddock, "Changing World," p. 107.

23. Paddock, "Changing World," p. 107.

24. Paddock, "Changing World," p. 107.

25. Paddock, "Changing World," p. 134. Paddock notes that at least three-quarters of the tuition for these students was paid for through taxation.

26. Wisconsin Constitution, *Wisconsin Blue Book 1997–1998*, p. 206.

27. Paddock, "Changing World," p. 135.

28. Paddock, "Changing World," p. 135.

29. Paddock, "Changing World," p. 135.

30. School district data are taken from Miller and Hawkins, "Local Government," p. 26. The authors list the relevant editions of the *Wisconsin Blue Book* as the original source for the data.

31. Crane and Hagensick, *Wisconsin Government and Politics*, p. 3.1.

32. Miller and Hawkins, "Local Government," p. 26.

33. Miller and Hawkins, "Local Government," p. 26.

34. One example is Fairfax County, Virginia. The county delivers public services to the population within its borders except for the residents of the independent city of Fairfax.

35. Number of counties, cities, villages, and towns: *Wisconsin Blue Book 2001–2002*, p. 728; number of school and technical college districts: "Municipal and County Finance," Wisconsin Legislative Fiscal Bureau, Informational Paper no. 16, January 2003; number of special districts: U.S. Department of Commerce, Bureau of the Census, *1997 Census of Governments*, table 3, 1999.

36. All county size and population data are from the *Wisconsin Blue Book 2001–2002*, p. 728.

37. "County Organization and Administration," Wisconsin Taxpayers Alliance, in *The Wisconsin Taxpayer* 65, no. 4 (April 1997): 8–9.

38. A vote of two-thirds of the county supervisors is needed to override the county executive's veto.

39. Miller and Hawkins, "Local Government," p. 27.

40. *Wisconsin Blue Book 1997–1998*, "Framework of Government," p. 231.

41. For a more comprehensive description of Governor Patrick Lucey's attempt to shift the costs of important services provided by local governments from the property tax to state taxes, see James K. Conant, *Executive Decision Making in the State*, Ph.D. diss., Department of Political Science, University of Wisconsin–Madison, 1983.

42. *Wisconsin Blue Book 1999–2000*, p. 526.

43. Miller and Hawkins, "Local Government," p. 31.

44. Miller and Hawkins, "Local Government," p. 32.

45. Paddock, "Changing World," p. 119.

46. Leon D. Epstein, *Politics in Wisconsin* (Madison: University of Wisconsin Press, 1958), p. 14.

47. Miller and Hawkins, "Local Government," p. 33.

48. Paddock, "Changing World," p. 119.

49. Villages with a population below 350 people can only have three trustees.

50. *The Framework of Your Wisconsin Government* (Madison: Wisconsin Taxpayers Alliance, 1997), p. 85.

51. Wisconsin Department of Public Instruction, Bulletin No. 95055, September 1994, p. 2.

52. Wisconsin Department of Public Instruction, Bulletin No. 95055, September 1994, p. 2.

53. "1999–2001 Biennial Report," Wisconsin Technical College System, October 15, 2001.

54. "FTE Student Headcount Summary by Course Aid Category FY 01–02," Wisconsin Technical College System, October 21, 2002.

55. "FTE Student Summary by Aid Category FY 01–02," Wisconsin Technical College System, October 17, 2002.

56. For a superb discussion of vocational-technical education in Wisconsin and the ways in which Wisconsin's vocational-technical education system is similar to and different from those in Europe, see Joel Rogers, Wolfgang Streeck, and Eric Parker, "The Wisconsin Training Effort," in James K. Conant, Robert H. Haveman, and Jack Huddleston, eds., *Dollars and Sense: Policy Choices and the Wisconsin Budget*, 2 vols., 2d ed. (Madison: The Robert M. La Follette Institute of Public Affairs, 1991), pp. 119–53.

57. "Technical Colleges: Old Idea, New Look," Wisconsin Taxpayers Alliance, in *The Wisconsin Taxpayer* 65, no. 5 (May 1977): 1.

58. "Framework of Government," *Wisconsin Blue Book 1995–96* (Madison WI: Joint Committee on Legislative Organization, 1995), p. 253.

59. *Wisconsin Blue Book 1997–1998*, p. 231; Miller and Hawkins, "Local Government," p. 36.

60. *Wisconsin Blue Book 1997–1998*, p. 231; Miller and Hawkins, "Local Government," p. 36.

61. Miller and Hawkins, "Local Government," p. 36.

62. U.S. Department of Commerce, Bureau of the Census, *2003 Census of Governments*, table 3, "Local Government and Public School system by Type and State: 2002."

63. "Municipal and County Finance, 1997," Wisconsin Legislative Fiscal Bureau, p. 7.

64. Beverly A. Cigler, "Trends Affecting Local Administrators," in James L. Perry, ed., *Handbook of Public Administration* (San Francisco: Jossey-Bass, 1990), p. 43.

65. See, for example, Patricia Hersh, *A Tribe Apart* (New York: Ballantine, 1998).

66. John Shannon, "The Return to Fend-for-Yourself Federalism: The Reagan Mark," *Intergovernmental Perspective* 13, no. 3 (1987): 34–37.

67. John P. Thomas, "Perspective on County Government Services and Financing," *State and Local Government Review* 19, no. 3 (1987): 119–21.

68. John Kincaid, "De Facto Devolution and Urban Defunding: The Priority of Persons Over Places," *Journal of Urban Affairs* 21, no. 2 (Summer 1999): 135–67.

11. STATE-LOCAL RELATIONS

1. Jack Stark, "Property Tax and Property Tax Relief in Wisconsin," in the *Wisconsin Blue Book 1991–1992* (Madison WI: Joint Committee on Legislative Organization, 1991), p. 104.

2. Stark, "Property Tax and Property Tax Relief," p. 110.

3. For example, in 1927, the state property tax allocated to schools was 0.7 of a mill; a legislative enactment that year raised the figure to 1.1 mills. For more detail, see Stark, "Property tax and Property Tax Relief," p. 124.

4. Stark, "Property tax and Property Tax Relief in Wisconsin," pp. 129–30.

5. Stark, "Property tax and Property Tax Relief in Wisconsin," p. 133.

6. Stark, "Property tax and Property Tax Relief in Wisconsin," p. 132.

7. Stark, "Property tax and Property Tax Relief in Wisconsin," p. 133.

8. Stark, "Property tax and Property Tax Relief in Wisconsin," p. 133.

9. Stark, "Property tax and Property Tax Relief in Wisconsin," pp. 136–37.

10. Stark, "Property tax and Property Tax Relief in Wisconsin," p. 137.

11. John Wyngard, *Green Bay Press Gazette*, February 3, 1971.

12. *Capital Times*, March 15, 1971.

13. Lucey Campaign Release, September 12, 1970.

14. James K. Conant, *Executive Decision Making in the State*, Ph.D. diss., Department of Political Science, University of Wisconsin–Madison, 1983, p. 150.

15. Kenneth Roesslein, *Milwaukee Sentinel*, October 28, 1971.

16. These data were provided in an article in the *Capital Times*, September 28, 1971.

17. *Capital Times*, February 25, 1971.

18. Conant, *Executive Decision Making*, p. 169; *Capital Times*, October 27, 1971.

19. Conant, *Executive Decision Making in the State*, p. 186.

20. *Milwaukee Journal*, May 21, 1972.

21. Lucey Press Release, October 27, 1972.

22. Conant, *Executive Decision Making in the State*, pp. 181–82, 189.

23. The inequities created by financing local schools through the property tax were highlighted in the *Serrano* case. The formal title of the Doyle Commission, named after its chair, Ruth Doyle, was the Governor's Task Force on Educational Financing and Property Tax Reform.

24. Conant, *Executive Decision Making in the State*, pp. 207–8. The takeover of Supplemental Security Income and Medical Assistance was to begin on January 1, 1974. The takeover of Aid to Families with Dependent Children was to begin January 1, 1975.

25. Among the leaders of this initiative was the president pro tempore of the Wisconsin Senate, Fred Risser.

26. Conant, *Executive Decision Making in the State*, p. 186.

27. Conant, *Executive Decision Making in the State*, p. 221.

28. Conant, *Executive Decision Making in the State*, p. 221.

29. *Biennial Report 1973–1975* and *Biennial Report 1981–1983*, Wisconsin Department of Revenue.

30. Conant, *Executive Decision Making in the State*, p. 277.

31. *Town, Village, and City Taxes 1966–1977*, Wisconsin Department of Revenue.

32. Conant, *Executive Decision Making in the State*, p. 284.

33. Stark, "Property tax and Property Tax Relief," p. 155.

34. Tommy G. Thompson, *Power to the People: An American State at Work* (New York: HarperCollins, 1996), p. 128.

35. *State of Wisconsin 1991 Annual Fiscal Report*, Wisconsin Department of Administration, October 15, 1991, p. 8.

36. Thompson, *Power to the People*, p. 136.

37. Thompson, *Power to the People*, p. 140.

38. Thompson, *Power to the People*, p. 136.

39. Thompson, *Power to the People*, p. 127.

40. Thompson, *Power to the People*, p. 140.

41. Thompson, *Power to the People*, p. 139.

42. Thompson, *Power to the People*, p. 139.

43. Thompson, *Power to the People*, p. 142.

44. Thompson, *Power to the People*, p. 141.

45. Thompson, *Power to the People*, p. 142.

46. *State of Wisconsin 1998 Annual Fiscal Report*, Wisconsin Department of Administration, October 15, 1998, pp. 10–11; *State of Wisconsin 1999 Annual Fiscal Report*, Wisconsin Department of Administration, October 15, 1999, pp. 9–10.

47. *State of Wisconsin Budget in Brief 1997–1999*, Wisconsin Department of Administration, February 1977, p. 17.

48. *State of Wisconsin 2001 Annual Fiscal Report*, Wisconsin Department of Administration, October 15, 2001, p. 9.

49. "Tax Law Changes Beginning in 1995," Wisconsin Legislative Fiscal Bureau, November 2002.

50. *State of Wisconsin 2000 Annual Fiscal Report*, Wisconsin Department of Administration, October 13, 2000, pp. 7, 9;

51. *State of Wisconsin 2001 Annual Fiscal Report*, Wisconsin Department of Administration, October 15, 2001, p. 7.

52. *State of Wisconsin 2000 Annual Fiscal Report*, p. 10; *State of Wisconsin 2001 Annual Fiscal Report*, p. 10.

53. *State of Wisconsin Budget in Brief 1997–1999*, Wisconsin Department of Administration, February 1997, p. 37.

54. *State of Wisconsin Budget in Brief 1997–1999*, p. 34.

55. A comprehensive study of Wisconsin's deficit can be found in James K. Conant, "Wisconsin's Budget Deficit: Size, Causes, Remedies, and Consequences," *Public Budgeting and Finance* 23, no. 2 (Summer 2003): 5–25. An excellent case study of another state's fiscal problems in the recent recession is Thomas P. Lauth, "Budgeting During a Recession Phase of the Business Cycle: The Georgia Experience," *Public Budgeting and Finance* 23, no. 2 (Summer 2003): 26–38.

56. Additional lessons gleaned from the state's fiscal problems are presented in Conant, "Wisconsin's Budget Deficit," pp. 5–25.

12. WISCONSIN IN THE FEDERAL SYSTEM

1. A thorough review of the case and its significance is presented in Joseph Ranney, *Trusting Nothing to Providence: A History of Wisconsin's Legal System* (Madison: University of Wisconsin Law School, 1999), pp. 95–107.

2. Deil S. Wright, *Understanding Intergovernmental Relations* (Pacific Grove CA: Brookside Publishers, 1988), p. 298.

3. Wright, *Understanding Intergovernmental Relations*, p. 299.

4. Daniel Elazar, *The American Mosaic: The Impact of Space, Time, and Culture on American Politics* (Boulder: Westview Press, 1994), p. 281.

5. Diane D. Blair and Jay Barth, *Arkansas Government and Politics*, 2d ed. (Lincoln: University of Nebraska Press, 2005). See especially chapter 11, "Arkansas in the Federal System: Cooperation and Conflict."

6. This impression is imparted in a dramatic way in books such as Melba Pattillo Beals, *Warriors Don't Cry* (New York: Washington Square Press, 1994).

7. As a U.S. senator, Robert La Follette pushed for this protective legislation. An interesting discussion of the national government's efforts to protect children is found in Arthur A. Ekirch Jr., *Progressivism in America: A Study of the Era from Theodore Roosevelt to Woodrow Wilson* (New York: New Viewpoints, 1974) pp. 79–82.

8. Among the Wisconsinites who played important roles in the development of national government legislation were John R. Commons, Edwin Witte, and Wilbur Cohen.

9. Among the Wisconsinites who contributed to the antipoverty programs were Professors Robert Lampman and Burton Weisbrod.

10. Gaylord Nelson, one of the state's two U.S. senators, played an important role in both governmental and nongovernmental actions during the early 1970s. In addition to his support for legislation to reduce air and water pollution, Nelson is often recognized as the founding father of Earth Day. Senator Nelson told the author of this book that he thought Earth Day was probably his single most important contribution to the environmental movement and governmental action to protect the environment.

11. Officials in both the Wisconsin Department of Industry, Labor, and Human Relations, and the Wisconsin Department of Natural Resources played important roles in implementing this legislation.

12. Journalist E. J. Dionne Jr. finds powerful parallels between the economic, social, moral, and political circumstances of America at the end of the nineteenth century and the end of the twentieth century. See *They Only Look Dead: Why Progressives Will Dominate the Next Political Era* (New York: Simon and Schuster, 1996), pp. 12–13, 45–50.

13. A description of urban life for immigrants during this era is in Jane Addams, *Twenty Years at Hull House* (New York: Macmillan Company, 1910).

14. A remarkable portrait of these conditions is in Jacob Riis, *How the Other Half Lives: Studies Among the Tenements of New York* (New York: Charles Scribner's Sons, 1890), and Jane Addams, *Twenty Years at Hull House.*

15. The quotation is taken from Ekirch, *Progressivism in America*, p. 107. There is of course a body of literature that emphasizes the "functional" dimension of these political machines. The machines are reported to have provided essential aid and services to people, including new immigrants, for whom there was little or no government assistance. Yet a third perspective on these machines can be found in William L. Riordan, *Plunkitt of Tammany Hall*, wherein George Washington Plunkitt, a Tammany ward boss and philosopher, argues that the men of the Tammany machine got rich through "honest" graft and never engaged in any "dishonest" graft.

16. Robert S. Maxwell, *La Follette and the Rise of the Progressives in Wisconsin* (Madison: Wisconsin State Historical Society, 1956), p. viii. An interesting discussion of Progressivism at the national level, particularly the emphasis placed on antitrust activities and regulation of the industrial economy, is in Jerold J. Duquette, *Regulating the National Pastime: Baseball and Antitrust* (Westport CT: Praeger, 1999).

17. Maxwell, *La Follette*, p. 5.

18. In addition to California, Oregon, and Wisconsin, those states included Washington in the West; Illinois, Iowa, Minnesota, Missouri, Ohio, North Dakota, and Kansas in the Midwest; Georgia, South Carolina, Arkansas and Mississippi in the South; and Maine, Massachusetts, and New York in the East.

19. Ekirch, *Progressivism in America*, p. 110.

20. Ekirch, *Progressivism in America*, p. 110.

21. Initiative and referendum are the subject matter of a recent book by journalist David Broder, *Democracy Derailed: Initiative Campaigns and the Power of Money* (New York: Harcourt, 1999).

22. This is especially true for the 1970s through the end of the twentieth century.

23. A Pulitzer Prize–winning biography of Teddy Roosevelt's life up to the point when he became president is Edmund Morris, *The Rise of Teddy Roosevelt* (New York: Coward, McCann, and Geoghagan, 1979).

24. George Mowry, *Theodore Roosevelt and the Progressive Movement* (Madison: University of Wisconsin Press, 1946), p. 33.

25. C. C. Regier, *The Era of the Muckrakers* (Gloucester MA: Peter Smith, 1957), p. 199. A comprehensive bibliography of Muckraker periodicals, authors, and articles is provided at the end of the book.

26. Regier, *Era of the Muckrackers*, p. 8. Regier says that more than 500,000 workers were killed or badly maimed each year. Among the best-known works on these topics were Upton Sinclair, *The Jungle* (Cambridge MA: Robert Bentley, Inc., 1946), and Ida Tarbell, *The History of the Standard Oil Company* (New York: Norton, 1969).

27. Lincoln Steffens is probably the best known of the Muckrakers who reported on corruption in the cities and the states. Among his best known exposes were: "Enemies of the Republic," *McClure's* 22 (March 1904): 587–99, and "Rhode Island: A State for Sale," *McClure's* 24 (February 1905): 337–53.

28. New York was the first state to have a legislative library. Wisconsin's Legislative Reference Bureau not only had a library but also bill-drafting and research services for legislators.

29. Ranney, *Trusting Nothing to Providence*, p. 284. Ranney also points out (p. 285) that McCarthy was careful to provide high-quality service to legislators of all political persuasions. Consequently, he survived even during the period between 1914 and 1920 when the Progressives did not control the statehouse.

30. Ekirch, *Progressivism in America*, p. 110.

31. Ely's views on government provoked sharp criticism by some. In fact a concerted effort was made by his enemies to get him fired from the university faculty. A fascinating description of Richard Ely's work—as well as his "trial" at the University of Wisconsin for fomenting "dangerous" ideas—is in W. Lee Hansen, ed., *Academic Freedom on Trial* (Madison: Office of University Publications, 1998).

32. Ekirch, *Progressivism in America*, p. 26.

33. Ekirch, *Progressivism in America*, p. 117.

34. Ekirch, *Progressivism in America*, p. 117.

35. *Wisconsin Blue Book 1999–2000* (Madison: Joint Committee on Legislative Organization, 1999), p. 244.

36. Donald O. Herzberg and Alan Rosenthal begin their *Strengthening the States* (New York: Doubleday, 1971) by noting that the key question to be answered is, what improvements are to be made to strengthen state legislatures? With the development of the Legislative Fiscal Bureau in 1961, Wisconsin had already provided a key part of the answer.

37. David C. Nice, *Federalism: The Politics of Intergovernmental Relations* (New York: St. Martin's Press, 1987), p. 14.

38. These data are reported in Susan B. Hansen, *The Politics of Taxation* (New York: Praeger, 1983), p. 149. Hansen reports the original source for the data on the personal income tax and corporate income tax as Clara Penniman, *State Income Taxation* (Baltimore: Johns Hopkins University Press, 1980).

39. Hansen, *Politics of Taxation*, p. 149.

40. Hansen does not provide reasons for the immediate diffusion of the policy outside of the geographic region (Midwest), but she does offer a couple of explanations for the timing of adoption in the different states. In addition to economic necessity, she cites "political opportunity" or unified government (party control of a state government's executive, legislative, and judicial branches). Discussion of this factor is provided in Hansen, *Politics of Taxation*, pp. 148–64.

41. Elliot W. Brownlee, *Progressivism and Economic Growth: The Wisconsin Income Tax 1911–1929* (Port Washington NY: Kennikat Press, 1974), p. 41.

42. Between 1929 and 1937 eighteen states adopted the personal income tax and nineteen states adopted the corporate income tax, as reported in Hansen, *Politics of Taxation*, p. 149.

43. In 1913 the Sixteenth Amendment to the U.S. Constitution was ratified by a sufficient number of states, and the statutory language needed to establish the income tax was agreed upon by both houses of Congress.

44. John Witte, *The Politics and Development of the Federal Income Tax* (Madison: University of Wisconsin Press, 1985), p. 78.

45. Hansen, *Politics of Taxation*, p. 86.

46. Regier, *Era of the Muckrakers*, p. 8.

47. Regier, *Era of the Muckrakers*, p. 203.

48. An articulation of the argument that Wisconsin's progressive income tax had a substantial, negative effect on the development of the state manufacturing industry is in Brownlee, *Progressivism and Economic Growth*, p. 41.

49. Among the Wisconsin governors who articulated frustration over this circumstance was Patrick Lucey. Yet less than a decade after he left the governorship, Lucey claimed permanent residence in Florida and thus avoided Wisconsin's income tax.

50. As reported in John F. Witte, "Wisconsin Income Tax Reform," 108–29, in Sheldon Danziger and John F. Witte, eds., *State Policy Choices: The Wisconsin Experience* (Madison: University of Wisconsin Press, 1988).

51. Witte, "Wisconsin Income Tax Reform," p. 127.

52. Witte, "Wisconsin Income Tax Reform," pp. 118–19.

53. Witte, "Wisconsin Income Tax Reform," p. 121.

54. The Earl administration's view was presented to the author by Earl's former policy director, Hal Bergan, during a discussion with the author about this initiative.

55. A complete description of the Reagan tax initiative is in Timothy J. Conlan, Margaret T. Wrightson, and David R. Beam, eds., *Taxing Choices: The Politics of Tax Reform* (Washington DC: CQ Press, 1990).

56. Jason DeParle, "Wisconsin Pledges to Exit U.S. System of Public Welfare," *New York Times*, December 14, 1993.

57. Avrum D. Lank, "Big business to escape state taxes," *Milwaukee Journal Sentinel*, June 13, 1999.

58. In the 1998–1999 executive budget, for example, only 20 percent of Wisconsin's total revenues were provided by the national government.

59. *The Book of the States 2001–2002* (Lexington KY: Council of State Governments, 2002), p. 69.

60. *Statistical Abstract of the U.S.*, U.S. Department of Commerce, U.S. Census Bureau (Washington DC: U.S. Census Bureau, 2002), no. 462, "Balance of Payments by State 1990–1999," p. 313.

61. The definition of "social welfare" employed here includes programs that might be placed in the category of public health, such as Medicaid.

62. *Wisconsin Atlas and Gazetteer* (Yarmouth ME: DeLorme, 1992), pp. 4–5. The national government also owns and manages three other modestly sized tracts of land: the Apostle Islands National Lakeshore (twenty islands and a section of shoreline along Lake Superior); the Ice Age National Scientific Reserve; and the St. Croix National Scenic Riverway (252 miles of adjacent banks along the Namekagon and St. Croix Rivers). Even with the addition of these properties, however, the national government's ownership of state lands is only about 5 percent of the total.

63. Thomas A. Heberlein, *Social Issues and Wildlife at The Horicon Marsh* (Madison: University of Wisconsin Press, 1987).

64. For more discussion of the marsh, particularly the origins of the efforts to restore it after it was drained for agricultural purposes, see Heberlein, *Social Issues and Wildlife at The Horicon Marsh*.

65. The United States Fish and Wildlife Service is the administering agency for the national government; the Department of Natural Resources is the state agency with administrative responsibility.

66. *Wisconsin Atlas and Gazetteer*, p. 12.

67. J. W. Moore, "Mandates Without Money," *National Journal* 18, n. 40 (1986): 2366–70.

68. A more complete discussion of the effects the Reagan initiatives had on the states is in James K. Conant, "The Growing Importance of State Government," in James L. Perry, ed., *Handbook of Public Administration* (San Francisco: Jossey-Bass, 1989), pp. 26–27.

69. Hal Bergan, who served as policy director under Governor Earl, provided an alternative explanation for the failure of Wisconsin's congressional delegation to secure changes in the transportation funding. Mr. Bergan argued that elected

officials from reformist states are not likely to be particularly interested in, or good at, the kind of log-rolling activity that is required to make such changes. Wisconsin's elected officials tend to gain their political experience in the state legislature or local government, and Wisconsin's politics tends to be oriented on issues rather than based on pork barrel or patronage.

70. The act was the Agricultural Marketing Agreement of 1937.

71. "97011: Dairy Policy Issues," Congressional Research Service (Washington DC: Government Printing Office), November 9, 1999.

72. Congressman Ron Kind, from the Third Congressional District of Wisconsin (including Eau Claire), compares this circumstance to having the national government attempt to create a lobster industry in the Midwest by salinating Lake Michigan. See "Michigan Lobsters," *Washington Post*, September 22, 1999.

73. For example, among the states that wanted to preserve the old system were Florida, New York, Texas, and Pennsylvania. The congressional delegations from these states voted almost uniformly in favor of HR 1402—a bill that kept the old system intact. The votes of these four states comprised almost six times the number of votes that the congressional delegations from Wisconsin and Minnesota could produce.

74. Congressman Rod Grams of Minnesota, as reported in "GOP Leadership Sour on Mild Reform," *Washington Post*, November 17, 1999, p. 4.

75. An excellent description of the tribes and their histories can be found Patti Loew, *Indian Nations of Wisconsin: Histories of Endurance and Renewal* (Madison: Wisconsin State Historical Society, 2001).

76. *Chippewa Off-Reservation Treaty Rights: Origins and Issues*, State of Wisconsin Legislative Reference Bureau, Research bulletin 91–1, December 1991, p. 6.

77. *Chippewa Off-Reservation Treaty Rights*, p. 6.

78. *Chippewa Off-Reservation Treaty Rights*, p. 6.

79. *Chippewa Off-Reservation Treaty Rights*, p. 7.

80. *Chippewa Off-Reservation Treaty Rights*, p. 7.

81. The cases and court rulings are summarized in *Chippewa Off-Reservation Treaty Rights*, pp. 11–12.

82. *Chippewa Off-Reservation Treaty Rights*, pp. 11–12.

83. The cases and the court rulings are summarized in *Chippewa Off-Reservation Treaty Rights*, pp. 7–10.

84. *Chippewa Off-Reservation Treaty Rights*, p. 19.

85. *Chippewa Off-Reservation Treaty Rights*, p. 18. The polls were conducted by faculty at UCLA and St. Norbert's College, Wisconsin.

86. *Wisconsin Blue Book 1991–1992* (Madison: Joint Committee on Legislative Organization, 1991), p. 898.

87. *Wisconsin Blue Book 1991–1992*, p. 915.

88. *Wisconsin Blue Book 1993–1994* (Madison: Joint Committee on Legislative Organization, 1993), p. 922.

89. *The Evolution of Legalized Gambling in Wisconsin*, Research Bulletin 00-1 (Madison: Legislative Reference Bureau, 2000), p. 23.

90. *Evolution of Legalized Gambling*, p. 22.

91. *Evolution of Legalized Gambling*, p. 11.

92. *Evolution of Legalized Gambling*, p. 22.

93. *Lac du Flambeau Band of Lake Superior Chippewa Indians v. Wisconsin*, 743 F.Supp.645 (W.D. Wis. 1990).

94. *Evolution of Legalized Gambling*, p. 22.

95. *Lac du Flambeau Band v. Wisconsin*, 770 F.Supp.480 (W.D. Wis. 1991).

96. *Evolution of Legalized Gambling*, p. 23.

97. *Evolution of Legalized Gambling*, p. 23.

98. *Evolution of Legalized Gambling*, p. 24.

99. (Milwaukee) *Journal Sentinel*, June 2, 2003.

100. *Evolution of Legalized Gambling*, p. 27.

101. *Evolution of Legalized Gambling*, p. 27.

13. CONTINUING TRADITIONS AND EMERGING ISSUES

1. Alice E. Smith, *The History of Wisconsin: From Exploration to Statehood* (Madison: Wisconsin State Historical Society, 1973), p. 655.

2. Robert La Follette Sr., *La Follette's Autobiography* (Madison: University of Wisconsin Press, 1960), p. 10.

3. John R. Commons was professor of political economy at the University of Wisconsin. He was the drafter of the civil service law, centerpiece of the Civil Service Act, and he is reported to have said that "administration was more important than legislation. Legislation furnished the authorization. Administration was legislation in action." See *Wisconsin: A Guide to the Badger State* (New York: Hastings House, 1954), p. 59.

4. Daniel Elazar, *American Federalism: A View from the States*, 3d ed. (New York: Harper and Row, 1984), p. 91.

5. Of course, some critics of those policy innovations believe that they have resulted in some very bad consequences for poor families, including increasing rates of homelessness and hunger.

6. Michael Feldman, "Clean State, Dirty Politicians," *New York Times*, October 24, 2002, p. A35.

7. Feldman, "Clean State, Dirty Politicians," p. 35.

8. Feldman, "Clean State, Dirty Politicians," p. 35.

9. Tom Loftus, *The Art of Legislative Politics* (Washington DC: CQ Press, 1994), p. 93.

10. This quotation derives from a confidential interview with a veteran observer of the Wisconsin legislature. Permission has been granted to the author to use the quotation but not to name the source.

11. James K. Conant, "Wisconsin's Budget Deficit: Size, Causes, Remedies, and Consequences," *Public Budgeting and Finance* 23, no. 2 (Summer 2003): 5–25.

12. James K. Conant, "The Bust Phase of the Boom and Bust Cycle, Again!" *Public Budgeting and Finance* 23, no. 2 (Summer 2003): 1–4.

Index

In the Politics and Governments of the American States series

Alabama Government and Politics
By James D. Thomas and William H. Stewart

Alaska Politics and Government
By Gerald A. McBeath and Thomas A. Morehouse

Arizona Politics and Government: The Quest for Autonomy, Democracy, and Development
By David R. Berman

Arkansas Politics and Government, second edition
By Diane D. Blair and Jay Barth

Colorado Politics and Government: Governing the Centennial State
By Thomas E. Cronin and Robert D. Loevy

Delaware Politics and Government
By William W. Boyer and Edward C. Ratledge

Hawai'i Politics and Government: An American State in a Pacific World
By Richard C. Pratt with Zachary Smith

Illinois Politics and Government: The Expanding Metropolitan Frontier
By Samuel K. Gove and James D. Nowlan

Kansas Politics and Government: The Clash of Political Cultures
By H. Edward Flentje and Joseph A. Aistrup

Kentucky Politics and Government: Do We Stand United?
By Penny M. Miller

Maine Politics and Government, second edition
By Kenneth T. Palmer, G. Thomas Taylor, Marcus A. LiBrizzi, and Jean E. Lavigne

Maryland Politics and Government: Democratic Dominance
By Herbert C. Smith and John T. Willis

Michigan Politics and Government: Facing Change in a Complex State
By William P. Browne and Kenneth VerBurg

Minnesota Politics and Government
By Daniel J. Elazar, Virginia Gray, and Wyman Spano

Mississippi Government and Politics: Modernizers versus Traditionalists
By Dale Krane and Stephen D. Shaffer

Nebraska Government and Politics
Edited by Robert D. Miewald

Nevada Politics and Government: Conservatism in an Open Society
By Don W. Driggs and Leonard E. Goodall

New Jersey Politics and Government: Suburban Politics Comes of Age, second edition
By Barbara G. Salmore and Stephen A. Salmore

New York Politics and Government: Competition and Compassion
By Sarah F. Liebschutz, with Robert W. Bailey, Jeffrey M. Stonecash, Jane Shapiro Zacek, and Joseph F. Zimmerman

North Carolina Government and Politics
By Jack D. Fleer

Oklahoma Politics and Policies: Governing the Sooner State
By David R. Morgan, Robert E. England, and George G. Humphreys

Oregon Politics and Government: Progressives versus Conservative Populists
By Richard A. Clucas, Mark Henkels, and Brent S. Steel

Rhode Island Politics and Government
By Maureen Moakley and Elmer Cornwell

South Carolina Politics and Government
By Cole Blease Graham Jr. and William V. Moore

West Virginia Politics and Government
By Richard A. Brisbin Jr., Robert Jay Dilger, Allan S. Hammock, and Christopher Z. Mooney

West Virginia Politics and Government, second edition
By Richard A. Brisbin Jr., Robert Jay Dilger, Allan S. Hammock, and L. Christopher Plein

Wisconsin Politics and Government: America's Laboratory of Democracy
By James K. Conant

To order or obtain more information on these or other University of Nebraska Press titles, visit www.nebraskapress.unl.edu.

CPSIA information can be obtained at www.ICGtesting.com
Printed in the USA
LVOW130720021111

253099LV00008B/8/P